THE WOMEN'S MOVEMENTS OF
THE UNITED STATES AND WESTERN EUROPE

In the series
WOMEN IN THE POLITICAL ECONOMY,
edited by Ronnie J. Steinberg

THE WOMEN'S MOVEMENTS OF THE UNITED STATES AND WESTERN EUROPE

Consciousness, Political Opportunity, and Public Policy

Edited by
Mary Fainsod Katzenstein
and
Carol McClurg Mueller

 TEMPLE UNIVERSITY PRESS · PHILADELPHIA

Temple University Press, Philadelphia 19122
Copyright © 1987 by Temple University, except Chapter 10, which is © Jo Freeman
All rights reserved
Published 1987
Printed in the United States of America

The paper used in this publication meets the minimum
requirements of American National Standard for Information
Sciences—Permanence of Paper for Printed Library Materials,
ANSI Z39.48-1984

Library of Congress Cataloging-in-Publication Data

The Women's movements of the United States and Western Europe.
    (Women in the political economy)
    Bibliography: p.
    Includes index.
    1. Feminism—United States. 2. Feminism—Europe. I. Katzenstein, Mary Fainsod,
1945–   . II. Mueller, Carol. III. Series.
HQ1426.W6655 1987   305.4′2′0973   86-30182
ISBN 0-87722-463-3 (alk. paper)

Table 1-1, p. 26, reprinted by permission of Philip Morris, Inc.
Table in n.12, p. 212, reprinted by permission of Yale University Press.

Contents

PART TWO
POLITICAL PARTIES AND THE STRUCTURE OF OPPORTUNITY

PART THREE
THE STATE AND FEMINIST POLICY OUTCOMES

Preface

This book focuses on the feminist movement of seven Western democracies. Our intent is not to present a profile of women's economic, social, or political status in these countries. We seek, rather, to chart the rich political terrain where feminist movements, gender consciousness, and political institutions converge and interact. The feminist movements of these seven countries share a common transformational agenda—the goal of transforming the activities, behavior, beliefs, and identities that constitute the basis of social life organized around gender hierarchy. This agenda has led to a common attack on culture as well as institutional practice, on consciousness as well as the distribution of resources. But feminist movements rarely confront identical political opportunities. The political options of these movements depend entirely on the varied and complex ways in which movement goals and consciousness intersect with the interests of political parties and state institutions. This book is about these political intersections.

We owe a very great debt to Sidney Tarrow, who was the initiator and lead organizer of the conference at Cornell that provided the initial ideas for this book. The support of the Council of European Studies, the Department of Government, and the Women's Studies and Western Societies programs was critical to that conference. We thank Delores Robinson and David Armstrong, who handled much of the typing and production work, and we gratefully acknowledge the support of the Murray Center at Radcliffe College, the Center for Research for Women at Wellesley College, and the Jonathan Meigs fund at Cornell.

Mary Fainsod Katzenstein
Carol McClurg Mueller

INTRODUCTION

Comparing the Feminist Movements of the United States and Western Europe: An Overview

MARY FAINSOD KATZENSTEIN

The life of social movements is thought to be cyclical: movements arise, flourish, and fade (Tarrow 1983). Later, under different societal conditions, when renewed social discontent develops and political opportunities present themselves, a generation of new social movements is reborn. Consistent with this cyclical theory is the image the popular media now present of a feminist movement on the downward swing of such a cycle. If the media are to be believed, the feminist movement's second wave has crested.[1] The relative infrequence of protests, demonstrations, marches; the dissolution of the earlier consciousness-raising groups; and the more audible self-criticism within the movement have signaled to some observers that contemporary feminism has spent its force.[2]

But this obituary is premature. Although many of the social movements born in the 1960s and early 1970s have expired, the feminist movement is one of the few survivors. If the health of the women's movement is to be accurately gaged, it is important to appreciate that some of the instruments that plumbed the strengths and weaknesses of other social movements are inappropriate as measures of the well-being of feminism. Membership figures, for instance, that give a reasonable indication of the well-being of trade unions tell little of the story of feminist movements. There are many feminist activists, not to mention supporters, who are neither dues-paying or card-carrying members of any particular organizational unit. Unlike the civil rights movement, moreover, whose strength was measured in large part by its very public protests and demonstrations, the women's movement even at the outset made less use of the "orthodox" tactics of disorder. It has instead pursued its often very radical agenda in less visible ways—through consciousness-raising groups, collectives, caucuses, and local organizations.

An assessment of the well-being of the women's movement must identify the mutiple networks through which feminist consciousness is purveyed and activism is promoted. Of particular importance here is the emergence of local and therefore less visible feminist organizations. The number of such organizations has

3

dramatically increased.[3] Even as the old consciousness-raising groups have dissipated, task forces, collectives, women's caucuses, women's centers, women's studies programs, and feminist publishing houses, in addition to the more conventional membership organizations, have taken over different movement activities. To mention only a few scattered but suggestive statistics: There are now over 200 feminist-run Women's Aid refuges in Britain (Pahl 1985). The readership of the German magazine *Emma* numbers over 300,000 (Altbach 1984, 7), three-fourths the circulation of *Ms.* in the United States (Ferree and Hess 1985, 73). In the Netherlands in 1977 (as Chapter 2, on the Dutch women's movement, notes), groups and organizations that identified with the women's movement could be formed in one-fourth of all Dutch towns. In the United States, the decade of the 1970s saw the development of some 452 women's studies programs and 30,000 women's studies courses (Howe 1984, x). Through the proliferation of these organizations, feminist ideas and feminist consciousness have found an ever broader and more accepting constituency in the last 15 years.

One purpose of this book is to offer a framework through which the present and future well-being of feminist movements can be assessed. This framework is built upon a cross-national comparison of seven countries (the United States, Great Britain, France, West Germany, Italy, Sweden, and the Netherlands). The differences in the successes with which the women's movements in these countries have mobilized a feminist constituency and have pursued particular policy objectives reveals more about the prerequisites of a movement's strengths than study of a single country could accomplish. But even more critical to this framework is its focus on the political institutions and state structures through which the feminist movements must operate if their agenda is to be realized. In this focus we seek to fill a void in the studies of women in the United States and Western Europe. There are now excellent comparative studies of family and employment policies that affect women (Adams and Winston 1980; Farley 1985; Kahn and Kamerman 1978, 1981, 1983; Ratner 1980). There are also comprehensive studies of particular political institutions: trade unions, voting, and elite representation (Cook, Lorwin, and Daniels 1984; Epstein and Coser 1981; Lovenduski and Hills 1981). However, there is little that focuses on the feminist *movement* cross-nationally and that links the feminist *movement* to political institutions and in turn to political outcomes.[4] Through the analytical strategy of exploring comparatively the political opportunities afforded the women's movements in different political systems, we seek to discover both a national logic and an institutional logic to the politics of feminist movements.

The chapters in this book set out to trace the complicated web that links feminist organizations to other political institutions. This institutional analysis focuses chiefly on the relationship of feminist organizations to political parties and to the role of labor within the state. It is out of these linkages that a feminist consciousness is formed and policy reforms are pursued. The complexity of these relationships among organization, consciousness, and state action are immediately evident. Political organization and consciousness, for instance, are far from isomorphic, as the contrasting politics of Black and white women in the United States amply demonstrates. There is a distinctly higher acceptance of feminist ideas among Black women than among white women (Gallup Poll 1986, 51). But the stronger commitment to feminist ideology of Black women is not accompanied by a concomitantly more active commitment to feminist organizations. Instead Black women (as Ethel Klein notes in Chapter 1) invest their political energies in such organized activity as welfare rights or the church.

We are similarly reminded of the nonlinear relationship between social movement organization and state responsiveness by the example of Sweden. There the government has evinced a higher level of commitment to gender equality than have most states in Western Europe or North America. Yet the feminist movement in Sweden is considerably less of a presence than in countries such as the United States or Italy where state policy lags well behind. This rich and complicated interplay between social movement organization, feminist consciousness, and state action constitutes the terrain for the theoretical explorations of this book.

An analysis of the feminist movement that addresses, as this book does, feminism in seven countries must begin with the recognition that we are discussing not one discrete organizational movement but rather a political force that even in a single country has broad ideological variety and a range of organizational expressions. The use of the singular in describing the feminist movement is nevertheless appropriate, given the unifying ideological embrace of a political goal that seeks to change a world that relegates women to a subordinated political, economic, and social status. But from that common theoretical core, a multitude of different feminist movements have sprung.

One reason for the diversity of feminism is the fact that the women's movement is a potentially *transformational* social movement[5] and thus draws supporters with a range of different agendas. The movement is transformational in the sense that it engages both a *broad* range of issues and a set of issues that can *deeply* affect the daily experiences of an individual's life. Thus, feminism addresses economic concerns (the existence of job discrimination; the valuation of women's work); sexual issues (the definition of sexual pleasure; the problem of rape, harassment, battering, and homophobia); family issues (the provision of child care; the division of labor in the household; maternity/parental leave; reproductive rights); and a range of matters less easily catalogued (the demilitarization of society; the deconstruction and critical analysis of language; the rewriting of women's history). What this "agenda" entails is nothing less than the reformulation of public life, the educational sphere, the workplace, and the home—that is, a total transformation of society.

This transformational character is common to feminist movements irrespective of their national origins. It explains their preoccupation with consciousness change because the restructuring of personal identities and relationships among friends, partners, parents, and children is reached only with difficulty by law or policy declamation. The transformative nature of the feminist agenda also accounts in part for the movements' impatience with policy reforms that are sometimes thought of as failing to touch the deep normative structures and values that brace the status quo. The transformational character of feminism, moreover, encourages contests over symbolic issues such as the Equal Rights Amendment in the United States; for both supporters and opponents, the ERA became the surrogate for a host of individual changes across the spectrum of electoral, economic, social, and family issues. The transformational character of the movement also makes it possible to absorb reversals on one flank while remobilizing political energies around another set of issues (by the same token, of course, the achievement of movement goals on one flank—as with suffrage—may at least temporarily siphon off groups of feminist activists who consider their agenda fulfilled).

These issues around the transformative agenda of feminism are examined at different points throughout the book. But there are three main themes that structure the intercountry comparisons and that are the principal subject of this volume:

1. The book advances several claims about feminist consciousness: That its dissemination has been widespread; that its diffusion is heavily influenced not just by social and economic changes but also by politics, by the strength of feminist organizations, and by the role of labor and parties of the left; and that the diffusion of feminist consciousness is absolutely critical to the success of feminist movements. This changing consciousness may occur at the individual level around issues involving personal identity and policy preferences. It may also be manifest at the institutional level in the changing ideas about what is admissible as subjects of legislative and policy treatment. At both levels, changing consciousness is a vital resource in the achievement of a feminist agenda.

2. The opportunity to influence policies by forging alliances with political parties depends on the particular parties involved and the degree of autonomy the feminist movement is willing to forgo. The socialist and communist parties of Western Europe have proven far more supportive of feminist concerns than the (Christian Democratic) Center or the Right. At the same time the leftist parties' own survival needs (as they see them) and the ideological privilege they give to class over gender concerns has made them problematic allies. This has confronted European feminist movements with one of their central strategic dilemmas. In the United States, by contrast, in the absence of a strong Left, the feminist movement has been less dependent on and less troubled by its relationship to political parties although some of the same concerns and trade-offs around autonomy and influence, nevertheless, obtain.

3. The nature of the state is as important to the type of reformist policies adopted as are the opportunities for party alliances. Policies sought by feminists are more likely to emerge from either centralized states with a strong

labor movement (Sweden) or decentralized, fragmented states with a weak labor movement (the United States) than from centralized states where the labor movement is a weak partner in state policy-making (Great Britain).

These three themes provide a logical sequence for the sections of the book: In Part One, on the dissemination of feminist consciousness, Ethel Klein compares the change in political consciousness in the United States and Western Europe during the last decade and a half. Martien Briët, Bert Klandermans, and Frederike Kroon explore the role of consciousness in precipitating and deterring women's decisions to join the Dutch feminist movement. Jane Jenson describes a change in elite consciousness—in what she calls the universe of discourse—that allowed the consideration and adoption of abortion reform in France. Carol Mueller links the growth of consciousness to the increase in women's political representation in the United States and assesses the way an appreciation of consciousness change requires a modification of existing theories of social movements.

Part Two, on parties and political opportunities, treats three countries with very different party systems. Judith Hellman explores the accommodation of the different strands of feminism to the "workerist" tradition in the labor stronghold of the Italian city of Turin. Stephen Hellman's essay, also on Turin, describes the feminist challenge to the "model of militancy" of the Communist party organization in the city. Karen Beckwith looks at the controversies between feminist organizations and leftist parties surrounding the passage of legislation in the Italian parliament. Myra Ferree investigates the genesis and weighs the consequences of the greater autonomy and radicalism of the West German women's movement as compared with the feminist movement in the United States. Jo Freeman and Anne and Douglas Costain analyze the relationship between the feminist movement and political parties in the United States.

Part Three, on state action and public policy, begins with Mary Ruggie's explanation of the celebrated Swedish record in forging egalitarian economic policies and contrasts the Swedish experience with the less effective and less egalitarian British policies. Joyce Gelb examines the relatively restricted opportunities for the women's movement to exert political influence and to penetrate state institutions in the United Kingdom as compared with those in the United States. Finally, in an upbeat concluding essay, Janet Flammang describes the political organizing around "comparable worth" in a California county and thus demonstrates the potential of local politics for successful feminist activism.

THE IMPORTANCE OF A CHANGE IN CONSCIOUSNESS TO THE WOMEN'S MOVEMENT

The feminist agenda embraces such a broad range of societal changes that the movement's success will depend critically on the acceptance of feminist values and ideas. This spread of consciousness is important not only in the sense that the creation of a collective identity is, as with all social movements, requisite to (and a result of) successful political mobilization. More particularly, because the feminist agenda targets "the private realm" along with the "public sphere," [6] it must place a particular reliance on consciousness as a tool of social change. Although the political programs of the environmental or peace movements, for instance, demand far-reaching changes in the structures of "public" power, the women's movement demands in addition a redefinition of the relations of power in daily life. The reshaping of friendship, of family, of love (in their abstract formulation), and of the decision structure around the relationships of sex, child care, and household financing (in its more concrete expression) is central to the feminist agenda. These are matters that can be reached only in part by legislation, public policy, and judicial action. They are, therefore, necessarily the business of consciousness change.

What we have loosely been referring to as a receptivity to feminist ideas or as a growth of feminist consciousness bears elaboration. A receptivity to feminist ideas may occur without the development of a full-blown feminist consciousness. The beginnings of such a receptivity may mean no more than an increase in the willingness to vote for a woman for public office, or it may be captured merely by such exclamations as "I'm no women's libber but you'll never find me bringing my husband his slippers." A receptivity to feminist ideas suggests, then, an inchoate rejection of societal discrimination and of the structures that cause women's subordination.

A feminist consciousness represents a deeper and more systematic receptivity to feminist ideas as well as a real identification with women as a group or sex-class. This gender consciousness includes the presence of at least two attitudinal conditions, identified by Patricia Gurin as: 1) discontent with the level of women's power and influence; and 2) the belief that gender disparities are illegitimate (Gurin and Townsend, 1984, 1–4).[7]

A feminist consciousness, however, is different from particular feminist ideologies. Feminist consciousness can best be thought of as a lens through which ideas, individuals, and relationships are newly viewed. Marilyn Frye (1983, 95) describes this lens as a "kaleidoscope . . . whose shapes, structures, and patterns alter with every turn of feminist creativity." By contrast, feminist ideologies that may be expressed, for instance, as radical feminism, liberal feminism, as ideologies of difference or ideologies of sameness, specify a particular set of goals and strategies.

There are of course a range of different ways in which feminist consciousness is manifest. It may appear as a changing sense of personhood that structures individual political aspirations (as Carol Mueller explores in Chapter 4). When feminist consciousness becomes part of the institutional arena of government, it may take the form of a changing public agenda or discourse (Jane Jenson's argument in Chapter 3). When it is manifest in policy preferences (as Ethel Klein discusses in

Chapter 1), consciousness has been narrowed down to a small set of ideological choices.

Although it may be a matter of contention whether the active life of feminist organizations has peaked, there can be little dispute over the existence of a growing feminist consciousness. Ethel Klein reports herein that feminist consciousness as tapped by potentially transformative policy preferences (concerning married women's employment, shared responsibilities in the home, equality of job opportunities and equal pay) is now widely diffused throughout the United States and Western Europe. The growth of support for the aims of the feminist movement reported in her chapter is underscored by the dramatic data recorded in a recent U.S. Gallup Poll (1986, 51). The poll shows 56 percent of all women in the United States identifying themselves as feminists and 71 percent observing that the women's movement has done either fairly well or very well in improving their lives.

There are, however, important national differences in the levels and kinds of gender consciousness expressed. Klein notes that support for feminism is higher in France, Italy, and Greece than in West Germany or the United Kingdom, indicating stronger feminist support in countries with active socialist or communist parties than in countries with a more social democratic tradition. The importance of a strong Left is further born out by the fact that on public opinion inquiries pertaining to equality of roles, Sweden, with its influential labor movement, ranks considerably higher than other nations.[8] The fact that high levels of feminist support come from societies as diverse as Sweden and Greece (with very different patterns of female labor force participation and fertility rates) points to the critical role that politics can play in shaping gender consciousness.

Political culture as well as institutions may shape the kind of gender consciousness expressed. Some suggestive evidence of this is reported in a cross-national poll that explored respondents' views on solutions to gender inequality. American opinion emphasized the role of individual effort, Swedish opinion the importance of reducing societal impediments, and Germans the role of juridical reforms (Hastings 1986, 709).

While Klein compares patterns of gender consciousness in the United States and Western Europe, the other three essays in Part One take up a different question. They assess the consequences of gender consciousness, exploring its importance to the feminist movement and policy reform.

The Briët, Klandermans, and Kroon essay on the Netherlands (Chapter 2) focuses on the relationship of consciousness to the movement's ability to attract a membership. Using a survey conducted in 1981–82, they assess the awareness of an interest in the women's movement among the female population of the town of Gouda. They conclude that agreement with the objectives of the movement is not a sufficient condition for participation. Klein makes the same point in discussing the disjuncture between Black and white women in support for the American women's movement. But the key argument of Briët, Klandermans, and Kroon is that a *lack* of consciousness can act as a serious deterrent to women's willingness to support feminism. The large number of women in the Netherlands who reject feminism constitutes one of the movement's most serious challenges.

Jane Jenson's discussion of the French women's movement (Chapter 3) also focuses on the consequences of consciousness—not for movement organization, as in the Dutch paper, but for the pursuit of feminist reforms.[9] Jenson's argument is that until a change in elite consciousness occurred, until the "universe of political discourse" was modified, women's claims continued to be relegated to issues of women's maternal and familial roles. Abortion reform was achieved only when a change in consciousness occurred such that the state had come to see women's interests as those of individual citizens whose voices could not be represented simply by spokespersons for the family.

Carol Mueller's essay (Chapter 4) addresses the importance of consciousness for political representation. She observes that the feminist debates of the 1970s over women's roles increased the sense of efficacy and thus the motivation among women who were poised to consider political careers. The women's movement thus created a consciousness among a pool of women who were in a position to enter electoral politics. No less important, Mueller argues, was the movement's effect in shaping the outlook of women officeholders. By the mid-1970s, women at the higher levels of state office were more likely than before to see their difficulties in terms of discrimination and to see women's caucuses and women's organized actions as necessary responses to those difficulties. A new consciousness had reached the voters, too, as evidenced by the greater readiness of the electorate to support women candidates. The dissemination of a political consciousness around gender, Mueller tells us, meant that the increased representation of women in public office would be dependent not on voter prejudice but instead on an increasing availability of candidates.

POLITICAL PARTIES AND THE "STRUCTURE OF OPPORTUNITY"

What a social movement will be able to extract from the state is not knowable from the character or membership of the movement itself. Much will depend on what has been called the "political opportunity structure," a term that Sidney Tarrow (1983, 28–34) defines in terms of access to state institutions, the stability of political alignments, and the relation to allies and support groups.

The relationship to allies and support groups is the focus of the second section of this book. The essays in Part Two reveal a sharp contrast between the European and American experience: in Italy (as in France) the parties of the Left together with the labor movements have repeatedly (if not consistently) supported efforts to introduce measures that advance women's equality. Although their support has fallen far short of what feminists hope for, the Left has been far more responsive than the Christian Democrats or the parties of the Right.[10] The dilemma for the feminist movement in these countries is that the Left is at once the movement's most promising ally and its detractor, insisting as it does that the priorities of class politics cannot be sacrificed to gender interests. Negotiating the line between seeking influence "in the system" and maintaining movement autonomy, however, does not occupy the same prominence in the strategic thinking of the American women's movement.

Judith Hellman (Chapter 5) discusses three types of women's organizations in the Left-dominated city of Turin. Although these organizations were not looking to the worker's movement for an alliance partner, they had to struggle to find a way of voicing feminist claims, Hellman says, in terms that would "fit within the restrictive framework of the workerist politics of Turin." The "workerist" tradition in Turin, she observes, proved to be both a catalyst and a constraint, stimulating feminists to reach out to working-class women on the one hand, but inhibiting "the development of women's self-knowledge and consciousness" on the other.

One source of feminist misgiving about the leftist organizations with which they might ally is explored by Stephen Hellman in his essay on the Communist party organization (PCI) in Turin (Chapter 6). He describes the debates over the party's expectations about the nature of an individual's dedication to party work ("the model of militancy"), and the tensions this creates around the non-party commitments to family and to "personal" concerns that party activists might have. Hellman suggests that the PCI may be readier to adapt its programs and agendas to external societal pressures than it is to suffer changes to the *internal* value structure of the party organization.

This dual opportunity-constraint relationship between the Left and the women's movement in Italy is also documented in Karen Beckwith's discussion of national politics (Chapter 7). As she observes, feminist issues raised in parliament are mostly the result of leftist party initiative. The Christian Democrats, who introduced a national referendum to reverse the abortion reforms, clearly failed the feminist movement. By contrast, the Socialist and the Communist parties were both ready to sponsor at least some versions of abortion reform and legislation prohibiting violence against women. But, as Beckwith reports, the versions of the policies that the Left was willing to endorse robbed the measures of much of their feminist content.

The political opportunity structure in Germany is more restrictive, or at least is perceived so by activists in the German feminist movement. As Myra Ferree notes in Chapter 8, the "autonomous women's movement" in West Germany is concerned with maintaining control, self-sufficiency, and independence from the institutions of the state. She contrasts this with the American women's movement, which far more readily finds allies in the Democratic party, the unions, the bureaucracies, and from a range of other quarters. Where the women's movement in the United States seeks out such allies even at the risk of co-optation, the German women's movement avoids entanglement even at the risk of reduced influence. The reason for this difference, Ferree suggests, lies largely in the historical weakness of the liberal institutions in Germany and liberalism's greater strength in the U.S. It may also be that because the major political actor on the Left in West Germany is the Social Democratic party, rather than the more radical Left of the French and Italian socialist and communist parties, the determination of the women's movement to stay outside "establishment politics" is seen as more rational in Germany than in France or Italy.

The feminist movement in America is different in organization and ideology from its European counterparts. Mainstream feminism in the United States, liberal in its political tenets, is the only movement of those described in this volume with a mass-based national organization run by a paid, professional staff. In no country in Western Europe is there a national organization analogous to the National Organization for Women (NOW). Far less chary than its European counterparts of seeking allies "within the system," the feminist movement in the United States has, as Anne and Douglas Costain observe, "tried virtually every routine and non-routine method to obtain political influence." This alliance strategy runs the same risk, Ferree notes, of drawing the women's movement into a cooptative relationship with the state; but at the same time the American feminist movement's multifront strategy of playing all levers gives it an independence that is lacking when a movement must depend on the support of one or two strong leftist parties.

The Costains' essay (Chapter 9) identifies three periods in the movement's alliance strategy: a period of protest and nonpartisan pressure on political elites (1966–72); a period of broadening and routinizing in which the movement mounted court challenges, lobbies, boycotts (1972–77); and a period of turning increasingly toward electoral politics as the impending defeat of the ERA, the Republican electoral successes, and the emergence of a women's vote brought NOW into a closer alliance with the Democratic party (after 1977).

The feminist movement's new partisanship is explored in Jo Freeman's discussion (Chapter 10) of the Republican and Democratic parties. She points out the paradox historically, that although feminist concerns found a greater affinity with Republicans than with Democrats, the reverse now holds. The political culture of the Democratic party, she contends, now makes it more accessible than the Republican party to the interests of organized feminism.

The political opportunity structure has thus shifted in the United States. It has pulled the feminist movement into a closer alliance with the Democratic party. Both Freeman and the Costains raise questions about the wisdom of such an alliance and offer examples of the autonomy that has been relinquished by the movement in its efforts to win concessions (such as the Geraldine Ferraro nomination) from the party. This new partisanship will continue to be debated in the United States, over the next years, but it is unlikely to reach the salience of similar debates in either France, Italy, or Germany.[11]

But the differences in political opportunities at present are perhaps less striking than the similarities among countries. In no country has the women's movement succeeded for any extended period in forming its own political party. Irrespective of whether the political environment is hostile or receptive to third parties, separate women's political parties have never been anything but short-lived. The National Woman's Party in the U.S. functioned only briefly as an electoral force, and the efforts of *Choisir* in France to run its own slate for the European parliament left it unable to clear the 5 percent hurdle (Sauter-Bailliet 1981, 415). The brief life of such undertakings speaks to the slim rewards earned as against the enormous expenditure of money and energy required.

If the women's movement were able to organize its own political party, the need for electoral allies or party sponsors for legislative initiatives would be reduced. In lieu of entering such an alliance, significant sections of the feminist movement in every country have opted to ignore electoral politics at some cost to movement goals (Katzenstein 1984). But for the most part, feminist organizations have sought allies, usually on the left of the political spectrum. This has been part of recent electoral history in France and Italy; it is also occurring in Britain and the United States, where the new conservatism of Prime Minister Margaret Thatcher and President Ronald Reagan has made a Left out of the center. Feminism has shed its party agnosticism in favor of a closer alignment with the Labour and Democratic parties respectively ("The Women's Movement and the Labour Party," 1984). As feminism in the United States and Western Europe establishes closer links to parties of the Left (or relative Left), the movements have come to face a parallel dilemma. Not only must they ask themselves what such alliances will cost them in their ability to adhere to their own agenda, but they must also satisfy themselves that there are sufficient rewards to be gained. The fate of the 1984 Ferraro candidacy in a race that had little chance of success and the fate of the Ministry of Women's Rights (Ozzello 1983–84) under the return of the Gaullist party to power in France could be read as negative answers to this stipulation of "sufficient rewards." But they are better seen as evidence that in conservative times, at least some victories are possible.

THE STATE AND FEMINIST POLICY OUTCOMES

There is no simple linear relationship between the level of movement organizing and government response to feminist activity. The relationship between the articulation of feminist interests and policy outcome is mediated not only by the opportunities for alliances with political parties but also by the relations of other organized interests to the state.

In the third section of this book, the authors address the relations of the state, labor, and feminist policy. The three countries discussed, Sweden, Britain, and the United States, suggest a common theme. Where the labor movement proves to be strong, economic policies responsive to women's interests are more likely to follow. This is the lesson at least of Sweden. Where labor is the lesser partner—as is true in Britain—in a still centralized state, feminist policies are less likely to be pursued. But where the state is fragmented (geographically and functionally), even though the labor movement nationally is weak, the feminist movement may discover a wide range of opportunities, as the American movement has, to influence decision-making.

Mary Ruggie's essay (Chapter 11) argues the case for understanding the relationship between labor and the state as critical to an account of the variation in state responsiveness to women's economic interests. The fact that labor has been a weak partner in Britain (its interests given lesser priority on the national agenda) has led to an incomes policy that has done little for low-income women workers. In Sweden, by contrast, where labor has been a more nearly equal partner within the state, the commitment to reduce income inequalities has been treated more seriously. This has proved of great benefit to women, who, in Sweden as everywhere, are at the low end of the wage-earning scale.

It is likely that the existence of a strongly centralized state with labor as an important partner is one reason why the feminist movement has been less organized in Sweden than in many other countries. A strong labor movement or strong Left—as we saw in the previous discussion of Italy—has costs for the women's movement as an organization. In Sweden, women have begun, as Ruggie notes, to insist that more attention be paid to women as women and not only to women as low-income workers. Nevertheless, she argues, "the situation of women workers in Sweden is so significantly better than the comparative situation in other countries, especially Britain, that attention must be paid to the route of these achievements."

Joyce Gelb's essay on Britain and the United States (Chapter 12) offers an analysis complementary to Ruggie's. Gelb argues that the structure and values of British political institutions have isolated the feminist movement from the state. The highly centralized British political system operates, she observes, as if behind closed doors. It is thus relatively unresponsive to pressures from social movements or interest groups. Union and labour party voices in the government, through which feminist pressure might be exerted, are also less efficacious than in Sweden because, as Ruggie argues, labor interests do not occupy the same standing as they do in the shaping of Swedish national policies.

In the United States where a relatively decentralized and institutionally segmented state structure obtains, the feminist movement has been less marginalized and has sought more persistently to operate as an active political interest. This greater political openness of the American state has allowed the women's movement, Gelb contends, to make more dramatic gains than its British counterpart.

Janet Flammang's study of one city and county in the United States (chapter 13) demonstrates the political advantage of a relatively decentralized political system. Feminist activists in San Jose, California, were able to press for re-evaluation and adjustment of city pay scales, heralding a major breakthrough in the new political territory of "comparable worth." This success was possible in part because national political parties did not exert tight control over the local machinery and partly, too, because the liberal union, AFSCME, was an active force.

The San Jose case instructs us in the potential influence that organized feminism can have in a politically fragmented state system where power is decentralized. But such conditions provide the opportunity, not the guarantee, of movement influence. Reforms in which authority devolved on the regions of Italy had different consequences for feminism in different sections of the country; for instance, in the South the Christian Democrat–controlled region was slower to establish abortion clinics (mandated by a 1975 national law) than were the labor-dominated regions of the North (Lovenduski 1985, 235). By the same token, feminist initiatives launched in San Jose may be more successful than such attempts elsewhere in the United States.

On the more sanguine side, opportunities for influence at the local level can be found even in a strongly centralized system. The Greater London Council, for instance, has witnessed the formation of an influential women's committee, which has undertaken innovative projects in health care, lesbian rights, transportation, housing, and so on. Whether this committee has a secure future is unclear. But it demonstrates that the possibility of feminist influence even in a centralized state structure should not be ruled out.

FEMINIST MOVEMENT SUCCESS AND POLITICAL SYSTEM VARIATION

The three themes of this book suggest an apparent paradox. The feminist movement appears to be most successful in political systems where the Left is either most or least strong. The relationship of the feminist movement to gender consciousness, party alliances, and state structures all point to this same message. Consciousness as expressed by support for the feminist movement is most widely diffused in the U.S., Sweden, France, and Italy; least so in Britain, the Netherlands, and Germany. Leftist political parties are quick to take on, and take over, feminist issues (even as their feminist content is diluted) in France, Italy, and Sweden. In these countries, the women's movement has greater connection to and influence over the party agenda than is true in Great Britain or West Germany. In the United States, the feminist movement has succeeded in helping define the electoral agenda of at least one of the two major parties in the 1980s, as the Ferraro nomination and Democratic party platforms suggest. Finally, with respect to many areas of public policy, the state structure is more productive of policy reforms in Sweden and in the United States than in Great Britain (although with respect to certain areas of health and family support policies, Great Britain would rank well ahead of the United States).

But there is, in fact, no paradox. In the one case, centralized state structures and a strong Left accomplish what in the other case is realized by a strong feminist movement. This is not to say that the nature of success is identical in both cases. If feminist movement "success" can be measured by its mobilizational achievements, by its access to power, and by its policy results,[12] the kind of success achieved by a strong Left as against a strong women's movement is certainly different. In Sweden, policy success is won at the price of feminist organizational weakness.[13] The impressive employment and wage reforms and the consciousness of role equity issues generated by the state's very explicit commitment to role equality have in a sense robbed feminism of its organizational rationale. In the United States, an argument could be made that political mobilization, debate, and consciousness-raising are sometimes pursued at the expense of policy success. The attention given, for instance, by NOW's ERA campaign to demonstrations and boycotts—as opposed to electoral strategies—right up to the last few years before the amendment's defeat suggests that, intentional or not, the process of mobilization was deemed of critical importance for its own sake and not just as a means to the passage of the reform (Boles 1982).

This is not to imply that American feminists lack for policy achievements. But here, too, there seems to be a tradeoff. Some American activists rightfully express frustration at the absence of a strong progressive force in the United States that would work to usher in the kind of radical policies (reduced unemployment, better-paid jobs, support for low-income households, paid maternity and parental leave) that have been associated with welfare-state policies in Europe. But a comparison of a range of other policies in this country with those in much of Western Europe puts this otherwise well-placed frustration in a somewhat different perspective. The studies of feminist movements in Europe point out that one source of the American movement's strength is unexpected in terms of previous theories of social reforms. Descriptions of the difficulties faced by European parties of the Left in incorporating feminist goals suggest that the "decline of ideology" and the absence of ideological party divisions in the United States are not as incapacitating in the feminist case as previous discussions of welfare-state politics would suggest. In the case of a feminist movement that does not fit the traditional left-right delineation, the absence of a leftist or ideological party system appears to encourage the reevaluation of a particular array of policies and practices. The American feminist movement has succeeded in bringing national attention to issues of harassment, battering, rape, and sexual freedom (with its attendant discussion of homophobia, pornography, sexual pleasure). There are important policy endeavors in the economic sphere as well, illustrated by the newer campaigns around comparable worth and the feminization of poverty. Still, there is simply no denying that policies that would alleviate the situation of poor women in the United States lag well behind those of Western Europe.

Although more successful/less successful comparisons must be informed by national (class and race) differences in movement goals and values, agnosticism about the relative success of feminist movements would be a mistake. Comparative assessments are necessary if the imaginations of feminist activists are to be spurred to think afresh about old questions of what is desirable and what is possible in a more feminist world.

NOTES

Acknowledgments: I am grateful to Michael Ames, Peter Katzenstein, Carol Mueller, Ronnie Steinberg, and Sidney Tarrow for their useful suggestions on earlier drafts of this chapter, and to Alice Cook for her generous loan of materials on Western Europe.

1. See, e.g., Betty Friedan 1985; "Feminism's Identity Crisis" 1986; D'Souza 1986.

2. Phyllis Schlafly's *Eagle Forum* (June 1986) celebrates the "flood of anti-feminist articles" noting that "all of a sudden the 'establishment' publications have discovered the truths about women's lib that you have been reading for years in the *Phyllis Schlafly Report."*

3. One example dramatizes this point. Tradeswomen, an organization that supports women working in blue-collar jobs, in its monthly publication, *Trade Trax,* lists blue-collar support groups in the San Francisco area. They include such nonpublicized groups as Bay Area Women's Carpenters Committee, City of San Francisco Blue-Collar Women, Blue-Collar Asian Women, Organization of Women in Landscape, Women Electricians Group, Women in Electronic/Computer Repair, Women in Telecommunications, Plumbers Caucus, Women's Maritime Association, Sonoma County Tradeswomen, and the Alice B. Toklas Democratic Club—in addition to the usual harassment, rape, etc., hotlines and organizations.

4. But see Lovenduski (1985), which provides an exhaustive survey of European women's movements. The book by David Bouchier (1984) does compare the feminist movement in Britain and the United States. Mary Ruggie's (1984) book on Sweden and Britain, although its focus is not the women's movement, provides an important model for comparative analysis of women's issues.

5. The characterization of the women's movement as transformative was suggested by Michael Lipsky at the Cornell workshop on which this volume is based and was critical to my thinking in this chapter.

6. The terms "private" and "public" that by convention demarcate extra- and intra-household spheres are placed in quotations because they are, and should be, distinctions under challenge. Much in so-called public life is kept private and much in so-called private life is directly shaped and influenced by law, state authority, and public opinion. And yet it should be recognized that although feminists are right to question the definition of what is public and what is private, matters that do involve individual relationships and the household are less *easily* shaped by public authority than are so-called public matters.

7. Gurin (1984) also includes a third dimension, a commitment to collective action as a solution to women's subordination, which may be closer to what we call here political ideology.

8. Swedish respondents rank as far more egalitarian than other national respondents on a number of measures. When asked, for instance, whether in the early training of children they felt it would better to teach a boy to behave like a boy and a girl to behave like a girl, only 6 percent of the Swedish respondents replied affirmatively compared with 63 percent of the Japanese, 28 percent of the Americans, 31 percent of the Germans, 20 percent of the British, and 20 percent of the Filipinos (Hastings and Hastings 1986, 715).

9. For good discussions of the way the political consciousness of French women has affected and has in turn been influenced by the elections of leftist parties, see Bashevkin (1984); Northcutt and Flaitz (1985); and Ozzello (1983–84).

10. The recent history of the Roudy ministry is a dramatic illustration of this dilemma. President François Mitterand, although less than fully responsive to certain feminist issues such as reproductive rights, appointed Yvette Roudy to head a newly created Ministry of Women's Rights. He thus brought women's interests back onto the French political agenda (Ozzello 1983–84). But with the return of the Gaullist party and the assumption of the prime ministership by Jacques Chirac in 1986, the Roudy ministry was removed from the cabinet and virtually disempowered by a reduction in the budget allotment.

11. It is reflective of the unimportance of this debate in the United States that in their recent fine study of the American Women's movement, Ferree and Hess (1985, 119–20) devote less than two pages to "playing party politics."

12. For a consideration of definitions of success, see Ergas (1982), Melucci (1984, 830), Tarrow (1983, 7–8).

13. The Frederika Bremer Association has about 8,000 members. The smaller and more radical Group 8 has come only recently to identify itself as feminist. Each of the parties except the Communist party of Sweden has women's organizations associated with them. Leaders of these women's groups have been very influential; indeed, Eva Moberg, the editor of the Frederika Bremer Association's bimonthly journal, is credited with having launched the debate over sex roles with her essay of 1961 on women's emancipation. Yet the ability of women's organizations to mobilize is surprisingly limited. As Hilda Scott (1982, 158) writes, "There is probably no Western country where hostility to 'feminism' as opposed to 'women's liberation' is so out of proportion to the strength and militancy of the avowed feminists in the women's movement." Scott also writes that feminist initiatives around academic programs, bookstores, refuges, cafes, etc., are more infrequently found in Sweden than in Denmark, the U.S., or Britain.

REFERENCES

Adams, Carolyn T., and Katherine T. Winston. 1980. *Mothers at Work: Public Policies in the United States, Sweden and China.* New York: Longman.

Altbach, Edith Hoshino. 1984. "The New German Women's Movement." In E. Altbach, J. Clause, D. Schultz, and N. Stephan, eds., *German Feminism: Readings in Politics and Literature,* 3–26. Albany: State University of New York Press.

Bashevkin, Slyvia B. 1984. "Changing Patterns of Politicization and Partisanship among Women in France." *British Journal of Political Science* 15 (no. 1): 75–96.

Boles, Janet K. 1982. "Building Support for the ERA." *PS* 15: 572–77.

Bouchier, David. 1984. *The Feminist Challenge: The Movement for Women's Liberation in Britain and the U.S.A.* New York: Schocken Books.

Cook, Alice Hanson, Val R. Lorwin, and Arlene Kaplan Daniels. 1984. *Women and Trade Unions in Eleven Industrialized Countries.* Philadelphia: Temple University Press.

D'Souza, Dinesh. 1986. "The New Feminist Revolt; This Time It's against Feminism." *Policy Review* 35 (Winter): 46–52.

Epstein, Cynthia Fuchs, and Rose Laub Coser, eds. 1981. *Access to Power: Cross-National Studies of Women and Elites.* London: Allen and Unwin.

Ergas, Yasmine. 1982. "1968–1969—Feminism and the Italian Party System: Women's Politics in a Decade of Turmoil." *Comparative Politics* 14 (no. 3): 253–79.

Farley, Jennie, ed. 1985. *Women Workers in Fifteen Countries: Essays in Honor of Alice Hanson Cook.* Cornell International Industrial and Labor Relations Report no. 11. Ithaca, N.Y.: ILR Press, Cornell University.

"Feminism's Identity Crisis." 1986. *Newsweek.* 31 March, 51.

Ferree, Myra Marx, and Beth B. Hess. 1985. *Controversy and Coalition: The New Feminist Movement.* Boston: G. K. Hall.

Friedan, Betty. 1985. "How to Get the Women's Movement Moving Again." *New York Times Magazine.* 3 November, 26ff.

Frye, Marilyn, 1983. *The Politics of Reality: Essays in Feminist Theory.* Trumansburg, N.Y.: Crossing Press.

Gallup Poll. 1986. *Newsweek.* 31 March, 51.

Gurin, Patricia, and Aloen Townsend. 1984. "Properties of Gender Identity and Their Implications for Gender Consciousness." Manuscript, author's copy.

Hastings, Elizabeth, and Philip Hastings, eds. 1986. *Index to International Public Opinion, 1984–1985.* Westport, Conn.: Greenwood Press.

Howe, Florence. 1984. *Myths of Coeducation.* Bloomington: Indiana University Press.

Kahn, Alfred J., and Sheila B. Kamerman, eds. 1978. *Family Policy: Government and Families in Fourteen Countries.* New York: Columbia University Press.

Kahn, Alfred J., and Sheila B. Kamerman. 1983. *Income Transfers for Families with Children: An Eight-Country Study.* Philadelphia: Temple University Press.

———. 1987. *Child Care.* Dover, Mass.: Auburn House.

Kamerman, Sheila B., and Alfred J. Kahn. 1981. *Child Care, Family Benefits, and Working Parents: A Study in Comparative Policy.* New York: Columbia University Press.

———. 1983. *Maternity Policies and Working Women.* New York: Columbia University Press.

Katzenstein, Mary Fainsod. 1984. "Feminism and the Meaning of the Vote." *Signs* 10 (no. 1): 4–26.

Klein, Ethel. 1984. *Gender Politics: From Consciousness to Mass Politics.* Cambridge, Mass.: Harvard University Press.

Lovenduski, Joni. 1985. Manuscript. "Women in European Politics." (Since published as *Women and European Politics.* Brighton, Eng.: Wheatsheaf Books, 1986.)

———, and Jill Hills. 1981. *The Politics of the Second Electorate: Women and Public Participation.* London: Routledge & Kegal Paul.

Melucci, Alberto. 1984. "An End to Social Movements?" *Social Science Information* 32 (no. 4/5): 819–35.

Northcutt, Wayne, and Jeffra Flaitz. 1985. "Women, Politics and the French Socialist Government." *West European Politics* 8 (no. 4): 50–71.

Ozzello, Yvonne Rochette, with Elaine Marks. 1983–84. " 'Mignonnes allons voir sous la rose. . . .' Socialism, Feminism and Misogyny in the France of Yvette Roudy, May 1981–May 1983." *Contemporary French Civilization* 8 (Fall/Winter): 202–27.

Pahl, Jan. 1985. "Refuges for Battered Women: Ideology and Action." *Feminist Review* 19: 25–43.

Ratner, Ronnie Steinberg. 1980. *Equal Employment Policy for Women: Strategies for Implementation in the United States, Canada, Western Europe.* Philadelphia: Temple University Press.

Rucht, Dieter. 1984. "Comparative New Social Movements: Organizations and Strategies in a Cross-Sectional and Cross-National View." Paper presented at EGOS conference, Aarhus, Denmark.

Ruggie, Mary. 1984. *The State and The Working Women: A Comparative Study of Britain and Sweden*. Princeton, N.J.: Princeton University Press.

Sauter-Bailliet, Theresia. 1981. "The Feminist Movement in France." *Women's Studies International Quarterly* 4 (no. 4) 405–20.

Scott, Hilda. 1982. *Sweden's "Right to be Human": Sex-Role Equality, The Goal and the Reality*. Armonk, N.Y.: M. E. Sharpe.

Tarrow, Sidney. 1983. "Struggling to Reform: Social Movements and Policy Change during Cycles of Protest." Center for International Studies, Western Societies Occasional Paper no. 15. Ithaca, N.Y.: Cornell University.

"The Women's Movement and the Labour Party: An Interview with Labour Party Feminists." 1984. *Feminist Review* 16 (April): 75–87.

Part One CHANGING
CONSCIOUSNESS

1 The Diffusion of Consciousness in the United States and Western Europe

ETHEL KLEIN

A political movement such as the women's movement is an expression of widely shared grievances. In the United States, women have lobbied legislators, initiated lawsuits, marched in demonstrations, and boycotted major corporations to secure their rights. These actions were not spontaneous expressions of political discontent. They were organized efforts by a large number of women who felt that the government had some responsibility to help remedy their problems.

The ideology, the problems, and even some of the solutions espoused by contemporary feminists have been around for a long time. Yet most women were not willing to support feminist activism until after the mid–1960s. Personal problems rarely gain a political voice. People often blame themselves for their difficulties. Only when they see that their problems are shared by other people like them, the group, can they attribute the source of the concerns to social conditions such as discrimination and look to political solutions. The belief that personal problems result from unfair treatment because of one's group membership rather than from a lack of personal effort or ability is known as group consciousness. The emergence and maintenance of this group consciousness is central to the formation and success of political movements (Klein 1984; Oberschall 1973; Useem 1975).

An insistence that women's roles are determined by society rather than biology lies at the heart of theories of patriarchy and women's powerlessness. As long as women believed that they belonged in the home with sole responsibility for the care of children, they did not question why they were not represented in business, government, or the arts. Only after women came to reject their traditional, biologically defined role could an alternative image based on gender equality be internalized and a new framework be made available for political change.

The feminist movement grew in response to the development of a new norm defining women's daily experiences. As the critical dimensions of women's lives—which were traditionally characterized by a stable family relationship centered on children and domestic production—were transformed by the demands of an

23

urban industrial economy, a new definition of womanhood emerged, placing increased emphasis on women as workers and less on women as mothers (Klein 1984). Approval for the employment of married women increased dramatically, from 25 percent in 1945 to 44 percent in 1967 and to 64 percent in 1972, while support for large families dropped from 45 percent in 1960 to 35 percent in 1966 and to 23 percent in 1971. The traditional view that becoming wives, homemakers, and mothers is women's natural destiny was no longer a matter of consensus by 1972. Many women, 41 percent, felt that they should have an equal role with men in the public sphere, as compared to only 25 percent who argued that women's place is definitely in the home. Women were almost evenly divided on the issue of biological determinism, with a sizable number (43 percent) believing that society defines women's roles (Klein 1984: 90).

Yet the acceptance of this new group identity did not automatically translate into political activism. An alternative group image merely provides a framework for new social comparisons. It facilitates the questioning of past criteria for the distribution of resources.

Political consciousness requires that the acceptance of social equality be coupled with a recognition and rejection of unequal and unfair treatment. People need to see themselves as objects of collective discrimination or as victims of inadequate social institutions before they can become politically active. This shift in criticism from the self to social institutions allows problems that were once thought to be personal to be seen to have a social cause and probably a political solution. In 1946, most women (72 percent) believed that there were sometimes good reasons to pay women less than men for the same job. By 1968, 66 percent favored equal pay, but only 33 percent thought that women faced discrimination. In 1970, 54 percent of women felt that a woman with the same abilities as a man did not stand an equal chance of becoming a corporate executive. A substantial number of women also felt that they faced discrimination in obtaining executive positions in business (50 percent), obtaining top jobs in the professions (40 percent), and getting skilled employment (40 percent). By 1972 many women (42 percent) ascribed at least some of their problems to society rather than to themselves, providing a mass-based constituency for the feminist movement.

DIFFUSION OF FEMINIST CONSCIOUSNESS IN THE UNITED STATES

The tremendous growth in feminist consciousness since the emergence of the women's movement rises out of the educational efforts of the movement itself, as well as out of the continued integration of women into nontraditional lifestyles. Feminist leaders have incorporated discussions of social equality and sex discrimination into a coherent ideology, which identified sex discrimination as women's problem, held the government responsible for ending this unfair treatment, and offered a plan of action to ease women's burdens. By 1980 the majority of men (54 percent) and women (58 percent) came to believe that differences in men and women's experiences were due to the way they were raised rather than to basic physical differences or innate abilities. Women were placing a higher priority on self-fulfillment. Only 48 percent of women in 1985, compared to 64 percent in 1974, regarded being taken care of by a loving husband as more important than making it on one's own. Most women in the late 1980s are working to help support themselves and their families, but the majority (66 percent) see their adult roles in the workplace and would continue to work even if they were financially secure.[1]

Americans have embraced many of the new roles brought about by the changing division of labor. When people think of the ideal ways to combine work, marriage, and children, a marriage where husband and wife share responsibilities is deemed preferable to the traditional division of breadwinner and housewife by the majority of men (50 percent) and women (57 percent) as compared to a scant minority of men (44 percent) and women (46 percent) in 1974. There is a general sense that women have gained more respect through recent efforts to change their status. When the movement first emerged, some men (40 percent) and women (38 percent) already felt that women were more respected in 1970 than a decade earlier. A decade later, 53 percent of men and women thought that women were more respected in 1980 than in 1970. By 1985 this assessment was even stronger, with 60 percent believing that women today are more respected.

People expect this trend toward greater role equality to continue. Most men and women (75 percent) believe that women's roles in the future will be very different from their roles in 1985 with only 10 percent believing that women will revert to more traditional roles. Moreover, most Americans (68 percent) believe that women's roles *should* continue to change, even if the consequences are unpredictable. This is a substantial increase from just five years earlier, when 57 percent favored continued change.

In the course of the last 15 years there has been a greater recognition of sex discrimination. In 1985 the majority of women felt that they did not have an equal chance with men in becoming business executives (57 percent), entering prestige professions (55 percent), or obtaining top jobs in government (57 percent). More women felt that they were excluded from leadership responsibilities in 1985 (46 percent) than in 1970 (31 percent), and the sense that women had less access to skilled jobs grew from 40 percent in 1970 to 51 percent in 1985. Overall, the percentage of women arguing that there are more advantages to being a man than a woman increased from 31 percent in 1974 to 49 percent in 1985.

Changing views on women's roles and opportunities have been accompanied by increased support for political efforts to strengthen women's status in general and the feminist movement specifically. Public support for efforts to advance women's rights increased from 44 percent of men and 40 percent of women in

1970 to most men (69 percent) and women (73 percent) in 1985. People were also considerably more positive toward the efforts of women's organizations than they had been in the past. In 1980 many more people (53 percent) felt that feminist organizations were helpful than had thought so in 1970 (34 percent). Public support for the women's liberation movement increased from 49 percent in 1972 to 60 percent in 1979. In 1985 most men and women (72 percent) strongly agreed that over the past 20 years the women's movement had helped rather than hurt working women, but many (42 percent) also believed that it made little difference in the lives of homemakers. Still, more people thought the movement had helped homemakers (33 percent) rather than hurt them (20 percent).

Trends in attitudes toward appropriate sex roles, perceived discrimination, and support for efforts to further women's rights reveal a tremendous growth and diffusion of feminist support between 1970 and 1985. Efforts toward improving women's status were initially endorsed by women with nontraditional experiences, but support then spread to other segments of the population (see Table 1-1).

Initially, the feminist movement found its greatest advocates among women who were single (53 percent) or divorced (61 percent), college educated (44 percent), young (46 percent), or living in urban areas (47 percent). It faced greatest resistance among traditional women. By 1985, support for feminist efforts had reached even higher levels among women who were single or divorced (84 per-

TABLE 1-1
WOMEN'S SUPPORT FOR EFFORTS TO STRENGTHEN WOMEN'S STATUS (% IN FAVOR)

	1970	1972	1974	1980	1985
Single	53	62	69	75	84
Divorced/separated	61	57	68	75	84
Married	38	46	55	64	70
Widowed	36	40	49	48	61
18 to 29	46	56	67	74	80
30 to 39	40	49	70	70	76
40 to 49	39	42	63	60	76
50 and older	35	41	56	55	64
Urban	47	52	64	62	
Rural	34	40	51	46	
White	37	45	55	62	72
Black	60	62	67	77	78
No high school	36	42	43	54	63
High school	38	43	56	63	72
College +	44	57	67	73	79

Source: 1985 Virginia Slims American Women's Opinion Poll.

cent), college educated (79 percent), or under 30 (80 percent). And resistance to feminist efforts decreased dramatically between 1970 and 1985 among more traditional women: support for improving women's status increased from 38 percent to 70 percent among married women; 36 percent to 61 percent among widows; 36 percent to 63 percent for women with less than a high school education; and 35 percent to 64 percent among elderly women.

Ideas of the feminist movement have long found support among Black women. Contrary to what is often heard in public discussion, Black women have been the most supportive constituency of feminist principles. In 1970, when only 37 percent of white women embraced feminist activism as necessary, 60 percent of Black women favored feminist efforts. This gap had narrowed by 1985, but Black women were still more favorable toward women's rights than white women (78 percent versus 72 percent).

Unlike white women, who had to reject biological definitions that circumscribed womanhood in terms of nurturance, passivity, and dependence, Black women have historically been socialized to be personally and economically independent. Few Black women fantasize about Prince Charming whisking them off to a happy-ever-after life. In the early years of the feminist movement, when women debated work versus marriage, white women were much more likely (67 percent) than Black women (47 percent) to opt for a loving husband to care for them rather than make it on their own. Ten years later, black women still showed greater preference for having a job over being a housewife, if given the option, than did white women (67 percent versus 43 percent). Black women have always been more supportive of feminist activism and more likely to see the efforts of the women's movement as helping them personally.

In the late 1970s the Equal Rights Amendment (ERA) became the symbol of the feminist movement. Black women have consistently supported the amendment in greater proportions than white women. ERA has been a much more controversial issue for white women because it represents a struggle over changing definitions of femaleness. When the amendment was defeated in 1982, few Black women (6 percent) were pleased. The majority were supportive but indifferent (54 percent), while a sizable number (40 percent) were displeased. White women were more polarized on this issue, with 27 percent pleased by its defeat; 46 percent supportive but indifferent; and 27 percent expressing serious discontent.

Adherence to the ideology of sex equality is not synonymous, however, with a sense of membership in the women's movement or an endorsement of all its policies. Most Black feminists are working outside of mainstream feminist organizations to create space for discussing the problems facing Black women. There are long-standing Black women's clubs, sororities, and organizations—such as the National Council of Negro Women—that were addressing the concerns of Black women prior to the emergence of the feminist movement. As the debate over women's place became more radical, Black women lent their voice by forming the

National Black Feminist Organization (1973), the National Alliance of Black Feminists (1976), and the National Association of Black Professional Women (1976). Black feminists also pressed for the establishment of the Mary McLeod Bethune Memorial Museum, the National Archive for Black Women's History, and the National Institute for Women of Color to establish the Black woman's rich history and enlighten discussion of current public policy. At the community level, most Black women address feminist concerns through their local clubs, churches, the YWCA, or neighborhood organizations rather than through newly established feminist groups (Giddings 1984; Hooks 1981).

White working-class women were initially much more resistant to the feminist ideology of self-determination and awareness of sex discrimination than Black or middle-class women. Many have been caught between religious and cultural values on the one hand that result in expectations of marriage and motherhood as a woman's primary role, and a rapidly changing economy and social environment on the other that require women to help support their families financially. During the early 1970s, working-class women were much more likely than middle-class women to believe that being cared for by a loving husband was more important than being able to work on one's own (73 percent versus 51 percent) and had a greater preference for a traditional marriage over a sharing marriage (69 percent versus 45 percent). In the early days of the movement, middle-class women favored feminist efforts (57 percent) much more than working-class women (42 percent).

By 1980 many more working-class women were supportive of feminist principles. In looking at the roots of sex role differentiation in society, working-class women were almost as likely as middle-class women to attribute the cause to socialization rather than biology (57 percent compared to 59 percent) and to argue that sex discrimination made it more advantageous to be a man than a woman (40 percent compared to 45 percent). These changes in role orientation and recognition of discrimination among working-class women increased support for efforts to strengthen women's role and status from 42 percent in 1970 to 54 percent in 1980 to 63 percent in 1985. Support among middle-class women increased from 57 percent in 1970 to 73 percent in 1980 to 79 percent in 1985.

Support for feminist goals among working-class women, as in the case of Black women, has not translated into involvement in feminist organizations or feminist politics directly, but the principles of feminism have found their way into recently formed working-class women's organizations. In 1975 the National Congress of Neighborhood Women (NCNW) was formed in the Williamsburg section of Brooklyn, New York, as a grassroots movement—composed primarily of Italian, Polish, and some Black and Hispanic women—to provide a voice for the concerns of women living in poor and working-class neighborhoods. The organization, founded by a feminist social worker and a radical feminist organizer, is now a national coalition of loosely related locally autonomous community groups. The NCNW sponsors courses focusing on job training, development of leadership skills, and legal rights; it funds shelters for battered women; it organizes consciousness-raising groups and provides classes in cooking, knitting, pre- and postnatal care, and Bible studies (Gelb and Klein 1983; Gittell and Naples 1982).

Working-class politics is traditionally linked to labor movements and trade union activism. Some feminist concerns have been incorporated into the labor movement through the Coalition of Labor Union Women (CLUW), founded in 1974 to increase the representation of women and women's concerns (such as flexible hours and affirmative action, which most unions oppose) and to organize women workers. CLUW has pushed for endorsement of comparable worth, paid maternity leave, child care allowances, and equity in pension programs as part of all collective bargaining agreements. The coalition does not define itself as a feminist organization however, but rather as a labor organization representing the interests of women within the larger labor movement. (Gelb and Klein 1983; Wertheimer 1977; Schroedel 1985).

Even with the formation of CLUW, the historic antipathy to women in the trade union movement and the resistance of many workers to unionization has prompted many working women, particularly clericals, to form independent organizations such as Union Women's Alliance to Gain Equality (Union WAGE), the Nine to Five National Association of Working Women, and Employed Women. These groups organize drives to upgrade salaries and promotion opportunities in banks, insurance companies, law firms, publishing houses, brokerage houses, and universities. Unlike unions that focus most of their energies on the collective bargaining contract, these organizations advance the interests of clerical workers through enforcement of affirmative action and anti-discrimination legislation, demonstrations against employers, and educational efforts. They provide workers with information about job rights and publicize occupational health and safety needs. While they build on legislation passed by the feminist movement and work for reforms that are part of the feminist agenda, they do not define themselves as feminist organizations and have only recently begun to develop more formal links to other activist women's organizations.

FEMINISM AND ELECTORAL POLITICS

The changing social and economic conditions that underlie the emergence of the feminist movement have also had consequence for electoral politics. As women entered the public world, their participation in the electoral arena increased. Historically, men voted in greater numbers than women, while women voters, we are told, voted like their men. By the mid-1980s, women's participation rates were greater than men's, and a women's vote has emerged (Baxter and Lansing 1983).

Women's policy preferences also now diverge from those of men (Clymer 1983; Ketter 1985; Klein 1984 and 1985; Shapiro and Mahajan 1986). These disparities are most evident on issues of peace, social services, consumer protection, political reform, and women's economic rights. The largest and most persistent differences are to be found on policy questions that have to do with violence (Frankovic 1982; Smith 1984). Thus, during the 1970s, women were less favorable than men to military intervention, defense spending, and the assumption of a tough posture toward the Soviet Union. Similarly, they were most likely to oppose the death penalty and the draft, and more likely to support gun control.

In a variety of domestic policy areas, women have tended to be more partial than men to government activism. For example, they have been more likely to favor shutting down nuclear power plants, the pursuit of environmental protection even at the cost of economic growth, jail terms for drunk drivers, bans on cigarette advertising, and measures to reform campaign practices. In addition, especially since the mid-1970s, women have been markedly more supportive than men of government efforts to help minorities and the poor. These differences in the perspectives and priorities of men and women have been the bases of the women's vote.

Studies of the 1980, 1982, and 1984 elections reveal that men and women cast their votes on the basis of different considerations. In 1980, there was an 8 percent difference between Reagan's proportion of the male vote and his share of the female vote. The 1982 elections demonstrated that the women's vote was a partisan phenomenon, or issue vote, independent of Reagan. Higher proportions of women than men voted for Democratic candidates in 73 percent of the 85 statewide races covered by the networks' polls. The 1982 National Election Study found a 6 percent gender gap in favor of Democratic congressional candidates; in districts where there was no incumbent running for reelection, the gap averaged 16 percent (Baxter and Lansing 1983; Klein 1984 and 1985; Miller and Malanchuk 1983).

The results of the 1984 elections reveal that the women's vote is part of a complicated process forestalling a political realignment in the United States. More women voted for Reagan than for Mondale, but women were less supportive of the president by a difference of 8 percent. Despite the size of Reagan's winning margin, the Democrats managed to gain two Senate seats and hold their losses in the House to 16 seats. The women's vote played a critical role in holding down a Republican surge. It was the key to victory for liberal Democratic candidates in four senate races: those in Illinois, Iowa, Massachusetts, and Michigan. The Democrats benefited from a gender gap in House races as well: 53 percent of women—compared to 47 percent of men—supported Democratic congressional candidates (Klein 1985).

However, this women's vote is not monolithic. The importance women place on issues and spending priorities is influenced by their race, class, and age. Middle-class women are most concerned about world peace, women's rights, and educational and economic opportunities; working-class women focus on social services, employment, and economic security.

The concerns of different groups of women during the 1982 nonpresidential

TABLE 1-2
WOMEN'S BUDGET PRIORITIES, 1982

Issue	Income	Race	Household Head	Age
Environment	−.05	−.13	.06	.19
Health	.07	−.16	.07	.07
Cities	−.02	−.20	.04	.08
Crime	.06	−.13	.03	.07
Drugs	.10	−.13	.04	−.07
Education	−.07	−.17	.00	.27
Blacks	.03	−.24	.07	.06
Defense	.09	−.05	.00	−.15
Welfare	.20	−.34	.14	.01
Social Security	.14	−.15	.03	.22
Food stamps	.19	−.38	.06	.16
Student loans	.04	−.27	.00	.32
Unemployment	.10	−.38	.02	.12
Handicapped	.00	−.29	−.03	.13

Source: 1982 National Election Study.
Note: Entries are Pearsonian correlation coefficients; $n = 784$.

campaign illustrates this point (Table 1-2).[2] Class differences, measured in terms of family income or being a female head of household, emerged on issues of welfare expenditures ($r = .20$) and food stamps ($r = .19$): women from higher-income families felt too much was being spent on these programs while low income women felt the government needed to guarantee jobs ($r = .20$). On the other hand, there were no class differences in women's assessments of how much money ought to be spent on the environment, health, crime, education, or defense.

The respondent's life stage also influenced assessments of spending priorities. Younger women more than older women favored increased allocations for environmental protection ($r = .19$), education ($r = .27$), student loans ($r = .32$), and Social Security ($r = .22$). There were no generational differences in assessing how much should be spent on health, cities, combatting crime and drugs, or welfare.

Minority women favored increased spending on non-defense-related items in much greater proportions than white women. The largest differences emerged on perceptions of the government's responsibility for aiding minorities ($r = .30$), guaranteeing jobs ($r = .32$), and spending on welfare ($r = .34$), food stamps ($r = .38$), student loans ($r = .27$), cities ($r = .20$), and unemployment ($r = .38$).

Electoral politics is being shaped by the emergence of an explicitly feminist constituency as well. Feminist women, those who were displeased with the defeat of the ERA, favored cutbacks in military spending ($r = .31$) and increases in aid to minorities ($r = .30$) and social services ($r = .20$); and they held the government responsible for providing jobs ($r = .20$). Yet there were race, class, and age differences even among feminist voters. Working-class feminists were more concerned than middle-class feminists with increasing spending for welfare ($r = .21$) and Social Security ($r = .20$). Younger feminists gave greater priority to funding environmental protection ($r = .19$) and student loans ($r = .33$) than did older ERA proponents.

Major differences emerge between minority and majority feminists. Black feminists were much more likely than white feminists to favor increased spending for welfare ($r = .41$), Social Security ($r = .26$), food stamps ($r = .44$), and unemployment ($r = .40$). There was agreement, however, on a host of issues, including environment, health, cities, education, aid to Blacks, and defense.

The agreements and disagreements on spending priorities found among feminists based on age, race, and class underscore the possibilities and problems for organizing a feminist constituency among the electorate. They parallel the differences in priorities that have made movement coalitions between feminist organizations and working-class and minority women's groups difficult. The diffusion of feminist consciousness and favorable assessments of feminist efforts across most social groups provides a broad-based constituency for feminist politics, but the proliferation of organizations aimed at addressing the concerns of diverse groups of women has made the passage of a feminist policy agenda more difficult.

Feminist issues such as pay equity, day care, reproductive rights, freedom from sexual violence, affirmative action, and political representation are widely supported by Black and working-class women. Yet a political partnership between women of different races and classes has been limited, in part because of differences in priorities. For Black women, issues of social services, health, and housing are more central concerns than they have been for the feminist agenda until recently. The women's movement has successfully raised many important health-related issues: protesting unnecessary hysterectomies, mastectomies, and caesarean sections; criticizing doctors for overprescribing tranquilizers; promoting a better understanding of menstruation, menopause, birth control, and women's mental health needs. While all women benefit from these efforts, Black women describe their health issues in terms of access to basic medical care, nutrition, and decent treatment. Feminists have succeeded in legally forcing landlords to rent to women, and banks to provide credits and mortgages, but policies targeted to the housing needs of inner-city women or female heads of households have not received the same attention. While feminist scholars have documented the feminization of poverty for years, questions of poverty and social services have only recently received primary attention from feminist activists.

The feminist movement lacks an organizational base that penetrates these various communities of women and is therefore currently incapable of aggregating and consolidating policy preferences across these groups. There have been some limited successes in this direction—such as the 1977 International Women's

Year Conference in Houston, the development of grassroots coalitions on such issues as domestic violence and economic justice, and voter registration efforts through the Women's Vote Project—but the absence of strong local parties or unions has meant the proliferation of women's groups aimed at addressing the interaction of race and class with sex rather than a consolidation of efforts around a focused set of demands. Over the last ten years women's organizations have been forming coalitions at the state and local levels with other labor, civil rights, welfare, and community groups, but this is a very slow and difficult process—particularly when local party organizations are unwilling or unable to promote or facilitate the compromises and coordination such efforts require. The organization of American politics around interest groups has allowed for the rapid emergence of women's groups concerned with a broad set of issues, but the absence of strong parties to coordinate these disparate concerns has made the passage of feminist policies, despite their broad-based support, much more difficult (Gelb and Klein 1983).

FEMINIST CONSCIOUSNESS IN WESTERN EUROPE

If feminism in the United States grew in response to dramatic changes in the sexual division of labor, then one would also expect women's movements to emerge in European countries. In fact, feminist organizations did surface in most Western European democracies during the early 1970s, including France, West Germany, Italy, Holland, and Great Britain. By the end of the 1970s feminist movements had appeared in Greece and Spain as well. All of these movements have raised the issue of role equality and sex discrimination. They have taken a variety of forms and met with different degrees of success (Hills and Lovenduski 1981; Randall 1982).

Feminist concerns have also made it onto the agenda of the European Community as a whole. The Commission of the European Communities has conducted three studies in an attempt to understand the attitudes of men and women toward some of the problems their countries face. In 1983 the commission conducted a study of men and women's attitudes on women's employment situation and their role in society. The findings of this study illustrate the extent of feminist consciousness in Europe and its possible roots and consequences for feminist politics.[3]

Feminism builds on the rejection of the traditional division of labor in favor of more egalitarian roles. Most citizens of the European Community (64 percent) agree that there should be fewer differences between the respective roles of men and women. Yet when it comes to choosing work and family roles, Europeans are less likely than Americans to see an egalitarian marriage as ideal (Table 1-3). Members of the European Community divide among three scenarios for job and family roles: one where both partners have absorbing jobs and share equally in household and child care (36 percent); another where the wife works at a less demanding job and thereby takes greater responsibility for the household (30 per-

TABLE 1-3
BEST DIVISION OF RESPONSIBILITIES (% EUROPEAN OPINION 1983)

	Equal	Wife Larger Share	Wife Purely Housewife	None of These	No Reply
BY AGE AND SEX					
Men					
15–24 years	47	31	17	2	3
25–39 years	38	36	21	3	2
40–54 years	26	34	34	4	2
55 and over	25	26	43	3	3
Women					
15–24 years	56	24	14	3	3
25–39 years	43	31	22	2	2
40–54 years	34	32	28	3	3
55 and over	29	27	37	3	4
BY COUNTRY					
Belgium	31	22	35	7	5
Denmark	46	30	16	5	3
Germany	26	34	30	4	6
France	40	26	29	3	2
Ireland	30	24	39	3	4
Italy	41	28	29	1	1
Luxembourg	25	21	47	4	3
Netherlands	38	25	29	5	3
United Kingdom	37	36	23	2	2
Greece	51	22	24	2	1
TOTAL	36	30	28	3	3

Source: *European Women and Men in 1983*. 1984. Brussels: Commission of the European Communities, 30.

cent); and the traditional division where the husband works and the wife runs the home (28 percent).

Support for social equality is related to changes in the sexual division of labor. Preferences for egalitarian marriages are shaped by age and the extent of non-traditional experience. A marriage in which both men and women share home and work responsibilities is seen as ideal by many young men (47 percent) and women (56 percent) between 15 and 24 years old, and by a substantial number of men (38 percent) and women (43 percent) between 25 and 39 years, but by few people (26 percent) of 50 years or older. This older cohort of men (43 percent) and women (37 percent) have the strongest preference for maintaining the traditional division of labor.

Employment arrangements also shape assessments of ideal roles. Men with employed wives are much more likely to prefer equality in the division of labor than those whose wives are not working (42 percent versus 23 percent). This support among men with wives in the labor force is somewhat conditioned by age: 59 percent of those between 15 and 24, and 48 percent between 25 and 39, prefer sharing roles—as compared to 36 percent of those 40 to 54 years old, and 40 percent of men of 55 years or older. Employed women are much more likely to idealize an egalitarian marriage than are housewives (51 percent compared to 33 percent). The preference for shared responsibilities is prevalent among working women of all ages: 56 percent of the youngest cohort and 45 percent of the oldest chose a sharing relationship as ideal.

Approximately one-third of women in the European Community are currently employed, yet two-thirds of women say that—given a choice—they would prefer to be employed. Most women (60 percent) in the labor force say they would continue to work even if they had enough money to live as comfortably as they wished. It is important to note, however, that a significant number of women in Europe work part time (39 percent) and that most of these women (78 percent) prefer to continue with part-time work.

These patterns are similar to those found in the earlier years of the feminist movement in the United States, when support for gender equality was first embraced by younger cohorts and men and women with nontraditional experiences, and later diffused to the more traditional segments of the population. European women—and to a lesser extent, men—no longer see traditional arrangements as viable or even ideal; they welcome women's entry into the workplace but have not, as yet, fully accepted women as equals in the marketplace. In fact, most men (61 percent) and women (59 percent) tend to agree that in a period of high unemployment a man has a greater right to work than a woman. Still, acceptance of work as man's privilege is influenced by a woman's age and education. Young women are much less likely to acknowledge men's prior right to employment than older women (33 percent compared to 73 percent). Similarly, women with high levels of education are less likely to grant men preference than women who are less educated (40 percent compared to 73 percent).

The overall pattern, then, of people's assessments of traditional roles versus gender equality is related to generational differences and exposure to nontraditional experiences. However, European attitudes on gender roles also vary a great deal from country to country. For example, while there is majority agreement that differences between men and women's roles need to be reduced, there is greater support for this proposition among citizens of Greece (75 percent), France (74 percent), and Luxembourg (68 percent) than in the Netherlands (62 percent), United Kingdom (58 percent), or Belgium (55 percent). Egalitarian marriages were much more popular in Greece (51 percent), Denmark (46 percent), and France (40 percent) than in Luxembourg (25 percent), Belgium (31 percent), or Ireland (30 percent).

The multiple causes underlying these national differences need to be explored further in order to understand the constraints and opportunities for feminism in Europe. Part of the explanation is structural, rooted in birth-rates, divorce rates, employment patterns, expansion of the industrial and service sector, and degree of urbanization. But this is only a partial explanation, since one finds tremendous support for feminist roles in Greece, a relatively less industrialized country with a higher birthrate and lower female labor force participation than the United Kingdom, where nontraditional roles are not as favored.

In countries such as Greece and Ireland, there is a significant domestic economy in which women produce goods, work in family businesses, and take in boarders. These activities contribute to both the family and the national economy but are not reflected in the rates of labor force participation. It would be important to explore the extent to which domestic production hinders or promotes the growth of feminism. Religion, as a means of tapping the penetration of traditional culture, is often offered as a factor hindering the acceptance of role equality and hence the emergence of feminist movements, yet one finds relatively strong feminist sentiments in such Catholic countries as France and Italy. There are undoubtedly political explanations: legal rights based on the family as opposed to the individual; the passage of social policies such as parenting leaves, family allowances, day care services, and antidiscrimination legislation that pre-empt political mobilization; or, from a more historical perspective, the political controversy surrounding the enfranchisement of women. These hypotheses raise a broad research agenda aimed at understanding both the general conditions that allow or push for a redefinition of women's roles—which is necessary for the emergence of feminism in any country—and country-specific constitutional and historical arrangements that facilitate or repress movement formation.

In the United States the basic tenets of feminism, belief in gender equality and acknowledgment of sex discrimination, are accepted by both men and women. While there has been little exploration of the significance of this male support, it has provided the American feminist movement with an important constituency (Klein 1984). It is unclear how feminist politics would have evolved in the United States in the face of male opposition to role equality. On the whole, European men and women also tend to agree on reducing role divisions and on images of the ideal marriage, but there are some countries where sex differences emerge. Women are considerably more egalitarian than men in Ireland (59 percent versus 71 percent) and Germany (58 percent versus 68 percent), while men are somewhat more egalitarian in the Netherlands (65 percent versus 59 percent) and the United Kingdom (62 percent versus 54 percent). The implications of these gender differences for the growth of feminism in these countries need to be explored.

The political consequences of the rejection of traditional role prescriptions depend on whether that rejection leads to the reevaluation of social and legal arrangements and a recognition of discrimination. Europeans acknowledge that men are more advantaged than women in the workplace. The majority of men

(57 percent) as compared to a minority of women (27 percent) say their sex is an advantage for the work they do; women are more likely to see their sex as a disadvantage (15 percent versus 2 percent). Women argue that sex makes no difference to their work more often than men (53 percent compared to 37 percent). Comparing these responses to people's assessments in 1977 of whether their sex was an advantage to employment reveals a large shift away from a sense that women are economically advantaged by their sex in Ireland (55 percent to 20 percent), Luxembourg (55 percent to 29 percent), Belgium (41 percent to 23 percent), and Germany (37 percent to 14 percent). European men have maintained their sense of advantage, with the exception of Belgium (60 percent to 40 percent) and Ireland (83 percent to 71 percent).

While most people agree that men have a prior right to work and that men are more advantaged in the workplace, there is also a sense that women face discrimination and that this needs to be remedied (Table 1-4). Europeans believe that women face discrimination when it comes to the number and range of jobs available to them (51 percent), salary (51 percent), prospects for promotion (51 percent), and, to a lesser extent, job security (42 percent).

Perceptions of discrimination were highest in Germany, Denmark, and France. These were also the countries where women were much more likely to be aware of discrimination than men. In Denmark, women see greater sex discrimination in salary (14 percent difference), job security (11 percent difference), and promotions (17 percent difference). German women are more likely to feel unfair treatment in the number and range of available jobs (13 percent difference),

TABLE 1-4
PERCEPTION OF DISCRIMINATION AGAINST WOMEN (% EUROPEAN OPINION 1983)

	Number and Range of Jobs		Extra Training		Salary		Job Security		Prospects for Promotion	
	Men	Wmn.	Men	Wmn.	Men	Wmn.	Men	Wmn.	Men	Wmn.
Belgium	46	51	27	33	49	50	41	50	44	61
Denmark	62	60	23	32	58	72	43	54	49	66
Germany	55	68	28	51	71	78	47	67	59	76
France	55	61	26	37	61	68	44	51	47	63
Ireland	50	42	39	39	40	45	25	30	49	52
Italy	53	49	40	40	22	33	39	44	40	43
Luxembourg	46	40	19	20	42	51	35	38	40	49
Netherlands	50	49	20	31	50	57	55	58	58	59
United Kingdom	45	31	29	28	34	39	21	25	39	41
Greece	41	39	30	33	45	42	30	29	30	27
Total	52	51	30	37	48	54	39	45	47	55

Source: *European Women and Men in 1983*. 1984. Brussels: Commission of the European Communities, 107.

training (23 percent difference), job security (20 percent), and promotion (17 percent); French women are more aware of discrimination in job security (7 percent) and promotions (16 percent).

Having acknowledged discrimination, 65 percent point out that there are laws in their country allowing women to demand equality of treatment at work; however, more than half (58 percent) believe that these antidiscrimination laws are not applied in practice. People who believe in gender equality and show concern over employment discrimination provide a constituency for feminist movements.

Women's movements are popular in some countries and highly unpopular in others. A substantial number of people (18 percent) have no opinion about movements for women's liberation in their country, but on the whole, positive assessments (45 percent) outweigh negative judgments (37 percent) among those aware of feminist activism. More women support the movement than oppose it (47 percent versus 33 percent), while men divide evenly for and against (42 percent versus 43 percent). Feminist movements find their greatest support among women who are 15 to 39 years old or have high levels of education, while resistance is strongest among men with high levels of education.

In rating movements for women's liberation on a four-point scale (4 is strongly positive, 1 is negative, and values of over 2.5 indicate favorable opinions), the citizens of Greece, Luxembourg, Belgium, France, Italy, and Ireland give their movement positive scores, while the British, Dutch, Danes, and Germans assign negative marks (Table 1-5). However, there are some important country-specific sex differences in assessments of feminist movements. Women support feminist politics in Ireland, Germany, and Denmark, while men do not. This is in part a debate between men and women on appropriate gender roles: in Ireland and Germany, men are less likely to want to reduce differences in social roles (20 percent difference in Ireland; 10 percent in Germany) and much more likely to argue that men have a greater right to jobs during periods of high unemployment. Differences in perceived discrimination also explain these tensions in Germany and Denmark, where there are large sex differences in assessments of women's work situation in terms of job availability (13 percent difference in Germany); training (9 percent difference in Denmark; 23 percent in Germany); salary (14 percent difference in Denmark; 7 percent in Germany); job security (11 percent difference in Denmark; 20 percent in Germany); and promotion (11 percent in both countries).

Europeans are much more likely to support the aims of women's movements than the movements themselves (Table 1-6). Most favor fighting against prejudice (68 percent), want to obtain true equality between men and women in their work and careers (81 percent), believe political parties should give women the same chances as men to reach positions of power (78 percent), argue for parenting leaves to care for sick children (67 percent), and agree that housewives should be compensated for caring for children (60 percent). Few people, however, favor organizing women into an independent movement aimed at transforming society (21 percent).

TABLE 1-5
APPROVAL OF WOMEN'S LIBERATION MOVEMENT (% EUROPEAN OPINION 1983)

	Men	Women
BY AGE		
15–24 years	2.48	2.76
25–39 years	2.43	2.65
40–54 years	2.45	2.57
55 and over	2.44	2.40
BY LEVEL OF EDUCATION		
Low	2.47	2.53
Medium	2.46	2.57
High	2.30	2.62
BY COUNTRY		
Belgium	2.53	2.75
Denmark	2.36	2.55
Germany	2.35	2.63
France	2.59	2.66
Ireland	2.35	2.64
Italy	2.51	2.69
Luxembourg	2.70	2.91
Netherlands	2.42	2.48
United Kingdom	2.24	2.27
Greece	3.00	3.12
TOTAL	2.45	2.58

Source: *European Women and Men in 1983*. 1984. Brussels: Commission of the European Communities, 42.
Note: Value over 2.50 indicates that favorable opinions dominate.

The majority of even the oldest and least-educated groups support feminist aims, but there is significantly greater feminist support among the young and better-educated. Sex differences emerge for 15- to 24-year-olds, with women taking a more feminist position than men on equality in politics (10 percent difference) and sharing the care of sick children (10 percent difference). Similarly, there is an average of 8 percent difference in fighting prejudice, equality at work and politics, and sick care among 40- to 54-year-olds. There are no sex differences on these four goals among people with low levels of education, but as education levels increase, women are on average (8 percent) more feminist.

In most of these countries, feminist movements grew out of the protest movements of the late 1960s and have continued to be much more radical and socialist than contemporary American feminism. Thus opinions of movements for women's liberation are more favorable in countries with active socialist movements, such as France, Italy, and Greece, than in those where socialist governments have been turned out of power, such as England and Germany.

All of these countries, however, have class-based parties that inhibit feminist

TABLE 1-6
SUPPORT FOR AIMS OF WOMEN'S MOVEMENTS (% EUROPEAN OPINION 1983)

	Fight against Prejudice		Equality at Work		Equality in Politics		Sharing Sick Child Care		Salary for Housewives		Transforming Society	
	Men	Women	Men	Women	Men	Women	Men	Women	Men	Women	Men	Women
TOTAL	66	70	79	83	76	80	65	69	59	61	18	23
BY AGE												
15–24 years	70	76	83	88	78	88	74	84	57	64	20	31
25–39 years	72	75	83	88	83	87	76	78	64	66	20	25
40–54 years	63	71	78	86	74	82	62	70	61	62	17	19
55 and over	60	62	74	73	71	68	51	52	54	56	17	18
BY LEVEL OF EDUCATION												
Low	60	63	75	76	72	72	58	59	60	60	19	21
Medium	67	74	81	89	77	86	66	76	57	61	17	24
High	78	84	84	93	86	92	75	80	60	65	13	18

Source: *European Women and Men in 1983.* 1984. Brussels: Commission of the European Communities, 50.

organizing, arguing that feminism is a special interest that undercuts the unity of the working class and undermines the strength of labor parties. Many feminist demands—including abortion, divorce, domestic violence shelters, and rape crisis centers—fall outside the agendas of most labor movements, which traditionally eschew taking stands on social policies. Economic issues are the primary concerns facing most Europeans, particularly in this period of high unemployment and inflation. When asked to rank the importance of sex equality as a political concern, the majority (55 percent) feel it has some importance, 20 percent rank it as very important, and 21 percent see it as having little importance. This is a decline in support since 1975, when 32 percent rated gender equality as a very important issue. This decline is partly in response to the growing fiscal crisis of European states and partly due to the belief that the situation for women has been improving.

Again, the importance attached to the problems of women is a function of age, education, and sex. The problem of women's situation is seen as more important in Greece, Italy, and France than in Denmark, the United Kingdom, or the Netherlands. To what extent are these political differences due to the strength of revived socialist movements as compared to that of long-standing labor parties? Are the differences due in part to social policies that have helped incorporate women into the labor force as part of an emphasis on workplace concerns rather than concern for women's rights?

There has been a greater diffusion of support for feminism, women's movements, and feminist politics in the United States than in Europe. There is, however, a sizable feminist constituency in Europe similar to that found in the United States in the mid-1970s. The rate of increase in feminist consciousness in Europe will depend partly on how fast and in what ways changes in the sexual division of labor force men and women to question traditional arrangements. High unemployment rates are likely to dampen movement toward feminism; increased divorces and female-headed households will accelerate the process.

The politicization of women's consciousness in the United States has been limited by the social diversity of women. The fact that the United States lacks institutions such as strong parties or unions has meant that the women's movement has been unable to aggregate and coordinate activities across its diverse constitutency base. This is particularly evident in efforts to organize the women's vote, where there is agreement on the overall policy agenda but serious differences—based on race and class—in the priorities given to these issues. Currently, there is no broad-based organizational vehicle—feminist organization, political party, or labor union—that is capable of organizing this vote to its full potential.

In Europe, the presence of strong socialist parties or labor unions provide potential organizational vehicles for implementing feminist policies. These organizations are often hostile to feminist claims, however, because such claims are seen to challenge the primacy of politics organized around issues of class. In those European countries where feminist movements have successfully organized outside the parties (Italy is a prime example), feminists have been able to exert enough pressure to change the political agenda in part by having their issues co-opted by the parties (Ergas 1982). Ironically, the future of feminist politics in the United States is dependent on the development of strong political organizations that can mobilize its diverse constituency, while in Europe it will require challenging strong institutions because they refuse to acknowledge interests that are not directly linked to traditional class-based issues.

NOTES

1. The data discussed in this section are largely from a series of surveys conducted by the Roper organization for the Virginia Slims American Women's Opinion Poll in 1970, 1972, 1974, 1980, and 1985.

2. This analysis is based on the 1982 National Election Study. The data presented in this section were made available by the Inter-Consortium for Political and Social Research. The data for the American National Election Study, 1982, were originally collected by the Center for Political Studies of the Institute for Social Research, the University of Michigan.

3. The analysis presented in this section is based on a study by the Commission of the European Communities entitled *European Women and Men in 1983*. The survey was conducted in ten countries of the European Community (at the request of the Directorate for Information of the Community) as a supplement to the Eurobarometer Survey no. 19, conducted in March–April 1983. The same questionnaire was put to representative samples of the population aged 15 years and over in each country. The total sample size was 9,790, all of whom were personally interviewed. The study was carried out by ten professional research companies, all members of the "European Omnibus Survey."

REFERENCES

Baxter, Sandra, and Marjorie Lansing. 1983. *Women and Politics: The Visible Majority.* Ann Arbor: University of Michigan Press.

Clymer, Adam. 1983. "If Anything, Gender Gap Is Becoming Even Wider." *New York Times,* 11 December, p. E5.

Ergas, Yasmine. 1982. "1968–1979—Feminism and the Italian Party System: Women's Politics in a Decade of Termoil." *Comparative Politics* 14 (April):253–80.

Frankovic, Kathleen. 1982. "Sex and Politics—New Alignments, Old Issues." *PS* 15:439–48.

Gelb, Joyce, and Ethel Klein. 1983. *Women's Movements: Organizing for Change in the 1980's.* Washington, D.C.: American Political Science Association.

Giddings, Paula. 1984. *When and Where I Enter: The Impact of Black Women on Race and Sex in America.* New York: Bantam Books.

Gittell, Marilyn, and Nancy Naples. 1982. "Activist Women: Conflicting Ideologies." *Social Policy* 12 (Summer):25–27.

Hills, Jill, and Joni Lovenduski. 1981. *The Politics of the Second Electorate: Women and Public Participation.* London: Routledge & Kegan Paul.

Hooks, Bell. 1981. *Ain't I A Woman: Black Women and Feminism.* Boston: South End Press.

Ketter, Scott. 1985. "Public Opinion in 1984." In Gerald Pomper et al., *The Elections of 1984: Reports and Interpretations* Chatham, N.J.: Chatham House.

Klein, Ethel. 1984. *Gender Politics.* Cambridge, Mass.: Harvard University Press.

———. 1985. "The Gender Gap: Different Issues, Different Answers." *The Brookings Review* 3 (Winter):33–37.

Miller, Arthur H., and Oksana Malanchuk. 1983. "The Gender Gap in the 1982 Election." Paper presented at the Annual MEH.

Oberschall, Anthony. 1973. *Social Conflict and Social Movements.* Englewood Cliffs, N.J.: Prentice-Hall.

Randall, Vicki. 1982. *Women and Politics.* New York: St. Martin's Press.

Schroedel, Jean Reith. 1985. *Alone in a Crowd: Women in the Trades Tell Their Stories.* Philadelphia: Temple University Press.

Shapiro, Robert Y., and Harpreet Mahajan. 1986. "Trends in Gender Differences in Policy Preferences." *Public Opinion Quarterly* 50 (Spring):42–61.

Smith, Tom W. 1984. "The Polls: Gender and Attitudes Toward Violence." *Public Opinion Quarterly* 48:384–96.

Useem, Michael. 1975. *Protest Movements in America.* Indianapolis: Bobbs Merrill.

Wertheimer, Barbara. 1977. *We Were There: The Story of Working Women in America.* New York: Pantheon.

2 How Women Become Involved in the Women's Movement of the Netherlands

MARTIEN BRIËT

BERT KLANDERMANS

FREDERIKE KROON

In the Netherlands, as in many other countries, feminism came to life again in the 1970s. The second feminist wave produced a diverse assembly of women's groups, organizations, and activities. Many of the initiators had previously been active in the student movement or the Vietnam movement. Initially, feminists directed their efforts at equal opportunities for men and women. Gradually, they came to the conclusion that women not only had unequal opportunities but were oppressed, and that this oppression was woven into the fabric and the culture of our society. Although there is no national Dutch organization similar to the National Organization of Women (NOW) in the U.S., the Dutch women's movement has evolved into a variety of decentralized groups and organizations that keep in touch with each other in various ways. This has resulted in the fishnet structure that Gerlach and Hine (1970) consider so typical of social movements.

The movement covers an extremely wide range of ideologies and concrete activities. There are political interest and pressure groups—women for peace, women for legalized abortion, women against sexual violence, women dependent on public support, and women's groups within political parties and unions. There are counseling, education, and training groups for women seeking radical therapy; groups for women in midlife; crisis hotlines; courses on society (the so-called VOS or "Women's Orientation to Society" course) for women with only a few years of secondary education. There are cultural groups such as women's cabarets and theaters, women's art galleries, women's publishing and printing companies, women's bookstores, women's newspapers and magazines. And there are more general groups and activities: women's houses or cafes, consciousness-raising groups, and women's groups in community centers. Not all of these activities are equally common, but some combination of them can be found in most Dutch towns. It should be pointed out that the movement has no fixed form. Groups disappear; others develop; newly discovered problems give rise to new groups. Right now, for instance, consciousness-raising groups have all but disappeared, while support groups and women's networks seem to be rising.

Empirical study of the women's movement has been sparse. In particular, there has been little research on how women become involved in the women's movement (but see Carden 1978; Ferree and Hess 1985, for exceptions). This paper presents a theory of how people become involved in a social movement and applies it to a study among women in an average Dutch town. Mobilization attempts by feminist groups in that town were registered for the period of one year. In October 1981 and again in October 1982, a survey conducted among a random sample of women asked questions about their knowledge of women's groups in their town, their intention to participate in one such group, and their actual participation. Between these two dates, smaller samples of women were interviewed about specific mobilization attempts. Results are reported on three types of activities: the women's house, women's groups in community centers, and the VOS course, each of which is an example of the way in which the Dutch women's movement manifests itself. But before discussing the theory and the study, we first present as background some facts about women in the Netherlands.

THE POSITION OF WOMEN AND THE WOMEN'S MOVEMENT IN THE NETHERLANDS

Generally, a relationship is assumed between the rise of the women's movement and the social, economic, and cultural changes that have taken place since the 1960s. The number of working women increased; the number of divorces increased; views about sexuality changed; the number of children per family decreased; and education became more accessible to women. These developments were not unique to the Netherlands, but the situation here differed in several respects from that in other Western countries. Some high points from the social statistics will make this clear (all data are taken from Oudijk 1983; for a summary, see Morgan 1984, 465, 476).

By the beginning of the 1980s, although the number of women at institutes for higher education had increased to one-third of the total enrollment, it was still the lowest in Europe. Women still primarily chose "female" majors and female professions; in fact, there were more men entering typically female occupations than women going into typically male occupations.

The percentage of women in the working population, which had been about 25 percent for three-quarters of a century, increased to 32 percent in the 1980s. In spite of this, it is still the lowest percentage in Europe. The increase is mainly due to the fact that more women did not quit working immediately after getting married but waited until their first child was born. Between 1960 and 1979, the percentage of married women who worked increased from 7 to 31 percent. Of the women with children, however, only 16 percent were working in 1979 if their children were under four, and 25 percent if their children were four or older. Most married women who work do so part time.

The work women do is concentrated in a few occupations: sales, secretarial, or nursing jobs and the like. The number of women in management positions is very low. Typically female occupations have less prestige.

When men and women have comparable occupations, educational levels, ages, and years of service, women earn less than men. Women are eligible for certain Social Security allowances only if they are breadwinners.

Although the number of women in political positions has doubled, in 1982 they held no more than 15 percent of these posts. And what posts they do hold are mostly low. The percentage is considerably smaller for the higher positions.

Radical changes have taken place in the area of marriage and morals. The number of divorces has shown a sharp rise: currently, one in three marriages ends in divorce. Views on the gender roles of husband and wife in the family and in society underwent a great deal of change between 1970 and 1980. Opposition to abortion decreased: the number of youths who were against abortion under all circumstances was cut in half in ten years' time (from 40 to 20 percent); among older people it decreased from 40 to 30 percent. The number of alternative households (other than family units) increased, and tolerance of alternative forms increased as well, although the integral family is still predominant.

On the whole, however, cultural changes seem to have gone further than social and economic ones. And the economic recession has not improved this picture. There is more unemployment among women than among men: 18 and 16.3 percent respectively in 1983. Besides this, more hidden unemployment of women not officially registered as unemployed is found among women. If this is taken into account, the percentage for women would be even higher.

In the Netherlands, as in other Western countries, these changes in the position of women were associated with the revival of the women's movement. After a spectacular start that obtained a lot of media coverage, the movement shifted somewhat out of the limelight in the late 1970s. This is not to say it had stopped growing: the movement continued to expand rapidly. For instance, in 1977, women's groups of various sorts were active in some 37 towns; by 1982, there were 158. This means that groups and organizations that reckoned themselves part of the women's movement were operating in one-fourth of the towns in the Netherlands at that time.

Although the Dutch women's movement adopted many ideas from its American counterpart, there are important differences. Most significant is the lack of a national feminist organization such as NOW. The national organizations that do exist cannot be defined and would not define themselves as part of the women's movement, even though many women within them (the leadership, particularly) are sympathetic to feminist goals. Some such organizations are foundations or institutions constituted because of the movement but not emerging from the movement base itself. The Emancipation Council (*Emancipatie Raad*) is one of these. Although there is a growing awareness of the need for movement coordination, and several national initiatives have been taken, thus far they remain somewhat weak.

What Myra Ferree notes in Chapter 8 about the West German women's movement also applies to the Dutch movement as compared to the movement in America. While "liberal" feminism is weaker here than in the United States, "socialist" and "radical" feminism are stronger. In this respect the Dutch women's movement shows more affinity with the German than with the American movement.

The strong decentralization of the Dutch women's movement and the lack of a national feminist organization are due in part to ideological causes. Many parts of the movement look upon hierarchical structures with antipathy. And yet ideology would be unable to determine the form of a movement in the long run if it were not enmeshed in the political opportunities structure. Two circumstances can help to explain why the Dutch women's movement concentrates on local organizing and why there are few national organizations: the party system and the decentralized welfare system.

In Dutch politics, political parties play an important role. Members of parliament for a certain party generally vote *en bloc*, so there is little use in lobbying aimed at individual members. If one hopes to influence the vote in parliament, one must influence the views of a party rather than the views of individual members of parliament. This fact has led to the formation of women's groups within each political party, the goal of which is to influence the position of their own party. Because of the ideological boundaries that separate parties, functional co-operation between women's groups of different parties is a laborious and tedious matter. There are exceptions: the women's groups of the small left-wing parties have joined forces, and the women members of parliament confer on a regular basis. But the interest of political parties in women's emancipation and the formation of women's groups in political parties was a result of the growth of the women's movement, not a cause of it. It took a long time to exert any influence on political decision-making in this way. As late as 1982, two government officials justifiably stated that the women's movement had not managed to present its demands as political issues until very recently (Dijkstra and Swiebel, 1982).

What was said about political parties applies to the unions as well. In a somewhat belated reaction and under pressure from their women members, unions have begun to show an interest in the position of female employees. But having been converted, unions now play a large role in the battle for equal rights for women at work and in social security. Women's groups in the unions are very important in this respect.

Another important factor was the decentralization, in the early 1970s, of the welfare system in the Netherlands. One result was that the fight for many of the facilities the women's movement was calling for had to be waged at a local level. A women's house, a subsidy for a VOS course, facilities for a women's group all had to be arranged with local officials. Any need for coordinating bodies was therefore chiefly local. For the groups within the women's movement, then, many of the issues were local as well, and this was where they turned their attention. In matters calling for national efforts, action was usually organized through the women's groups in political parties or unions.

And yet we must take care not to conclude that the Dutch women's movement is inconsequential. A great deal of its influence is almost invisible because it is exerted in political and social organizations at the local level, but it exists. In addition, more and more women are coming to occupy positions where they can influence policy. Nor is it safe to conclude from the absence of spectacular events that the movement is on its way out: witness the quadrupled number of towns with women's groups between 1977 and 1982. Nevertheless, because of its form, the Dutch women's movement clearly must rely (more than many other movements) on the active participation in all these groups of women who set out to influence either local politics or, through political and social organizations, national politics.

Theorists writing on social movements have commented that political strategies must include a combination of personal transformation and societal change (Turner, 1983). But there is no necessary bond between personal transformation and social manipulation. Some women's activities emphasize the former (e.g., radical therapy groups), others the latter (e.g., women's groups in political parties). Participation in the women's movement comprises both elements, although one or the other, depending on the group in which a person participates, will be in the foreground. Participation in the movement is not a necessary condition for personal transformation, but as we will see below, personal transformation is an important condition for participation. This article does not treat the process of personal transformation per se but rather emphasizes the process of joining a women's group or organization.

BECOMING INVOLVED IN A SOCIAL MOVEMENT

Snow, Zurcher, and Ekland-Olson (1980) draw attention to the simple fact that people cannot be mobilized by a social movement unless there is some sort of contact between them and the movement. They established that the chance of such contact taking place is greater if people have ties to social networks that are allied with the social movement. The contacts themselves can vary from lengthy face-to-face meetings with a representative of the movement to indirect contact via the mass media or direct mail.

We will call these contacts mobilization attempts, a concept basic to our analysis of how people become involved in a social movement. A mobilization attempt sets in motion a process of consideration that may result in a decision to participate in a movement. Not all mobilization attempts are equally effective. The literature on persuasive communication leads us to suppose that multimedia approaches, combining mass media appeals with face-to-face interaction, have the best results (Rogers 1983), but the means to carry out such a strategy may not be available. If the infrastructure needed for face-to-face interaction is lacking, then one must resort to mass media appeals (McCarthy 1983). If no means are available for mass media appeals, then one must rely on face-to-face interaction. Gerlach and Hine (1970) showed that face-to-face contact was a necessary condition for recruiting members in the Black Power movement and the Pentecostal movement. But McCarthy (1983) showed that environmentalists managed to mobilize considerable resources by utilizing direct mail.

It is our assumption that this must be seen in relation to the nature of a movement. The more fundamental and far-reaching is the decision-threshold to join, the more important is face-to-face contact. We may suppose that face-to-face contact plays an important role for the women's movement in this respect. Elsewhere (Briët, Kroon, and Klandermans 1984), in a report of retrospective research among participants in the women's movement, we concluded that for many women, joining the movement was a matter with far-reaching consequences. It changed their way of life and the image they had of themselves. They started to interpret their existence differently and to see their past with different eyes. Of course, such consequences will not be of equal magnitude for all groups in the women's movement. In every movement there are gradations in the extent to which groups change the lives of their members. The greater the change, the more important face-to-face contact will be in recruiting participants.

But the type of contact is not the only determinant of whether a consideration to participate will take place. People hold prior beliefs about a social movement and its goals. If these beliefs place the movement in the latitude of rejection (Petty and Cacioppo, 1981; Sherif, Sherif, and Nebergall, 1965), it is not very likely that people will ever ask themselves whether or not they should join, not even after face-to-face contacts. It is simply a lost cause. No consideration takes place at all. This, too, will vary for different movements and for groups within a movement. Some groups, often the more radical ones, will meet with more rejection than others.

So the absence of mobilization attempts, in effective forms of contact, or an attitude of rejection toward a movement and its goals can explain why people do not even stop to consider joining a movement. If no such barriers are present, a mobilization attempt will lead people to weigh the costs and benefits of participation.

Perceived costs and benefits can be classified under two headings: collective and selective. Selective costs and benefits can be further divided into social and nonsocial (Klandermans 1984). A person has expectations about all three, and the result is three types of motives to participate: (a) *goal motives* or *collective motives,* related to the achievement of the collective good; (b) *social motives,* having to do with the expected reactions of significant others; (c) *reward motives,* having to do with the anticipated nonsocial costs and benefits of participation. Each of these motives makes it own contribution to the willingness to participate. Weighing perceived costs and benefits leads to an intention to participate or not to participate. After this, circumstances beyond the control of those intending to participate (illness, no babysitter, and the like) may prevent them from carrying out their intention.

So the process of joining a social movement depends on several conditions. A person must form (or already hold) positive attitudes about the movement and its goals. This may be a very lengthy process in which mass media, opinion leaders, significant others, and salient events interact in a complex manner (Gamson and Modigliani 1983). Once this condition is fulfilled, mobilization attempts lead people to consider the perceived costs and benefits of participation. Their success depends on their nature (face-to-face or mass media) and the level of participation required. People's positions in social networks can increase or decrease their chances of being exposed to mobilization attempts. Consideration of costs and benefits results either in an intention to participate or in an intention not to participate. Practical circumstances can prevent people from carrying out their resolve.

THE RESEARCH METHOD

Because to become active in the Dutch women's movement usually means becoming active in one of the groups or activities in one's place of residence, we were able to select an average town for our study without losing much information. In our research we utilized the fact that movements have seasons. All activities get underway in September, and around June the summer recess begins. Each season's rhythm of attempts to activate women are initially intensive and then gradually decrease in frequency and intensity. At the start of the season, one can study to what extent women are familiar with women's groups in their place of residence and how seriously they are considering taking part in one of them. After the season is over, one can investigate whether changes took place in these figures and whether women who were intending to participate actually did so. More generally, one can investigate whether women were aware of and participated in the concrete activities that took place. We studied the 1981–82 season in this way.

The Women's Movement in Gouda

We chose the town of Gouda because it offered an average range of women's activities. Important women's groups were present, and they were active enough that we could count on their undertaking mobilization attempts. There was a women's bookstore, a women's telephone line, courses on society (VOS courses), groups for women in midlife, feminist radical therapy groups, a women-for-peace group, women's groups in political parties and union locals, and many women's groups and activities in the town's community centers. All of these worked together in Gouda's women's council. The high point of the season we studied was the opening of a new women's house in the spring of 1982, an occasion for many festivities.

This paper examines mobilization attempts for three types of activities in Gouda:

1. *The women's house.* Women's houses are gathering places for the women's movement. They are open only to women, and they provide space for all sorts of groups and activities. At the start of the second feminist wave, they often served as a sort of retreat where women in the movement could go in search of support and inspiration. Later, they became centers for a great variety of activities, ranging from classes in carpentry to assertiveness training. More than any other single activity, the women's houses are associated with the women's movement.

2. *The VOS course.* In the early 1970s there was an initiative in the women's movement to start courses for women who, for whatever reason, never had a chance to complete their education. Participants must have had no more than a few years of high school. The classes cover such topics as politics, general social science, health education, social security, work, and budgeting. They were an immediate success and are currently given in dozens of towns every year. Although their ties with the women's movement are evident, the organizers try not to put too much emphasis on this connection for fear tht it will act as a barrier.

3. *Women's groups in community centers.* As a result of the movement, many community workers set up women's groups in their centers. They organized such activities as coffee mornings, women's clubs, creative clubs, film evenings, discussion evenings. They tried to focus on the position of women in society. So although those who organized them established a link to the women's movement, they also did their best to reduce the threshold of resistance to women's activism by stressing the concrete programs of these groups.

Each of these activities is an example of the way the Dutch women's movement manifests itself. From the point of view of comparing mobilization attempts, they are an interesting trio. On the one hand there is the women's house with its explicit ties to the feminist movement; on the other, two types of activities whose ties are much less pronounced. On the one hand there is the VOS course with its specific goal and its specific target group; on the other, two activities whose goals are much broader and which do not focus on any particular category of women. Together the three provide an opportunity to test the hypotheses we formulated in the theory section.

Design
In the fall of 1981 and the fall of 1982, representative samples of the female population of Gouda were questioned. One sample was interviewed twice; two

samples were interviewed once, in 1981 and 1982 respectively. In this way we could control for repeated measurement. In the intervening period several specific mobilization attempts were studied in greater detail. Trained female interviewers met with respondents in their homes, using questionnaires with prestructured answers.

In 1981 we surveyed 613 respondents; in 1982 we surveyed 631. They were obtained by sampling street addresses. Since women with young children are more often at home, they are overrepresented in the sample.

The questionnaire asked about the women's groups and activities in Gouda: familiarity with these activities, the way in which the women had become aware of them, whether they had considered taking part in a particular activity, motives to participate, whether they actually had taken part, reasons for not participating despite their resolve. There were also questions about (a) *respondents' attitudes toward the women's movement,* toward the women involved, the goals of the movement, and its consequences for the respondent's own life; (b) *respondents' satisfaction with their own position as women,* whether they ever felt deprived, were irritated by typically female role behavior, believed financial independence important; (c) *demographics,* including age, education, income, number of children living at home, activities and work outside the home.

THE RESULTS

During the 1981–82 season the women's house, the VOS course, and the community center groups tried to involve women in their activities in all kinds of ways. To do this, they made use of several mass media as well as face-to-face contact.

For the women's house the opening of the new building was an event that received a lot of attention. As the subject of much controversy between proponents and opponents, it filled the columns of Gouda newspapers for days on end. During the rest of the year, too, the women's house made use of the local press (both the newspaper and various door-to-door advertising papers) to announce its activity program. Its organizers also publicized their activities by putting up posters and stickers in places where many women come. Besides all these written forms of communication there was, of course, mouth-to-mouth advertising by women who told one another about the women's house.

Women used a variety of means of communication for the VOS course as well. They distributed folders in doctors' waiting rooms, nursery schools, and clinics for babies and toddlers. Posters were put up in schools and stores. Participants in a previous course told about it at community centers. Short announcements were placed in the local papers, and two of them devoted a series of articles to the new setup the course would have that year. The teachers urged participants to tell others about the course.

For the community center groups the most important means of publicity were their respective neighborhood newspapers. They also put up posters in stores and at health clinics, and made use of the fact that community centers are meeting places for the neighborhood. One center tried to engender mouth-to-mouth publicity by telephoning women who lived in the neighborhood.

Familiarity

We assumed that a woman who was not familiar with a group, even when it was mentioned by name, had not been exposed to a mobilization attempt by that group. Table 2-1 gives the percentages of respondents who were *not* aware of the existence of the women's house, the VOS course, or the community center groups. This percentage was the lowest for the women's house, which was to be expected in view of the publicity it had received. Nonetheless, two-fifths of the women questioned had never heard of the women's house. Slightly less than half the women had never heard of the VOS course, slightly over half knew nothing about the community center groups. This means that these women had not been reached by the means utilized. They were not exposed to mobilization attempts by these groups.

In all three cases, many more women had read about a group (over 80 percent) than had heard about it (over 40 percent). Articles in the local papers were much more effective in this respect than posters and folders. Women who had heard of an activity mentioned acquaintances most often as their informants. The fact that acquaintances turned out to be more important in this respect than friends or family confirms the assumption that people who do not have very strong ties with one another nevertheless often act as channels through which information about new phenomena in society is spread (Granovetter 1983).

Table 2-2 shows the significant differences in demographic variables between women who were and who were not aware of a group. It is apparent that women with a higher socioeconomic status were better informed. This is a correlation familiar in the communication literature: people with a higher socioeconomic status make more and better use of information sources. The same proved to be true of information about the women's movement. It is interesting to note that women who were familiar with these activities more often had children living at home and/or activities and work outside the home. We presume that in both these

TABLE 2-1
WOMEN NOT FAMILIAR WITH WOMEN'S ACTIVITIES IN GOUDA

Activity	%
Women's house	38
VOS course	46
Community center groups	54

Note: The data for the VOS course stem from women with a lower educational level ($n = 358$), the other data from the entire sample ($n = 613$).

TABLE 2-2
COMPARISON OF WOMEN FAMILIAR AND NOT FAMILIAR WITH WOMEN'S
MOVEMENT ACTIVITIES

Variable	Women's House	VOS Course	Community Center Groups
Education/income	+	+	+
Number of children living at home	+	+	+
Activities or work outside the home	+	+	
Age	−	−	

Note: All variables were scored in the direction of a higher value on the dimension. A + indicates that women who are familiar with an activity have a significantly (ANOVA, $p < .05$) higher value on a variable than women who are not familiar with the activity. A − indicates a significantly lower value. A blank entry means the absence of any significant correlation.

circumstances the women had more numerous and more frequent contacts with others and were thus informed earlier about what was going on around them. Table 2-2 also shows that younger women are more familiar with the women's house and the VOS course. This is primarily due to the fact that it is the younger women who have children living at home and activities outside the home.

In order to gain an impression of the joint influence of these factors on women's knowledge of the groups, we performed regression analyses. With these variables, 8 percent of the variance in knowledge of the women's house and 10 percent of the VOS course could be accounted for, while this figure was 3 percent for the community center groups. The attitude toward the feminist movement and the satisfaction with one's own position as a woman were of little importance in this respect, adding only a few percentage points to variance accounted for.

Consideration

The fact that a person is aware of a group in the women's movement does not automatically mean that she will consider participating. The figures in Table 2-3 are very telling in this respect. Very large percentages of women did not even consider taking part in these activities. The percentage was highest for the women's house and lowest for the VOS course, with the community center groups occupying an intermediate position. The great decline for the women's house is in accordance with our assumption that it would encounter the highest threshold of resistance to participation; the percentages for the community center groups lead us to suspect that they have a higher threshold of participation than the VOS course. Whether this is the case or whether other causes can be pointed out for the lower percentages among these groups will become apparent in the following paragraphs.

In our theoretical introduction we mentioned two reasons why a person might

TABLE 2-3
WOMEN WHO HAD CONSIDERED PARTICIPATING

Activity	%
Women's house ($n = 380$)	6
VOS course ($n = 164$)[a]	19
Community center group ($n = 332$)	11

[a] For the VOS course, the data stem from women with a lower educational level.

not even consider taking part: the way in which a woman became aware of the existence of a group may not have been very effective from the point of view of mobilization; or she might have taken a negative attitude toward the women's movement. We also hypothesized that the more strongly allied with the women's movement a group is, the more handicapped it is in recruiting.

MASS MEDIA VS. FACE-TO-FACE CONTACT. Table 2-4 shows in what way women who did or did not consider participating had become aware of the activity. These results yield some interesting conclusions. We know from the literature on communication that a multimedia approach is the most effective. The results in Table 2-4 confirm this: most of the women who had considered participating had both heard *and* read about the activity of their preference. The majority of the women who had not considered participating had only read about it.

The figures confirm our assumption about the interaction of the nature of the contact and the nature of the group. The percentage of women who had considered participating and who had both read and heard about an activity is the largest for the women's house. As the activity with the highest threshold of participation, the women's house requires a more broad-based approach than the VOS course or a community center group. The figures for the two latter activities lend support to the suggestion that community center groups have a higher threshold than the VOS course.

ATTITUDES TOWARD THE WOMEN'S MOVEMENT. Fifty-five percent of the women questioned took a positive stand on the women's movement, 25 percent were indifferent, and 18 percent were negative. The respondents did not think negatively of the women in the women's movement: only one-fourth of all the women questioned agreed with the statement that women in the movement are loud-mouthed man-haters. Thirty-eight percent of the women felt that improvement of the social position of women was necessary; 35 percent felt it to be somewhat necessary; and 27 percent felt it was not necessary. Fifty-seven percent agreed with the statement that such improvements can be brought about only if women fight for them together. The younger a woman was and the better her

TABLE 2-4
INTENT TO PARTICIPATE IN TERMS OF INFORMATION SOURCE (IN PERCENT)

Activity	Read about It	Heard about It	Read and Heard about It
WOMEN'S HOUSE			
Considered (n = 24)	29	8	63
Not considered (n = 356)	60	16	23
VOS COURSE			
Considered (n = 31)	29	13	58
Not considered (n = 133)	63	17	20
COMMUNITY CENTER GROUP			
Considered (n = 39)	30	30	40
Not considered (n = 297)	60	15	25

education, the more positive was her attitude toward the women's movement. Altogether, more than half of the women took a positive attitude toward the movement, its goals, and its strategy.

When we asked whether the women's movement was also important or necessary for the person being questioned herself, whether the problems the movement fights against also affected her, we obtained an entirely different picture. Then it turned out that 78 percent of the women regarded the women's movement as unnecessary. Closely related to this finding was the fact that the women thought the position of women in general ought to be improved but excluded themselves: 88 percent were satisfied with their own position. Neither gender roles in the household nor questions of financial independence nor feelings of being deprived caused problems for much more than 15 percent of the women.

To summarize, three-fourths of the women evidently saw the women's movement as something from another world. Of course, there are a lot of women who are very badly off, they admitted, and they thought it a good thing that the women's movement stand up for these women, but they did not consider themselves members of this group.

We must not expect that mobilization attempts by the women's movement among women who do not feel the movement is necessary for themselves will be very effective. The figures in Table 2-5 confirm this. This table summarizes the significant differences in attitude toward the women's movement and satisfaction with their own positions as women between women who had and who had not considered participating. The results are clear. Women who did not consider participating were less positive toward the women's movement, less convinced of the necessity of the movement for themselves, and more satisfied with their own position as women. The ties of each of the three activities with the women's movement mean that the attitude toward the movement has an influence on the

TABLE 2-5
COMPARING ATTITUDES OF WOMEN WHO HAD AND HAD NOT CONSIDERED
PARTICIPATING, REGARDING THEIR VIEWS OF THE WOMEN'S MOVEMENT AND SELF-
SATISFACTION

Variable	Women's House	VOS Course	Community Center group
ATTITUDE TOWARD THE WOMEN'S MOVEMENT			
positive attitude	+	+	
positive opinion of women in the movement	+		
improvement of the position of women is needed	+	+	+
the women's movement is necessary for me	+	+	
SATISFACTION WITH ONE'S OWN POSITION AS A WOMAN			
I am not taken seriously as a woman	+	+	+
I missed something because I am a woman	+	+	+
financial independence is important	+		

Note: See Table 2-2.

consideration to participate. This influence was the greatest for the activity most strongly allied with the movement, the women's house; it was less for the VOS course and least for the community center groups. The results of regression analyses confirm this. In the case of the women's house, the indexed variables jointly accounted for 15 percent of the variance; in the case of the VOS course, 10 percent; in the case of the community center groups, 4 percent.

These results confirm our hypothesis about the interaction of the nature of an activity and the attitude toward the women's movement in relation to the consideration of whether or not to participate. They also confirm the assumption we formulated on the basis of Table 2-4 that community center groups have the lowest resistance-threshold and the VOS course a higher one.

A confirmation of the fact that the connection with the women's movement prevents many women from taking part in a VOS course is provided by one of the smaller studies we carried out during the 1981–82 season. In that study 20 women were interviewed solely about the VOS course, so that we could go into the views about this course more deeply. Fifteen of the 20 women had never considered taking part in a VOS course. The connection with the women's movement and/or the fact that only women attended played an important role in this.

The question remains why fewer women considered going to a community center group if it was not a question of a higher resistance-threshold. The most obvious reason is lack of interest. For many women, the community center groups lay not so much in the latitude of rejection (as did the women's house and the VOS course) as in the latitude of noncommitment. The women were indifferent about these groups. Several shorter studies of the community center groups confirmed this, showing that the groups fell outside the sphere of interest for most women.

To Participate or Not to Participate

The fact that women considered participating did not automatically imply that they actually took part. Table 2-6 shows what percentages of the women who considered participating actually did so. For the women's house this was half; for the other two activities, about one-third.

There are two sorts of reasons for a person's failure to participate: the motivation to participate may be insufficient, or objective circumstances can prevent even someone who is motivated from participating. Although the motivation to participate is an individual matter, a social movement can exert influence on it, and it can try to remove obstacles that keep motivated persons from participating. As to motivation, the nature of the contact between movement and person is again of importance: in face-to-face contact, dialogue permits the representative of the movement to counter the objections a person brings up. Mass media do not have this advantage.

TABLE 2-6
WOMEN WHO CONSIDERED PARTICIPATING AND DID SO

Activity	%
Women's house ($n = 24$)	50
VOS course ($n = 31$)	39
Community center group ($n = 35$)	30

TABLE 2-7
PARTICIPATION IN TERMS OF INFORMATION SOURCE (IN PERCENT)

Activity	Read about It	Heard about It	Read and Heard about It
WOMEN'S HOUSE			
did go ($n = 12$)	8	17	75
did not go ($n = 12$)	50	8	42
VOS COURSE			
did go ($n = 11$)	18	18	64
did not go ($n = 20$)	35	10	55
COMMUNITY CENTER GROUP			
did go ($n = 11$)	27	45	28
did not go ($n = 24$)	42	36	24

The data in Table 2-7 show that the nature of the contact also affects the decision to participate. Of the group of women who had only read about an activity, almost none actually did participate. And here, too, there turned out to be an interaction between the nature of the contact and the nature of the group. The women's house had to rely the most on the intensive approach (reading *and* hearing), the community center groups the least.

MOTIVES TO PARTICIPATE. Table 2-8 summarizes the motives to participate that the women mentioned. We took a reference to what the group wants to achieve or to the fact that it involves joint activities of women as a reference to the *collective* benefits of participation. More individually tinged wishes—such as contact, having something to do, or educating oneself—we took to be *selective* benefits of participation. For all three groups we see a combination of collective and selective benefits, yet some nuances are related significantly to the nature of the group. Women who considered going to the women's house more often mentioned the collective benefits as a motive to participate; women who considered going to a VOS course or a community center group gave more weight to the selective benefits. For the VOS course, it is understandable that the desire to develop oneself further was most often mentioned.

The figures in Table 2-8 also provide an explanation for the fact that, despite the higher threshold of resistance, comparatively more women had started going to the women's house. This can be accounted for by a stronger motivation, both collective and selective. The women who considered going to the women's house

TABLE 2-8
MOTIVES TO PARTICIPATE (IN PERCENT)

Motives	Women's House (n = 24)	VOS Course (n = 31)	Community Center Groups (n = 35)
COLLECTIVE BENEFITS			
What the group wants to achieve is important	29	13	11
It is attractive to do something together with other women	50	30	37
Total Collective Benefits	79	43	48
SELECTIVE BENEFITS			
I want to meet other women	30	16	26
I feel like doing something	42	20	32
I want to educate myself	29	48	26
Total Selective Benefits	101	84	84
Total Benefits[a]	180	127	132

[a]Respondents could mention more than one motive.

TABLE 2-9
AVERAGE NUMBER OF MOTIVES PER WOMAN

Motives	Women's House		VOS Course		Community Center Groups	
	Did Go	Didn't Go	Did Go	Didn't Go	Did Go	Didn't Go
Collective benefits	1.10	0.50	0.73	0.25	0.63	0.41
Selective benefits	1.30	0.75	1.00	0.75	0.82	0.84
Total	2.40	1.25	1.73	1.00	1.45	1.25

mentioned many more motives than the women who considered going to the VOS course or a community center group.

Table 2-9 shows how many motives on the average were mentioned per woman, classified as to women who did participate and women who did not. First of all, this table shows that women who ultimately did participate indeed associated more benefits with participation. Comparison of the three groups shows that the difference in motivation between participants and nonparticipants is largest for the women's house and smallest for the community center groups. The VOS course occupies an intermediate position.

Comparison of the collective and selective benefits indicates that all three groups of participants see more collective benefits than do nonparticipants. This means that collective benefits are important motivators; in the case of the community center groups they even seem to be decisive.

The differences in expected collective benefits between participants and nonparticipants are largest for the women's house and smallest for the community center groups. As far as the selective benefits are concerned, it is striking that they show no difference between participants and nonparticipants for the community center groups, a slight difference for the VOS course, and a large one for the women's house. In this respect it is important to remark that for women with a low educational level there was no alternative available to the VOS course, obviously, selective benefits will make a difference in such a case. In contrast, the selective benefits of participation in the women's house or the community center groups could have been found elsewhere.

CIRCUMSTANCES THAT PREVENT PARTICIPATION. Apart from a lower motivation, outside circumstances can be the reason a person ultimately does not participate. The reasons primarily given by nonparticipants were that they were too busy, they were too much tied up at home, or the time at which the activity took place was not convenient for them. Although these are ostensibly circumstances that prevented women from participating, such reasons also imply that other things have higher priority. This confirms what we already established in the section on motivation, that the women who did not participate were less motivated. A person can try to remove the obstacles to her participation, but the effort to do so would also increase the costs of participation. Less motivated people are not willing to pay these costs.

DISCUSSION

We have here applied to the women's movement a theory about how people become involved in a social movement. As a frame of reference, we used resource mobilization theory (Oberschall 1973; Zald and McCarthy 1979) and the social psychological expansions given by Klandermans (1984). We emphasized that the process of considering the costs and benefits (an essential part of these theories) is not set in motion under all circumstances. It may be that mobilization attempts do not reach a person, or that they are not effective. Ideological rejection of the movement can keep a person from considering participation. Groups and organizations vary in how susceptible they are to these factors.

The theory presented and the research results based upon it once again point up the role of ideology. Our research also shows that agreement with the ideology of a movement is not a sufficient condition for participation. In this respect it confirms resource mobilization theory. But it also draws attention to an entirely different role of ideology, as a condition for nonparticipation. As long as many people reject a movement's ideology, as is true at present of the Dutch women's movement, that movement has its work cut out for it: its ideology must become more widely accepted.

If mobilization attempts take place in groups with a certain affinity with a movement, ideological barriers play only a small role. Studying ideologically homogeneous populations can yield a one-sided picture of the influence of ideological factors. This is also true if mobilization attempts aimed at one single group or at groups equally sensitive to these factors are studied. Insufficient control of these factors may have caused underestimation of the significance of ideology to participation in a social movement. The implications of our study are an incitement to more research on interaction between the ideological composition of the target group, the means of communication used, and the characteristics of the mobilizing movement's organizations.

The results on the relative significance of collective and selective benefits confirm the results of previous research (Carden 1979; Gamson 1975), which showed that both collective and selective benefits are important motivators. Collective benefits even seemed to be decisive in one of our three groups, and understandably so. Selective benefits are often aspecific; that is, they can also be acquired in groups outside the movement. Nonparticipants may value the selective benefits of participation just as highly as participants do but prefer a group outside the movement because the collective benefits of participation in the movement have less appeal for them. In this respect it was significant that for the activity that did yield specific selective benefits (the VOS course), these benefits made a real difference. Results such as these are another rebuttal to Olson's (1977) assertion that only selective benefits can bring a person to participate in a social movement.

What this all points to is that different groups of women have very different reasons for not taking part in the women's movement. Besides women who are not familiar with a given group in the movement, there are women who were reached by the group's publicity but not very effectively. There are also women whose attitude toward the women's movement is one of rejection and who thus tend to give less consideration to participation the more strongly a group is allied with this movement. Then there are women who consider participating but decide not to because their motivation is not strong enough to put something else aside for it or to cross certain barriers.

It is clear that entirely different approaches are needed to mobilize each of these groups. An obvious place to start would be among the women who consider participating but have too little motivation. Success with this group alone would more than double the number of present participants. Either mobilization attempts with more motivating power or ways of removing barriers will first have to be found.

It is much harder to get at the group that did not consider participating because of ideological rejection. Data from Ferree and Hess (1985) suggest that this group is larger in the Netherlands than it is in the United States—presumably because of differences both in the position of women and between the movements in the two countries. On the one hand the demographic transformation of women's role (Klein, 1984) is less far-reaching in the Netherlands; on the other, "radical feminists" are more important to the Dutch movement. These two differences reinforce each other in producing more negative attitudes toward the women's movement in the Netherlands. It will be difficult to change these attitudes in the short run. The women's movement itself will probably have little success, since it will not be a credible source.

Finally, by improving publicity, one can try to reach women who have not been reached at all. But let us not be too optimistic about this effort. Of all the groups involved in our research taken together, only 11 percent had never heard of a single group. Besides, the women thus reached will split into women who do consider participating and women who do not. And that ratio will probably be less favorable than in the mobilization attempts studied, because we may assume that there has been a bias in mobilization up to now (Ferree and Hess 1985), reaching many women who already had an affinity with the movement.

REFERENCES

Briët, Martien, Frederike Kroon, and Bert Klandermans. 1984. "Vrouwen in de vrouwenbeweging." In R. van der Vlist, ed., *Sociale psychologie in Nederland,* deel IV. Deventer: van Loghum Slaterus.

Carden, Maren L. 1978. "The Proliferation of a Social Movement: Ideology and Individual Incentives in the Contemporary Feminist Movement." In Louis Kriesberg, ed., *Re-*

search in Social Movements, Conflict and Change, 1: 179–96. Greenwich, Conn.: JAI Press.

Dijkstra, Tineke, and Joke Swiebel. 1982. "De Overheid en het vrouwenvraagstuk: emancipatiebeleid als mode en taboe." *Socialisties-Feministiese Teksten* 7: 17–31.

Ferree, Myra Marx, and Beth B. Hess. 1985. *Controversy and Coalition: The New Feminist Movement in America*. Boston: G. K. Hall.

Gamson, William A. 1975. *The Strategy of Social Protest*. Homewood, Ill.: Dorsey Press.

Gamson, William A., and A. Modigliani. 1983. "Political Culture and Cognition." National Science Foundation Research Proposal. Unpublished paper. Boston College/ University of Michigan.

Gerlach, Lattier, and Virginia H. Hine. 1970. *People, Power, Change: Movements of Social Transformation*. Indianapolis, Ind.: Bobbs-Merrill.

Granovetter, Mark. 1983. "The Strength of Weak Ties: A Network Theory Revisited." In Randy Collins, ed., *Sociological Theory 1983*, 201–33. San Francisco: Jossey-Bass.

Klandermans, Bert. 1984. "Mobilization and Participation in a Social Movement: Social Psychological Expansions of Resource Mobilization Theory." *American Sociological Review* 49: 583–600.

Klein, Ethel. 1984. *Gender Politics: From Consciousness to Mass Politics*. Cambridge, Mass.: Harvard University Press.

McCarthy, J. D. 1983. "Social Infrastructure Deficits and New Technologies: Mobilizing Unstructured Sentiment Pools." Working paper, Department of Sociology and Center for the Study of Youth Development, Catholic University.

Morgan, Robin, ed. 1984. *Sisterhood Is Global: The International Women's Movement Anthology*. New York: Anchor/Doubleday.

Oberschall, Anthony. 1973. *Social Conflict and Social Movements*. Englewood Cliffs, N.J.: Prentice-Hall.

Olson, Mancur. 1977. *The Logic of Collective Action: Public Goods and the Theory of Groups*. Cambridge, Mass.: Harvard University Press.

Oudijk, Corinne. 1983. *Sociale atlas van de vrouw*. s. Gravenhage: Staatsuitgeverij.

Petty, R. E., and J. T. Cacioppo. 1981. *Attitudes and Persuasion: Classic and Contemporary Approaches*. Dubuque, Iowa: W. C. Brown.

Rogers, Everett. 1983. *Diffusion of Innovation*. New York: Free Press.

Sherif, C. W., M. Sherif, and R. E. Nebergall. 1965. *Attitude and Attitude Change: The Social Judgment-Involvement Approach*. Philadelphia: W. B. Saunders.

Snow, David A., Louis A. Zurcher, Jr., and Sheldon Ekland-Olson. 1980. "Social Networks and Social Movements: A Microstructural Approach to Differential Recruitment." *American Sociological Review* 45: 787–801.

Turner, Ralph H. 1983. "Figure and Ground in the Analysis of Social Movements." *Symbolic Interaction* 6: 175–181.

Zald, Mayer, and John D. McCarthy. 1979. *The Dynamics of Social Movements: Resource Mobilization, Social Control and Tactics*. Cambridge, Mass.: Winthrop.

3   Changing Discourse, Changing Agendas: Political Rights and Reproductive Policies in France

JANE JENSON

The modern women's movement has challenged those responsible for setting the agenda of French politics since the late 1960s. This social movement has insisted on introducing a new collective actor—women—onto the political scene and inserting the needs and interests of women onto the policy agenda. These changes were possible because the modern women's movement took as its fundamental goal specification of a new collective identity; it wanted not only to reform women's condition but also to construct a new consciousness. Earlier manifestations of "feminism," especially during the interwar years, accepted the definition of the female condition shared by all political actors. Whereas the contemporary women's movement strives to develop a politics of "women," the earlier movement saw women in a traditional familial and/or national context; this meant, usually, that women were defined by maternity.

This essay assesses the importance of this difference in discourse by examining two issue areas: acquisition of citizenship rights, and reproductive policies. From the comparison the conclusion emerges that the fundamental contribution of the modern women's movement was its ability to alter the "universe of political discourse" and thus to press its goals in ways quite different from those of earlier mobilizations of women.

Recent writing on social movements stresses the external social and political setting within which they arise: changes in the basic social relations of production (Touraine 1981); the development of new state forms, especially the welfare state (Offe 1984); the role of the state in mediating relations among social movements and their adversaries (Pizzorno 1979); the availability of political space due to competitive conditions among elites (Piven and Cloward 1979); and the "political opportunity structure" (Tarrow 1983). This chapter continues this direction of inquiry by emphasizing the fundamental importance of external

This study is part of a larger project supported by a Research Fellowship from the German Marshall Fund of the United States, whose aid is gratefully acknowledged.

conditions to the mobilization, character, and success of the women's movement in France.

The contemporary women's movement rose in the political firmament of France at the end of the 1960s, as did similar movements in most advanced capitalist societies (Guadillo 1981; Leger 1982). Women who had been touched in one way or another by the wave of social and political mobilization that occurred about that time—opposition to the Algerian War, the New Left, student uprisings, and the resurgence of class conflict—came together in small groups and large demonstrations to press for changes in the rights and condition of women. In a short time the social movement was sufficiently visible to have acquired a label in the eyes of the world, the MLF (*Mouvement pour la libération des femmes*), and to be considered one of the credible and legitimate actors on the complicated political scene of post–1968 France.[1] Parties of both Right and Left as well as other social actors began to take notice of the women's movement and to react to it.

Nevertheless, the story of the French women's movement demonstrates that it is not enough to appreciate its mobilization of resources within a particular context of institutions, alignments, and alliance possibilities. It is also necessary to consider an important external factor that profoundly affects the prospects of any new social movement: this is the universe of political discourse within which it acts.

THE UNIVERSE OF POLITICAL DISCOURSE

What is the universe of political discourse? At its simplest it comprises beliefs about the ways politics should be conducted, the boundaries of political discussion, and the kinds of conflicts resolvable through political processes. In the vast array of tensions, differences, and inequalities characteristic of any society, only some are treated as "political." Thus, whether a matter is considered a religious, economic, private, or political question is set by this definition. Invisibility can exist for those questions that are, for whatever reasons, never elevated to the status of being "political."

The universe of political discourse functions at any single point in time by setting boundaries to political action and by limiting the range of actors that are accorded the status of legitimate participants, the range of issues considered to be included in the realm of meaningful political debate, the policy alternatives feasible for implementation, and the alliance strategies available for achieving change. Thus, the universe of political discourse filters and delineates political activity of all kinds. Ultimately, its major impact is to inhibit or encourage the formation of new collective identities and/or the reinforcement of older ones. Within a given universe of political discourse, only certain kinds of collective identities can be forged; for more to be done, the universe itself must be challenged and changed.

In the broadest sense, the universe of political discourse is a consequence of the basic social arrangements in any society. Changes in the mode of production create new occupational categories and alter the relations of production, setting forth the possibility that new collective identities will emerge. Most obviously, and by way of example, mobilization around a working-class collective identity could occur only after industrial capitalism was sufficiently advanced to make available a group of workers for whom that collective identity had meaning. Similarly, the degree of societal religiosity and/or secularization strengthens or weakens the bases upon which certain collective identities can be constructed. It is clear that for women the postwar labor market, characterized by increased demand for relatively inexpensive labor (especially but not exclusively in the service sector), and the expansion of the welfare state are important factors shaping the universe of political discourse within which the contemporary women's movement has created its own collective identity and pursued its demands for change.

However, these basic social arrangements provide only the limiting conditions for the delineation of a universe of political discourse. Moreover, they are only facilitators, not guarantors, of change in the prevailing discourse. For example, just as it is obvious that working-class movements can be mobilized only in industrial societies, it is also obvious that not all industrial societies experience that mobilization in the same way or to the same extent. Whether the mobilization of the working class *qua* class occurs or not is a profoundly *political* outcome, dependent in large part on the activities of political parties and other organizations of the labor movement that alter the language of politics (Brodie and Jenson 1980, chap. 1).

Because the universe of political discourse is a political construct, its character is determined by ideological conflict. Social arrangements can be described in terms that may serve as the rallying cry for mobilization around a collective identity and a set of demands. For example, "exploitation," "class struggle," and even "the working class" are terms that take on popular meaning within the labor movement only *after* political struggle and *after* the hegemonic ideology has been breached by the world views propounded by organizations of workers (Przeworski 1980). Thus, the universe of political discourse changes as a result of political struggle.

Moreover, influence over the universe of political discourse is a prize much sought after and jealously guarded. This means that any collectivity attempting to introduce new actors, issues, and policy alternatives must overcome the resistance of political formations already in place and effectively acting as guardians of the political discourse. Since the universe of political discourse acts as a gatekeeper, excluded actors may not be able to construct a collective identity at all (Brodie and Jenson 1980, 9–10).

For some social movements, recognition is no longer a problem. Since the late nineteenth century, for example, politics in Europe have taken place within a universe of political discourse in which conflict between classes and the mobilization of protest by workers against capital, the capitalist system, and the capitalist state are widely expected. Thus, the protests of "workers" are immediately named as such. Similarly, peace movements, whether as cross-class alliances or as emanations of the working class, are easily recognized within the prevailing universe of political discourse. Not so for other movements, in particular "new social movements." The concerns that we now label those of the new social movements were until the late 1960s usually dismissed as being "nonpolitical" cultural or private matters, beyond the legitimate reach of politics. Only recently have these new movements succeeded in redefining politics so as to place their concerns on the agenda.

For all of these reasons, then, the universe of political discourse should not be seen as fixed. It changes in response to social change, to political action, and to struggles by organizations and individuals seeking to modify the restrictive boundaries of the political imagination. However, the possibilities of modification are not always equal. At some moments—when social change has altered the patterns on which the existing universe of discourse was founded—challenges to it *may* be successfully mounted. When, in addition, traditional actors do not succeed in adapting their discourse to new conditions, challenges from other actors *may* be successful in mobilizing protest within a new discourse. Finally, the more extensive and pluralistic the challenges mounted are, the more likely it becomes that changes in the universe of discourse will be lasting and far-reaching, altering in a major way the definition of politics and its credible actors.

RESEARCH STRATEGY

The notion that the universe of political discourse is one of the important external conditions within which social movements operate—one, moreover, that performs a gatekeeping function—implies a specific research strategy for the examination of social movements. It may be that the effect of the universe of political discourse will be to block the development of a new identity. Then, political actions that appear from the perspective of the present to represent actions by a particular actor may, from the perspective of those involved, actually have represented something quite different. Matters that are for contemporary observers clearly within the range of policies crucial to the status of women may not have been on the political agenda in that form for the actors at the time, when the same matters may have represented foreign policy or family policy, for example.

Starting with policies rather than assuming the existence of any particular actors makes it possible to circumvent the problem of employing the limiting definitions utilized by historical actors and the effects of outdated universes of political discourse. Tracing the policy and not a specific actor, the analysis can describe the actors and discover the names and characteristics given to them within their own universe. This research strategy also means that it is necessary to preface a description of the balance of political forces that a social movement faces with a specification of the character of the movement itself. Doing this means examining the ideological terrain and the ways it affects social movements by constraining the constitution of particular collective subjects.

In the current universe of political discourse, both policy areas dealt with here—the acquisition of suffrage and the reform of reproductive policies (legal access to contraception and abortion)—are firmly within the realm of "women's issues." However, as case studies show, even these seemingly straightforward examples were not always defined as having to do with women.

There are, then, two external conditions to be examined in the analysis of a mobilization of women at any point in time. The first is the character of the social movements that led to protests and demands for reform; it must be asked in particular whether any of them defined "women" as their collective subject. The second external condition is the balance of political forces in French politics; it must be asked whether and how issues touching on the "female condition" were permitted on the agenda and which actors were involved in the conflict. The process of reform can, then, be mapped by examining these two conditions, and the outcomes can be understood in consequence. Using a research strategy that focuses on these two external conditions, this essay examines three case studies of reforms that have had profound effects on French women.

CASE I: ACQUISITION OF POLITICAL RIGHTS

Granting full citizenship to women, after years of exclusion, seems to represent a straightforward example of placing "women" on the political agenda. Yet history is not so straightforward. Instead, this case study delineates the effects of a political discourse virtually unanimous in its depiction of women as childlike, inferior to men, fundamentally maternal, and without an individual claim on or need for political rights. Moreover, no challenge to this unanimity could be mobilized, in large part because of a balance of political forces in which even those who might have argued for the justice of women's voting were prevented from doing so because of fear for their own political futures. In other words, the external conditions faced by the feminist movement in the interwar years were such as to make the emergence of any new collective identity unlikely and thus to locate the rationalization of any reforms in the needs of collectivities other than women.

Although female suffrage was advocated, it was primarily the votes of "mothers" rather than "women" that were pressed. Despite the fact that the feminist movement agitated in favor of an expanded franchise, it sometimes promoted a "family vote" in which wives' and husbands' ballots would be linked. Female suffrage was rarely presented as a way of expanding equality; it was frequently debated exclusively in terms of its contribution to competing visions of French society as Republican or Catholic. When French women were finally granted the vote in 1944, the feminist movement had been moribund for more than half a decade; the instigator of the reform was a political party that had its own quite particular definition of the social category "woman"; and the decision was rationalized as a reward for service in the Resistance, not in terms of any fundamental right of women to full equality and citizenship. While the balance of political forces had altered enough to expand the franchise, no real change in the universe of political discourse—which might have brought other improvements in women's situation—had been effected.

Ironically, just prior to World War I, French feminists seemed close to achieving universal suffrage. The movement had developed in the latter part of the nineteenth century, growing with the modernization, urbanization, and secularization of nineteenth-century French society. It shared roots with movements for secular public education, and it was ideologically linked to republicanism and liberal democracy. Its social base was primarily and increasingly bourgeois (Bouchardeau 1977, 73ff.; Hause and Kenney 1981). The movement seemed, then, well suited to a Third Republic France dominated by the Radical-Socialist party, which prided itself on representing the best of provincial, petit bourgeois, republican, and democratic traditions.

Again in May 1919 the goal seemed within reach. An act passed in the Chambre des Députés by a large majority (344 to 97) would have given women the same rights as men in elections. However, after an inordinately long delay, in 1922 the Senate overruled the Chambre's decision. This legislative scenario was repeated three times in the interwar years. Finally, in 1944 the wartime Constitutive Assembly in Algiers voted for the proposal of Communist Fernand Grenier and gave women full political rights in liberated France. The constitutions of 1946 and 1958 enshrined this equality in their articles. This tardiness in granting full citizenship to women in the country that pioneered universal manhood suffrage cries out for explanation.

The Universe of Political Discourse of Movements and Parties

A large number of actors—social movements and political parties—had views on female suffrage and contributed to a universe of political discourse within which there was widespread agreement that women and men were fundamentally different because of their family roles. The first actor was, of course, the feminist movement. A number of organizations were concerned with the condition of women in interwar France, although they were never exclusively concerned with gaining the vote (see Bouchardeau 1977, 235–37 for a catalogue).[2] The feminist movement was not united in the rationale for the demand for women's right to vote. A small number of feminists who might be termed "individualist feminists" claimed the vote for women in the name of equality.[3] This position was very much a minority one, however (Offen 1984, 654). Much more common were feminists who can be characterized as "familial feminists."[4] Their social vision, emphasizing the differences between women and men, was based on a sexual division of labor that gave women primary responsibility for safeguarding the family, as well as the health and well-being not only of their own children but of society as a whole.

In other words, women needed to vote so they could inject nurturing and social concerns into a political process that confronted profound social problems and dislocations as a result of industrialization, urbanization, and the development of liberal and libertarian values. For these familial feminists, who dominated the largest federation of feminist groups, the Conseil National des Femmes Françaises (CNFF), women were first and foremost *mothers,* and it was their maternal values that should be allowed to find expression in politics. For example, a 1938 article entitled "Why Women Must Vote" in *La Française* (the newspaper of the CNFF) listed the advantages of female suffrage, ranging from specific programs that only female voters could be counted on to advocate to the very general view that voting women would bring "the triumph of justice, of social progress, and of Childhood, Motherhood and Peace" (*La Française,* 30 April 1938). This was obviously, then, a discourse of difference rather than of equality, and one emphasizing maternity to the exclusion of almost all other roles.

Catholic feminists were the third wing of the interwar feminist movement. Organized primarily in the Union Féminine Civique et Sociale (UFSC), created in 1925 after the Pope advocated female suffrage, their goal was to educate future female voters about their duties. This group emphasized the complementarity of the social roles of women and men and the "true feminism" of Catholic women, in which "behind the woman, one sees the family" (Bouchardeau 1977, 52, 40; Rebaut 1978, 236ff.). It, too, highlighted the connection between women and maternity at the same time as it sketched a vision of the family as naturally and appropriately patriarchal. This was the kind of family that the Catholic Church defined as the fundamental social unit. For Catholic feminists, female suffrage could provide a bulwark against the secular, individualist (and often collectivist) male-dominated Left, which would overturn traditional family and religious values. Female suffrage would help to create a politics more attuned to Christian principles.

Because of their familial feminism, these last two tendencies of the movement could be tempted into an alliance with the family movement, the second major contributor to the universe of political discourse around female suffrage in the interwar years. When it became increasingly clear that votes for women were not likely to pass the Senate, feminists were induced to sign on to support the family movement's notion of the "family vote." [5]

The family movement after World War I pressed the state to provide encouragement and support for large families, with tax advantages for fathers of large families, redistributive programs to reallocate wealth from the childless to those with many children, and symbolic recognition of the patriotic contributions of parents. For this movement, since the family was the basic social unit, the individual per se had no legitimate existence in politics (Talmy 1962, 42–45). The *mouvement familial* thought of women only as mothers and agitated for benefits for those families in which mothers were performing their roles well: that is, raising many healthy children within wedlock, and not getting divorced (Bouchardeau 1977, 58).

Movement activists argued that only if families had a greater weight in elections could the state be expected to enact the demanded reforms; thus, the family vote has been described as the most important demand of this movement (Talmy 1962, 6ff.). In proposing the family vote the movement vacillated, in fact, between a proposal to give the family's whole vote to the father and one to allow mothers to vote independently. The proponents of the paternal vote feared family discord if mothers could decide for themselves, while the proponents of mothers' votes saw this as, among other things, a way of creating an alliance with the feminist movement to push the reform (Talmy 1962, 40–41). For a time the promoters of the second position succeeded, and some feminists allied with the family movement to demand the family vote. The non-Catholic feminists withdrew from this alliance rather quickly, however, recognizing that their allies' fundamental focus remained on family improvement rather than on women (Louis-Levy 1934, 22ff.).

Another major actor of the interwar period that contributed to a universe of political discourse almost unanimously focused on mothers rather than women was the movement against the falling birthrate (*dépopulation*) of France. Motivated only by the goal of reversing the decline, this movement had the narrowest definition of women of all the actors considered here. For it, women had no identity beyond their wombs, which would bring forth children for France. It was unconcerned about family status—advocating state support of both married and unmarried mothers—or women's contribution to the reproduction of any societal values. All the repopulators wanted was babies, and they would support any changes in the conditions of motherhood that might contribute to that end. Therefore, in debates about reform they weighed in on the side of social change to improve the situation of childbearing women; this, in turn, encouraged feminists to concentrate their efforts in that direction as well, because the repopulators were politically very powerful in the years of buildup to World War II (Tomlinson 1983).

Other important actors both influencing and acting within the universe of political discourse were, of course, the political parties, which had the ability to actually enact legislative reform. Both Right and Left shared the assumption that women, and most particularly wives, were minors in law if not in potentiality. The weight of the legal position of women that followed from the Napoleonic vision of women—*la femme est donnée à l'homme pour qu'elle fasse des enfants, elle est donc sa proprieté, comme l'arbre à fruit est celle de jardinier* (the woman is given to the man to have children, and she is therefore his property as the fruit tree is the property of the gardener)—enshrined in the Civil Code was such as to reinforce, for all married Frenchmen, the idea of women as subordinate. Moreover, the Roman-French legal tradition incorporated a notion of *offices viriles* (masculine responsibilities), which had come to mean that men were defined as the public representatives of the family unit (Offen 1977, 17).

In part as a consequence of this legal tradition, one important theme in the attitude of both the Left parties and the Radicals—those parties which in other countries were important allies of the women's suffrage movement—was the need for long education and a slow process of bringing women up to the standards of male citizens. They were expected to learn their civic duties by acquiring their rights slowly. Thus Raymond Poincaré (1921, 4–5), a member of the *comité d'honneur* of the Ligue Française des Droits des Femmes (LFDF), one of the major mainstream feminist organizations, proposed a step-by-step procedure.[6] He congratulated feminists for being reasonable and not expecting to be immediately given access to the Chambre des Députés, and proposed that suffrage be extended to women for municipal elections. This was typical of the kind of learning experiences that were proposed, along with special age restrictions and other constraints to be imposed before full suffrage could be achieved (Bouchardeau 1977, 47–49). Part of the process involved women's "proving themselves." Thus, for Poincaré again (1921, 6), their patriotic actions in the war of 1914–18 had given women the right to municipal suffrage.

Another crucial aspect of the Left parties' and Radicals' vision of women was that, as a group, they were particularly susceptible to being misled. Supposedly as yet somewhat childlike, women were considered open to political machinations and the influence of priests.[7] It was thought likely that this susceptibility would be overcome with time, but meanwhile, only "proven" women could accede to greater responsibility. Léon Blum, for example, argued that women should gain political access from the top rather than from below; accordingly, he appointed three female junior ministers in the Popular Front Government in 1936.

A further aspect of the Left parties' view of women, important throughout this period, was the denial that women constituted a separate collective subject. Beginning from the position that society was composed of collectivities and that one of these—class—superseded all others in importance, some socialists and most communists denied the importance of gender as a revolutionary force. While women were identifiable as a social category—as were youth, the aged, and others—they were always most profoundly affected by their class position (Engels, cited in Bell and Offen 1983, 74–81). Thus, while a Marxist analysis implied that political struggle for equality between women and men should go forward, it simultaneously argued that struggles taking gender as a starting point were diversionary, especially those that clearly emerged from the bourgeoisie, as did French feminism in the interwar years. This interpretation of the articulation of class and gender predominated in the Socialist and Communist parties in the interwar years and meant that a stable and fruitful alliance between feminists and the Left was never constructed (Rabaut 1978, 292; Sowerwine 1982, chaps. 7–8).

All three of these aspects of the parties' ideological construction of women contributed to a universe of political discourse in which women did not achieve a collective identity in their own right. Marxists denied the specificity of women's condition and, thinking of society as composed of collectivities, conceived of classes as the only actors of any real import. Social Democrats and Radicals— the equivalent of liberals in other countries who were often convinced by equal rights arguments and who in France believed in democracy for men—could see women not as free-thinking individuals but only as minors and/or as part of that frightening collectivity, Catholics.[8] Meanwhile, for the political Right, women were submerged in the family, acquiring rights only as part of the family unit or because of the special qualities of maternal women.

From this discussion of the actors involved in the creation of the universe of political discourse, it can be seen that the debates about female suffrage took place within a discourse that was more familial than individualistic, that was concerned with national well-being more than individual self-fulfillment, and that was seldom egalitarian. Throughout the interwar years, political discourse emphasized the differences between women and men. This difference provided a justification for the lack of gender equality: women could best serve the family, the nation, or the Church by being "mothers of citizens."

The Balance of Political Forces

The universe of discourse within which the feminist movement operated shaped the structure of the movement as well as its immediate goals. Feminists emphasized those aspects of women's condition—especially maternity and family responsibilities—that could be reformed within the terms of the prevailing discourse at the same time as they discarded themes of individuality. The universe of discourse also had profound effects on the response the movement evoked from the political process, limiting and shaping the kinds of alliances that could be concluded. The feminist movement was tilted toward the Right. Socialist and Communist women were not active in the movement to any appreciable extent in the interwar years, because of the Marxist judgment that class exploitation far surpassed gender oppression in needing political attention. The rightward tilt also pushed the feminist movement into the alliance, described above, with the family movement and Catholics, and this alliance reinforced the Left and Radical vision of women as synonymous with Catholics.

The lack of reliable and/or influential left-wing allies, as well the character of their right-wing allies, was a very great obstacle to the feminist movement's achievement of female suffrage. The Third Republic has been described as a "stalemate society" with a profound division over the legitimacy of the secular Republic (Hoffmann 1963). While passions were frequently inflamed by religious quarrels, the delicate balance of stalemate continued until it was finally destroyed by occupation, resistance, and liberation. The Radicals were, throughout the Third Republic, the axis of almost any parliamentary coalition. This party, self-described as based in the petite bourgeoisie of republican France, was harassed from the Right by parties dedicated to overturning the anticlerical character of the Radicals' Republic and from the Left by the ascendant parties of the organized working class—first the Socialists (SFIO) and then, after 1920, the Communists. Caught between demands for a return to traditionalism and pressures for economic redistribution, if not revolution, the Radicals could not be expected to take to heart any proposal that might unblock the stalemate. The party feared that an expanded franchise would do just that and opposed it continually on the grounds that female suffrage would enhance the power of the Church-dominated Right.[9] Moreover, once the Pope supported female suffrage in the 1920s, the opposition of the Radicals stiffened (Charzat 1972, 171; Michel and Texier 1964, 2: 104–10).

Only the PCF was willing to make an outright and forceful commitment to the cause of female suffrage; it included calls for the vote and for gender equality in the resolutions of its Congresses throughout the interwar years (Charzat 1972, 171; Michel and Texier 1964, 2: 104). Yet because the Parti Communiste Français (PCF) adhered to a Bolshevik vision of the transition to socialism, votes for either gender were no more than educational in value, and the PCF's original strategy of pristine workerism and class-against-class politics prevented it from making an alliance with any party or movement to bring about female suffrage. Only when it moved to united frontism in the 1930s could the PCF undertake more realistic political action around female suffrage. Then, however, it ran up against the opposition of the Radicals and the ambivalance of the Socialists.

The SFIO equivocated on the issue of female suffrage for more than four decades, its basic position being support in principle without much concrete help (Rabaut 1978, 192ff; Sowerwine 1982, chaps. 7–8). While individual Socialists advocated female suffrage, the party as a whole did little more than vote in the Chambre for various proposals that ultimately died in the Senate. Moreover, in 1936 the Socialist-led Popular Front Government did nothing to push the issue— adopting a position of "neutrality"—and allowed the Radical-dominated Senate to block the proposal yet again (Charzat 1972, 171; Rabaut 1978, 297ff.).

In 1944, when the balance of political forces was vastly different, women finally acquired the right to vote in French elections. The Right of the Third Republic had been virtually destroyed as a legitimate political actor in consequence of its behavior in the Vichy regime. The Constitutive Assembly in Algiers, which voted suffrage, leaned decidedly leftward. Moreover, one crucial actor was the PCF in its most united-frontist phase, supporting a broad progressive movement around a reformist program. For the PCF, women (along with soldiers, peasants, and other social categories) were a necessary component of this united front. Therefore, it proposed and the newly rejuvenated SFIO and the Gaullists concurred in granting women the vote and full eligibility in all elections after the war (Dreyfus 1975, 17–18; Grenier 1970, 279ff.).[10]

We see from this case study that by 1944 one external conditioning factor for the social movement had altered, but not both. Therefore, while France had universal suffrage, the needs of "women" *qua* women were no more on the policy agenda than in the interwar period. The composition of the universe of political discourse had not changed. Women gained the vote because of the exemplary actions of a social category, rather than because of any notion that women as individuals had any universal right to citizenship. The political parties never moved beyond their fear that women were Catholics and/or part of the bourgeoisie. The Catholics', the repopulators', and the familial feminists' vision of women in the family had overwhelmed any movement claiming universal, individual suffrage. To obtain any political allies, no matter how ineffectual in the final analysis, feminists had utilized the only concept of women that was recognizable within the prevailing discourses. Therefore, the collective identity fostered by this feminist movement described women first and foremost in their familial roles and rationalized the extension of the franchise as a way of inserting "maternal" values into the political process. In consequence, their natural allies became the Church, the family movement, and the repopulators—all of which recognized this description of women—as well as the PCF, which saw women only as ungendered workers or, in its united-front phase, saw mothers as a social category to be incorporated into a broad social alliance.

The postwar period was marked by the particularities of this victory. Wives remained legally subordinate to their husbands in many everyday areas until the 1960s, when mothers finally acquired authority over their children equal to that of fathers, for example, and wives were fully able to pursue educational and work activities without their husbands' approval. After the war, major steps were taken toward the establishment of the French welfare state, yet the new social policy addressed women either as workers or mothers. Moreover, with family policy established as its cornerstone, the French welfare state shored up and cemented a family structure within which wives and children were dealt with as minors and appendages of men. Finally, since family policy was designed to perpetuate the definition of childbearing as a national duty—a definition that left no room for a notion of women as "nonmothers"—restrictions on access to birth control and abortion were made even more severe (Jenson 1986). Only much later did a movement promoting a collective identity for "women" gain any purchase in the universe of political discourse.

CASE II: REPRODUCTIVE POLICIES—THE REGULATION OF CONTRACEPTION

Motivated by a concern for population decline, in 1920 the French government passed legislation that severely punished anyone obtaining, providing, or aiding an abortion *and* anyone advocating the use of or providing contraceptive devices (Bell and Offen 1983, 309–10). The Law of 1920, particularly the aborton sections, was widely abused, and the population curve continued downward throughout the interwar years. This extremely harsh and repressive law was challenged increasingly after World War II, resulting in reform of the provisions relating to contraceptive devices and information in 1967 and 1974, and those relating to abortion in 1974 and 1979. This case study traces the process that resulted in repeal of the provisions of the Law of 1920 related to contraception.

The Universe of Political Discourse of Movements and Parties

Case I has already documented the notions of women in the universe of political discourse during the interwar years, when there was an overwhelming tendency to see women only as part of the family unit and without independent rights. The discussion in 1920 took place as if the law had nothing to do with women. Abortion and contraception were dealt with solely within a discourse of traditional familialism and patriotism, considering the nation's needs for a large population to combat the prolific Germans and to keep France a strong presence on the European scene. Analyses of population decline focused on the financial hardships that children imposed on families and/or on the moral degeneration of the working class that resulted in a lack of responsibility in matters of the family (Talmy 1962, 16–21). To the extent that any individuals were deemed guilty of acts leading to depopulation, they were thought to be men who preferred the easy life of the cabaret and cafe to that of *père de famille*. To combat these difficulties, financial and other inducements were proposed, including a system of awards and medals that would publicly recognize large families. Often these awards went to the *père de famille,* indicating clearly that the role of women in the whole enterprise was not much considered (Bouchardeau 1977, 119–20).

Not even feminists (with a few exceptions) spoke out against population politics. This is not surprising, given the social and ideological composition of the feminist movement described above. Women on the Left, too, paid little attention to the law: in 1920 when the infamous act was passed, women writing in *L'Humanité* were more concerned with other proposals than about the law relating to contraception and abortion (Bouchardeau 1977, 125). In large part, this lack of opposition was due to the fact that the discourse around contraception was the exclusive preserve of a very particular and quite marginal political movement.

The only opposition to the hegemonic analysis of the problems of the birthrate came from the anarchist-led neo-Malthusian movement, which advocated contraception as an act of defiance against a nation-state supposedly interested in children only as cannon fodder (Ronsin 1980, pt. 1). This movement to disseminate information about and devices for contraception came into being before World War I. It promoted its cause with three arguments: that the state could be weakened if women refused to bear children destined for the capitalists' factories or imperialist wars; that contraception would free women and men from the fear of unwanted pregnancy, thus making truly liberated love possible; and that the poor could never escape their grinding poverty as long as they were compelled to bear children year after year.[11] The anarchism of the neo-Malthusians meant that they were politically marginal and isolated—from the Right for obvious reasons, but also from the Left, which rejected the notion of the *grève des ventres* (strike of wombs).[12] Discussion of contraception unfolded as a debate within the Left about revolutionary tactics as well as a line of cleavage between Left and Right. In all of this there was little room for any consideration of women and their needs. The idea that "wombs" and not "women" were on strike is extraordinarily exemplary here, of course.

It is obvious that there was little space for considering women *qua* women in the discourse of contraception. The act of childbirth was interpreted as a patriotic and/or family act redounding to the credit of the father, who was the *chef* of the social unit both in law and in ideology. Mothers were important, but for all actors (the repopulators being the only exception) they were always supposed to be married women, encased within a stable and healthy family. There was, then, the same emphasis on the family in this policy area as in the discourse of suffrage. In fact, the two policies were linked by, among other things, the concept of the family vote.[13]

Restrictions on contraception were the first areas of the Law of 1920 that reformers took up; success was achieved, eventually, without any fundamental change in the notions of women in the universe of political discourse. Contraceptive reform was justified as a triumph for the French family as it struggled to control the conditions of its life. Reform came only with change in the notion of what this family was and what the nation needed from families. Over time, the emphasis on the large family as the backbone of the nation weakened, in part because of the population boom after World War II. Because of the diminished importance of the repopulation movement and the partial transformation of the family movement into one concerned with child rearing more than childbearing, there was space within the political process for a new analysis of the family. However, until after 1967 the discourse remained a discourse about families, not about women.

A new birth control movement appeared in the 1930s, out of a very different social location from that of the neo-Malthusians. Inspired in part by activities in the United Kingdom and the United States, the movement presented itself as interested in "family planning," rather than in controlled reproduction intended to frustrate the warmongering goals of the state. This movement also had more middle-class roots—although one of the earliest and best-known clinics before World War II was in the Socialist-controlled municipality of Suresnes (Paillard 1973, 93–94).

A small movement in the interwar years, by the mid-1950s it had become a mass movement, beginning in 1956 with the organization of Maternité Heureuse, the precursor of Planning Familial (the French affiliate of Planned Parenthood), created in 1958 (MFPF 1982, chaps. 6–7). After 1945, France experienced rapid social and economic change, which profoundly altered the life conditions of families. Rural-to-urban migration shifted a huge percentage of the population in a single generation from farm to city, out of agricultural work. Consumerism put new lifestyles within the reach of many as automobiles, greater leisure time, and longer paid vacations became widely available. At the same time, more women entered the salaried labor force, moving into new jobs in the service sector especially. Educational opportunities opened for both genders, and university education became more common. Secularization and the decline of religious practice spread. In all this, family situations changed in major ways. Nuclear families separated from their extended families as young people settled in the cities away from their childhood homes. Better-educated working women bore children.

This kind of social change swelled the categories of the population that have been—in all advanced industrial societies—in the vanguard of contraceptive use. That is, the number of urban, well-educated, and prosperous couples was on the increase. Not surprisingly, dissent from existing reproductive policies appeared. An additional factor making such reform pressing was the growing evidence that many Frenchwomen were resorting to illegal (and very dangerous) abortion as their primary method of birth control (Michel 1961).

The Planning Familial movement between 1962 and 1967 increased its membership from 17,000 to 100,000, opened over 100 clinics all over France, and achieved major media attention and popular support (MFPF 1982, chap. 8). It was a mixed organization with a heavy emphasis on professional medical expertise from both male and female doctors (Bouchardeau 1977, 136–37). Its public spokespersons were, for the most part, health professionals.

The goals of Planning Familial were specified clearly at the beginning and did not change over the decade of greatest mobilization until the reform of 1967. Its primary intent was to help families control their fertility in order to meet family goals of material well-being and emotional support for children (Paillard 1973, 97). The emphasis was clearly and always on having children, not on childlessness. The clinics were willing to counsel any couple with any religious beliefs to help find the most suitable contraceptive technique, and therefore the movement adamantly denied that it challenged anything in traditional, even Catholic, family ideals or contributed to French population decline. In order to achieve its goals, however, it was absolutely essential that legal restrictions on contraceptive practices and dissemination of information be repealed.

It can be seen from this description that Planning Familial did not attempt to alter the notions of women in the universe of political discourse; they were still considered only within families, and it was the well-being and prosperity of the family that concerned the movement most. While the family would ideally be more egalitarian (given the recognition of female sexual pleasure made possible by the elimination of fears of pregnancy, repeated childbirth, and punishing abortion) and enlightened, the world for the activists of Planned Parenthood was still made up of couples who were planning families.

The Balance of Political Forces

Between 1956 and 1967 the balance of political forces that the movement faced was in rapid evolution, including the transition from the Fourth to the Fifth Republic and the beginnings of the United Left, which eventually moved the PCF out of its Cold War ghetto and helped to create the polarized party system of the Fifth Republic. However, when Planning Familial began in the mid-1950s, the Left was divided in its support. The SFIO and other leftist groups were generally favorable if not enthusiastic—it was such Socialist-led municipalities as Grenoble that welcomed the first clinics—but the PCF was vehemently opposed. Only when the Left became more united, not only about its position on reproductive policies but more generally, could the Law of 1920 be changed.

Somewhat surprisingly, perhaps, the question of contraception was first raised in the PCF as an issue affecting the liberation of women. In 1956 a Communist militant, Jacques Derogy, wrote a book advocating the repeal of the Law of 1920 as the beginning of the liberation of women (Mossuz 1966, 922). The response of the PCF leadership to this book and its argument was that it represented neo-Malthusian, pro-American, anti-Communist, and reformist positions. As the secretary-general of the PCF wrote to Derogy: "It seems necessary to recall that the route to the liberation of women is via social reforms and not via abortion clinics," (quoted in Mossuz 1966, 922). In this way, a battle was engaged between the leadership and much of the rank and file of the PCF, which produced the alienation of many Communist militants—including a large number of doctors—from their party. Another result was the difficulty of mounting a successful legislative challenge—in the absence of support from the PCF and the 1956 Mollet Government (despite earlier promises)—to change the Law of 1920.

By the mid-1960s, however, the balance of political forces was very different. the PCF was launched on a united-front strategy involving alliances with other Left forces, while the non-Communist Left learned relatively quickly in the Fifth Republic that a centrist strategy would no longer work and that leftist allies were necessary. Thus, during the 1965 presidential campaign, in which he was the sole Left candidate, François Mitterrand announced his support for changing the law's provisions about contraception in order to allow family life to flourish (Charzat 1972, 196). The Communists supported this position, too. At the same time, parts of the Right were beginning to recognize the political benefits of altering reproductive policies. The new law, the *loi Neuwirth,* was proposed by a Gaullist deputy, although it was opposed by many members of his own governmental coalition.

Legislative discussion originated, however, with a proposal by the *haut comité consultatif de la population et de la famille* for legislation to "regulate childbirth." In other words, the title itself indicated the political issues involved and the effort of the participants to find an acceptable discourse (Cayla 1968, 225). Debate in the National Assembly made use of the traditional discourse, emphasizing the impact of legislative changes on the national birthrate and family life. The compromise that was worked out defined contraception as an abnormal medical act, surrounding it with special provisions to be met by consumers, doctors, and pharmacists. For example, while the purchase of most medication in a pharmacy required only the presentation of a doctor's prescription, contraceptives were much more controlled. Besides age restrictions (girls under 18 needed parental permission, written on the prescription form), products were available to unemancipated (that is, single) minors between 18 and 21 only with a special prescription, more complicated even than that required for narcotics (*stupéfiants*; Cayla 1975, 2). The consequence of this restriction was to place on doctors and pharmacists the responsibility for establishing and guaranteeing the age and civil status of their clients—which they were reluctant to assume—and to make contraceptives readily available only to married women and women whose age was not in question.

In addition, all propaganda of an antinatalist variety was officially prohibited by the *loi Neuwirth* (Cayla 1968, 238). This provision had the effect of eliminating virtually all advertising about the use and effectiveness of contraceptives; even "indirect" publicity—recommendation by a family planning association, for example—was prohibited(Cayla 1975, 2). Once again, only already well-informed couples or those willing to make the effort to search out information themselves would be likely to become acquainted with the possibilities of contraception.

Legislators concerned about the continuation of family values (parental authority as well as sex confined to marriage) wanted to make these products unavailable to young, unmarried women. Those concerned about the nation's birthrate could accept contraception only if it was intended for family planning, not to allow widespread and easy childlessness. These concerns could be accommodated by the reform movement, led by Planning Familial, because it too was most concerned about the needs of married couples and families. There was not much here, however, designed to meet the needs of women with an identity other than that of potential mothers.

CASE III: REPRODUCTIVE POLICIES—THE REGULATION OF ABORTION

The universe of political discourse had changed dramatically by 1974, when the *loi Neuwirth* was revised. At that time the special age and procedural restrictions were removed, and advertising of contraceptive products became possible (Cayla 1975). The differences between the two versions of the law can be explained only by the changing discourse within which the debate took place, which in turn reflects the impact of the modern women's movement. The changed universe was most visible in the debate around legalizing abortion, or permitting *l'interruption voluntaire de la grossesse* (voluntary end to pregnancy), which is the term used in the new discourse.

The Universe of Political Discourse of Movements and Parties

Mobilization for reform of the provisions of the Law of 1920 relating to abortion was very different from that for birth control. Throughout the earlier discussion the matter of abortion had been delicately avoided. It was raised only with reference to the negative effects of lack of access to contraception, when it was asserted that improved policies would end the massive resort to illegal abortion; little was heard about legalizing abortion. Liberalization of abortion laws arrived on the agenda only after the modern women's movement developed in conjunction with the wave of protest of May–June 1968. This development both reflected and contributed to a fundamental change in the notions of women within the universe of political discourse.

The French women's movement came into being in France, as in other countries, at the end of the 1960s, after more than a decade of steady increase in the rate of female participation in the paid labor force and in postsecondary education. Well-educated working women had become visible in "public" life in ways that women of earlier generations had not been. Moreover, rising divorce rates and other changes in lifestyles challenged traditional expectations about the family structure. All these kinds of social change made less credible the treatment of women in the existing universe of political discourse—that their needs and responsibilities were satisfactorily met with policies directed towards families. With the women's movement came a new discourse that seemed better suited to these unfamiliar situations and modern women.

There were substantial changes in popular reactions to women. Obviously, radical feminism attracted attention, especially in the student milieu (Gaudillo 1981).Some mainstream Left political parties and trade unions responded by developing a new understanding of women's oppression separate from that of class. Existing women's organizations and representatives became more conscious of new types of female roles, separate from familial ones. From the Estates General of Feminism (organized by *Elle* magazine) to the PCF, which finally disassociated women from children in its mobilizational work, many actors began to adopt new understanding of and discourse about women's place in French society.

This new discourse, and the collective subject that made primary use of it, developed in large part as a logical consequence of the growth of the New Left, which emphasized democratic themes and could be used by women to understand their situation. It also came partially as a result of the changes in the political process following from the experience of politics with new social movements, an experience that challenged the notion of politics organized solely around class cleavages and class politics. The French New Left created a new political discourse emphasizing democracy and accommodating identities beyond those of class. According to its analysis, an expansion of democracy—in the workplace, in society, and in political organizations—was crucial to the creation of conditions for socialism.

Once the New Left had successfully implanted the themes of democracy and the movement had experienced a series of massive protest mobilizations, ideological space was created for a new inquiry into all forms of oppression. As that happened, women's specific oppression was placed on the agenda of the New Left and those parts of the Old Left still hoping to appeal to the social forces so attracted by the new themes. In this way the universe of political discourse was fundamentally altered: for the first time, women alone and outside a family frame of reference became the subject of political discourse.

The development of an analysis of the everyday workings of male domination introduced issues specific to women into a discussion already focused on democracy. Thus, women's demands for the control of their own bodies and the modification of the bourgeois family were included along with demands for meaningful equality and democratic participation in work and social relations. In this analysis, the oppression of women could no longer be reduced to exploitation in the capitalist relations of production. Women had specific disadvantages to struggle against, without men and in alliance with all women. In other words, an autonomous movement of women, dedicated to destroying the structural and ideological factors oppressing women, was essential. The Old Left's goals of equal rights, which emphasized the similarities of men and women, were replaced by greater attention to difference and specificity.

The campaign for abortion reform was organized primarily by women and by groups without a mixed membership (or ones in which male activists were very unlikely to be prominent public representatives). It was not a campaign of professionals; rather, the only thing that seemed to bind the membership was that they were all "women." Claims were made for the liberation of all women—married or single, teenagers or older, paid workers or housewives—and, most particularly, their right to decide *for themselves* whether to bear children. The question was less *when* (as it had been for the earlier campaign) and more *whether* to have a child at all.

Of course, this new entry into the universe of political discourse did not spring completely unexpectedly from the activities of the modern women's movement. Behind the official discourse utilized in the birth control campaign, for example, there had been evidence that popular understandings and reactions were in flux, often ahead of those of the movement's leaders. In 1961, Andrée Michel (1961, 1217) found in a public opinion survey that many more respondents were concerned about the effect of contraception on women than about the family consequences, despite the care taken by Planning Familial not to surpass traditional family discourse. Thus, a receptive public already existed for the discourse that Simone Veil, minister of health, finally used in 1974 when she described the further changes to the *loi Neuwirth* as a process of normalization to meet the needs of modern women (Cayla 1975, 3).

The Balance of Political Forces

Because most legislators' views, however, were still rooted in the traditional discourse of patriotism and family, the family planning movement had felt compelled to restrain itself in order to achieve success. This restraint was not evident in the actions of the new women's movement when it mobilized around the issue of abortion rights.

Traditional organizations of all kinds increasingly ran into problems in accommodating the new discourse as abortion reform came to symbolize nothing less than a change in women's status and their relation to their own bodies and the state. A telling example of this organizational tension is provided by the experience of Planning Familial, which immediately after the "victory" of 1967 lost a number of activist doctors—including its founder—who were opposed to pushing further toward complete repeal of the Law of 1920 (MFPF 1982, chaps. 9–10). Another effect of this new discourse, both inside such organizations and more generally, was to push aside the taboos surrounding abortion (hence the spectacular publicity events) and to force "personal" problems of women onto the political agenda.

Radical feminists and more moderate groups like Choisir and the Mouvement de Libération de l'Avortement et de la Contraception (MLAC) all used their willingness to reveal themselves as lawbreakers as a principal tactic. In 1971 the *Manifeste des 343* was published. This remarkable document was a public acknowledgment by 343 prominent women in the arts, intellectual circles, politics, and the professions that they had all had at least one abortion. It was followed in 1973 by a public letter issued by doctors acknowledging that they had performed abortions. MLAC and other women's groups publicly organized trips to countries where abortion was legal as well as practicing abortions themselves with the Karman method (Mossuz-Lavau 1984, 2). Thus, in addition to the more everyday actions of lobbying, demonstrating, organizing public debates, and seeking media attention, these women challenged the state's ability to maintain social control.

In 1972 the spectacular and symbolic *procès de Bobigny* took place, in which a teenage girl, her mother, and some of her mother's colleagues were charged under the Law of 1920. The Bobigny case was argued by Gisèle Halimi, a lawyer who became one of the leaders of Choisir. In discussion among several women's groups, the defense was prepared as an explicit attempt to put before the public the case for reform of the Law of 1920 (Halimi 1973, chap. 3; Turpin 1975).

Bobigny is a good example, then, of new content in the universe of political discourse: that is, real consideration of the situation of women. Yet it is important to note that the resolution of the Bobigny case was also based upon themes that were part of a discourse having little to do with women. The final result displays both the insertion of new identities into the universe of political discourse and the continuing importance of traditional forms of address.

The first of these traditional themes was the state's ability to maintain social control by enforcing the law. As it became increasingly obvious to observers—and especially to important parts of the judicial establishment—that the law as written was unenforceable and that more frequent public violations could be expected, the pressure for reform mounted (Turpin 1975, 38–41).

The lack of enforcement was connected closely to a second theme, that of inequality (Turpin 1975, 42ff.). With the frequent publication of information about illegal abortions and foreign travel to obtain abortions, it became clear that it was the poor who were being restricted by the Law of 1920; the rich could afford the costs of special arrangements. The class implications were especially visible in the *procès de Bobigny*, which brought to trial a teenage girl and a mother who had been abandoned years before by the father of her infant children and who worked for the equivalent of the minimum wage to support her children and herself. Famous and usually wealthy women stated in the *Manifeste de 343* that they had aborted and gone free (thus mocking the state's inability to prosecute), while this poor child and her struggling mother faced fines and imprisonment. The press, the Left, and feminists could all agree that this was a gross inequity, although for many the inequity was one of class rather than gender.

Finally, in a profoundly interesting way, Bobigny allowed feminists to expose the contradictions within a discourse that assigned women primary responsibility for the family. A major theme in defense of the mother, who had arranged the abortion for her daughter, was that she was "performing her duties *as a mother.*" Only if she freed her daughter from the life that was bound to follow her unwanted pregnancy (the life she herself had been forced to live) would she be a true and loving mother. She argued that she had failed to teach about and provide her daughter with contraceptive methods—which she would now surely do for this daughter and the others—but that if she had not arranged the abortion, she would have failed even more. This argument, which was an important theme in the public discussion of the *procès,* reveals clearly the way the universe of discourse had changed to accommodate not only a new understanding of the right of women to avoid unwanted pregnancy but also new notions of family responsibility in preparing children for the modern world.

The *procès de Bobigny* reveals, then, the changes as well as the continuities in the universe of political discourse within which the repeal of the Law of 1920 took place and which influenced the reform process. By 1974, themes of women's right to control their own bodies were part of the legislative debate, as were discussions of equity, fairness and family planning (Mossuz-Lavau 1984, 4–9). In 1973 the minister of justice announced that the government was prepared to revise the law to permit abortion on demand, paid for by the Social Security system. Right-wing opposition from pronatalists, Catholics, and cultural conservatives in the National Assembly blocked this very liberal proposal; in fact, quite restrictive legislation was all that could be passed. Obtaining an abortion was no longer a crime per se, and in this way the state relieved itself of the problem of an unenforceable law. However, because strict and relatively short time limits were set, the reform benefited most those women who were least equivocal and/or most informed about their pregnancy—likely to be those who were older or poorer and able to recognize the burden an unwanted child might bring. Moreover, instead of giving women complete freedom to decide for themselves, the legislators insisted upon a compulsory waiting period "for reflection" between the first consultation with the doctor and performance of the procedure. Finally, the promoters of the law succumbed to opposition to greater freedom for women by not including the procedure within the Social Security system. In effect, abortion was labeled an act different from all other medical acts because it was not covered by the state's health program.

In the parliamentary committees and the corridors of the National Assembly, the old discourse about women still held a great deal of influence. Still, the 1974 *loi Veil* was less restrictive than the *loi Neuwirth* passed in 1967. Times and notions of women's rights had changed. For example, when the PCF first tried to confine abortion to cases of social need (poor mothers of more than three children—a remnant of the discourse of equality with respect to women used by the PCF for years), the proposal was immediately rejected, not only by feminists but also by women within the party who criticized the proposal as failing to recognize a fundamental right. The PCF gave up its reticence and joined the Socialists in support of the government's bill. It was, in fact, only because the opposition voted almost unanimously that the *loi Veil* passed over the objections of the majority.

The women's movement had been successful in raising within a broad Left constituency a new way of talking about women. This new identity did not banish all other female identities, however. The universe of political discourse was composed of a mixture of themes, including the liberation of women, equality, and the legitimacy of the state.

CONCLUSION

This essay has looked at several cases of reform in France which appear to have a great deal to do with "women." Closer examination shows that in only one of them, and only in most recent times, did the social movements agitating for reform ascribe to themselves the collective identity of "women." For the rest, the universe of political discourse had no space for female identities beyond the family. Other categories of women—unmarried women, girls, non-Catholics—did not predominate in the minds of the reformers. In consequence, new policies were not designed to nor could they extract "women" from their family situations.

The assumptions of the universe of political discourse were important influences on the process (or lack) of reform and the effects that reforms had on women's condition. Throughout the interwar years, the right to vote could be denied women because according to the hegemonic discourse their needs were met by the political action of their fathers or husbands. Feminists, sharing the same notions of the sexual division of labor, could not successfully challenge such assumptions. Therefore, when the extension of citizenship rights after World War II occurred, it was within a universe of political discourse in which female voters continued to be defined by all political actors either as ungendered members of classes, as mothers, or as Catholics. Similarly, the movement for birth control advocated reform for families, not for women, and that is what it won. The needs of unmarried and especially young women were not met in 1967.

Only as a result of the actions of the contemporary women's movement has the universe of discourse accommodated a dialogue among competing notions of women's place in society. This dialogue created a dynamic that allowed the women's movement to have some influence within the political process and to take advantage of the political resources it controlled in a partisan situation in flux. *L'interruption voluntaire de la grossesse* was achieved in part because of a new acceptance by some political actors that women had the right to decide, voluntarily, to bear children. For other actors, however, women remained either the means by which the state could guarantee its international position or the key to the reproduction of a traditional set of values. Because these actors are still politically influential, only vigilance on the part of the women's movement and its political allies can prevent a return to an older universe of political discourse, a return to the patriotic and familial versions of women's condition that have for so long kept them in the shadows.

NOTES

1. MLF was first used as a generic label, developed by the press. Only in 1979 was the title officially granted as a trademark to one radical feminist group within the movement.

2. Reforms advocated usually included greater civil rights for married women, equal pay for working women, improved education for girls, better conditions of childbirth and infancy, and programs to overcome tuberculosis, alcoholism, and other social scourges.

3. For example, the group La Femme Nouvelle, which was close to the Radical party, demanded the vote, followed by abolition of "the injustices of the Napoleonic Code," equal pay for equal work, and women's right to be magistrates on tribunals dealing with children's welfare.

4. These terms are from Bouchardeau (1977, 52) who uses language current in the interwar years.

5. See Talmy (1962, 39ff.) for details of the family movement's position on suffrage. See also *La Française*, 5 June 1937, for a self-critical evaluation of the CNFF's advocacy of the family vote.

6. Some feminist organizations also thought women's ideas contributed to their own subordination. Yet by the late 1930s many feminists argued that women had reached a level of education sufficient to vote. See the LFDF's *Le Droit des femmes*, December 1938, p. 3; June 1939, p. 89.

7. This view has a long historical life reaching at least from the writings of Michelet in the mid–nineteenth century to contemporary views held by the French Communist Party (PCF) (Jenson 1982).

8. Some Radicals subscribed to a social theory that was more collectivist than individualistic—solidarism. This theory led them to see men as acceptable political representatives of their wives and children (see Bourgeois 1902; Hayward 1961; Offen 1984, 664–68).

9. As Hause (1977) has shown, the Radical party was profoundly divided on this issue, but in the Senate, at least, the supporters of traditionalism and/or anticlericalism prevailed.

10. Even at this time, when their activities in the resistance had supposedly shown women's ability to assume full civic responsibilities, the Radical party opposed full suffrage, voting only to allow women to run for office (Grenier 1970, 279ff.).

11. This movement was termed "neo-Malthusian" because its activities promoted contraception and controlled reproduction rather than abstinence and late marriage, as Thomas Malthus had done (Ronsin 1980, chap. 4).

12. A common reason for opposition was the critique made of Malthus by Marx—that poverty had its source in capitalism, not in fertility, and that teaching the poor to regulate their fertility was a diversion from the real problem.

13. In Durand (1923), for example, the first remedy proposed for the birthrate problem was the family vote.

REFERENCES

Bell, S. G., and K. M. Offen, eds. 1983. *Women, the Family and Freedom.* Vol. 2. Stanford, Calif.: Stanford University Press.

Bouchardeau, Hugette. 1977. *Pas d'histoire, les femmes . . .* Paris: Syros.

Bourgeois, Léon. 1902. *Solidarité.* 3d ed. Paris: Armand Colin.

Brodie, M. J., and Jane Jenson. 1980. *Crisis, Challenge and Change: Party and Class in Canada.* Toronto: Methuen.

Cayla, J. S. 1968. "La Loi du 28 décembre 1967 relative à la régulation des naissances." *Revue trimestrielle de Droit sanitaire et social* 4 (no. 15): 225–40.

———. 1975. "Les Nouvelles Dispositions legislatives relatives à la régulation des naissances." *Revue trimestrielle de Droit sanitaire et social* 11 (no. 41): 1–8.

Charzat, Gisèle. 1972. *Les Françaises: Sont-elles les citoyens?* Paris: Denoel Gonthier.

Dreyfus, F.-G. 1975. *Histoire des Gauches en France, 1940–1974.* Paris: Seuil.

Durand, E. M. 1923. *Des Mésures prises par le législateur français pour encourager la natalité.* Paris: Librairie Générale de Droit et de Jurisprudence.

Gaudillo, N. G. 1981. *Libération des femmes, le MLF.* Paris: PUF.

Grenier, Fernand. 1970. *C'était ainsi.* Paris: Editions Sociales.

Halimi, Gisèle. 1973. *La cause des Femmes.* Paris: Livres de Poche.

Hause, S. C. 1977. "The Rejections of Women's Suffrage by the French Senate in November, 1922: A Statistical Analysis." *Third Republic,* nos. 3–4: 205–37.

Hause, S. C., and Anne Kenney. 1981. "The Limits of Suffragist Behavior: Legalism and Militancy in France, 1896–1922." *American Historical Review* 86 (no. 4): 781–806.

Hayward, J. E. S. 1961. "The Official Social Philosophy of the French Third Republic: Leon Bourgeois and Soliarism." *International Review of Social History* 6: 19–48.

Hoffman, Stanley, ed. 1963. *In Search of France.* Cambridge, Mass.: Harvard University Press.

Jenson, Jane. 1982. "The Modern Women's Movement in Italy, France, and Great Britain: Differences in Life-Cycle." *Comparative Social Research* 5: 341–75.

———. 1986. "Gender and Reproduction; or Babies and the State." *Studies in Politics and Economics* 20 (Summer): 9–46.

Leger, Danielle. 1982. *Le Féminisme en France.* Paris: Sycomore.

Louis-Levy, M. 1934. *L'Emancipation politique des femmes*. Paris: Librairie Feydeau.

MFPF (Mouvement pour le planning familial). 1982. *D'une revolte à une lutte: 25 ans d'histoire du planning familial*. Paris: Tierce.

Michel, Andrée. 1961. "A propos du Contrôle des naissances." *Les Temps modernes* 16: 1201–18.

Michel, Andrée, and G. S. Texier. 1964. *La Condition de la française d'aujourd'hui*. Paris: Gonthier.

Mossuz, Janine. 1966. "Les Régulations des naissances: Les aspects politiques du débat." *Revue française du Science politique* 5: 913–39.

Mossuz-Lavau, Janine. 1984. "Pouvoir de droite, pouvoir de gauche et problème de l'avortement en France (1973–1983)." Paper presented at the European Consortium for Political Research, Salzburg, Austria.

Offe, Claus. 1984. *Contradictions of the Welfare State*. London: Hutchison.

Offen, K. M. 1977. "Introduction: Aspects of the Woman Question during the Third Republic." *Third Republic*, nos. 3–4: 1–19.

———. 1984. "Depopulation, Nationalism, and Feminism in Fin-de-Siècle France." *American Historical Review* 89: 684–76.

Paillard, Bernard Nicole. 1973. "La Brèche féministe du planning familial." In N. Benoit et al., *La Femme majeure*. Paris: Seuil.

Piven, Frances Fox, and Richard Cloward. 1979. *Poor People's Movements: Why They Succeed, How They Fail*. N.Y.: Vintage.

Pizzorno, Alessandro. 1979. "Political Exchange and Collective Identity in Industrial Conflict." In Colin Crouch and Alessandro Pizzorno, eds., *The Resurgence of Class Conflict in Western Europe Since 1968*, vol. 2, 277–99. London: Macmillan.

Poincaré, Raymond. 1921. *Pour le suffrage des femmes*. Paris: LFDF.

Przeworski, Adam. 1980. "Social Democracy as an Historical Phenomenon." *New Left Review* 122: 27–58.

Rabaut, Jean. 1978. *Histoire des féminismes français*. Paris: Stock.

Ronsin, François. 1980. *La Grève des ventres: Propagande néo-malthusienne et baisse de la natalité en France, 19e–20e siècles*. Paris: Aubier-Montaigne.

Sowerwine, Charles. 1982. *Sisters or Citizens? Women and Socialism in France since 1876*. Cambridge: Cambridge University Press.

Talmy, Roger. 1962. *Histoire du mouvement familiale en France (1896–1939)*. Annales de la Faculté de Droit et de Science Politique, vol. 2. Paris: UNCAF.

Tarrow, Sidney. 1983. *Struggling to Reform: Social Movements and Policy Change during Cycles of Protest*. Center for International Studies, Western Societies Occasional Paper no. 15. Ithaca, N.Y.: Cornell University.

Tomlinson, Richard. 1983. "The Politics of *Dénatalité* during the French Third Republic." Thesis, King's College, Cambridge, 1983.

Touraine, Alain. 1981. *The Voice and the Eye: An Analysis of Social Movements*. Cambridge: Cambridge University Press.

Turpin, Daniel. 1975. "La Décision de libéraliser l'avortement à France." *Annales de la Faculté de Droit et de Science Politique*. Clermont, 12: 3–170.

4 Collective Consciousness, Identity Transformation, and the Rise of Women in Public Office in the United States

CAROL McCLURG MUELLER

Evaluating the success of the contemporary women's movement presents a task of a new order of magnitude for social movement theory and research. Not only does the women's movement claim a majority of the nation's citizens as its constituents; it also supports goals that range from transforming the subtlest details of social interaction to the redistribution of political power and economic well-being. Despite the scope of these goals, they cannot be discounted by social movement theorists as the utopian visions of idle dreamers. They have been pursued in the programmatic plans of organized activists whose political influence still continues to grow after almost 20 years (Gelb and Palley 1982; Boles 1982).

Because of the magnitude and diversity of the women's movement and because of several inadequacies in social movement theory, it is more likely at present that the movement will inform theory than the reverse. Social movement theory in this paper refers to a divergent literature describing the mobilization and allocation of resources on behalf of social movement goals. This literature stems largely from the work of Gamson (1975), McCarthy and Zald (1973; 1977), Oberschall (1973), and Tilly and his associates (see, e.g., Shorter and Tilly 1974; Tilly 1969; Tilly, Tilly, and Tilly 1975). Similarities in many assumptions lead many observers to characterize the literature as a single paradigm despite differences in emphasis, terminology, and empirical focus (for a thorough review and critique, see Jenkins 1983). This resource mobilization paradigm is discussed in terms of its adequacy for describing and understanding the current women's movement and its successes.

Although the process of informing theory has already begun, a systematic analysis of the women's movement from the perspective of social movement theory has not been attempted. Such analyses of women's movement "success" as do

This paper was formerly titled "Women's Movement Success and the Success of Social Movement Theory."

exist tend to evaluate public policies in terms of interest group theory (Boneparth 1982; Freeman 1982; 1975; Gelb and Palley 1982) or conflict theory (Boles 1979). Although these works express increasing interest in social movement theory, their interest has not yet been realized. Costain's work (1980; 1982) explicitly draws together theoretical perspectives from interest group and social movement theory but does not incorporate the more recent work on resource mobilization.

In the interest of contributing to this collaboration as well as enhancing social movement theory in general, the present paper has two goals: to identify two major issues in social movement theory that bear on our understanding of women's movement success, and to relate these issues to one specific goal of the movement. The first issue is that of distinguishing between means (resources) and ends (outcomes) in identifying what constitutes success. The second issue concerns the role of collective consciousness both as a resource and as an outcome of social movement activity. I argue that the distinction between resources (means) and outcomes (ends) is an arbitrary theoretical device that ignores historical evidence suggesting that the most successful outcomes provide generalized resources for future mobilization. I argue further that one of the most important generalized resources is the development of collective consciousness.

I illustrate the importance of these two issues for understanding the fate of one goal of the contemporary women's movement: increasing the number of women in public office. Women public officials are selected as my focus because a considerable literature exists describing their state of consciousness both before and after the mobilization of contemporary feminism.

THEORETICAL ISSUES

Means and Ends in Defining Success

Evaluating either protest or social movement success is a relatively new enterprise. In the mid–1960s, Eckstein (1965, 135) reached a pessimistic conclusion after a review of existing knowledge on the outcomes of internal wars and violent protests: "Curiously enough," he noted, "the later the phase, the less there is to read about the issues involved." Ten years later, summarizing the broader issues concerning the outcomes of social movements, Marx and Woods (1975) were not noticeably more optimistic. Again, in 1983, Tarrow summarized a growing but diverse literature on the outcomes of internal wars and social movements with a sophisticated definition of success, a set of hypotheses, and a research agenda incorporating internal and external influences on outcomes. Yet consensus among researchers on the meaning and measure of success continues to elude us.

Despite Tarrow's excellent review and another by Gurr (1980) on the outcomes of violent conflict, a major—perhaps unresolvable—issue remains. This is the question of whether a consequence of social movement activity is defined as a "success" in its own right or merely as a means to some other goal that serves the ends of either protesters or elites. Tarrow (1983, 67–69) points to one important aspect of the issue in identifying two historical approaches to cycles of policy reform. He observes that students of Western social history such as Bendix (1964) and Marshall (1964) conceive of reform as an irreversible causal chain in which the extension of political rights of suffrage and association are a necessary prelude to the extension of other citizenship rights. In contrast, he suggests that scholars like Piven and Cloward (1971, 1977) argue that reforms are reversible once outbreaks of civil disorder have subsided.[1] To reconcile these two viewpoints, Tarrow (1983, 70) suggests that "a basic hypothesis is that reforms producing institutionalized participation are both more durable and more productive of further reforms than substantive rights." This hypothesis suggests that one major dimension of social movement success is that in which outcomes are evaluated in terms of the resources they provide for further mobilization.[2]

Piven and Cloward's well-known analysis of the civil rights movement falls well within the range of Tarrow's hypothesis as well as the tradition of Marshall and Bendix—their reversibility argument of reform notwithstanding. Thus, Black manhood suffrage was one "success" of the abolition movement even though it was denied to most southern Blacks from Reconstruction until it was won again in the 1960s. Nevertheless, by the 1950s, Black voting strength in northern cities (and its potential in the South) was a key resource in generating electoral instability. The increase and volatility of the northern Black vote, together with the protests of the civil rights movement, helped assure elite support from presidents Dwight Eisenhower, John Kennedy, and Lyndon Johnson for civil rights legislation (Piven and Cloward 1977, 195–258). Two of these victories were the Voting Rights Act of 1965 and the increase in federal protection of southern Black suffrage. These successes, in turn, made possible the election of increasing numbers of Black officials in the South and ultimately a sharp curtailment in white terrorism. Thus, the success of one movement or movement phase is recycled as a resource for a second movement phase.

Tarrow's observations on cycles of reform have more general application, however, in informing our understanding of social movement success. It is not only reforms and policy innovations that differentially empower further movements and further reforms. Some aspects of mobilization may constitute "successes" for one movement or movement phase, which can be rechanneled as a resource in a later movement or movement phase. Social movement organizations are the resources that have been most widely debated in terms of future use as a movement resource. This seems to be the major issue raised for instance by Piven and Cloward's *Poor People's Movements* (1977). They argue that social movement organizations are inevitably co-opted and thus do not serve their constituents. Controlled by elites, they cannot serve as resources for future movements or reforms, either. This argument is hotly contested in major reviews of their book by Jenkins (1979), and Lipsky (1979). It is also undercut by the uneven support it receives from Piven and Cloward's four case studies. Evidence on the National Workers Alliance of the unemployed and the National Welfare Rights Organization of welfare mothers is considerably more convincing than that on industrial unions or the Black civil rights organizations. In his review, Jenkins (1979)[3] explains the difference in resistance to co-optation of the unemployed and industrial workers in terms of the functional importance of the mobilized actors for the political-economic system. We note that centrality to the political system is equally important. Unlike the unemployed, industrial workers are central to the economic system. In contrast to welfare mothers, black voters of the 1950s had become crucial to Democratic control of the presidency.

Organization is not the only mobilization resource that can be viewed as both a successful outcome of one mobilization phase and a resource for further mobilization and policy reform. Equally critical for evaluating the mobilization and success of the women's movement is the creation of a shared (collective) consciousness among segments of the potential constituency, allies, and/or general public, which incorporates varying degrees of approval for the movement's grievances and goals. As a generalized resource, the creation of a collective consciousness is critical for converting activists, for enlisting the support of third parties (Jenkins and Perrow, 1977; Lipsky, 1968), for mobilizing movement activists (Mueller and Dimieri, 1982; Mueller and Judd, 1982), and for notifying members of the general public such as Olson's (1968) "free riders" of potential opportunities (see, e.g., Cancian 1979 on women's accelerated entry into business schools after 1970). The collective consciousness is important, though often unspecified, at every phase of mobilization and strategic interaction with elites or targets. The development of a collective consciousness is itself a "successful" social movement outcome.

Collective Consciousness and Social Movement Theory

"Collective consciousness" refers here to a transforming set of ideas that legitimate opposition to traditional norms, roles, institutions, and/or the distribution of scarce resource. New sets of revised rights and privileges are articulated on behalf of each category or community seeking to enhance its status as well as its share of scarce goods and services. These ideas are transforming in the sense that they envisage a social world that does not currently exist. In recent history the authority of the social sciences or the loyalties of race or nationality have served most frequently to justify the new beliefs. The collective consciousness is internalized with (probably) decreasing intensity, consensus, and support as one moves from core activists to the movement's potential members/constituents; to potential allies or third parties; to the general public and even opponents (see Mueller and Dimieri 1982 for the distinction between pro- and anti-ERA activists and the general public).

To argue that a particular social movement relies on the creation of a new collective consciousness implies immediately that its rationale lies initially outside the prevailing consensus of community or society. To some extent, its believers will be treated not as political opponents but as ridiculous, dangerous, heretical, or crazy elements of society. It also implies that much of the "work" of the movement will involve the recreation of its own history, the reappropriation of cultural symbols, and the resocialization of adults. Its programmatic goals will emphasize control of the instruments of socialization as well as access to scarce values. One indicator of "success," then, comprises the degree of diffusion of the collective consciousness, the transformation of culture, and the appropriation of the apparatus of socialization.

The process by which a collective consciousness is developed in opposition to prevailing norms, roles, institutions, or the distribution of scarce values was a major issue for classical Marxist theory and continues to be of central interest in studies of protests and social movements outside the resource mobilization framework. It is the key intervening variable in Piven and Cloward's analysis of poor people's movements (1977, 3–4); in Gitlin's (1981) study of the media's transforming effect on Students for a Democratic Society (SDS) during the sixties; in Rudé's (1980, 15–38) recent study of popular protests in history; and in numerous interpretations of recent worker insurgency in Europe (Mann 1973; Melucci 1980; Pizzorno 1978). The role of consciousness also emerges as central to recent conceptualizations of powerlessness and political quiescence in the works of Gaventa (1980) and Lukes (1974), which draw on the earlier work of Antonio Gramsci.

Despite abundant evidence of continuing interest in the creation, diffusion, and use of collective oppositional consciousness (or its absence), resource mobilization theory has minimized its importance. Arguing that attention to consciousness overestimates the importance of members and potential members to recent social movements, McCarthy and Zald's classic paper states:

> We stress a different approach. Our "resource mobilization" approach emphasizes the resources, beyond membership consciousness and manpower, that may become available to potential movements. These resources support the growth and vitality of movements and movement organizations. This view does not necessarily deny the existence of grievances. It stresses the structural conditions that facilitate the expression of grievances. (1973, 1)

While McCarthy and Zald are careful to indicate that their paradigm is complementary to the "hearts and minds" approach, others have not been so cautious.[4] Jenkins and Perrow (1977, 250) for instance, attack those theories which contend that "social movements arise because of deep and widespread discontent." Instead, they argue, "what increases, giving rise to insurgency, is the amount of social resources available to unorganized but aggrieved groups, making it possible to launch an organized demand for change." Grievances, we are told, are a constant fact of life. Resource mobilization research and theory argue that grievances and/or discontent can be taken for granted. The process by which grievances are defined and legitimated is not problematic for these social movement theorists. It is assumed that groups which do not mobilize are short on resources or third-party support and a favorable political environment.

While resource mobilization theory and research have created a valuable paradigm for calling attention to professional leadership, organizational resources, technological innovations, and political constraints, the neglect of consciousness has proved a major liability in understanding social movements based on a massive shift in collective consciousness. Yet such a shift of consciousness is one of the defining characteristics of the contemporary women's movement, as indicated in the extensive treatment it receives in *all* the major works that attempt to describe the movement as a totality (see, for instance, Carden 1974; Cassell 1977; Deckard 1975; Evans 1979; Hole and Levine 1971).[5]

Only if the central role of consciousness is recognized can we understand several otherwise anomalous characteristics of the movement: why a primarily symbolic issue like the Equal Rights Amendment (ERA) became the unifying focus of the movement; why a woman's control of her body is considered more valuable than the life of a fetus; why an army of women are laboring in women's studies to redefine the canons of art, art history, and literature; why women at the highest levels of electoral office are beginning to talk about feminizing the nature of political leadership. These goals reflect the general thrust of the movement toward elevating the status of women while feminizing culture and power. Such goals fall outside the liberal consensus in that they focus on directly enhancing women's status as a group rather than indirectly raising the status of women by expanding opportunities for individual women. In this respect, the American women's movement is similar to those European movements of collective identity described by Melucci (1980).

If the women's movement differs from many contemporary American movements in its pursuit of a massive shift in consciousness, and if social movement theory is inhospitable to evaluating the role of collective consciousness, what is the most productive strategy for scholars of the movement? Past work on the women's movement has essentially separated the study of consciousness from the study of mobilization or policy outcomes. Policy analysis by political scientists has evaluated the landmark legislation of Congress during the early 1970s (Freeman 1975; Murphy 1973); the campaign for the ERA (Boles 1979; 1982); and, more recently, the varying success of specific policies that differ in their emphasis on role equity or role change (Gelb and Palley 1982). The analysis of consciousness has usually focused on either the ideological literature of the movement (e.g., Yates 1975) or the analysis of mass survey data (Baxter and Lansing 1980; Fulenwider 1980; Klein 1984).

Increasingly there are points of overlap. Klein's early (1979) analysis of survey data also offers a social learning theory of why the consciousness of the women's movement developed when it did. Her later research (1984) goes further and shows its importance for the development of a women's voting bloc. Survey studies of the beliefs of activists also identify segmented views of the feminist consciousness at the point where it enters the political process (Arrington and Kyle 1978; Mitchell, McCarthy, and Pearce 1979; Mueller and Dimieri 1982; Rossi 1982; Tedin et al. 1977). Costain's (1980; 1982) work goes even further in attempting to bridge the gap between social movement and interest group in explaining the lobbying efforts of the movement.

What is lacking, however, is sustained research based in a common theoretical orientation. The most promising orientation, from my perspective, remains that of resource mobilization, despite its current hostility to the study of consciousness.[6] This judgment is based on four observations. First, the literature frequently cited as compatible with the resource mobilization theory already uses notions of collective consciousness as unexamined parameters. Thus, Freeman's (1973) frequently cited paper on the origins of the women's movement refers to the congruence in consciousness or values when she describes the "co-optability" of networks from which movement activists were drawn. Jenkins and Perrow (1977) also depend on the change in consciousness of liberal third parties to account for the greater success of farm worker organizing in the 1960s than in the 1940s. Lipsky (1968) is more straightforward in pointing to the symbolic manipulation engaged in by protest leaders seeking the sympathy and support of third parties.

Second, disavowal of the "hearts and minds" approach within resource mobilization stems largely from discrediting "discontent theory" (Shorter and Tilly 1974; Tilly, Tilly, and Tilly 1975), which relied on fluctuations in grievances to explain riots, strikes, and other forms of collective action. Methodologically, however, these recent studies based on aggregate data are no more convincing in their "proof" regarding states of consciousness than were earlier studies based on aggregate data, which argued in favor of the discontent theories (see, e.g., Gurr 1969; 1970). Far more convincing are Moore's (1966) and Rudé's (1952) careful descriptions of the mobilization of city mobs and peasants based on fluctuations in the price of bread and other specific grievances that became linked to the broader issues of the French Revolution. One does not need to bring in the excesses of Smelser's (1963) irrational, magical beliefs to study the role of consciousness, beliefs, or grievances.

Third, the explicit consideration of collective consciousness within the resource mobilization framework has already begun. McCarthy (1982) argues convincingly that the pro-choice (abortion) movement has compensated for a weak grassroots infrastructure by mobilizing supportive public opinion ("an unstructured sentiment pool") through the sophisticated use of direct mail techniques. These techniques made it possible to raise money, enlist members, and exert political pressure on Congress. Thus, the "sentiment pool" is the most generalized resource available to the pro-choice movement. Understandably, its existence is not problematic from McCarthy's perspective. Yet in evaluating the successes and failures of the movement, the peculiar weaknesses of public opinion on this issue (as well as the ERA) and its connection to McCarthy's "thin" infrastructure are of concern.

Fourth, as McCarthy's study shows, there is no inherent incompatibility between the study of consciousness and organizational resources as components of social movements. Furthermore, outside the resource mobilization framework, they are found to be intimately connected. Thus, Gitlin (1980) finds that media manipulation of the image of SDS transformed the membership as well as the goals and tactics of SDS. Gaventa (1980) finds similarly that the cultural discontinuity between atheistic union organizers and fundamentalist miners in central Appalachia proved disastrous for coalition efforts.

I am concerned here with demonstrating the role of consciousness in realizing one goal of the contemporary women's movement: the increased election of women to public office. The role of consciousness as it influenced the self-perceptions of women on the threshold of public office and the norms of appropriateness held by voters are compared with the more tangible resources made available by feminist organizations.

FEMINIST CONSCIOUSNESS AND THE RISE OF WOMEN IN PUBLIC OFFICE

The Rise of Women in Public Office

From the beginning, one goal of the contemporary women's movement has been to increase the number and influence of women in elective office. This was part of the 1966 statement of purpose of the National Organization for Women (NOW) when it sought to bring women "into the mainstream of American life." Looking at a simple correlation between goal and social change, the movement appears to have been wildly successful. The number of women elected to state and local office has increased remarkably since 1970. In state legislatures, the number of women elected has risen from 305 in 1969 to 1,130 in 1987, or from 3.5 to 15 percent. The election of women at the local level has increased even more dramatically. From 1975 until 1981 the number of women serving as mayors or governing officials of municipalities and townships rose from 4,650 to 14,672, or from 4 to 14.3 percent. In 1981 there were 1,707 women mayors (making up 7 percent of the total), compared with 244 (1 percent) in 1971 and just 10 in 1951. (Data are unavailable from the states of Illinois, Indiana, Kentucky, Missouri, Pennsylvania, and Wisconsin; Center for the American Woman and Politics, 1986.)

The timing of women's increased election to public office in the early 1970s corresponded closely with massive insurgent collective action; with the "media blitz" that signaled the public phase of the movement; with the increasing size of the National Organization for Women; and with the creation of a feminist organization dedicated to the goal of increasing women's electoral influence—the National Women's Political Caucus (NWPC). August 1970 marked the turning point as massive demonstrations were held across the country on the fiftieth anniversary of women's suffrage. Women who had not been active before marched and picketed, attended rallies and teach-ins. Feminist protests spread through the churches, the professions, academic disciplines, labor unions, sports, art, the armed services, government bureaus, and the national press corps. Media coverage increased exponentially. Cancian and Ross (1981) found that the proportion of the *New York Times* index devoted to women in general increased from 0.05 percent in 1969 to 0.36 percent in 1977. The average number of items related to women on the three major television networks rose from 18 in 1969 to 53 in 1970 and 1,924 in 1975. Membership in NOW grew rapidly from 3,000 in 1969 to 46,500 in 1974. By the late 1970s, the four major feminist organizations (NARAL [National Abortion Rights Action League], NOW, NWPC, and WEAL [Women's Equity Action League]) had a combined membership of about 250,000 (Gelb and Palley 1982, 50). Public support for improving the status of women grew dramatically.

The question of concern here is which of the factors associated with this explosive growth in activity, organizational strength, media coverage, and public support contributed most heavily to the increase of women in public office. Current social movement theory would argue in favor of organizational resources. Certainly there was organizational activity toward this goal.

Organizational Resources

In 1966, the National Organization for Women stated its general commitment to bringing women into public life. In 1971, members of NOW led in forming the National Women's Political Caucus, which sought a more focused effort for women's full participation in electoral politics. NWPC stated that its purpose was opposition to "racism, sexism, institutional violence and poverty through the election and appointment of women to public office, party reform and the support of women's issues and feminist candidates across party lines" (Feit 1979, 185). The celebrity status of caucus founders (Betty Friedan, Bella Abzug, Gloria Steinem) assured media coverage of its activities, particularly as they focused on party reform and the forthcoming 1972 presidential conventions. Eight years later, one NWPC Caucus founder claimed the following accomplishments for the organization:

> Aside from helping to place women in public office or to win legislative and party fights, the Caucus can justly claim credit for a much more basic accomplishment, creating women as a political interest group. At the time the Caucus was born, women as a group were not a political factor of any importance. The issue of how many women were serving in political leadership roles had not scratched the public

consciousness. No one, in fact, monitored or knew how many women there were in public office nationwide. The representation of women at national party conventions was of interest only to a small group of reformers, and the concept of women's issues as a sub-group of political issues did not exist. There were no national campaign funds for women candidates and no one was lobbying for the appointment of women to public office. The Caucus was the leader in changing all of this. (Feit 1979, 187)

While some of these accomplishments can properly be credited to the caucus, it is not unusual for social movement leaders to make extravagant claims. How much credit should be given to the resources of organized feminism for the dramatic increase of women in public office?

Early social science evaluations of the role of the feminist organizations and their resources were quite generous. After interviewing 200 women involved in politics across the country, the Tolchins (1973) reported that the movement had unleashed a massive outpouring of organizational resources to work for the election of women to public office. Later attempts to find evidence of these organizational resources have reached more modest conclusions. It now appears that until the late 1970s the feminist organizations were only a minor influence in making resources available to women running for office. This is true in terms of providing its own members as candidates, in funding campaigns, and in encouraging women to run for office.

The most obvious resource that feminist organizations could contribute would be their own members. Bella Abzug's career in the early 1970s as caucus founder, congresswoman, and Senate candidate from New York provided a spectacular model for this route into politics. Since women have usually been more likely than men to enter politics through work in voluntary organizations, entree through reform-oriented social movement organizations would not have proved a radical innovation. Yet most of the newly elected women did not belong to feminist organizations. According to a 1977 survey (Johnson and Carroll 1978), 4 percent of city council members, 4 percent of mayors, and 13 percent of county commissioners belonged to feminist organizations like NOW, NWPC, or WEAL. Only at the state level, where the number of women is much smaller, is there a significant minority of women who belong to feminist organizations (31 percent in state legislative and 26 percent in state executive branches). Even at the state level, however, the proportion belonging to feminist organizations is lower than for any other category of women's groups.

Although most of the new women in public office do not come directly out of the feminist organizations, other resources from these organizations may have facilitated their increasing numbers. Most critical would be campaign funds, the Achilles heel of many women's candidacies (Mandel 1981, 181–201). With the amount of money spent in campaigns increasing by quantum leaps, women's lack of access to major sources of funding could be overcome by campaign contributions from feminist organizations. Again, however, the data indicate only a modest impact, and that in the late 1970s and early 1980s as the campaign for ERA ratification intensified.

The Women's Campaign Fund, an offshoot of the National Women's Political Caucus, is the only national feminist organization that exists solely to fund women's political campaigns. In its first year, 1974, it distributed $20,800 to 27 candidates. By the fall of 1980 this sum had increased to $112,758 divided among 93 candidates; the average per candidate had increased from $770 to $1,212. In 1976 the national caucus could contribute only $25,000 to women candidates across the entire country and $45,000 in 1978. Much larger sums were made available to elect pro–ERA legislators in unratified states. The NWPC/ERA fund gave about $350,000 in 1976 and 1978 (Mandel 1981, 216). By 1982, NOW, which distributed $110,000 to pro–ERA candidates in 1978, had earmarked $1 million for state and local races and $2 million for federal contests (Palley 1982, 589). By 1983, 16 women's political action committees (PACs) had been created nationwide to support women's candidacies (Kleeman 1983).

While it has been widely acknowledged that the growing ERA campaign funds from the major feminist organizations may have been a significant factor in electing more women to office, they have only been available in the last two years before the ratification deadline in June, 1982. During the mid-1970s, when the rate of increase was greatest, the feminist organizations then had little money to offer, and though these small sums were crucial in some races (Mandel 1981, 217), they can hardly account for the overall increase.

If feminist organizations did not contribute either members or money in quantities sufficient to account for women's rise in public office, perhaps their influence was felt through encouraging other women to run. Historically, women have been more likely than men to require encouragement before seeking office, and one original goal of the NWPC was to find likely candidates and encourage them to run. Yet contrary to the prevailing image that women have to be asked, the best data available suggest that by the mid-1970s, women had become "self-starters." Carroll's (1980, 64–65) study of women who ran for state and congressional offices in the 1976 primaries and general elections found that one-third of the total sample and almost half (48 percent) of those who ran for Congress decided to run on their own. For those who were urged to run by someone else, friends were the most important influence, then family, followed by officeholders and party officials. Feminist groups were at the bottom of the list, along with coworkers and voters. An even higher proportion of self-starters was found in a 1976 survey of women state legislators by Lex: almost half ran because of the contribution they thought they could make to public life. For those who ran because of encouragement from others, the most important organizations were the League of Women Voters and school-related groups. Feminist groups ranked along with church groups and service clubs.

On the basis of the evidence for actual resources—members, campaign funds, and encouragement—contributed by feminist organizations, they appear to be an increasingly important factor which, nevertheless, cannot account for the dramatic increase in women's officeholding throughout the 1970s. Rather, what emerges from this and other data is the transformation in consciousness of women in traditional organizations like the League of Women Voters. Located at the threshold of elective office, their self-perceptions changed, and they also found high levels of support from families, friends, and voters.

The Role of Consciousness in Identity Transformation

Despite inadequate baseline data on women officials during the 1960s, the proportion of self-starters identified in the mid-1970s suggests that the widespread public debate on the role of women that occurred after 1970 greatly increased the sense of efficacy and the motivation for a political career in the identities of women close to politics. These were women active in civic affairs, in the political parties, in all of the voluntary organizations that serve as "feeders" for women who run for office.

Among women running for office, this change of consciousness seems to occur in three steps or stages.

Stage One: *Career Feminism*—a change in perceptions regarding ambition for public office. Women decide that it is legitimate to have a political career. They reject traditional beliefs that women are emotionally or psychologically unsuited for the competition of political contests. They also reject the idea that being a wife and mother presents insurmountable obstacles to a political career or that women can have more real power and influence "behind the throne," using feminine charm and diplomacy.

Stage Two: *Structural Feminism*—a perception that the obstacles to women's full participation in political institutions is not legitimate. Exclusion is regarded as discrimination, whether the obstacles come from party officials, fellow legislators, the media, or funding sources. Women no longer agree that they have as much opportunity as men, and they identify chauvinism, stereotyping, exclusion from important committee assignments, and informal influence as major difficulties of officeholding.

Stage Three: *Group Feminism*—a sense of group identification with other women and with the women's movement. Women support specific policy proposals of women's movement organizations, such as the ERA, government-funded child care, social security for homemakers, and opposition to limitations on the right to and availability of abortion.

Prior to 1970, the few existing studies indicate that only a few women—such as Congresswoman Martha Griffiths, chief strategist for Title VII of the Civil Rights Act of 1964 and congressional passage of the ERA in 1972—would have had a positive score on any of these dimensions. Almost every woman who achieved office prior to 1970 was appointed to fill a vacancy caused by the death of her husband or someone else. Of the 94 women who served in Congress through 1976, 50 were there to fill seats vacated in each instance by the death of the incumbent (Kincaid 1978). Few could be described as self-starters. While acknowledging that they were cut out of the major centers of power by their male colleagues, most denied that this influenced their effectiveness. Most were party loyalists in their voting (Francovic 1977) and disavowed any interest in issues related to the status of women; they were horrified at the thought of constituting themselves as a "women's bloc" (Gehlen 1969). A similar pattern of consciousness was found in the 1960s among women officials at the state and local levels (Mueller 1982).

A somewhat different pattern appeared first in a study of 50 women legislators selected by civic organizations around the country as "highly successful" (Kirkpatrick 1974). These women, 15 percent of the 330 serving in 1972, were considered the most effective and influential women state legislators in the country. In terms of the three stages of feminist consciousness, almost all had cleared the first step but few had gone further. They were overwhelmingly self-starters, but like most women officials in the 1960s, they did not regard the exclusionary treatment they received from their male colleagues as illegitimate discrimination. Nor did they look with favor on the women's liberation movement. They did not consider themselves to be representatives of women as a group, nor did they have an interest in women's issues per se.

By the mid-1970s, most studies show, there was development of all three stages of consciousness among women elected to office, with variation in the three stages based on level of office. In the Johnson and Carroll study (1978), all women who reported any difficulties in their role of public official focused on illegitimate sources of discrimination against them as women, or what I have described as "structural feminism." What varied was the proportion who experienced such difficulties—from 58 percent of local officeholders to 78 percent of state senators. Women at the local level were more likely to feel that women have just as much opportunity as men to become leaders (agree strongly: mayors = 35 percent; local council = 31 percent; state senate = 16 percent; state executive = 15 percent). Similarly, for the third stage, or "group feminism," support for feminist-identified policies was strongest from women in state executive and state senate offices and weakest from women in local councils.

Thus, the women's movement seems to have created a consciousness that legitimated ambition for a political career among a pool of women who were on the doorstep, ready and eligible to run for office. The higher they aspired, however, the more obstacles they found (see Mueller 1982). Again, the new consciousness was there to provide an explanation. Exclusion was no longer the necessary price for chivalry. It was discrimination; it was unfair; and it should be opposed through creating an organized presence of women officials in caucuses and informal networks (Mueller 1983b). The movement had also adopted a program of policy changes, and women officials increasingly supported them, as well. As Klein (1984) has argued in another context, these women already had many of the necessary resources for political mobilization, but they—as well as the public—lacked a legitimating set of ideas before 1970.

The Changed Consciousness of Voters

The increased readiness of women to run for office would have had no effect if a change in consciousness had not occurred among voters as well. In a 1976 survey, women serving in state legislatures were asked to give their opinion as to why there had been an increase in the election of women to public office. Far ahead of any other reason was the change they attributed to the electorate. Almost half said that the most important reason was "the electorate's developing a greater degree of confidence in the ability of women to assume political roles." In other studies asking women officials to name their biggest problems in reaching office, very few considered the voters prejudiced against women candidates. This is in sharp contrast to the attitudes of most women officials before 1970. It also contrasts sharply with the continuing sentiments of their male colleagues (Johnson and Carroll 1978).

Surveys of public opinion support this perception of voters by women officials. Public office was one of the first nontraditional careers for women to receive widespread public acceptance after 1970. Repeated surveys have found increasingly large majorities supporting the hypothetical election of a woman for president (Ferree 1974; Schreiber 1978). Public support for women's participation in politics continued throughout the 1970s despite conservative trends on other public issues (Mueller 1983a).

Early election studies that examined actual voting behavior in a limited sample of elections found that there were few significant differences in the success of male and female candidates once party and incumbency were controlled (Darcy and Schramm 1977; Karnig and Walters 1976). A more recent study examining 6,000 state legislative races in six states from 1970 to 1980 found that women fared better than men in the primaries but not as well in the general elections for the first half of the decade (Welch, Clark and Darcy 1982). After 1975, however, gender was no longer a significant factor once incumbency and party were controlled. These findings support the argument that (for the state legislative offices studied) the election of women is no longer dependent on decreasing voter prejudice against women but depends instead on the availability of women candidates. Similar findings are reported where women ran as major party candidates for high-level office in five 1982 elections (Zipp and Plutzer 1985).

For the state legislatures studied by Welch, Clark, and Darcy, the proportion of women candidates increased from 7.9 percent for the 1970–75 period to 12.1 percent for the 1975–80 period. By 1980, 14.8 percent of the candidates were women. Presumably, the increase in the number of women candidates began with the change in consciousness at the beginning of the decade, which is now augmented by the many models of successful women officeholders and the actual availability of resources from feminist organizations.

CONCLUSIONS

Beginning in 1970, a dramatic change occurred in the representativeness of the American electoral system: for the first time, women were being elected to state and local offices in significant numbers. Increasingly, they have considered women their constituency and women's issues their issues. This change is one of many "successes" achieved by the American women's movement in the last 20 years. Yet current social movement theory is ill equipped to explain either why more women began to run or why voters elected them to office. This is true for a simple reason. The rise of women in public office reflects a massive change in consciousness regarding the norms of acceptable behavior for women, as well as a redefinition of the appropriate characteristics of officeholders by voters. Thousands of women decided to stop "lickin' and stickin' " for the election of men and to become candidates in their own right. Thousands of other women helped them campaign, and millions of voters supported them. It is a success based on the resource of least interest to resource mobilization theory—membership consciousness.

Despite indicating the importance of consciousness in activating electoral mobilization and voter acceptance, I have not specified a mechanism by which the changes occurred. Was it the series of protest demonstrations that spread across the country in 1970–71; was it the heightened importance paid to women in general by the media; was it a sense of group efficacy that followed congressional passage of ERA and the legislative victories of the Ninety-second Congress; was it the dramatic role of feminists from the National Women's Political Caucus at the 1972 presidential conventions? All of these are plausible explanations, given our current lack of theory and research on the relationship between social movement events, the way they are covered by the media, and their consequences for consciousness among relevant subgroups like women on the threshold of public office. It seems very unlikely, however, that this level of change in self-perceptions and voter acceptance could have come about without large-scale mobilization and collective actions. That is, the new forms of mobilization made possible by the technologies of direct mail and computerized mailing lists may be the most efficient means of exploiting McCarthy's "unstructured sentiment pools," but it has yet to be demonstrated that such clusters of public opinion can be created by the new technologies. Despite the professionalization of social movements, it appears that actual "movement," collective action, and media events are still necessary.

I have operationalized the notion of consciousness here only in the most rudimentary way (see also Klein 1984). There is, however, one advantage in this strategy. Looking at only these three levels of changing self-perceptions has made it possible to utilize an unusually rich but varied body of data from political scientists on the development of consciousness among a significant group of key actors during a critical period of change. Although the studies I have described are not strictly comparable, they do offer a glimpse of changing consciousness which is not available in such detail for any other group of women entering nontraditional roles during the 1970s.

Ultimately, however, we appear to evaluate any social movement success in terms of how much it contributes to further mobilization, further successes. Thus, we will want to know what policy changes follow from having more women in public office. I have not attempted to answer this question systematically because at present I know of no research that evaluates the difference it has made to increase the proportion of women in state and local office by 10 percent. There are casual claims by the NWPC that every major piece of legislation for women passed by Congress was introduced by a women. If this is largely true, it strongly suggests the importance of women officials as necessary if not sufficient resources for further social movement successes. Lack of surveillance makes a comparable judgment difficult at state and local levels. We do know that greater numbers have created a critical mass of women officials who are increasingly organized in caucuses and informal networks to increase women's influence and legislative successes at all levels. The degree to which this particular social movement success will nourish further mobilization and successful outcomes remains to be seen.

NOTES

1. Piven and Cloward (1982) have acknowledged that by the late 1970s reversibility of relief rights in the U.S. may have become less susceptible to elite manipulation. As the second Reagan administration progressed, the limits of welfare state retrenchment were not yet clear.

2. The distinction between substantive reforms and outcomes that create resources for future mobilization may prove more fruitful than Gamson's (1975) distinction between an outcome that provides new advantages and one in which the challenging group is either "accepted" or "rejected."

3. Jenkins (1979) argues—mistakenly, I believe—that electoral instability had "neutralized" the state. It seems more likely that the support of three presidents for civil rights legislation and enforcement was a positive factor, not a neutral one, in civil rights victories.

4. In the process of establishing a new paradigm, the shift in emphasis away from questions of belief, ideology, or consciousness is not difficult to understand. As the resource mobilization paradigm developed, it was Smelser's *Theory of Collective Behavior* (1963) which was the most visible and vulnerable treatment of the collective behavior approach to social movements. Smelser's treatment of magical and irrational generalized beliefs as the chief means of identifying collective behavior as well as differentiating its major types was highly questionable. In contrast, resource mobilization emphasizes diversity rather than homogeneity in motives and the continuities between collective actions and routine, everyday behavior (Currie and Skolnick 1970; Oberschall 1973, 22).

5. The work of Jo Freeman is the one possible exception. Her major contribution, *The*

Politics of Women's Liberation (1975) contains no references to consciousness, ideology, or beliefs. Yet her later papers (1979, 1982) devote extensive coverage to the ideology of this women's movement and the cultural assumptions associated with gender discrimination.

6. The achievements of the new paradigm are considerable, although they are, with few exceptions, confined to the study of mobilization. Collective actions such as strikes, protests, and demonstrations have been severed from their Durkheimian connection with forms of deviance such as crime. Further, the conditions for collective action have been identified with successful political mobilization rather than the destabilization of social relations that Smelser (1963) and others associated with urbanization and economic development. Thus, political as well as religious movements are found to expand and draw in new members through preexisting social networks, not through the mobilization of alienated and atomized individuals as claimed by mass society theorists. Large-scale structural changes are found, instead, to affect the forms of collective action which, in their targets and organizational structure, have paralleled the expansion of national markets and the consolidation of the nation-state.

REFERENCES

Arrington, Theodore, and Patricia Kyle. 1978. "Equal Rights Amendment Activists in North Carolina." *Signs* 3:666–80.

Baxter, Sandra, and Marjorie Lansing. 1980. *Women and Politics*. Ann Arbor: University of Michigan Press.

Bendix, Reinhard. 1964. *Nation-Building and Citizenship*. New York: Wiley.

Boles, Janet K. 1979. *The Politics of the Equal Rights Amendment*. New York: Longman.

———. 1982. "Building Support for the ERA." *PS* 15:572–77.

Boneparth, Ellen. 1982. "A Framework for Policy Analysis." In Ellen Boneparth, ed., *Women, Power and Policy*, 1–14. New York: Pergamon.

Cancian, Francesca M. 1979. "Meaning and Social Change: Women Students in Business Schools." Social Sciences Research Reports, #22. School of Social Sciences, University of California, Irvine.

Cancian, Francesca M., and Bonnie L. Ross. 1981. "Mass Media and the Women's Movement: 1900–1977." *Journal of Applied Behavioral Science* 17, no. 1:9–26.

Carden, Maren Lockwood. 1974. *The New Feminist Movement*. New York: Russell Sage Foundation.

Carroll, Susan. 1980. "Women as Candidates." Ph.D. diss., Indiana University.

Cassell, Joan. 1977. *A Group Called Women: Sisterhood and Symbolism in the Feminist Movement*. New York: David McKay.

Center for the American Woman and Politics. 1986. Private communication from Deborah Walsh.

Costain, Anne. 1980. "The Struggle for a National Women's Lobby." *Western Political Quarterly* 33:476–91.

———. 1982. "Representing Women: The Transition from Social Movement to Interest Group." In Ellen Boneparth, ed., *Women, Power and Policy*, 19–37. Elmsford, N.Y.: Pergamon Press.

Currie, Elliott, and Jerome Skolnick. 1970. "A Critical Note on Conceptions of Collective Behavior." *Annals of the American Academy of Political and Social Science* 391:34–45.

Darcy, Robert, and Sarah Slavin Schramm. 1977. "When Women Run against Men." *Public Opinion Quarterly* 41 (Spring): 1–12.

Deckard, Barbara Sinclair. 1975. *The Women's Movement.* New York: Harper and Row.

Eckstein, Harry. 1965. "On the Etiology of Internal Wars." *History and Theory* 4: 133–63.

Evans, Sara. 1979. *Personal Politics.* New York: Random House.

Feit, Rona F. 1979. "Organizing for Political Power: The National Women's Political Caucus." In Bernice Cummings and Victoria Schuck, eds., *Women Organizing,* 184–209. Metuchen, N.J.: Scarecrow Press.

Ferree, Myra Marx. 1974. "A Woman for President? Changing Responses: 1958–1972." *Public Opinion Quarterly* 38 (Fall): 390–99.

Francovic, Kathleen. 1977. "Sex and Voting in the U.S. House of Representatives: 1961–1975." *American Politics Quarterly* 5 (July): 315–30.

Freeman, Jo. 1973. "The Origins of the Women's Liberation Movement." *American Journal of Sociology* 78:792–811.

———. 1975. *The Politics of Women's Liberation.* New York: McKay.

———. 1979. "The Women's Liberation Movement: Its Origins, Organizations, Activities, and Ideas." In Jo Freeman, ed., *Women: A Feminist Perspective,* 2d ed., 557–74. Palo Alto, Calif.: Mayfield.

———. 1982. "Women and Public Policy: An Overview." In Ellen Boneparth, ed., *Women, Power and Policy,* 47–67. New York: Pergamon.

Fulenwider, Claire Knoche. 1980. *Feminism in American Politics.* New York: Praeger.

Gamson, William A. 1975. *The Strategy of Social Protest.* Homewood, Ill.: Dorsey Press.

Gaventa, John. 1980. *Power and Powerlessness.* Chicago: University of Illinois Press.

Gehlen, Frieda. 1969. "Women in Congress." *Transaction* 6 (October): 36–40.

Gelb, Joyce, and Marian Palley. 1982 (rev. ed., 1986). *Women and Public Policies.* Princeton, N.J.: Princeton University Press.

Gitlin, Todd. 1980. *The Whole World Is Watching.* Berkeley: University of California Press.

Gurr, Ted. 1969. "A Comparative Study of Civil Strife." In Hugh Graham and Ted Gurr, eds., *Violence in America,* 572–32. New York: Bantam Books.

Gurr, Ted Robert. 1970. *Why Men Rebel.* Princeton: Princeton University Press.

———. 1980. "On the Outcomes of Violent Conflict." In Ted Robert Gurr, ed., *Handbook of Political Conflict: Theory and Research,* 238–94. New York: The Free Press.

Hole, Judith, and Ellen Levine. 1971. *Rebirth of Feminism.* New York: The New York Times; Quadrangle Books.

Jenkins, Craig. 1979. "What Is to Be Done: Movement or Organization?" *Contemporary Sociology* 8:222–28.

———. 1983. "Resource Mobilization Theory and the Study of Social Movements." *Annual Review of Sociology* 9:527–53.

Jenkins, Craig, and Charles Perrow. 1977. "Insurgency of the Powerless: Farm Workers Movement (1946–1972)." *American Sociological Review* 42:249–68.

Johnson, Marilyn, and Susan Carroll. 1978. *Profile of Women Holding Office.* Vol. 2. New Brunswick, N.J.: Center for the American Woman and Politics, Rutgers University.

Karnig, Albert, and B. Oliver Walters. 1976. "Elections of Women to City Councils." *Social Science Quarterly* 56 (March): 605–13.

Kincaid, Diane. 1978. "Over His Dead Body: A Positive Perspective on Widows in the U.S. Congress." *Western Political Quarterly* 31 (March): 96–104.

Kirkpatrick, Jeane. 1974. *Political Woman*. New York: Basic Books.

Kleeman, Kathy. 1983. *Women's PACs*. New Brunswick, N.J.: Center for the American Woman and Politics, Rutgers University.

Klein, Ethel. 1979. "A Social Learning Perspective on Political Mobilization." Ph.D. diss., University of Michigan.

———. 1984. *Gender Politics: From Consciousness to Mass Politics*. Cambridge: Harvard University Press.

Lex, Louise. 1976. Data tape from doctoral diss., "Women in State Legislatures." Dept. of Political Science, University of Iowa. Housed at Murray Research Center, Radcliffe College, Cambridge, Mass.

Lipsky, Michael. 1968. "Protest as a Political Resource." *American Political Science Review* 73: 1144–58.

———. 1979. Review of Piven and Cloward, *Poor People's Movements*. *American Political Science Review* 23: 597–98.

Lockwood Carden, Maren. 1974. *The New Feminist Movement*. New York: Russell Sage Foundation.

Lukes, Steven. 1974. *Power: A Radical View*. New York: Macmillan.

McCarthy, John. 1982. "Social Infrastructure Deficits and New Technologies: Mobilizing Unstructured Sentiment Pools." Paper presented at the annual meeting of the American Sociological Association, San Francisco.

McCarthy, John, and Mayer Zald. 1973. *The Trend of Social Movements in America: Professionalization and Resource Mobilization*. Morristown, N.J.: General Learning Corporation.

———. 1977. "Resource Mobilization and Social Movements: A Partial Theory." *American Journal of Sociology* 82 (May): 1212–39.

Mandel, Ruth B. 1981. *In the Running: The New Woman Candidate*. New York: Ticknor & Fields.

Mann, Michael. 1973. *Consciousness and Action among the Western Working Class*. London: Macmillan.

Marshall, T. H. 1964. *Class, Citizenship and Social Development*. Garden City, N.Y.: Doubleday.

Marx, Gary, and James L. Woods. 1975. "Strands of Theory and Research in Collective Behavior." In Alex Inkeles, et al., *Annual Review of Sociology*. Palo Alto: Annual Reviews, Inc. 1: 363–428.

Melucci, Alberto, 1980. "The New Social Movements: A Theoretical Approach." *Social Science Information* 2: 199–226.

Mitchell, Robert, with John McCarthy and Kathy Pearce. 1979. "The National Abortion Rights Action League: Report on a Membership Survey." Unpublished NARAL report, Washington, D.C.

Moore, Barrington. 1966. *Social Origin of Dictatorship and Democracy*. Boston: Beacon Press.

Mueller, Carol. 1982. "Feminism and the New Women in Public Office." *Women and Politics* 2 (Fall): 7–21.

———. 1983a. "In Search of a Constituency for the New Religious Right." *Public Opinion Quarterly* 47 (Summer): 213–29.

———. 1983b. "The New Critical Mass: Women Organizing in State Legislatures." Unpublished report to the Center for the American Woman in Politics, Rutgers University.

Mueller, Carol, and Thomas Dimieri. 1982. "The Structure of Belief Systems among Contending ERA Activists." *Social Forces* 60:657–75.

Mueller, Carol, and Charles Judd. 1982. "Belief Constraint and Belief Consensus: Toward an Analysis of Social Movement Ideologies." *Social Forces* 60:182–87.

Murphy, Irene. 1973. *Public Policy on the Status of Women.* Lexington, Mass.: Heath.

Oberschall, Anthony. 1973. *Social Conflict and Social Movements.* Englewood Cliffs, N.J.: Prentice-Hall.

Olson, Mancur. 1968. *The Logic of Collective Action.* New York: Schocken Books.

Palley, Marian L. 1982. "Beyond the Deadline." *PS* 15 (Fall): 588–91.

Piven, Frances Fox, and Richard Cloward. 1971. *Regulating the Poor: The Functions of Public Welfare.* New York: Pantheon Books.

———. 1977. *Poor People's Movements: Why They Succeed, How They Fail.* New York: Pantheon.

———. 1982. *The New Class War.* New York: Pantheon.

Pizzorno, Allessandro. 1978. "Political Science and Collective Identity in Industrial Conflict." In Colin Crouch and Allessandro Pizzorno, eds., *The Resurgence of Class Conflict in Western Europe since 1968,* 2:277–98. New York: Holmes & Meier.

Rossi, Alice. 1982. *Feminist in Politics.* New York: Academic Press.

Rudé, Georges. 1952. *Paris and London in the Eighteenth Century.* New York: Viking Press.

———. 1980. *Ideology and Popular Protest.* New York: Pantheon.

Schreiber, E. M. 1978. "Education and Changes in American Opinions on a Woman for President." *Public Opinion Quarterly* 42 (Summer): 171–82.

Shorter, Edward, and Charles Tilly. 1974. *Strikes in France, 1830–1968.* New York: Cambridge University Press.

Smelser, Neil. 1963. *The Theory of Collective Behavior.* New York: Free Press.

Tarrow, Sidney. 1983. *Struggling to Reform: Social Movements and Policy Change during Cycles of Protest.* Center for International Studies, Western Societies Occasional Paper no. 15. Ithaca, N.Y.: Cornell University.

Tedin, Kent, David Brady, Mary Buxton, Barbara Gorman, and Judy Thompson. 1977. "Social Background and Political Differences between Pro and Anti-ERA Activists." *American Politics Quarterly* 5: 395–408.

Tilly, Charles. 1969. "Collective Violence in European Perspective." In Hugh Graham and Ted Gurr, eds., *Violence in America,* 4–45. New York: Bantam.

Tilly, Charles, Louise Tilly, and Richard Tilly. 1975. *The Rebellious Century.* Cambridge, Mass.: Harvard University Press.

Tolchin, Susan, and Martin Tolchin. 1973. *Clout: Womanpower and Politics.* New York: Coward, McCann & Geoghegan.

Welch, Susan, Janet Clark, and Robert Darcy. 1982. "The Effect of Candidate Gender on Electoral Outcomes: A Six-State Analysis." Paper presented at the annual meeting of the American Political Science Association, Denver, Colorado.

Yates, Gayle Graham. 1975. *What Women Want: The Ideas of the Movement.* Cambridge: Harvard University Press.

Zipp, John F., and Eric Plutzer. 1985. "Gender Differences in Voting for Female Candidates: Evidence from the 1982 Election." *Public Opinion Quarterly* 49:179–97.

Part Two   # POLITICAL PARTIES AND THE STRUCTURE OF OPPORTUNITY

5 Women's Struggle in a Workers' City: Feminist Movements in Turin

JUDITH ADLER HELLMAN

Italian feminism emerged in the early 1970s, like feminism elsewhere in Europe and North America, as both an outgrowth of and a response to the ideology and activities of the New Left. Virtually every form that the women's movement has taken in advanced industrial society has developed—with greater or lesser impact and staying power—among Italian women. In Italy, the 1970s witnessed the emergence of small consciousness-raising groups, specialized collectives focused on single issues (women and the law, women and medicine, and the like), women's bookstores, women's publishing cooperatives, lesbian rights groups, and so forth. Except for the degree of emphasis given to the impact of the Catholic Church on the lives of women, Italian feminism closely resembled other radical women's movements in the West in its critique of the patriarchial nature of capitalism and of the sexual division of labor. The early forms of feminist activity were self-consciously patterned on experiments in the United States and to a lesser extent on those in France, England, and Germany. Only the experience of women in the Italian trade unions provides an exception to this generally derivative pattern.

THE UTILITY OF AMERICAN/ITALIAN COMPARISONS
The presence of mass parties of the Left is perhaps the most important feature of the overall political environment that distinguishes the Italian "mobilizational field" from that encountered by social protest groups in the United States (Garner and Zald 1981, 3–4; Tarrow 1983, 13). The involvement of political parties in defining the terms of social protest, if not in the actual organization of protest movements, is a characteristic of the Italian context that has no counterpart in the activity of American political parties (Oberschall 1978). Likewise, the political presence of the Italian labor confederations and—after the labor struggles of 1968—their increasing involvement in social issues beyond the factory gates have almost no parallels in contemporary American politics.[1] In general, the

111

literature on protest movements in North America rests on the assumption that radical groups on the Left operate in a broader context that is hostile to their fundamental goals. Therefore, these frameworks are inadequate to conceptualize an Italian situation in which a large number and assortment of left-wing groups, forces, and formations often compete vigorously for the chance to articulate leftist demands or represent radical positions.

The new social movements that emerged in Italy in the late 1960s and the 1970s often developed in political environments in which either the Left held power or left-wing and union activism was deeply rooted and widely viewed as legitimate. In many cases, the emergence and growth of new social movements were influenced by enduring traditions of dissent within a subculture dominated by the Italian Communist party (Barbagli and Corbetta 1978; S. Hellman 1980).

However, the presence of such a traditional leftist subculture does not necessarily enhance the chances of new social movements for success in the political arena (P. D. Schumaker, cited in Tarrow 1983, 28). On the face of it, it would seem a great advantage for a protest movement to develop in a context in which the parties of the Left are strong and the unions and their traditions of struggle are deeply embedded in the political subculture. In the case of Italian feminism, however, the strength of a leftist subculture represented at times a help but at other times an impediment to the mobilization of women.

TURINESE WOMEN'S MOVEMENTS

My working hypothesis is that feminist organizations are shaped in their ideology and practical activity by long-standing traditions and by the specific political environment of the Left peculiar to the city in which they emerge. In the five Italian cities I have examined, specific characteristics of the local political context influence and delimit the possibilities for the successful mobilization of women.[2] Local and regional variations in political subculture and, above all, the relative strength and cohesion of the parties of the Left and of the trade unions to a great extent define the range in which new social movements may operate.

An exceptionally clear example of this limitation of the boundaries of political and social action (the *spazio politico*, "political space," in the activists' own terms) is provided by the experience of women's organizations in Turin. The Turinese case permits us to examine (1) a women's movement springing directly from the communist tradition of mass organizations, (2) an assortment of small collectives representing the full development of the New Left/neofeminist forms of organization, and (3) a factory-based women's organization that became the voice of radical feminism within the trade union movement. With this case study we can identify the degree to which these three types of organizations—each the local expression of broader national movements—were influenced by their development in a city characterized by "workerist" politics: that is, by a tradition of left-wing politics that places the working class and its goals at the forefront of all popular struggle. As we shall see, in the most working-class of Italian cities, a new social movement, feminism, was conditioned by the workerism (in Italian, the *operaismo*) that shapes all activities on the Turinese Left. In Turin, women's organizations were not looking to the workers' movement as an alliance partner. Rather, they were struggling to find a way of defining or redefining the issues raised by feminists elsewhere in Italy (and in Western Europe and North America) in terms that fit *within* the restrictive framework of the workerist politics of Turin.

OPERAISMO

The development of the Turinese workers' militant political tradition is one of the most exciting and inspiring chapters in modern Italian history.[3] Turin witnessed the emergence of a highly conscious, compact, and cohesive working class; the first urban general strike in Italy; the development of the Factory Council movement under the leadership of Antonio Gramsci and his comrades; the occupation of the factories during the "red biennium," the period of labor struggles beginning in 1919; worker militance under fascism; and proletarian participation in the Resistance (Bates 1974; Cammett 1967; Gramsci 1955). The postwar history of Turinese struggle centers on the expansion of the gigantic Fiat autoworks during the economic boom years and its recruitment of a labor force comprising impoverished and politically quiescent southern Italians. It was marked by the *anni duri* (the "hard years") at Fiat. Coinciding with the Cold War, this was a period of extreme class polarization during which the industrial bourgeoisie pursued a strategy of union busting and overt repression and intimidation of Communists and Socialists (Gianotti 1979; Golden 1983; Lanzardo 1971; Pugno and Garavini 1974).

The *anni duri,* it can be argued, created in Turinese workers a defensive posture that tended to place the factory at the center of all political struggle. This episode fostered a mentality that led workers to view all of society as organized against them and all struggle as consisting essentially of holding their ground in the factories, defending their jobs and place in production. The experience of the *anni duri* reinforced a tradition of *operaismo* that was not brought into question until the "Hot Autumn," the period of intense labor strife that swept Italy in 1969.

The Hot Autumn struggles of 1969 held particular significance for Turin, not merely because of the leading role of the Turinese workers in these events—the entire history of the Turinese working class would lead us to expect that—but because the Hot Autumn defined for the first time a wider arena for class struggle in Turin. The protests centered not so much on factory conditions as on the inadequate social conditions in which workers lived their lives outside the factory. Broad, radicalizing demands for housing, transport, educational reform—for institutional changes at every level of society—gave content to the claim that the working class would serve as a mobilizing force not only in the workplace but also in the streets. Thus, the Hot Autumn took shape, led by workers in alliance with some of the "new political actors" of the period: the student and youth movements. And all of this activity unfolded "in society" rather than behind the factory gates.

This, then, is the environment in which the Turinese women's movements developed. The New Left was in ascendancy, even in Turin, but functioned in this workers' city in the context of a political tradition that required workers to stand in the vanguard of all popular movements. To be sure, the centrality of the factory as an arena for class confrontation was challenged by the events of the Hot Autumn. But even as the focus of struggle shifted outward from the shop floor to the universities and schools, the public institutions, and the street, the industrial working class as a class still determined the lines of struggle. Thus, the same themes of protest were sounded in Turin as were heard in settings like Milan, a middle-class city with a political tradition of petty bourgeois leadership in radical politics. But in Turin, the critique of civil society was articulated, above all, by the leaders of the working class and was framed in the language of the labor movement.

UNIONE DONNE ITALIANE (UDI)

The constraints imposed by *operaismo* on the development of Turinese women's organizations are clearly illustrated by the history of the Italian Women's Union, UDI (L'Unione Donne Italiane). UDI was the first women's movement of the Left to appear in Turin. It developed here, as elsewhere, out of the nucleus of the *Gruppi di Difesa,* the Resistance units staffed by women. Turin was hit particularly hard by the postwar economic dislocations that afflicted all of Italy, and the city became the scene of a series of popular "bread riots" that were marked by the massive participation of women. As had occurred so often in Turinese history, the parties of the Left were unable to give orientation or a sense of discipline to these spontaneous demonstrators. Thus, one of the major impulses stimulating Palmiro Togliatti, head of the PCI (the Italian Communist Party), to push for a national women's association like UDI was the uncontrolled, unmediated mass participation of women in the Turin riots (Camparini 1981, 555–57).

A mass organization with 15,000 members after the war, UDI soon declined numerically in Turin, as elsewhere in northern Italy, under the impact of the sectarian politics of the Cold War. Given its origins in the Resistance, in the immediate postwar period UDI's ranks had been swelled by a substantial membership of Catholic and other non-Communist women. However, with the coming of the Popular Front period, the Christian Democrats pulled most Catholic women out of the organization, and by the 1950s even the Socialist women had withdrawn, with a few remaining *a titolo personale*: that is, as a matter of individual choice. Thus, through the 1950s, the Turinese UDI followed the same pattern as the national organization. Communist women gained uncontested hegemony over a steadily shrinking base, and the organization pursued activities in line with the policies of the PCI, which it served—not all that effectively, to judge from the small turnout at demonstrations and mass mobilizations of various kinds—as the classic flanking organization.[4]

In those years, UDI was shaped not only by its designated task of drawing women into political activities in line with PCI policy but by the very limits on the concept of "women's politics" that prevailed in that period, a concept that essentially extended women's nurturing role in the family out into the public sphere (J. Hellman 1984). After the phase of postwar reconstruction and the inevitable international solidarity efforts, UDI settled into a pattern of initiatives labeled by its leaders themselves as "*assistenziali*": that is, in aid and support of others. Thus, UDI in Turin, as elsewhere in Italy, assisted the families of war veterans and striking workers; agitated for day care, schools, communal laundries, and other social services directly connected to women's traditional tasks; and mobilized, as did Communists everywhere, for peace and against the Marshall Plan, NATO, and the Bomb.

But given their location in Turin, in addition to carrying out the standard UDI "initiatives" the Turinese UDI women were concerned with establishing an organizational presence and visibility in the factories and in the workers' struggles. Their efforts met with little encouragement, however, even when they were not directly rebuffed by the unions, including the Communist's own labor confederation, the CGIL. The unionists' indifference or hostility toward UDI's overtures stemmed from the fact that they were jealous of their primacy among the workers and under brutal assault from management during the *anni duri* at Fiat. The union view of "women's specific demands" was that such demands undercut the unity of the working class and undermined the strength of the workers' movement. Thus the trade unionists' position was at odds with the thrust of UDI's organizational efforts in Turin. For the 1950s and early 1960s were the years in which UDI, as a national organization, was struggling to stake out an "authentically female" area of political activity. And given the Communist view that women's emancipation would come through their insertion into the workplace and their consequent economic independence, it was logical that UDI should focus on "women and work" as the main terrain for mobilization and political initiatives.

This, then, was the period of UDI's major campaigns for legislation on equal wages for women, equal employment opportunities, equal access to civil service and teaching jobs, protection for working mothers, prohibition of the layoff of women when they marry, and the regulation of piecework manufacturing in the home. Yet ironically, in the great industrial city of Turin the political reversals suffered by the unions left UDI little room for political work among factory women. Furthermore, even though the system of domestic piecework was in expansion throughout the region and the national organization was pushing hard for mobilization around this issue, UDI's appeal to struggle actively for regulation of *lavoro al domicilio* was generally ignored at the base everywhere in Italy and particularly in Turin (Camparini 1981, 5589–90). Thus, in the 1950s we find that in this "workers' city" the only national UDI goal for which an effective local mobilization was mounted was the demand for pensions for housewives.

In Turin, UDI registered—although in modified form—the two major transformations that were to reshape the national organization. The first was the prolonged struggle for greater autonomy from the PCI: a break with the "transmission belt" model of activity which, throughout the 1960s, was also under attack in the Communist Youth and other flanking organizations. The desire for such independence had been expressed from the 1950s onward, but it was most explicitly articulated at the National Congresses in 1966 and 1969. At these meetings the national leadership openly asserted UDI's claim for complete autonomy from the PCI, initiated the search for "a new orientation and new political activities," and began a process of self-criticism that would not be completed for more than a decade (Alloisio 1974, 34–37; Ascoli 1979, 138–41; Manoukian 1969, 36–40).

The second period of transformation occurred in the 1970s as the UDI's national leadership embraced feminism. UDI's leadership, almost entirely Communist, received the feminist message slowly but with far greater openness and enthusiasm than inside the PCI, where female Communists were locked into an organizational power structure dominated by men and by male values (J. Hellman 1984). Since the UDI leadership did not depend on a hierarchy of male comrades, it proved more receptive to the feminist critique of traditional Left organizations and to the formation of alliances with some of the less antiorganizational feminist groups. That such cooperation ultimately served the PCI alliance strategy does not take away from the autonomy displayed by the national UDI leadership in December 1976, when for the first time UDI took to the streets of Rome, together with the Movimento per la Liberazione delle Donne (MLD) and other feminist groups, in a massive march in favor of liberalized abortion.

UDI was also more inclined to genuinely rethink and incorporate fundamental aspects of the feminist critique into its own analysis of society. This openness to feminist thinking is clearly reflected in the pages of the organization's magazine, *Noi Donne*—which increasingly published articles that tackled questions of sexuality, physical and emotional self-knowledge, male/female relations in the family and society, and a host of other issues central to the discussions of feminism—and in the themes taken up by the National Congress of 1978 (UDI 1978).

The problem for the Turinese UDI was that these transformations at the national level were modified by local traditions and conditions, above all by the *operaismo* of Turin, in such a way as to cause the Turinese organization to fall between two stools. On the one hand, it was too "feminist" to be taken seriously by the local PCI organization. Generally treated by the Communist comrades in an offhand manner, it was usually ignored but occasionally called out on parade when the Turinese PCI federation organized a demonstration or rally and wished to show massive "popular adhesion" or the presence of women "as women" rather than as PCI militants. On the other hand, it was seen as too sectarian and Communist dominated, too unreconstructed, too marked by the old masculine forms of doing politics to attract or hold large numbers of new feminists.

As a consequence, the upsurge in women's political activism throughout the 1970s did not bring about a corresponding increase in UDI membership or strength in Turin; the membership remained almost constant through the 1970s with roughly 200 members in the city and another 200 in the province. And more important than the stasis indicated by membership figures was the organization's failure to attract and hold the fluid groups of young feminists who did so much to rejuvenate UDI in the other cities in Italy. Elsewhere, new feminist participants, while eschewing formal affiliation with UDI, introduced feminist analyses and egalitarian political forms into the organization and stimulated fresh and lively political initiatives. In this way the young feminists—formal members or not— helped to make UDI, as a national organization with a national network, a key force in the most important women's battles of the 1970s: the struggles around divorce, abortion reform, women's clinics, and rape legislation.

But the pattern for Turin differed in a number of ways. Under pressure from local feminism, some of the old traditional political forms that had shaped the Turinese branch of UDI were eclipsed. For example, characteristic of the "old-style politics" was the General Meeting, opening with a long address by a leader to set the theme and tone of the proceedings, followed by a series of often eloquent but unconnected interventions from the floor, and closing with "concluding remarks" by the same or another organizational functionary. After the Hot Autumn, this format—so much a formula for the traditional parties of the Left, with its emphasis on the orientation of the masses by the leadership and the careful, disciplined mode of discussion—gave way to somewhat looser, informal, spontaneous, and democratic forms. Even in the Turinese UDI there was talk of the need to break down large meetings into small discussion groups in which each woman would feel encouraged to express herself. In fact, some of the style of consciousness-raising groups—of personal testimony and self-revelation— crept into UDI meetings in Turin, and some of the forms developed by feminists (such as the circle discussion) were attempted, even though a number of the older comrades were made intensely uncomfortable by the personal revelations flying back and forth.

But in the end, a core group of a dozen or so highly sectarian Communist women prevailed over the women who were most open to the new feminism. This faction worked to cut off spontaneous discussion and to restore leader-dominated traditional political forms by evoking, whenever possible, memories of the Resistance and the *anni duri* at Fiat. In reality, only one or two of the hardliners were actually old enough to have experienced these events at first hand, and only two had actually worked at the Fiat plant. Nonetheless, the sectarian core was largely successful in preserving the "purity" of the Turinese UDI by driving away independent feminists who were in search of an organizational structure in which their feminism could take an active, concrete political form.

A pattern soon developed in which younger women, especially students, would sit in on one or two meetings, participating somewhat tentatively but soon concluding—in some cases, with considerable regret—that this was not a forum in which their voices would be heard or their ideas be welcome. The "old guard" sectarian women effected this rejection whenever discussion threatened to "get out of hand": that is, when the PCI itself came under attack as a sexist institution, when some directive suggested to UDI by the PCI came under criticism, or when UDI's autonomy from the Communist Party was questioned. In moments like these, the hardliners would take up the theme of the "heroic years of the Resistance" or the persecutions suffered by comrades at Fiat, speaking, often very movingly, of the "traditions of Turin, the workers' city." In this way, further feminist discussion was effectively cut off.

Thus, in the most active, expansive, and creative years of Italian feminism, despite the best efforts of a few leaders in the local and national organization to open up, revitalize, and attract new members to the Turinese provincial organization, UDI in Turin remained small in membership, closed in on itself, and generally cut off from exciting initiatives promoted by other women's groups in the city. And yet UDI was not entirely marginal to developments in the women's movement in Turin. It formed part of a significant and respected national organization with its own history and place in Italian politics. In Turin it enjoyed legitimacy and prestige because of its connection with the Resistance. It had a fixed address, an ongoing organizational presence, its own headquarters, and public recognition. In a city governed by Communists, UDI could posit itself as a point of contact between the "masses of women" and the local administration. Therefore, it retained a weight in the political scene disproportionate to its size or the number of political initiatives it actually carried out.

Ironically, in light of its small membership, the great face-saving justification shared by Turinese UDI militants and essential to their organizational self-respect was their claim—quite sincerely believed—that while independent feminists represent and wish to represent no one more than themselves, "we, in contrast, speak for all the silent women out there, the housewives, working-class women, and factory workers who are locked into their own private domain or who have not yet found their political voice" (personal Interview with a UDI activist, May 1979). While this assertion by a group of 25 or so active UDI women may seem preposterous, the fact of a fixed, stable political presence based upon the financial support of a national organization that was self-supporting in other regions of Italy, if not in Turin, did give UDI some weight on the local scene. With the ebb and flow, the appearance and disappearance of other women's organizations, the continued presence of UDI as a point of reference took on potentially greater significance than membership figures alone would suggest. Thus, however small, UDI continued to be an element of the women's movement to be taken into account in any analysis of women's organizations in Turin.

THE FEMINIST MOVEMENT: THE COLLECTIVES

The second women's movement to appear in Turin comprised a series of small feminist collectives that developed in this city in response to the same forces that brought them to life and to political prominence in the other major political and cultural centers of Italy. As in Rome and Milan, Turinese feminism was stimulated above all by women's experience as participants in the generalized anti-authoritarian struggles of 1968–69, and by direct and indirect contact with North American feminism. Indeed, in Turin the very first feminist group, the Collettivo delle Compagne, was formed by women who had been involved, together with male comrades, in Communicazioni Rivoluzionarie (CR), a New Left organization founded late in 1970. CR collectives focused on exchanging information with political groups in the United States; groups in Rome, Milan, and Turin collected, translated, and summarized information on the Black Panthers, the Young Lords, and the extensive network of antiwar organizations. By spring of 1971, the Turinese women in CR had typed, run off, and addressed enough American "movement" material to know that they were no more willing than their American sisters to live out their political lives as typists, staplers, and envelope lickers. A steady flow of early feminist literature sent by a Turinese woman who had settled in Boston completed the work of politicization, and feminism had set down roots in Turin.

Assorted women's collectives succeeded this first group, and the pattern was set; the earliest feminists were veterans of the student movement of 1968 and the extraparliamentary Left, and their attraction to feminism was a response largely to their disillusionment with the place occupied by women in those movements (Gramaglia 1979; Menapace 1979; Spagnoletti 1978). In the early days of Turinese feminism, militant women generally defined themselves as Marxists, and their view of the interrelationship between Marxist and feminist commitments was most succinctly expressed in their slogan: "There is no revolution without the liberation of women; there is no liberation for women without revolution." Coming mostly from New Left groups of marked workerist tendencies, the first Turinese feminists generally "believed firmly in the leading role of the working class and the centrality of the struggle in the factory" ("Come siamo nate" 1978, 8) and thus found themselves in substantial harmony with the *operaista* tradition of Turin. Although they were mostly highly educated middle- and upper-class women, the neofeminists nonetheless groped for ways to justify their political positions and activities in terms of the relevance of their demands to their working-class sisters. Indeed, some went so far as to insist on the primacy of economic over sexual oppression (Ibid). Given this economic emphasis, the early feminist collectives were soon torn between those who maintained that only working-class women are oppressed and newcomers to the movement who held that all women, regardless of social class, suffer discrimination as a subordinate caste.

Soon even these differences, divisive as they had become, were eclipsed by fundamental conflicts over the "practice of feminism." In summary, a schism developed between women who wished to emphasize "external activities" (propaganda and letters to the media; encounter and confrontation with public institutions, political parties, unions, and so forth) and those who gave priority to "internal activity"—that is, to consciousness-raising (*autocoscienza*) within the group. The conflict over external versus internal activities—which in practice often came to a split between feminists who wished to pursue *both* and those who wanted to focus exclusively on consciousness-raising—was played out everywhere in Italy. In Turin, however, the lines were particularly sharply drawn because the *operaista* tradition, as we have noted, tended to delegitimize activities that did not focus on the working class and did not occur in the setting of the factory. And if ever there was a political practice that fell outside the boundaries of workerist politics, it was feminist consciousness-raising. As one feminist collective wrote, "We all feel the weight of Turinese workerism that threatens to suffocate the emergence of any diversity and of any activity that does not figure exclusively as a factory struggle or a struggle for employment." Meanwhile, another lamented "the time wasted by many comrades in the effort to convince men that feminism is a serious political practice." The essential problem was that workerism "imposed goals and externally determined priorities" rather than allowing women to recognize and respond to their own needs and set their own agenda for struggle (*Chi Brucia?* 1977, 1).

Still, there is no question that Turinese feminism—in counterdistinction to the psychologically oriented feminism of Milan—was marked by the workerist tradition characteristic of its immediate political environment. For example, the Collettivo di Liberazione della Donna (CLD), formed about 1972 by women with a New Left background, was typical of some of the well-intentioned if somewhat tortuous responses to the workerist pressures at play in the Turinese context. CLD women posited that their own middle-class origins and educational and social advantages permitted them to perceive and analyze the contradictions of capitalist society, "facilitating their awareness of themselves as women and as an oppressed group." In contrast, they noted, "there are other strata of women such as workers and housewives who have great difficulty in recognizing the problems they face as women because they must give priority to the resolution of their material and economic problems." Accordingly, the CLD women concluded that their task was

> to approach these [proletarian] women, sensitizing them to their specific problems as women, thereby promoting feminist consciousness, broadening the base of the movement, enriching our analysis with the inclusion of the point of view of women from social strata different from our own, and drawing them into the movement once they have reached feminist consciousness. (CLD Manifesto 1980)

Thus CLD posed itself as a "feminist vanguard" prepared to bring consciousness to the female masses.

The setting of such political priorities in Turin—as compared with other cities like Milan, where internally oriented groups preoccupied with highly personal forms of *autocoscienza* held sway—helps us to account for the strength and significance of the movement to establish women's clinics, or *consultori,* in Turin. Growing out of a feminist demand for free and accessible contraception, abortion, and general gynecological treatment, coupled with a push to break down the barriers between women and medical authority, the *consultori* began in Turin as spontaneous local initiatives carried out by feminists in working-class quarters of the city. Frequently, the first stage was the occupation by feminists of some vacant public building suitable for use as a makeshift clinic. Once the facility was spruced up, its organizers were able to reach out into the quarter, inviting the local women to a series of meetings, speeches, and discussion groups on female sexuality. The voluntary services of a qualified gynecologist were sought not only for the public information sessions but also for direct medical examinations. A key part of the feminists' strategy to raise the consciousness of working-class women was the "preexamination discussion," conducted by feminist militants on either an individual or a group basis. Attendance at these discussions became for working-class women the admission ticket to a free, and often desperately needed, physical examination.

The feminists involved in this kind of clinic were usually movers, or at least supporters, in the struggle to win legislation establishing *"consultori pubblici."* This legislation would oblige the regional governments throughout Italy to assume responsibility for setting up public clinics to provide, free of charge, the same services that were being supplied on a voluntary basis by the feminist activists and their medical comrades. In July 1975 such a law was approved, and after years of further agitation to pressure for its implementation, 11 publicly funded clinics gradually appeared in Turin. Of course, the establishment of publicly funded *consultori* represented a victory for the feminists, who had chosen a form of struggle that reached out to working-class women and at the same time confronted the institutions of the state. Yet the new legislation also brought defeat as the feminists' "people's clinics" were replaced by city-run official institutions. For even when the locale remained the same and the voluntary gynecologist stayed on as a remunerated public employee, the feminists found their role and influence eclipsed by the formal structure.

While the *consultori* in popular neighborhoods and the collectives that regarded themselves as a feminist vanguard for the working class were perhaps the most distinctively Turinese of the feminist groups that emerged, they were by no means the only kinds of feminist activities or experiences to develop in the 1970s. In sharp contrast with the would-be vanguardist stance of a group like the CLD was the approach of Alternativa Femminista (AF), the earliest of the new type of feminist collective to develop in the 1970s. The first Turinese group to take the word "feminist" in its name, AF focused initially on *autocoscienza,* but it differed from similar groups formed in the same period in Rome, Milan, and Florence in that it attempted to combine "externally oriented" activities with the raising of individual consciousness. In formulating this external program, however, Alternativa Femminista militants rejected the CLD model, arguing that any attempt to play a vanguard role among working-class women placed each feminist in the position of carrying forward a struggle *on behalf of* others—that is, an extension of women's nurturing role—rather than *for* herself. Thus Alternativa Femminista's external initiatives did not follow the CLD pattern of reaching out directly to proletarian women in an effort to lead them to a higher level of consciousness. Instead, they concentrated on formulating demands directed to state institutions (for example, the legalization of abortion, protection of prostitutes, and legislation benefiting "working parents" to replace that which protected "working mothers"), and they opened dialogues with the parties of the traditional and extraparliamentary Left (with letters to the Communist daily, *L'Unitá*, and the extraparliamentary newspaper *Il Manifesto,* public debates in PCI-sponsored encounters, and so forth).

By the mid 1970s the Alternativa Femminista pattern had become the more or less standard compromise adopted by a wide variety of collectives that combined some consciousness-raising with external activities. Women's caucuses also developed within several extraparliamentary groups. Collectives of law students, of medical students and doctors, and of women trained in the physical sciences sprang up. There was Donne Informazione, a group dedicated to facilitating communication among women's collectives through the publication of a newsletter. A cooperatively owned women's bookstore, consciously modeled after the famous Libreria delle Donne in Milan, opened in 1978. And in 1979 a *casa delle donne,* a women's center, opened; it was housed first in an abandoned insane asylum that had been occupied by feminists but moved to more suitable quarters provided by the city government in 1980.

Apart from these collectives that engaged chiefly in structured activities while devoting some energies to consciousness-raising, there were innumerable small groups dedicated exclusively to *autocoscienza.* Strongly influenced by developments in Milan, and to a lesser degree by contact with radical lesbianism in the United States and France, these feminists focused on the problems of sexuality and the rediscovery of the body. They emphasized working out "alternative lifestyles." Essentially, this meant "new ways of living among women," insulated from contact both with men and with "masculine institutions"—a designation that encompassed effectively all facets of the larger Italian society.

These small consciousness-raising groups had short lifespans. They tended to disintegrate in Turin, as elsewhere, as a casualty of their own internal dynamic. On the one hand, they were under increasing strain from the growing "overdetermination" of intense relationships among group members in what essentially amounted to a leaderless therapy group. On the other hand, they suffered, not from the classic "recruitment crisis" of attracting new members, but from the problem of integrating newcomers into a structure based on the shared past experience of longer-term members. Furthermore, with the mobilization of a broad leftist coalition around the crucial issues of enabling legislation for divorce and legalized abortion, feminist groups that conscientiously and systematically eschewed "external activity" were left in an awkward position. Those feminist collectives that were censorious of relations with men or with the institutions of the state—in short, with all relations other than with women—were rent by conflicts between members who felt referenda campaigns for such reforms required their public participation and other members who continued to reject all involvement outside the group.

These, then, were the problems that Turinese feminists shared with small consciousness-raising groups throughout Italy. In addition, of course, they faced the handicap peculiar to their immediate environment: *operaismo,* with its exclusive emphasis on workers, the workplace, and bread-and-butter issues. As the 1970s drew to a close and the feminist collective as a political form was in decline everywhere in northern and central Italy, Turinese feminists tended to view the difficulties they faced in sustaining their activity and group cohesion in terms of a struggle to swim against the tide of workerism. Increasingly, too, the workers' movement and the trade unions themselves were seen by feminists as exhibiting a particularly virulent strain of the sexism that infected all Italian social and political institutions. But while the small *autocoscienza* group crumbled under the weight of its own internal contradictions, the external pressure of the mobilization around divorce and abortion referenda, and the specific limitations of the Turinese political context, other militant feminists were responding very differently to the workerist pressures and were carrying the women's struggle into the heart of the trade unions themselves.

FEMINISM IN THE UNIONS

The feminist movement that developed within the trade unions represented a highly original contribution of Turinese women, not only to Italian feminism in general but to women's movements in advanced capitalist society. This women's organization has counterparts at the national level in Rome and elsewhere in Italy. But the Turinese women's coordinating committee (*coordinamento*) was the original local organization, and it was undoubtedly the workerist tradition of Turin that made the automobile capital the logical starting point for such a movement.

The key year in the development of union feminism in Turin was 1974, which marked the referendum on divorce, an issue directly affecting women *as women.* It was also an issue around which all the political actors in society—the state institutions, the parties, and the trade unions, as well as the Catholic Church and its flanking organizations—were obliged to take a stand and mobilize their respective forces. During the divorce referendum campaign, the union leadership was pressured to take a clear position and, for the first time, to open an area of debate for noneconomic, social issues. This opening of discussion within the unions corresponded to the demand of the New Left forces in the Hot Autumn of 1969 that the unions move the focus of their concerns out of the factory and into society. It also corresponded to the insistence of feminists within the union that the critique of the family be placed on the agenda (Cavagna et al. 1979, 5).

In the aftermath of the divorce referendum, in the winter and spring of 1975, two kinds of women's groups began to form more or less spontaneously within the trade union confederations. The first groups were composed of women who had already had some experience in small feminist collectives; the others comprised full-time union workers and elected representatives to the Factory Councils (roughly comparable to shop stewards). Women elected to represent different trades or "categories" within the broad labor confederations saw this as the appropriate moment to bridge occupational divisions, to meet together to share their experiences as women unionists, and to push their respective trade unions and confederations to positions of greater sensitivity to women's needs (Bocchio and Torchi 1979, 19, 25). The leadership in Turin was provided by women in the FLM, the metalworkers' union. Most were employed as secretaries and clerks at Fiat, jobs that gave them ample contact with industrial workers in the workplace.

The women who participated in these first initiatives generally accepted a radical critique of society and of the union movement as an expression of the sexist nature of advanced capitalist society. But what was significant about these groups, and what distinguished their initiatives from those of other radical feminists of that period in Italy and elsewhere in the West, was their choice "to remain as feminists within the union . . . adjusting to the timing, methods, rites, and priorities of union politics" (Bocchio and Torchi 1979, 48).

The goals of feminists within the union could be divided into two general categories. The first included those efforts aimed at transforming the union as an organization: democratizing its overall structure, increasing rank-and-file participation, making it more responsive to demands from the base (above all, the demands of its least articulate members: women), and inserting more women into the leadership apparatus at every level. Beyond the obvious need for more female stewards, more women in the union bureaucracy, and more power for those women already serving in key posts, this last objective implied dramatic changes in the conception of union militancy. For the greatest obstacle to female participation at all levels, from the Factory Council representatives through the whole union hierarchy, was the traditional model of militancy calling for a kind of full-time, day-and-night commitment that few if any married women or working mothers could give. Hence the call for greater democratization of the union through more genuine participation of women was a profoundly transformative goal insofar as it implied a radical change in the pattern of activism and leadership recruitment in the trade unions.

The feminist trade unionists further challenged their organizations' hierarchy with a demand for complete autonomy from union authority. They insisted on full access to the material support system of the union so that they might formulate positions, make public statements, and issue publications. What these demands amounted to in practice was the assertion by women of their rights to meet separately from male unionists, in meeting rooms provided by the union at union headquarters, and to be supplied with the paper and duplicating materials to run off and distribute pamphlets, notices, and posters in which the women's positions on a variety of issues could be put forward. As if the implications of these demands weren't challenging enough to male comrades, the women also demanded the right to march separately from the men at mass demonstrations under banners displaying slogans chosen by the women, with no veto given the union authorities. Furthermore, the feminist unionists insisted on their right to run formal meetings in plants having a largely female labor force, with no male union officers present to lay down the line. This practice gave the women's *coordinamento* real impact among female workers in the auto parts and electronics industries located in the industrial belt around the city of Turin. Extreme as some of these demands may seem, it is important to set them in context by noting that in the 1970s they represented only a few new "autonomous initiatives" among many that formed part of the broader antihierarchical, decentralizing leftist thrust within the Italian workers' movement.

The second set of goals were those that pressured the unions to insert into the list of priorities in contractual negotiations a series of demands designed to transform the condition of women's lives both in the factory and in the social world outside its gates. Some of these were demands dealing directly with women in the workplace and, as such, were more readily accepted by the union leadership. For example, feminists called upon union leaders to press for the implementation of the parity law providing equal pay for women and equal access to jobs, the reservation of a fixed percentage of new jobs for women, and guarantees of women's admission into courses designed to upgrade job skills. The feminists also pushed for the unification of the hiring lists at Fiat, which would mean that women laid off from factory jobs would be rehired strictly according to the date they were let go, without reference to the number of men unemployed at that moment or to the type of work carried out in the sector where a new job might become available. This demand was particularly controversial: it meant that the lighter work normally reserved in all-male departments of the factory for older or partially disabled male workers would now go to newly hired women. (Indeed, the problems raised by the "unified hiring lists" were only a few among the many contradictions of labor legislation that provided for equal opportunity at the same time that it preserved protective codes for women: limits on shift and night work, age of pensioned retirement, and so forth.) Finally, the union women pressured their organizations to become more involved in the protection of women employed on a piecework basis in their own homes or in small shops: that is, women who formed part of the nonunionized, submerged labor market.

In pressing these work-related demands, feminists could count on at least the verbal support of the more progressive male comrades, if not their wholehearted collaboration. But they met a much more serious level of "incomprehension" when they began to press for contractual provisions that were related to the workplace but had broader social implications for the traditional role of women in the family and in society. Included in this category were demands for (1) 40 hours of paid leave to care for sick children, for which either the mother or the father could apply; (2) day care centers supported by employer contributions but run by a committee of workers; (3) the extension of school hours to a full day, with after-school supervision for children of working parents; and (4) as a logical extension of these other demands, the call for more flexible working hours for all adults. In their struggle for changes that challenged the sexual division of labor, feminists received support from those male unionists who were active in efforts to turn the unions' concern outward into society (such as involving the union in the reform of education, social services, and other public institutions). The strength, however, of this tendency varied markedly from one union to the next, and nowhere were the "antieconomistic" forces strong enough to place these kinds of demands at the top of the list of priorities for contractual negotiations with management.

If these proposals with their transformative social implications met with some incomprehension on the part of male comrades, total bewilderment or outright hostility often greeted the feminists when they raised issues touching on women's sexuality. The giant labor confederations, wary of losing whatever unity they had been able to foster among Communists, Socialists, Christian Democrats, practicing Catholics, and secular elements, had been reluctant enough to allow debate on the divorce referendum. Now, in the late 1970s, feminists in their own ranks were trying to force the unions to sponsor factory assemblies on the topic of abortion law reform and to take a public position in favor of liberalized abortion legislation. Union feminists even reached the point of insisting that the unions demand that *consultori* be opened in all popular quarters of the city and that Pap tests be available in factory clinics.

Feminists emphasized the legitimacy of these concerns by pointing to the traditional preoccupation of the union with health and safety guarantees, particularly regarding hazards affecting women's reproductive capacity. Indeed, the expression "white abortion" was coined in union circles to denote a miscarriage induced by work on a vibrating platform or exposure to noxious fumes or other hazardous elements in the work environment. Thus, feminists attempted to override male opposition to these proposals by linking their call for union participation in the movement for *consultori* to the union's broader struggle for health care facilities and other social services for the families of workers.

But for all the originality and incisiveness of the issues raised by union feminists in this period, the most exciting opportunity for feminist mobilization arose not through a demand posed by feminists and accepted by the union but by the use to which women were able to turn one of the great concessions that the metalworkers' union, the FLM, had won for workers at Fiat in the period of labor militance following the Hot Autumn. Perhaps the most far-reaching effect in the lives of working women has been the change made possible by the "150 Hours" program.

In another essay I have examined the contractual agreement for 150 hours of paid educational leave won by the metalworkers at Fiat, and the transformation of this workers' victory into a major advance for the women's movement, first in Turin and eventually throughout Italy (J. Hellman 1982; also see Balbo 1981, and Caldwell 1983). The creation of women's studies courses under the rubric of the 150 Hours program was probably the single most significant achievement of feminists in Turin. The courses were originally designed to enable workers to upgrade their skills and level of literacy—the better to serve the needs of modernized and restructured Italian industry. However, the FLM's recognition of the lack of female involvement in the 150 Hours courses, and its acknowledgment of women's absence as a major shortcoming of the program, opened the door to all kinds of organizational possibilities for feminists, both in the union and in the schools and universities. Once the 150 Hours program was in place, women unionists were able to make a forceful and ultimately successful case for all-female courses, run by women for women with—they hoped—the full democratic participation of the workers and housewives who would enroll.

At the start, the vision of what end these courses might serve was fairly limited. They were sometimes proposed to union officials as leadership training to prepare rank-and-file workers for more active participation in union politics, and to give working-class housewives a more progressive perspective on political issues (Cavagna et al. 1979, 13). However, the courses were loosely structured, and the participants themselves were supposed to determine much of the content. Inevitably, this meant that as they developed, the courses moved away from traditional political themes toward discussions of topics well beyond factory and emancipationist concerns. Under the broad rubric of "Women's Condition," courses were offered on health, family relations, women's historical identity, psychoanalysis and women's sexuality, body language, and women in literature—as well as the more predictable themes of "women and union militancy," "women and the labor market," "women and the meaning of work," and so forth.

Overall, the program offered an opportunity for teachers, female union activists, and university students to come into sustained contact with working-class women in an egalitarian and highly supportive setting. With the development of these courses and the activities of the feminist unionists in the broader community—especially in the movement to establish *consultori* in every popular neighborhood—Turinese feminism moved beyond the exclusive domain of sophisticated, highly educated middle- and upper-class women in the heart of the city. The activities of the union women in Turin, and the similar initiatives stimulated elsewhere in Italy by the Turinese example, served to *decentralize* feminism and to alter its class character. To a large degree, women based in the Turinese unions managed to translate their feminist consciousness into a series of union-sponsored activities that enabled them to realize, at least in part, the fondest dream of any Marxist feminist: real and organic links with working-class women as women.

CONCLUSIONS

This survey of three types of women's activism in Turin in the 1970s provides some clear evidence of the conditioning influence of local political tradition on a new social movement. Given the *operaismo* that shapes all political activity on the Left in Turin, it is not surprising that it was the expression of feminism within the trade unions, rather than the feminist collectives or UDI, that found the most ample political space in which to operate. Turin's tradition effectively dictates that political initiatives be taken with the leadership of or in alliance with or— minimally—in the *name* of the working class. The antiinstitutional stance and consciousness-raising practiced by the small feminist collectives was, quite obviously, antithetical to this tradition. Their psychological orientation and individual focus clashed directly with the Marxist, collectivist, associative tendencies of Turinese political tradition. Likewise, the inability of the Turinese UDI to grow and develop in response to the stimulus of change in the national organization was due mostly to the reluctance on the part of a crucial minority to accept new organizational goals and styles or methods of operation that lay outside the workerist tradition.

The impact of a new social movement on the larger society serves as an important measure of its success. With the exception of a few small, internally oriented feminist collectives, all of the women's organizations under study hoped to reach out to other women and, generally, to improve the position of women in Italian society. Defining their goals in these terms, the activists' own evaluations of their achievements were mixed. UDI women were positive about their role in pressing for legislative reform: the abortion law, the legislative proposal on sexual violence, the provisions for publicly funded women's clinics, and so forth. The feminists involved in the struggle for the *consultori* generally assessed their efforts as unsuccessful insofar as they lost control of the clinics as "women's places" once the clinics were officially established and administered by committees appointed by the regional authorities. The union women readily acknowledged that they had little or nothing to show for their efforts to alter the sexist features of the trade union organizations, but they appraised the 150 Hours program as a major success because of the links it permitted them to forge with working-class women.

It is important to note that even in the participants' internal evaluation of the outcome of their efforts, the local context figures as a key variable. In Turin, the success of a movement is largely measured in terms of the capacity of that group to articulate working-class demands and mobilize sectors of the working class in support of its goals. Generally, this requires the formulation of demands in *operaista* terms. Thus, the women working within the unions saw themselves as "successful" because, in the framework of Turinese politics, their capacity to reach both unionized women and working-class housewives represented a great organizational triumph. This is not to say that the collectives built around *auto-coscienza*, which "only" managed to raise the consciousness of the middle- and upper-class women, should be dismissed as a "failure" in any broader analysis of women's experience in this period. The women who developed through their participation in these collectives were transformed by the experience; indeed, some went on to provide leadership in the *coordinamento* or to teach in the 150 Hours program. But the fact remains that only the feminists who worked within the unions could be said to have made strides along lines broadly recognized as politically significant in the workerist environment of Turin.

These, then, are three suggestive examples that indicate the degree to which local political environment may be a crucial variable conditioning the growth, survival, and degree of success of a new social movement like feminism. In Turin, a deeply rooted tradition of workers' struggle proved to be both a stimulus to and a brake on the development of the women's movement. On the positive side, the Turinese workerist subculture pushed feminists to broaden their appeal, reaching out to working-class women located—both literally and figuratively— on the margin of the city and of society. This is something that few women's movements anywhere in Western society have attempted or succeeded in doing, and there is no doubt that Turin's *operaista* tradition encouraged and provided an underpinning for feminists' efforts to popularize their movement. However, as we have seen, *operaismo* proved to be an inhibiting and limiting tradition as well. Other important goals of feminism—above all, the development of women's self-knowledge and consciousness—were submerged as a consequence of the pressure to tie women's struggle to the workers' movement.

Thus, in Turin, the presence of a subculture of the Left legitimized and encouraged the efforts of feminism to reach the popular masses but also inhibited the organization of women and, indeed, of other new social actors. Because the new social movements tended to be defined by the mass parties and the unions of the Old Left as narrow special-interest or single-issue groups, they were out of place in a political subculture that recognizes the legitimacy only of universalistic class appeals.

NOTES

1. The United Auto Workers (UAW) provides an exception to the rule.

2. The five cities are Turin and Milan in the advanced, industrialized Northwest; Verona in the "white region" of the very Catholic and traditional Veneto; Reggio Emilia in the heart of the Communist-governed "red belt"; and Caserta in the South.

3. In English see Cammett 1967; Golden 1983; and S. Hellman 1980. In Italian, see Agosto and Bravo 1981; Musso 1980; and Spriano 1958 and 1960.

4. Often referred to as a "front" in more hostile, anti-Communist parlance, a "flanking

organization" is designed to carry the influence of the party to those people who may share the party's goals and vision of a new order but who are not yet ready to commit themselves to partisan political activity. Flanking organizations enlarge the party's sphere of influence and serve as a "school" for political formation. They extend the base of the party and constitute a source of future party members (Manoukian 1969). In Italy the term is used to refer to organizations associated not only with the PCI, the Christian Democrats, and other political parties but even with the Catholic Church.

REFERENCES

Agosti, Aldo, and Gian Mario Bravo, eds. 1981. *Storia del movimento operaio del socialismo e delle lotte sociali in Piemonte.* Vol. 4. Bari: De Donato.

Alloisio, Mirella. 1974. "L'Udissea: Storia lunga trent'anni di una associazione femminile." *Noi Donne* 29, no. 49 (15 December): 23–45.

Alloisio, Mirella, and Marta Ajo. 1978. *La Donna nel socialismo italiano: Tra cronaca e storia (1892–1978).* Cosenza: Edicioni Lerici.

Ascoli, Giulietta. 1979. "L'UDI tra emancipazione e liberazione (1943–1964)." In Giulietta Ascoli et al., *La Questione femminile in Italia del '900 ad oggi.* Milan: Franco Angeli, 109–59.

Balbo, Laura. 1981. "Women's Access to Intellectual Work: The Case of Italy." *Signs* 6 (Summer): 763–69.

Barbagli, Marzio, and Piergiorgio Corbetta. 1978. "Partito e movimento: Aspetti del rinnovamento del PCI." *Inchiesta* 8 (January-February): 3–46.

Bates, Thomas R. 1974. "Antonio Gramsci and the Soviet Experiment in Italy." *Societas—A Review of Social History* 6 (Winter): 37–54.

Bocchio, Flora, and Antonia Torchi. 1979. *L'Acqua in gabbia: Voci di donne dentro il sindacato.* Milan: La Salamandria.

Caldwell, Lesley. 1983. "Courses for Women: The Example of the 150 Hours in Italy." *Feminist Review* 14 (Summer): 72–83.

Cammett, John M. 1967. *Antonio Gramsci and the Origins of Italian Communism.* Stanford, Cal.: Stanford University Press.

Camparini, Aurelia. 1981. "Lotte e organizzazioni delle donne dalla liberazione agli anni Sessanta." In Aldo Agosti and Gian Mario Bravo, eds., *Storia del movimento operaio del socialismo e delle lotte sociali in Piemonte.* Vol. 4, 555–606. Bari: De Donato.

Cavagna, Christina, et al. 1979. *La Spina all'occhiello: L'esperienza a Torino dell' intercategoriale donne CGIL-CISL-UIL attraverso i documenti 1975–1978.* Turin: Musolini Editore.

Chi Brucia? 1977. May, 1–4.

CLD Manifesto. 1980.

"Come siamo nate." 1978. *Bollettino delle Donne* (Turin): 7–9.

Garner, Roberta, and Mayer N. Zald. 1981. "Social Movement Sectors and Systemic Constraint: Toward a Structural Analysis of Social Movements." Center for Research on Social Organization, Working Paper no. 238. Ann Arbor: University of Michigan.

Gianotti, Renzo. 1979. *Trent'anni di lotte alla Fiat (1948–1978).* Bari: De Donato.

Golden, Miriam. 1983. "Austerity and Its Opposition: Italian Working Class Politics in the 1970s." Ph.D. diss., Cornell University.

Gramaglia, Mariella. 1979. "1968: Il Venir dopo e l'andar oltre del movimento femminista." In Giulietta Ascoli et al., *La Questione femminile in Italia del '900 ad oggi*, 179–201. Milan: Franco Angeli.

Gramsci, Antonio. 1955. "La Funzione storica delle città." *L'Ordine Nuovo*, 1919–20. Turin: Einaudi Editore, pp. 319–22.

Hellman, Judith Adler. 1982. "Feminism in the Italian Trade Union Confederations." Paper presented at the American Political Science Association Meetings, Denver, Colorado. September.

———. 1984. "The Italian Communists, the Women's Question, and the Challenge of Feminism." *Studies in Political Economy* 13 (Spring): 57–82.

Hellman, Stephen. 1980. "Il PCI e l'ambigua eredità dell'autunno caldo a Torino." *Il Mulino* 29 (March–April): 246–95.

———. 1986. "Italian Communism in Transition: The Rise and Decline of the Historic Compromise in Turin, 1975–80." Manuscript.

Lanzardo, Liliana. 1971. *Classe operaia e Partito Comunista alla Fiat: La Strategia della collaborazione, 1945–1949*. Turin: Einaudi.

Manoukian, Agopik, ed. 1969. *La Presenza sociale del PCI e della DC*. Bologna: Il Mulino.

Menapace, Lidia. 1979. "Le Cause strutturali del nuovo femminismo." In Giulietta Ascoli et al., *La Questione femminile in Italia del '900 ad oggi*. Milan: Franco Angeli, 161–76.

Musso, Stefano. 1980. *Gli operai di Torino, 1900–1920*. Milan: Feltrinelli.

Oberschall, Anthony. 1978. "The Decline of the 1960's Social Movements." in *Research in Social Movements*, I, ed. Louis Kriesberg, 257–90. Greenwich, Ct.: JAI Press.

Pugno, Emilio, and Sergio Garavini. 1974. *Gli anni duri alla Fiat: La resistenza sindacale e la ripresa*. Turin: Einaudi.

Schumaker, P. D. 1975. "Policy Responsiveness to Protest Group Demands." *Journal of Politics* 37: 488–521.

Spagnoletti, Rosalba, ed. 1978. *I Movimenti femministi in Italia*. Roma: Savelli.

Spriano, Paolo. 1958. *Socialismo e classe operaia a Torino dal 1892 al 1913*. Turin: Einaudi.

———. 1960. *Torino operaia nella grande guerra (1914–1918)*. Turin: Einaudi.

Tarrow, Sidney. 1983. "Struggling to Reform: Protest and Policy Innovation in Advanced Industrial Democracies." Center for International Studies Occasional Paper no. 15. Ithaca, N.Y.: Cornell University.

UDI (Unione Donne Italiane). 1978. *Atti del X Congresso Nazionale*, 19–20 January.

6 Feminism and the Model of Militancy in an Italian Communist Federation: Challenges to the Old Style of Politics

STEPHEN HELLMAN

Traditional parties of the Left and the new movements that arose in the 1960s and 1970s have not, to put it mildly, always enjoyed a smooth relationship. Italy in the 1970s provided a clear example of tension between the major party of the Left—the Italian Communist party (PCI)—and the bulk of the progressive, secular forces in society. Although the relationship would have been difficult in any event, this one was aggravated by a very specific factor. In 1973, the PCI formally adopted the *compromesso storico*, its strategy of "historic compromise" (Lange 1979; S. Hellman 1977). The strategy proposed long-term collaboration between the PCI and the party that had ruled Italy since World War II: the Christian Democrats (DC). Those committed to secular reform had least reason of all to cheer the PCI's proposal or its subsequent actions. Its willingness to avoid antagonizing intended allies soon had most of them convinced that the PCI's priorities were at odds with their own. As should be clear from this summary, Italian feminists had special cause for concern and resentment in this period, which witnessed blatant foot-dragging by the Communists on critical reforms like divorce, family law, and abortion.

Such a summary is accurate as far as it goes, but it does present a simplified portrait of the PCI. On the one hand, the tendencies that became so pronounced in the period of the historic compromise were in fact there long before the strategy was articulated—and they remained after the strategy was effectively abandoned (in 1980). But on the other hand, the PCI is a *mass* party with 1.7 million members, an extensive presence in Italian society, and an activist orientation. It may attempt to stand apart from and direct social ferment to its own ends, but it is very much a part of the environment it seeks to affect. Its structures get penetrated by many of the demands the party tries to manipulate, and these demands then challenge the party's most entrenched attitudes and practices.

This essay tries to show how such penetration takes place, with reference to themes that have grown directly out of the women's movement. I argue that the PCI's increasing openness to new issues in the 1970s cannot be understood as merely a political calculation by the national party leadership. There *were* calculations, to be sure. But change also occurred because of the *internal* dynamics of the PCI's grassroots interaction with a society in flux. Pressures for change were found even in the most insulated parts of the party machinery, once veterans of recent struggles and younger activists who had grown up in a dramatically altered society were recruited into important leadership positions. Bearing values that clashed with entrenched beliefs in the PCI, these newcomers generated and continue to exert considerable pressures for change within the party.

This study examines one important PCI organization, the Provincial Federation of Turin,[1] and analyzes two related developments since the late 1960s. The primary focus is on the tension between the PCI's traditional operational code and the new values that have spread in the wake of new social movements, particularly feminism. Of special importance is the challenge to what I call, following PCI usage, the party's "model of militancy." This is a set of attitudes, rooted in the party's Leninist past, that persists in spite of Italian Communism's notable evolution away from the old "vanguard party" ideal. These attitudes assign an absolutely central role to the party and thus implicitly deny any *real* autonomy—or legitimacy—to individual needs or to collective actors outside the party's own array of forces in society.

These entrenched attitudes have been challenged, on the Left, by views of social and political life that refuse to assign a secondary role to the private sphere—or that reject altogether a rigid separation of public and private. These views are part of the broader legacy of the New Left, and the most forceful expression of the challenge is clearly embodied in the feminist slogan, "The personal is political." We will see how the new attitudes have eroded entrenched values within the PCI, even within the innermost reaches of the party organization.

The second development examined is the Turinese federation's altered way of addressing women's issues, in society and within its own organization. This brief review is necessarily a synthetic treatment, but it serves two useful functions. It furnishes important background information on the federation and thus a context for our discussion of the leaders' attitudes. It also shows how—against formidable odds—certain themes first made their way into the local party's discourse and how the party reacted, in concrete terms, to issues raised by and on behalf of its own female cadres.

Examining these issues in a single locale avoids too high a level of abstraction while permitting us to observe the way new themes actually "percolate" through the party organization. Moreover, because Turin represents one of the *least* receptive terrains for these new themes, it is an especially important case to study. Evidence of their penetration here will be compelling proof of the permeability of the party in a much more general sense.

THE PCI'S OLD MODEL OF MILITANCY AND ORIENTATION TO "SOCIAL FORCES"

What exactly is the implicit and often explicit code governing the behavior of activists that I have called the party's model of militancy? It certainly goes much further back than the *compromesso storico*. Anyone familiar with the history of the international Communist movement knows that militance consisted of immense doses of dedication and sacrifice, often at great personal cost to the activist. Its origins are to be found in the original strategy of the movement, which was insurrectionary as well as revolutionary: a semimilitary notion of service to a cause in which one's life might well be at stake clearly could be nothing less than total. While the insurrectionary goal officially faded in the 1940s, variations on the theme persisted among many members of the PCI rank and file until well into the 1960s, when most of the cadres who favored a very hard line began to fade from the scene. But for good historical reasons, many aspects of the old model of militancy remained powerfully entrenched. The anti-fascist Resistance in Italy during World War II, in which the PCI was a prime protagonist, fanned old myths and clearly put a premium on "Bolshevik" virtues. Then the Cold War, which reached virulent and often hysterical levels of anti-Communism in Italy, created conditions that led the PCI to adopt an extremely tough, defensive stance simply for the purpose of survival. If we add to these factors the ideological pressures emanating from the U.S.S.R. and the "pure" imperatives of organizational maintenance, it is not surprising that the ideal of total dedication survived nearly intact through the 1960s.

And this is true in spite of the PCI's extensive destalinization at the end of the 1950s (S. Hellman 1975, 99–106). Even the younger, more flexible cadres who replaced the Stalinist old guard at the middle and top ranks of the party remained very much the products of earlier experiences. Many of the young leaders of the 1950s had lived through the Resistance, and all were socialized into party life during the Cold War. These "renovators" helped the party through a critical stage of its history. They wanted a less ritualistic and sectarian party, and their idea of a socialist Italy was a long way from what their Soviet comrades thought such a phenomenon should resemble. But they remained deeply committed to a notion of revolutionary transformation, and they continued to believe in a model of militancy that was close to the traditional one.

Some voices for change were heard within the PCI at a relatively early date, however. One of the most radical renovators, Lucio Magri, articulated the most distinctive aspects of Communist militancy even as he went on to suggest what ought to be changed:

> By the term *revolutionary militancy* we mean here a particular relationship between the member and the party, which distinguishes Bolshevism from any other type of political formation. . . . it does not sanction the division between private and public spheres, nor does it allow substantial absenteeism by members with the

corresponding domination of a bureaucratic-representative apparatus. On the contrary, it is based on the involvement of the whole personality of the militant, involving his life-long conception of the world in the complex work of building the new society. It becomes itself, therefore, a new way of being men and entering into contact with other men. (Magri 1970, 122)

As a revolutionary, Magri had no objection to the commitment demanded by this type of militancy, but he did strongly object to the separation of the public and private spheres that it demanded. He noted that this separation had historically led the Left to believe that the public or political realm was morally superior to the private, and thus to conclude that "a deeper sense of personal realization is only possible when serving the revolution." He labeled this a "Jacobin" notion, and criticized it sharply, calling instead for a conception of Marxism and the party that would bring these artificially separated spheres together and eliminate the abstract and moralistic character of militancy in the Bolshevik tradition (Magri 1970, 123).

As Magri's observations show, it is difficult to criticize the PCI's orientation toward its own militants without immediately raising questions about its general outlook on society. And in fact, as the 1960s progressed and confronted Italy with new forms of militancy from familiar groups (workers, for example), as well as unexpected demands from *new* groups (especially students, women, and young people in general), it was increasingly difficult to ignore the party's outlook. From the 1960s on it paid lip service to the growing richness and complexity of society and to the need to respect the autonomy of new social actors and movements. Pluralism, in other words, was integrated more fully into the PCI's descriptive vocabulary as well as into its projections for the future. This was a necessary part of the Communists' "maturation" as they moved toward a governing role and sought to reassure doubters. But at the same time, the PCI often continued to adopt a condescending attitude toward phenomena that fell outside what it viewed as the "real" political sphere, and its actions made clear that it had little patience with groups and demands it could not immediately and easily organize, or at least recruit to its own agenda. Where groups or demands threatened to complicate or undermine that agenda, they were not simply ignored but treated as inchoate, immature, or "prepolitical."

The Jacobin style that Magri denounces was much in evidence in the period of the historic compromise. The party line was often defended with old-style invective, a practice that is relatively rare in the PCI and understandably aggravated many long-standing suspicions. For example, in 1973, when the Italian feminist movement had been an undeniable force for several years, some of the party's top theorists—including the head of the national party school—were ripping into it as petty bourgeois and individualistic, a mere mirror of American trends and hence irrelevant to the *real* concerns of Italian women (Gruppi 1973). It would take an additional three years, and considerable pressure from women both within the party and in the sort of organizations it *was* inclined to recognize, for the PCI to admit that many of the issues raised by Italian feminists were both legitimate and urgent.[2]

Thus there are contingent and more deep-rooted explanations as to why the PCI might react unenthusiastically to a host of items that would crowd or complicate its own agenda. And as the 1970s proceeded, criticism was increasingly directed against the party's *general* attitude toward "the social" and its apparent ambition to bring all of civil society under the control of existing institutions (Donolo 1978; Fedele 1979; Pasquino 1982, 863–66; Stame 1977, chaps. 4–5). Perhaps most important, criticisms were increasingly heard from *within* the PCI on these very themes, even from those who accepted the idea that the party should assume a governing role in the country. As one younger leader put it, it was absurd for a party with governing ambitions to continue to view normal citizens as "incomplete militants"; they were just voters with a variety of motivations that did not happen to fit the party's pigeonholes (Petruccioli 1979). Others drew an explicit link between the PCI's view of new subjects and its internal model of militancy, deriding the idea that these groups were raw material to be shaped by the party, or that their demands were irrational simply because they focused on private rather than public concerns (Bolaffi 1981, 156ff.; Izzo 1977). Thus, by the end of the 1970s, a very important part of the PCI's identity crisis related to whether or not the party could develop a more flexible and pluralistic vision of itself and the world outside. To do this while maintaining a distinctive profile as a force for change is quite a tall order. Five years later, as this essay was being written, the PCI appeared no closer to a satisfactory solution.

THE PCI IN TURIN

A Difficult Setting

Let us turn to the Provincial Federation of Turin in the 1970s. Turin is an interesting research site for many reasons, all of which relate to its specificity: it is the archetypal blue-collar, one-company town. Its class profile, its urbanization and immigration rates (and therefore its social problems and forms of social militance) have tended, historically, to be extreme. It is many things, but it is *not* typical of other places in Italy. On the contrary, it is fascinating because it is a sort of laboratory case of unfettered advanced capitalist development. In the history of the country and its workers' movement, things generally occurred earlier and in more starkly defined terms in what used to be called "Italy's Petrograd." This was certainly the case during the intensive mass mobilizations and renewed militance that began in the late 1960s and ran well into the 1970s.

A few basic points can summarize the trajectory of capitalist development, and the party/movement dynamic in Turin. (1) Turin's industrial concentration has given the large factories of the area, and the blue-collar workers employed in them, pride of place in the analyses of local left-wing parties and unions; with a peak of 500,000 industrial workers employed in over 1,200 factories in the province, this is hardly surprising (Associazione Piemonte Italia 1974, 23–29, 38–52; Castronovo 1977, 639–43, 690). It has, nonetheless, meant that the discourse of the Left has often been almost vulgarly economistic, viewing as essentially irrelevant or "merely superstructural" any phenomena that were not *direct* expressions of society's productive forces. (2) The *rate* of development since World War II—particularly very rapid urbanization and southern immigration— utterly pulverized the old social and organizational bases of left-wing parties and unions alike. The destruction wreaked by these "objective forces" was aided by a brutal and direct onslaught against the Left, and by the Left's own sectarian attitudes and behavior, at least into the 1950s (Accornero and Rieser 1981; Berta 1981, 123–34; Pugno and Garavini 1974). (3) This combination of organizational weakness and a highly volatile social setting led the workers' movement to evolve a stance toward social conflict that is quite radical and militant. Since it generally cannot control extensive conflict directly, it tries to avoid being outflanked to the Left, at least verbally, as a means of maintaining its legitimacy with the working class.

These factors help us understand how Turin could be a center of militancy yet how the Left in general, including the PCI, might pay much less attention than they should to women as a new social and political force in the aftermath of the struggles of the late 1960s and early 1970s (see Chapter 5). Neither the themes nor the protagonists of the modern women's movement neatly fit the class categories that so totally dominate the Turinese scene. One could add another consideration, which at least two ranking leaders of the federation pointed out during interviews.[3] If the Piedmontese working class had never been prepared to go much out of its way on women's issues, the situation was certainly not improved when the local proletariat's ranks swelled with southern immigrants. Ambivalence over even the more *traditional* framing of "the woman's question"— women's right to work, to equal pay, or to birth control—was often exacerbated by the presence of so many workers in the party who brought north a distinctly retrograde set of attitudes. At the very least, this circumstance served as an alibi for a party organization that was not inclined to take much action on issues relating to women, but it probably had a real impact on the internal dynamic of the federation.

Finally, it should be added that while Turin certainly witnessed an important women's movement in the 1960s and 1970s, the most extensive and dramatic social mobilizations there involved *other* new subjects (as well as new forms of action by old subjects, such as workers). Aside from the extremely explosive workers' actions in this period, it was the student movement, extraparliamentary groups, squatters' occupations of public (or vacant) housing, and more generic urban movements that made Turin distinctive. (The feminists made their most notable impact in Rome and Milan.)

The resurgent militancy of the 1960s and 1970s eventually led to impressive gains for the Turinese Communists: by the mid-1970s their vote had risen to a point (40 percent in the capital, 37 percent in the entire province) that allowed them to gain control of every significant local office in the province. The federation's membership rose from 30,000 to 47,000 between 1969 and 1977, a growth rate matched in very few places in the entire PCI (S. Hellman 1980, 256–87). So much fresh blood revitalized the party in ways no one had thought possible just a few years earlier. At the peak of its growth in 1976–77, nearly 60 percent of the federation's entire membership had joined the party since 1969. But even this period saw the Turinese federation among the weakest, in *relative* terms, in the entire country—relative to total population, and relative to the number of votes obtained for every member.

The party's revitalization in the 1970s was skewed in ways that reflected its own history as well as its success in responding to the various movements of the "hot" period of intensive mobilization at the end of the 1960s and into the 1970s. It did best in recruiting workers, new white-collar groups, and young people. Rank-and-file party structures multiplied—but the emphasis, as always, was very much on factory organizations. This meant that most working-class militants—and they form the vast majority of the militants in a federation like Turin—had their energies channeled to the shop floor, rather than to broader party activities in civil society.

One area, however, where the local party's recruitment efforts were conspicuously *unsuccessful* was among women. Prior to the Hot Autumn (1969), the Turinese PCI had the same percentage of women among its members as did the party as a whole (23 percent). But as recruitment skyrocketed in the 1970s, this percentage fell drastically and then rose to roughly 20 percent, where it remained for the rest of the decade as overall party membership declined. By 1985, both national and local figures for female members had crept upward: for the whole PCI it was 27 percent; for Turin it was 24 percent (PCI 1986, 14, 18). Like the party in general, the federation had undoubtedly done quite well in winning women's votes—especially those of younger women (Sani 1977, 110–20). It clearly had less success in getting large numbers of women to take out a party card.

Women's Issues in the Turinese Federation of the PCI
We have seen a number of phenomena that would lead us to expect the Turinese PCI, in spite of being in the eye of the storms of the 1970s, to slight *la questione femminile*. But the Hot Autumn left two things in its wake that opened the party to new themes. First, all movements in Turin were strongly antiauthoritarian, even more so than their counterparts elsewhere. While this would by no means guarantee a more positive reception to ideas growing out of the modern women's movement, it would at least work in favor of one. The second, and related, positive legacy of the Hot Autumn for the PCI's reaction to women's issues lies in the immense influx of new blood into the party in the 1970s. Although initially

underrepresented, younger women did eventually join the party in large numbers. So did disproportionate numbers of young people in general, many of whom were very rapidly promoted in a party organization that badly needed new leaders. At the very least, these trends brought the party into closer contact with themes that were increasingly found in the everyday discourse of the broader society, and made the PCI more receptive to them.

But the overall balance in Turin would have to be considered more negative than positive on the question of receptivity to women's issues. The evidence, showing a good deal of evolution over time, has to be viewed against both an extremely poor starting position and changes that were taking place in the party as a whole.

The easiest way to survey this evolution is to highlight the attention women's issues received in the federation, primarily by referring to key party congresses held between 1969 and 1979. Although they are often ceremonial events, congresses do serve important functions. They give a sense of how the party leadership defines the "great issues" facing it every few years—usually in the form of precongressional documents and the party leader's opening address. The subsequent debate and final documents then permit one to measure the reaction of the lower levels of the leadership and of common militants to the way issues have been posed. Finally, congresses also elect the new leaders who will run the party until the next congress, which is generally two years away. In the PCI, as in most mass parties, there are certain sham aspects to the selection of the top leaders, but on questions such as the composition of the broadly defined elite of the federation, the information gleaned from elections can be quite helpful.

The 1969 congress was held close to the peak of the Hot Autumn. Radical themes were in the air, but they were mainly linked to the working class and the factories. The course of events, combined with the traditional orientations of the PCI in Turin, are reflected in the extremely low figures for women's participation in all aspects of federation activity: for example, only 8 percent of the delegates to the congress were women. Many speakers criticized the party on this issue, pointing to the absence of a full-time head of the Women's Commission as proof of a more general lack of interest in or even scorn for women's problems (Pastore 1969; see also Ayassot 1969, and Griotti 1969).

The federation responded to the strongest charges by initiating some changes, but these were slow and often halfhearted. The new leadership did include more women (14 percent vs. the earlier 10 percent), and a promise was made to bring women's issues more systematically before the entire federation in the future ("Mozione organizzativa" 1969, items 6, 7). But the latter point remained a dead letter, for the Turinese leaders never followed through on it. As one informant put it, this inaction communicated a lack of interest to the rest of the organization.

There were, if anything, signs of hostility from the top leadership in the early 1970s. In 1971, activists in the recently revived Women's Commission decided that a debate on abortion at the provincial Festival of the Party Press would be valuable in light of the issue's growing national importance as well as the increasing activities of the Italian women's movement in that period. The federation's leaders—all men—simply blocked the initiative. In the words of the head of the Women's Commission at the time, "As you can see, women's problems were not welcome in this organization then." [4]

By 1970 the federation had hired a full-time head of the Women's Commission. But it would be a long time before a female functionary occupied a leadership role that was not one of those "reserved" for women (such as the Women's Commission, Social Security, and Health). In 1975, as the local party's personnel needs expanded enormously, a second woman was hired; in 1977, a woman became secretary of the party's Youth Federation. This appointment followed a partywide trend, but the fact remains that it was done in Turin. Thus, by the end of the decade, there were three women in the apparatus out of some 40 functionaries in all. This was not even 10 percent of the total—but seven years earlier, there had been none.

Subsequent congresses continued to emphasize the lack of discussion of women's problems and the underrepresentation of women in the higher reaches of the party organization. For many reasons, the 1975 congress marked a watershed in the articulation of women's problems in the federation. Issues relating to women were raised more frequently and aggressively. Feminists were no longer dismissed wholesale or viewed at best as middle-class crusaders with no sense of the demands of working-class (read "real") women. Even some of the top-ranking men in the federation felt compelled to pay homage to the positive contributions of the women's movement.

The major external explanation for this development was that the 1974 divorce referendum had led to a resounding victory, much to the PCI's surprise. While fully supporting the maintenance of divorce in Italy, the PCI had desperately tried to avoid an open vote; it was worried about the outcome and knew that a polarization of the country along religious lines would not help its compromise strategy. But in the voting, Turin had led all major Italian cities in its support of divorce, with a whopping 80 percent. These results made it impossible to fall back on the old argument that the country was "not yet ready" to confront the issues regularly raised by many women's groups.

Yet not all the external signs were positive. Since the historic compromise had first been spelled out in 1973, the PCI's cautious behavior toward the DC, and the Catholic world in general, had alarmed many people inside as well as outside the party. And while the feminist movement remained strong in society at large, a very long series of maneuvers was already well underway over abortion, which would not be legalized for three more years. In spite of the divorce referendum, the Communists displayed extreme caution on abortion. They would eventually have to be goaded and threatened into a more courageous position by women within the party and its flanking organizations.

Several speakers at the 1975 congress, including the federation secretary, lauded the mass character of the women's movement, which earlier had usually been dismissed as elitist or petty bourgeois (Ariemma 1975, 69). Another topic that received considerable attention at the congress was the PCI's relationship to the Union of Italian Women (UDI), the Left's traditional flanking organization (J. Hellman 1984). Given the importance of women's issues, the party was going to have to stop delegating all these questions—especially those that one militant referred to as "hot potatoes"—to UDI. The secretary openly admitted that the party had "put the brakes on" women's participation in the PCI in the past (Ariemma 1975, 69–70).

The question of tone is best illustrated by example. An outstanding cadre who would shortly be elected to high public office ripped into the party's practices and did not even spare the secretary-general, Enrico Berlinguer. More than a year before the national leaders officially acknowledged the positive contribution of feminists (see note 2), she argued that feminism had too hastily and automatically been dismissed. She also had harsh words for the party's stand on abortion, which she called "timid." In a more general reference to the PCI's legislative proposals, including those on abortion, in the era of the historic compromise, she concluded that they "appear to respond more to tactical exigencies than to an effective intervention aimed at freeing women from constraints that reduce their full autonomy and responsibility" (Rosolen 1975; see also Berruto 1975).

The 1975 congress also included a lively floor fight over nominations both to the party's top organs and to the national congress. It included exchanges over the relative merits of quotas and affirmative action. The debate even provided the unusual spectacle of the federation secretary publicly "inviting" the electoral commission to reconsider the proportion of women sent to the national congress (12 percent) and included in the top leadership of the federation (15 percent).

The reason I have called this congress a watershed is hardly that it marked a turnaround of the Turinese party as a whole, or even of the bulk of its top leadership. The increasing numbers of female functionaries and the achievement of the proportional representation of women in the broadly defined leadership organs of the federation by 1977 should not be lightly dismissed, but they surely do not constitute evidence of a cultural revolution in the Turinese PCI. Rather, what I consider most significant about the party's evolution, apparent at the 1975 congress, is that it had found itself forced to address broader societal and "movement" themes, and to address them in ways that would have been beyond the ken of most leaders and militants five years earlier. The divorce referendum, which signaled profound social change, clearly was a critical factor. But so was the mass nature of the PCI: however weak it was in Turin, thousands of women passed through it in this period, and they had an impact on its collective consciousness. The same can also be said of the much more limited number of women who rose to prominent positions in the 1970s. As impressive as the victory for divorce was, it could not, by itself, have so completely altered the way *all* women's issues were raised—and received—by the federation. For all the grumbling about quotas (from traditionalists) and tokenism (from radical critics), the increased role for women in the higher reaches of the organization sped up the articulation of these issues in the Turinese PCI.

Words matter in such issues, for different definitions tend to legitimize different perspectives. It is therefore important to note that by the end of the decade, authoritative voices in the federation—and not only critical militants—were using terms like "liberation" and "feminist" without qualifiers or disclaimers when referring to the contributions of the women's movement (Minucci 1977; PCI 1979, sec. 4).

Legitimizing language was very much in evidence in an important document prepared for the 1977 congress. The top organs of the federation named committees from their midst to address the major areas of party activity, with the aim of reporting out a summary document that would then be submitted to the provincial congress. The committee assigned the theme "Party and Movement" held special seminars on the factories and unions, *and on the women's question.* Each seminar was "sanctified" by the presence of a top national leader of the PCI. The extensive preparatory groundwork for these gatherings involved most of the federation's top activists from each sector. The final document distributed at the congress contained about 50 pages of discussion of specific social issues and movements; nearly half was devoted to the women's question (C.F. e C.F.C., Seconda Commissione 1977, 22–48). The Women's Commission of the federation, which was strongly represented on the committee, obviously did not want to let a golden opportunity pass. It is questionable whether many delegates bothered to read the ponderous final document. But it did represent a statement that had received the formal imprimatur of the entire federation, and such official sanctions count for a lot in the PCI. The women's question would, in the future, have to be addressed in terms much more acceptable to the female militants of the organization.

But words and documents tell, at best, only part of the story. The period 1975–77 saw notable advances in the party's analysis of new ideas and movements, but this was also the period in which Communist *practice,* following a jump in the PCI vote, consisted of the most concerted efforts at a rapprochement with the DC. By 1980, the PCI had all but abandoned its historic compromise strategy and was back in the opposition. But until the line actually changed, the leaders of the Turinese PCI did not hesitate to intervene heavily in women's (and others') activities when the party's immediate political agenda was threatened.[5]

It therefore remains an open question how strongly the PCI (in Turin or elsewhere) will try to put into practice its assurances to women's groups and other new subjects that it does not wish to hegemonize them or channel their activities to its own ends (PCI 1979, sec. 4). If the party eventually comes forward with a strategy that genuinely tolerates and respects the autonomy of new subjects, then the painfully slow changes we have traced will stand a good chance of becoming consolidated in spite of the powerful forces of conservatism that are entrenched in the party's traditions and organization. If it revives some variant of the *compromesso*, or even if it continues to flounder in search of an alternative, as it has for several years, then it is likely to fall back on its old patterns and view new forces as masses to be maneuvered or obstacles to be neutralized. Obviously, in the latter case, changes in its outlook on and actions toward society will be much slower in coming, if they come at all.

The Party Apparatus and the Model of Militancy

Discussions of the Communist apparatus usually conjure up images of a corps of gray bureaucrats slavishly carrying out orders from on high. But the Turinese apparatus at the end of the 1970s was a far cry from a stereotyped party bureaucracy.[6] It included seasoned veterans, but more than half its members were 30 or younger, and nearly half had joined the party in the 1970s. A third of the entire apparatus—and *half* of those who joined the party in 1968 or later—had been active in either the student movement or an extraparliamentary group prior to becoming Communists. This is more early political experience than is the norm for PCI militants, and reflects the impact of the "hot" events in Turin on the local party (Sebastiani 1983, 105). Finally, although a majority of the functionaries were workers before joining the apparatus (and fully two-thirds came from working-class families), this was a well-educated group. Nearly three-quarters had gone to high school, and just under half had had at least two years of university training.

This background information helps explain how themes that challenge the prevailing model of militancy can quickly find their way into the apparatus. Until very recently, the PCI recruited and socialized functionaries according to a pattern common in working-class parties—which made it easy to insulate an apparatus against the outside world. Functionaries tended to be poorly educated workers whose hard work and political loyalty were rewarded (modestly, in strictly monetary terms) by their party. The bulk of their formal training was also provided by the party. The result was a material and psychological network of dependency on the organization that had given them a status they otherwise would have been very unlikely to achieve (Michels 1959). An important recent study of the PCI found that for functionaries over 35, the old standards still applied: the vast majority were workers who had not gone beyond junior high school (Sebastiani 1983, 117–19, tables 12 and 14).

But traditional mechanisms were eroded by the 1970s. With extensive political experience outside the PCI and high levels of education, new functionaries entered the party in a much less "unformed" state. They obviously felt less need to pass through strong socializing agencies such as party schools: in the 1960s, four out of five Turinese functionaries had attended party school (Bonazzi 1965, 54–55), whereas only two of five had done so by the late 1970s. It is therefore logical to expect that the new leaders would also hold a range of views different from those of their older or more traditionally socialized comrades. But will these views directly challenge the basic assumptions of the existing model of militancy? Or do the party's selection and socialization mechanisms remain so strong, in spite of recent changes, that they can dilute or deflect any such challenges? It is one thing to show that the apparatus—especially its more recent arrivals—has qualities that *ought* to translate into internal tensions within the party. It is quite another thing to demonstrate that such tensions actually exist and to assess their implications if they do.

The old model of militancy, as we have seen, posits a rigid separation between the private and public spheres, both in society and in personal life. If anything, the private is subjugated to the public: witness the puritanical, or at least Victorian, values often demanded of Communists. Although historically framed in terms of revolutionary discipline and sacrifice (the revolutionary was assumed to have no personal life at all), these values are really rooted in the maturing industrial proletariat of the late nineteenth and early twentieth centuries—and, ironically, reflect the success of the bourgeoisie in at least partially disciplining the nascent work force.[7] They persist in places like Turin because the industrial proletariat is so large (and often idealized), but also because they are so functional to the organizations of the workers' movement.

To be sure, "functional" has strongly sexist connotations, for activities are structured in ways that assume either that the militant has no broader personal obligations or that these obligations can be fulfilled by a partner. Meetings take place at the beginning or end of a shift, or they are held in the evening right after dinner. This obviously tends to discourage all but the most dedicated (or relatively well-off) women with family obligations. The governing assumption is clearly that of a traditional two-person relationship, with one partner charged with the maintenance of the personal sphere while the other is active outside, having little time for wife, children, and household responsibilities. And if this is the standard for activists at the grassroots, it applies doubly to full-time party militants, whose schedule must permit attendance at rank-and-file meetings. Functionaries not only put in very long days and work on weekends; they are also called to the hustings three or four evenings per week (Sebastiani 1983, 138).[8] The heavy personal costs of the PCI's compulsive activism is reflected in a well-worn joke: "The Italian Communist Party unites the proletariat and divides the family."

This attitude still exists in the PCI, but it no longer passes unchallenged. To someone who has done extensive research on the party organization since the late 1960s, one of the most notable changes has been the degree to which personal matters now make their way into conversations and interviews. When these issues arose prior to the mid-1970s, they were almost inevitably framed fatalistically: "This is a terrible job from the perspective of family life. I am very lucky to have such an understanding wife." When functionaries raise these issues *now,* they do so in a much less resigned way. Many admit to having had deep doubts about taking on the job because they knew what it would do to their personal lives. Some confessed to having debated whether marriage or having children could be compatible with joining the apparatus. "Job burnout" was openly and widely discussed and recognized as producing genuine tragedies; in the past, the tendency would have been to see these "failures" as people who "just couldn't make it."

In the course of systematic interviewing, the functionaries were asked what aspect of their work they liked least. Just over half (56 percent) responded with references to the crushing work load. What is interesting is not only that this complaint outdistanced all others by a factor of three, but that when the same question was put to functionaries in 1969 and 1973, *only 12 percent* complained strongly about the brutalizing schedule and pace of party work (S. Hellman 1973, 394). The functionary's job has changed little, if at all, over this period, but individual expectations certainly have.

It is extremely important to understand that these were not the grumbles of overworked party bureaucrats who wanted more leisure time. They were, on the contrary, thoughtful criticisms of the way the PCI functions. Underlying almost all criticism was an alternative notion of what militance in the PCI *should* mean. By its nature, party work is often unpredictable, and excessive demands have to be expected occasionally. But when a breakneck pace becomes the norm, something clearly has gone wrong with the party's ability to order its priorities. "Burnout" is not tragic only because of the terrible personal costs it inflicts on individual militants; it also reflects the profound tragedy of a party that does not know how to utilize the human material at its disposal. What these functionaries are lamenting most of all—and they are in the best position to know—is that the party's entrenched codes work against creating the type of militant most needed at this stage of Italy's, and the PCI's, maturation.

Within this broader context, the most striking thing about the functionaries' criticisms of their work load was the degree to which personal concerns found their way into the discussion. A third of the members of the apparatus injected personal considerations into their comments. While complaints about the work place were voiced fairly equally throughout the apparatus, the tendency to personalize was almost uniquely limited to those under 35. Very significantly, ex-workers were as likely as others to inject these concerns into their comments. To lend a human dimension to a problem that a statistical summary renders abstract, I have excerpted from my field notes examples of the way members of the apparatus voiced some aspects of the problem.

1. *Ex-worker (male), 28 years old.* When asked to leave his job to work full-time for the PCI, he had very strong doubts about whether he should get married, or later have children. "Your sense of responsibility as well as a common sense of justice make you want to be a full participant in your own family." This is a problem strongly felt by all functionaries, but we never raise it in the party. "What kind of revolutionary, after all, cannot even arrange and live his own life according to decent principles?"

2. *Ex-worker (male), 27 years old.* "The whole concept of the functionary is in crisis now. Many new things are in the air, but the constant pressure we have been under has kept most of that out of our experience." The breakdown of old forms of militancy has not been replaced by anything, even though the "new" party we are supposed to be is more than 30 years old. There is a crisis everywhere in our families, especially when there are children. Younger functionaries usually are a lot more sensitive to these issues. [Left the apparatus in 1980]

3. *Ex-technician (male), 30 years old.* He recounts "personal agonies" before deciding to join the apparatus; very long talks with his wife ended six months of indecision. He was recently offered the chance to go to party school in Rome for a six-month course and has been in a severe personal quandary ever since. He has already put in three years as a functionary ("and they feel like ten"), and he had planned to spend a total of only five years in the apparatus. With this new investment in him, the party will make a much greater demand on his time in the future, and he in turn will feel obligated to provide it. The sense of pressure is terrible. [Left the apparatus in 1979]

4. *Ex-clerk (female), 36 years old.* Does not want to be a functionary permanently. "We are constantly told that this is a different type of party than the old clandestine, insurrectionary one. But the basic model is still one that invades your entire life [*totalizzante*]." That leaves little room for personal development which is an absolute necessity. "Your human development cannot be determined by your political life. I have effectively stopped reading literature, going to the theater, and having a personal life since becoming a functionary." [Shifted from the apparatus to public office in 1980]

5. *Ex-clerk (male), 34 years old.* "The politics of 'the personal' is *not* a false problem. Ninety percent of functionaries have crises in their own families." He names several people who were burned out by party work and ended up with broken relationships or marriages. He feels that in the past you could do this job while avoiding personal questions. But the problem is simply kept quiet in the PCI. "You know, this eliminates a whole area of human existence in our cadres, and cadres are supposed to be able to relate to people and their problems."

Such testimony casts additional light on the internal dynamics of the federation. How can some issues be felt so strongly and yet be ignored collectively? The most obvious answer is that the organizational implications of a serious review of the model of militancy would be too threatening. Could the party really call its operational codes into question without simultaneously rethinking its entire structure and mode of relating to the social and political system? To raise these questions would represent nothing less than a fundamental challenge to the whole PCI's—not just the Turinese federation's—entire way of being.

Moreover, even if there were a willingness to face this challenge on its merits, the matter is enormously complicated by generational differences inside the federation. At the time of this study, the top leaders were often no more than ten years older than the newcomers. But most of these veterans had been socialized into the party when the old values were taken for granted. They are not insensitive to the concerns expressed by their younger comrades. Yet there are such wide generational gaps in outlook and lifestyle in the federation that younger functionaries' complaints are usually met with genuine incomprehension, not to mention embarrassment that such issues are voiced at all. This does not mean that the older leaders are all simply traditionalists or chauvinists. Many have managed to reconcile their private lives with their political commitment in admirable fashion. But they view these solutions as *personal*—which of course perpetuates the radical division between public and private that the younger generation finds so problematic.

Because these differences tend to be pushed aside in the normal operations of the federation, they create a lot of tension within the party machine. When the unwritten ethic is one of compulsive activism, those leaders who try to order their priorities in a different way find themselves in a state of near-constant anxiety. As we have seen, when they attempt to balance their private and political obligations, they meet with little sympathy from the center and feel they are letting the party down. But even when they try to choose among the many political and organizational demands heaped upon them, they have a sense of never doing enough.

This is frustrating in itself but it generates outright resentment when it becomes clear to the functionaries that comrades who follow the old model and throw themselves headlong into their work, ignoring the personal costs, are those viewed with most favor at headquarters. This, of course, is the key means by which the organization can reproduce itself without changing the price it extracts from its operatives. But it does not pass unnoticed. One younger leader, who dropped out of the university to work in the apparatus, said that the ethos in the federation could at times be quite crude: those who read or try to study issues in depth are often viewed as "not really working." And many members of the apparatus echoed the thoughtful comments of another young functionary:

> We are after all only a party of human beings, so it is natural for the leaders to identify most with those who are most like them. But there is a very strong feeling that the [promotional] criteria are highly subjective, and that it is usually those who are more compulsively active, and not those with the best abilities, who advance most rapidly in the Party. (Interview, May 16, 1978.)

On one occasion, the complaints I have been documenting received a public airing. In the autumn of 1977, a meeting of the apparatus spontaneously turned into a general discussion of the intolerable pressures felt by many of the functionaries. Several people recounted exactly the same scenario to me: the veteran leaders listened to the complaints and criticism very politely, quietly, and with what some described as acute embarrassment. No one felt that there had been any real communication about the issue, and the matter was never brought up directly again.

At the end of 1980 the federation did undertake an extensive series of changes in personnel assignments and organizational practices, with the expressed goal of more satisfactorily matching people to jobs and eliminating at least some of the duplication that keeps the apparatus frantically running in circles. This certainly was not an effort to address the broader issue, but it did openly acknowledge that the demands put on the apparatus were unacceptable. It also suggests that the leaders of the federation had finally begun to realize that the older, presumably "functional," style of operation was breaking down.

WIDER IMPLICATIONS AND CONCLUSIONS

If the PCI has had a strong suit over the years, it has been flexibility and adaptability. The party may not have changed enough to satisfy its sharpest (internal and external) critics, but it definitely has changed. And this flexibility is obviously a (if not *the*) key reason for its continuing political success: with 29 percent of the vote nationwide, it is by far the largest Communist party in the Western world. Moreover, for all its limits and caution, it has, when necessary, decisively thrown its weight and mobilizing capacities into the fray. The case of abortion is instructive. The party would have gladly settled for a weaker law than the one now on the books; it supported some of the law's more progressive aspects only when strongly pushed by its own (female) militants. And the PCI definitely did everything it could to avoid the 1981 referendum that tried to revoke the abortion law, but it fought very hard to maintain abortion once the referendum became inevitable, and the dimensions of the final victory—68 percent voted to keep the law—could never have been obtained without the PCI's decisive contribution.

A good deal of the party's flexibility must be attributed to the extremely able, politically sophisticated leadership it has had over the years. But I have argued, and tried to demonstrate, that the PCI has also adapted to a changing reality from the bottom up and from the inside out. These alterations are, to be sure, slow and incomplete. Yet they do indicate that as long as the PCI remains a mass activist party with strong social roots, there is no way it can keep society's most powerful progressive currents from eventually penetrating its own structures. This was apparent in the way the Turinese federation eventually became more responsive to women's issues, and it was also evident in the younger functionaries' unwillingness to accept some of the fundamental assumptions of the old model of militancy. When we recall that Turin is far from an ideal setting for such themes to be voiced and heard, cautious optimism might even be an appropriate reaction with respect to the PCI's future.

But even this guarded optimism must immediately be qualified. I would distinguish between the likelihood of the party's adopting more open attitudes toward society versus changing its model of militancy, and note that the former is much more probable than the latter. And I would also emphasize that, even with regard to society, the *degree* of change that can be expected is relative. Both qualifications go to the very heart of what the PCI is, and is not.

The PCI is likely to continue to evolve in its attitudes toward society because it is a political party whose social presence is a vital part of its continuing identity. It simply cannot afford to get too far out of touch with the main progressive currents of Italian society, or it will lose both the electoral and mobilizational leverage that make it the major party of the Italian Left; such a loss occurred during the period of the *compromesso storico,* and the party has not yet fully recovered. The PCI's own militants, as we have seen, ride these currents enough to generate internal pressures that tend to keep the party relatively "honest."

But precisely because the PCI is a large mass party, it has an agenda and projects that are exquisitely *political.* Its constituencies are much broader than any single movement (workers included), and its projects will always reflect this fact. Its positions will never please all the components of a single movement— assuming that any such position could exist—and they certainly will never please the most advanced part of a given movement (again, workers included). For the women's movement the party is likely to be—under the best of circumstances and by no means at all times—a less reluctant ally than in the past; it will undoubtedly become a less sexist institution, but there is no chance that it will adopt a thoroughly feminist platform. Indeed, because the most advanced parts of the women's movement are not found inside the party at all, it will rarely have to face internal pressures that push it to take positions it considers too radical.

Internally, there is even less cause for optimism, although we have seen strong evidence that a refusal to accept the traditional public-private dichotomy has penetrated even the party apparatus and is part of the consciousness of working-class as well as middle-class cadre. This is an extremely important finding; it suggests that the PCI will now permanently have to live with a fundamental challenge to its entire way of being. But precisely because this is such a basic threat, it is hard to see how the party's response can be other than limited, and probably evasive. Sheer inertia will probably keep most of the old model of militancy intact for a long time to come; as we also saw, those who adopt the established style are favored within the organization—not because of any conscious conspiracy but because they are by definition "more productive" according to the reigning criteria. Yet some evidence suggests that if the PCI persists in its old ways and is too selective in its promotions, or too slow to react to new ideas, it may find itself with a dwindling pool of potential leaders.

Here we see the PCI's basic dilemma: the flexibility that accounts for so much of its success is one of the major causes of a serious threat to its continued internal operations. It absorbs new impulses from society, at times in spite of itself. But the more deeply it absorbs them, the more they undermine the mechanisms by which it functions successfully as a party. It can undoubtedly continue to operate by making only limited concessions to the new challenges that confront it on this level; in doing so, however, it mortgages its future. If the PCI does not eventually alter its internal model of militancy, its very engagement with the social sphere threatens to put it increasingly out of step with many of the most vital forces in society.

NOTES

1. In the PCI, provincial federations are the key level of organization below the national level. Confusion occasionally arises from the fact that provinces and their capital cities bear the same name in Italy. To avoid confusion, all references to "Turin" in the text will refer to the capital city (pop. 1.2 million) unless clearly qualified. General references to "the party organization" should be understood in terms of the entire federation; i.e., the province (pop. 2.4 million).

2. It is generally accepted that the turning point in the PCI's attitudes toward feminism took place at the party's National Conference of Communist Women in 1976. Numerous speakers and the conclusions of a top-ranking leader (Gerardo Chiaromonte) linked the issues of emancipation and liberation, and indicated unprecedented openness on the part of the Communists toward many of the more radical themes of the women's movement (Ravaioli 1977, 5; for more details, see Ergas 1982).

3. The interviews took place on 8 February and 31 May 1978.

4. Interview, 24 February 1978.

5. I personally witnessed, in March 1978, a successful effort by the head of the Women's Commission and members of the federation secretariat to keep UDI from joining other women's groups in Women's Day celebrations. The party wanted UDI to join the funeral cortege for a Turinese policeman killed by the Red Brigades. This was the period during which Aldo Moro was being held hostage, and the PCI was throwing all its weight behind a hard line against terrorism, at least in part to further legitimize itself as worthy of inclusion in a national governing coalition. UDI did not take part in the Women's Day activities and did send a delegation to the funeral.

6. The bulk of the material reported here was gathered in 1978; biographical references have been standardized to that date. At the time, the apparatus had 43 or 44 members (the number was constantly in flux); 41 interviews were carried out.

7. For a fascinating and well-documented discussion of the German case, see Roth (1964, chap. 5); for a wider-ranging analysis of the Italian movement's culture pertaining to work and workers, see Accornero (1980).

8. For the PCI as a whole, 60 percent of all functionaries and 20 percent of all activists reported, in 1979, that they spent at least three evenings per week in party-related activities (Sebastiani 1983, 138).

REFERENCES

Accornero, Aris. 1980. *Il Lavoro come ideologia*. Bologna: Il Mulino.

Accornero, Aris, and Vittorio Rieser. 1981. *Il Mestiere dell'avanguardia*. Bari: De Donato.

Ariemma, Iginio. 1975. *L'Impegno dei comunisti torinesi per uscire dalla crisi, per cos-*

truire un'Italia democratica e antifascista nella prospettiva del socialismo. Turin: GEP.
Associazione Piemonte Italia. 1974. *I Comuni del Piemonte 1974.* Turin: Stamperia Artistica Nazionale.
Ayassot, Giovanni (RAI technician). 1969. "Intervention in Federazione provinciale torinese del PCI, XIII Congresso Provinciale." Mainly unpaginated typescript, Turin: Archives of PCI Federation.
Berruto, Luciana (worker at Fiat Mirafiori). 1975. "Intervention in Federazione provinciale torinese del PCI, XV Congresso Provinciale." Unpaginated typescript, Turin: Archives of PCI Federation.
Berta, Giuseppe. 1981. "Il Neocapitalismo e la crisi delle organizzazioni di classe." In Aldo Agosti and Gian Mario Bravo, eds., *Storia del movimento operaio del socialismo e delle lotte sociali in Piemonte,* 4: 123–72. Bari: De Donato.
Bolaffi, Angelo. 1981. "Nuovi soggetti e progetto operaio: La 'forma' partito nelle crisi di governabilità." In Pietro Ingrao et al., *Il Partito Politico,* 147–62. Bari: De Donato.
Bonazzi, Giuseppe. 1965. "Problemi politici e condizione umana dei funzionari del PCI: Una indagine sulla federazione comunista di Torino." *Tempi Moderni* 8 (July–September): 43–77.
Castronovo, Valerio. 1977. *Il Piemonte: Storia delle regioni dall'Unità ad oggi.* Vol. 1. Turin: Einaudi.
C. F. [Comitato Federale] e C.F.C. [Commissione Federale di Controllo], Seconda Commissione. 1977. "Nota Congressuale: Partito—Movimento, XVI Congresso della Federazione torinese del PCI," 16–20 March, 22–48. Archives of PCI Federation. Mimeograph, Turin.
Clark, Martin, David Hines, and R. E. M. Irving. 1974. "Divorce—Italian Style." *Parliamentary Affairs* 27 (Autumn): 333–55.
Donolo, Carlo. 1978. "Le Forme della politica nella crisi sociale." In Alberto Martinelli and Gianfranco Pasquino, eds., *La Politica nell'Italia che cambia,* 329–50. Milan: Feltrinelli.
Ergas, Yasmine. 1982. "1968–1979—Feminism and the Italian Party System: Women's Politics in a Decade of Turmoil." *Comparative Politics* 14 (April): 253–79.
Fedele, Marcello. 1979. "Complessità sociale e partiti di massa." *Democrazia e diritto,* 19 (January–February): 25–38.
Griotti, Luciana (ILMAS worker). 1969. "Intervention in Federazione provinciale torinese del PCI, XIII Congresso Provinciale." Mainly unpaginated typescript, Turin: Archives of PCI Federation.
Gruppi, Luciano, 1973. "Matrici ideali e sociali delle formazioni neo-femministe." *Donna e Politica* 17 (May): 22–26.
Hellman, Judith Adler. 1984. "The Italian Communists, the Women's Question, and the Challenge of Feminism." *Studies in Political Economy* 13 (Spring): 57–82.
Hellman, Stephen. 1973. "Organization and Ideology in Four Italian Communist Federations." Ph.D. diss., Yale University.
———. 1975. "Generational Differences in the Bureaucratic Elite of Italian Communist Party Provincial Federations." *Canadian Journal of Political Science* 8 (March): 82–106.
———. 1977. "The Longest Campaign: Italian Communist Strategy and the Elections of 1976." In Howard R. Penniman, ed., *Italy at the Polls: The Parliamentary Elections of 1976,* 155–82. Washington, D.C.: American Enterprise Institute.

————. 1980. "Il PCI e l'ambigua eredità dell'autunno caldo a Torino." *Il Mulino* 29 (March–April): 246–95.

Izzo, Francesca. 1977. "Personale e politico in un impegno di tipo nuovo." In Giorgio Amendola et al., *I giovani e la crisi della società*, 57–65. Rome: Editori Riuniti.

Lange, Peter. 1979. "Crisis and Consent, Change and Compromise: Dilemmas of Italian Communism in the 1970s." *West European Politics* 2 (October): 110–32.

Magri, Lucio. 1970. "Problems of the Marxist Theory of the Revolutionary Party." *New Left Review* 60 (March–April): 97–128. (Originally published in *Critica marxista* 1 [September–December 1963]: 61–102.)

Michels, Roberto. 1959. *Political Parties*. New York: Dover.

Minucci, Adalberto (Regional Secretary of Piedmont). 1977. "Federazione provinciale torinese del PCI, XVI Congresso Provinciale." Typescript, Turin: Archives of PCI Federation.

"Mozione organizzativa." 1969. "Federazione provinciale torinese del PCI XIII Congresso Provinciale." Mainly unpaginated typescript, Turin: Archives of PCI Federation.

Pasquino, Gianfranco. 1982. "Il PCI nel sistema politico italiano degli anni settanta." *Il Mulino* 284 (November–December): 859–97.

Pastore, Lia (5th Section). 1969. "Intervention in Federazione provinciale torinese del PCI, XIII Congresso Provinciale." Mainly unpaginated typescript, Turin: Archives of PCI Federation.

PCI. 1979. Federazione torinese. *Documento per il XVII Congresso della federazione torinese del PCI*. Turin: PCI.

————. 1986. Sezione statistica, documentazione e vicerea. *Organizzazione dati statistiche*. Rome: ITER.

Petruccioli, Claudio. 1979. "Democrazia statuale e democrazia di partito." *Democrazia e Diritto* 19 (January–February): 5–17.

Pugno, Emilio, and Sergio Garavini. 1974. *Gli anni duri alla Fiat: La resistenza sindacale e la ripresa*. Turin: Einaudi.

Ravaioli, Carla. 1977. *La Questione femminile: Intervista col PCI*. 3d ed. Milan: Bompiani.

Rosolen, Mariangela (Fiat officeworker). 1975. "Intervention in Federazione provinciale torinese del PCI, XV Congresso Provinciale." Unpaginated typescript, Turin: Archives of PCI Federation.

Roth, Guenther. 1964. *The Social Democrats in Imperial Germany*. Totowa, N.J.: Bedminster Press.

Sani, Giacomo. 1977. "The Italian Electorate in the Mid-1970s: Beyond Tradition?" In Howard R. Penniman, ed., *Italy at the Polls: The Parliamentary Elections of 1976*, 110–20. Washington, D.C.: American Enterprise Institute.

Sebastiani, Chiara. 1983. "I Funzionari." In Aris Accornero et al., *L'Identità comunista: I Militanti, le strutture, la cultura del PCI*, 79–177. Rome: Editori Riuniti.

Stame, Federico. 1977. *Società civile e critica delle istituzioni*. Milan: Feltrinelli.

7 Response to Feminism in the Italian Parliament: Divorce, Abortion, and Sexual Violence Legislation

KAREN BECKWITH

A crucial and troubling question in evaluating the impact of feminist movements concerns the responsiveness of governments to the legislative demands of those movements. To what extent can feminist movements expect to influence non feminist, or even anti feminist, parliaments to produce legislative relief for employment, housing, and education discrimination based on sex; for sexual harassment and violence against women; for inequitable and oppressive economic conditions among women; for women's lack of access to safe contraception and abortion; and for women's inferior status within the family, religious institutions, and the larger society? If parliaments are one of the appropriate arenas in which feminists should militate for change, then how ought we to evaluate the success of feminists who bring pressure upon parliaments?

This essay examines the case of the Italian parliament and its responsiveness to the demands of the Italian feminist movement; in particular, it focuses upon three major issues of special importance to Italian women: the liberalization of divorce, the legalization of abortion, and the proposal to reform the Italian penal code to allow the state to deal effectively and positively with violence directed against women.

An evaluation of this relationship requires, first, a definition of what constitutes "feminist issues" as a special and separate group of concerns; second, an understanding of what is meant by responsiveness; and third, a measure of the responsiveness of parliament, including a consideration of the forces to which parliament is responding (that is, to the feminist movement, to political parties, or to something else).

By "feminist issues," in this essay, we will understand a collection of political concerns, the commonality of which is their challenge to the existing legal, eco-

A slightly different version of this paper was presented at the Conference Group on Italian Politics meeting on "Institutional Performance in Italy," 14–19 June 1983, sponsored by the National Science Foundation, the Rockefeller Foundation, and the Consiglio Nazionale di Ricerche of Italy.

153

nomic, and social relationships between women and men in Italian life. In addition, the direction of this challenge is feminist; that is, these issues benefit women primarily or specifically, by seeking either to promote greater measures of equality between the sexes or to offer a wider variety of life options for women (Giele 1977, 3–5) by addressing the particularities of women's lives. Examples of issues that seek to promote greater measures of equality between the sexes include the law on employment parity and, in part, divorce legislation that makes adultery of the husband grounds for divorce, as well as adultery of the wife. Examples of issues that promote a wider variety of life options for women include abolition of protective or paternalistic laws, the repeal of *matrimonio riparatore* laws,[1] the 1978 abortion legislation, and the promotion of legislation against sexual violence.

It has been the case in Italy that women and the feminist movement have not always been the initiators of feminist legislative proposals; feminist issues that have been raised in parliament are often the result of initiatives by the Italian Left, rather than by the Center or Right parties, although this need not always be the case.[2] Therefore, classifying an issue as feminist is not dependent upon its introduction into parliament by female legislators or the feminist movement, nor is the classification itself intended to limit discussion to the parties of the Italian Left.

"Responsiveness" concerns the connection between mobilization in support of an issue and its legislative success. First, to what extent have feminist issues been promoted in the Chamber of Deputies? Second, have these issues been the result of pressures from female deputies, from political parties, or from the feminist movement? That is, is the promotion of these issues the result of mobilization and, if so, of whom: feminists, *deputate,* or parties?[3] Third, has the promotion of certain specific issues been more successful as the result of mobilization of one of these groups rather than another or others?

We can speak of greater or less responsiveness by examining feminist issues according to their source and their success. Greatest responsiveness is achieved when mobilized women make demands to which the Chamber responds; least responsiveness occurs when a mobilized group's demand is rejected or ignored or when the Chamber on its own enacts legislation concerning feminist issues.

In evaluating responsiveness, we will focus on three feminist legislative issues: divorce, abortion, and sexual violence. These represent major feminist issues of the 1970s and 1980s in Italy and offer a good test of responsiveness, since women, feminists, female legislators, and political parties were mobilized to different degrees in support of these proposals. Before turning to a discussion of these issues, however, we require a brief outline of the relevant political forces in postwar Italy.

The Italian Republic was founded in 1946 with the establishment of the Constituent Assembly, whose dual responsibilities were to govern a nation defeated in war and to write a republican constitution[4] for a state whose political experience from 1922 to 1943 had been monolithically fascist. After liberation, the

TABLE 7-1
PERCENTAGE OF SEATS IN THE CHAMBER OF DEPUTIES, FOR SELECTED PARTIES

	Christian Democrats	Communists	Socialists	Republicans	Liberals	Radicals
1948	53.3	22.8	9.1	1.7	2.6	—
1953	44.4	24.2	12.7	0	2.4	—
1958	45.8	23.7	14.8	0	3.0	—
1963	41.3	26.3	9.8	1.0	6.0	—
1968	42.1	27.1	14.4[a]	1.4	4.9	—
1972	42.1	27.8	9.7	2.4	3.2	—
1976	41.6	35.2	9.0	2.2	1.0	1.0
1979	41.6	30.6	9.7	2.5	1.4	2.7
1983	35.7	27.3	11.6	4.6	2.5	1.7

Source: *I Deputati e Senatori del Nono Parlamento Repubblicano* (Rome: La Navicella, 1983), lxxxi–lxxxiv.
[a]The Socialist Party and the Social Democratic Party submitted joint lists in 1968 as the Unified Socialist Party (PSU).

Communist (PCI) and Socialist (PSI) parties sprang from the ashes of two de-cades' prohibition on political parties, with the return of activists exiled in the Soviet Union, France, and elsewhere. The confessional Christian Democratic party (DC), whose early precursor was the Partito Popolare, was established, based on the militants of Catholic Action, a "non-political" Catholic organiza-tion that had managed to maintain itself during the fascist period as a result of the DC's agreements to the Lateran Pacts.[5] Other smaller parties, such as the Repub-lican and Liberal parties, reconstituted themselves. This yielded the party bal-ance in the Constituent Assembly shown in Table 7-1, with the DC, PCI, and PSI attracting the bulk of the votes.

The election of members to the Constituent Assembly involved what may have been the most important feminist issue in Italian postwar history: the enfranchisement of women, which came as the result of an agreement between Alcide De Gasperi, leader of the DC, and Palmiro Togliatti, head of the PCI. The results of this arrangement were that Italian women were enfranchised without having first mobilized themselves around the issue, and that the parties of the Left were, at least for several decades, electorally disadvantaged because large numbers of women cast their first votes for the Christian Democrats, as they were widely expected to do (Beckwith 1981; Dogan 1963; Galli and Prandi 1970).

The parties that would come to dominate Italian political life—the DC and PCI—each sought to mobilize and to educate the masses of Italian women as Italy was liberated from the Germans at the end of the war, the DC founding the Center for Italian Women (CIF) and the Communists and Socialists organizing the Union of Italian Women (UDI). While neither the DC, PCI, nor PSI has been a feminist party, the first two each has its own unique position (or positions) on the role of women in Italian social and political life; each party considers women crucial to the Italian political scene, although in different ways. Through CIF and UDI, the two major parties sought to mobilize Italian women in support of their parties, primarily in terms of electoral support, although activism in UDI has occasionally been a route to a PCI seat in the Chamber (Beckwith 1979; 1981).

While the Christian Democrats have always controlled at least a plurality of seats in parliament, one of the major issues of postwar Italy has been the possibility that the Communist party, the largest in Western Europe, might constitute the government. The Socialist party, which submitted a joint list with the PCI in the first parliamentary elections, was then the major party of the Left, but in the 1953 elections the PCI was able to gain the dominant position on the Left that it has held ever since. The tensions between the DC and the PCI, their electoral competition (where the votes of women have become increasingly important), and the various strategies of the PCI in its attempt to enter government (such as the "historic compromise"; see Chapter 6) all mark the contemporary Italian political scene and hence condition the possibilities for feminist influence in political life and in parliament.

Since 1962, however, another major question has concerned the role of the PSI in government; it participated in the 1963–66 governments as part of the DC's "opening to the Left," primarily as a way of forestalling PCI political and electoral advances. The first non-DC prime minister was elected in 1981 (the Republican Giovanni Spadolini) and the first PSI prime minister, Bettino Craxi, was elected in 1983, after parliamentary elections that gave the PCI 29.9 percent of the vote to the DC's 32.9 percent, the DC its most severe electoral defeat, and the PSI a very minor but significant increase in seats. The PSI under Craxi had been responsible for the fall of the Fanfani government and the call for new elections as part of its strategy for claiming the prime ministership, a project on which the party had been working since Craxi's assumption of PSI leadership in 1976. The PSI, a middle-class-oriented, left-of-center party which, like the French Socialists, has made appeals to teachers and other white-collar workers, has sought to integrate members of the political movements that arose in Italy in the 1970s— including women—but that effort has been strikingly unsuccessful (Pasquino 1977).

In sum, a political culture with multiple cleavages—class, ideological, subcultural, religious (in the sense of a religious-secular split), and regional, among others—has given rise to multiple political parties, two of which have always considered women important, if inferior, political actors; their attention to women as a group has been limited by the fact that women's political influence and activism were not given emphasis, aside from women's ability to affect electoral outcome. This limited attention, however, has provided women with explicit, if unenforced, constitutional protections, as well as a basis for laying claim to rights to political influence and power. That claim has been most visible and most dramatic throughout the 1970s and 1980s, with the rise of a mass-based feminist movement, the increased representation of women in the Chamber (primarily as left-wing-non-Socialist deputies), the defection of female voters from the DC, the internal political and ideological transformation of UDI, and the relative proliferation of legislation and referenda on women's issues. It is to a consideration of three of these major issues that we now turn.

FEMINIST INFLUENCE: DIVORCE, ABORTION, AND SEXUAL VIOLENCE

To reiterate, responsiveness to feminist issues is the extent to which the Chamber of Deputies enacts legislation as the result of pressure from Italian women, whether members of the feminist movement or female party activists (either functionaries or *deputate*). The three major issues under consideration—divorce, abortion, and sexual violence—are especially useful for examination, since they span two decades of Italian politics (1965–84) and the period of development and growth of the contemporary feminist movement. Each of these issues fits the definition of a feminist issue, since legislation and legislative proposals concerning each has benefited women, whether by promoting greater sex equality, by expanding women's life options, or both. In examining divorce, abortion, and sexual violence, we will consider the source of the legislative proposal, the interaction between the source and the parties in parliament, and the legislative result. The DC is excluded from this examination, since the party has opposed reform on all these issues; we will focus on the behavior of the PCI and the PSI in response to women's demands.

Divorce

Until legislation provided for civil divorce in 1970, divorce in Italy was regulated by the Catholic Church, empowered by Article VII of the constitution, which incorporated the Lateran Pacts negotiated under Mussolini into the document. Divorce reform legislation was introduced in parliament in 1965 by Loris Fortuna,[6] a PSI deputy; his bill would have provided for civil divorce after five years' legal separation. The bill, while not actively supported by the PSI, was not opposed by it, and a number of laical groups and parties mobilized support for the proposal through the Italian League for Divorce (Lega Italiana per il divorzio, or LID), an interparty single-issue group organized in 1966. LID, using political pressure tactics that have become the trademark of the Italian Radical party (whose secretary, parliamentary deputy and charismatic leader Marco Pannella, was LID's first secretary), organized a mixed, extraparliamentary coalition of intellectuals, white-collar workers, and members of the middle class. As a result of these efforts, the Chamber approved the proposal in 1969, the Senate a year later (Clark, Hine, and Irving 1974; Marzani 1980; Teodori, Ignazi, and Panebianco, 1977).

During the three years that LID was mobilizing, its major focus was on achieving divorce reform as a necessity in a modernizing society, and on rearranging (or recognizing the rearrangement of) the relationship between Catholic and lay forces in Italian society. In addition to the achievement of legal civil divorce, a second success of LID and the "new Radicals" was the establishment of a new form of doing politics, one that was both parliamentary and extraparliamentary and characterized by "individual deputies or senators, with a formula of 'elected-represented' rapport with the people, much closer to the Anglo-Saxon tradition than to [the Italian, where] all is centralized in party mediation or in corporate interest groups" (Teodori, Ignazi, and Panebianco 1977, 82).

The legislative divorce struggle, though it concerned a feminist issue, was not a case of parties or parliament responding to the demands of women.[7] While some women were involved in the leadership of the Radicals (Teodori, Ignazi, and Panebianco 1977, 98–99), the legislative proposals were organized and promoted primarily by men, either in the Chamber or through LID; the thrust of the divorce reform, which had the effect of benefiting women specifically and particularly, was to reorder church-state relations and to provide relief for the thousands of Italians who were already legally separated or divorced de facto.[8] Organizationally and in terms of propaganda, the woman question was not at issue whatsoever.[9] While Teodori and his colleagues (1977) mention the youth and student movements as being part of the fervor of the time, the feminist movement had not yet resurfaced, and there was no organized women's group pushing for divorce reform. It was neither initiated by women, nor in the legislative struggle, supported by women, organized or not.

A referendum to repeal the reforms in 1974 did reveal surprisingly widespread support among the female mass public for the legislation (which was by that time four years old and had been in discussion in parliament and the nation for almost a decade), but there was less evidence that the female mass public supported the proposal for civil divorce *before* it became law (Fabris 1977, chap. 3); it was feared that the traditionally DC-supporting female electorate would, following the instructions of priest and party, vote "yes" for the defeat of the law in the 1974 referendum.

Nevertheless, given the lack of clear female involvement in the legislative struggle for divorce, this case is not one of party responsiveness to women.[10] Despite the fact that divorce is part of the woman question in Italy, its liberalization occurred without significant female involvement.

Abortion

The abortion issue is more clearly a feminist issue by virtue of the specificity of procreation to women and the impact of pregnancy and birth upon women's life options. Unlike the divorce issue, the debate surrounding legislative abortion reform was concomitant with the reemergence of the feminist movement and with the aftermath of the success in defending the divorce law in the 1974 referendum.[11] In large measure because of the experience of that referendum, the abortion reform struggle was marked by the involvement of a variety of organized women's groups: the MLD (Movimento della Liberazione della Donna, associated until 1978 with the Radical party), UDI, independent feminists, and female activists in the major Left parties. During the period of legislation on the issue

(1973–78), the position of the female mass public was unclear; it was not until the 1981 abortion referenda results that the pro-abortion sentiment of Italian women was clarified (Fabris 1977, 151–53). The involvement of organized women continued in the abortion referenda; while parts of the MLD were split and in opposition to other organized women, the "Committee for the Defense of Law 194" was formed in 1980 by female activists from the PCI, the PSI, and other Left and lay parties, who coordinated their efforts with UDI and part of the MLD. The committee proposed to "assume the initiative for the entirety of the law and to commit women to repel the various attacks" to which the law had been subject (Comitato di Difesa della Legge 194, 1982).[12]

Abortion reform was first proposed in 1972, when the PCI introduced a resolution which—according to a female PCI functionary in the Women's Commission—was a rotten piece of work, opposed by women in the party, and quickly withdrawn. The PSI, through Loris Fortuna, introduced a bill on abortion reform in 1973, and in 1975 the PCI and the Social Democratic Party (PSDI) introduced their own proposals. That same year, the Constitutional Court declared Article 546 of the penal code unconstitutional, thereby legalizing abortion in cases where the woman's health was placed in jeopardy by the pregnancy. In April 1975 the Republican Party, the Liberal Party, and the DC submitted their own proposals on abortion, and debate of the various resolutions began in the Health and Justice committees of the Chamber. The latter half of the year was marked by the Radicals' circulation of petitions calling for a national referendum to annul the old abortion law (written by the fascists) and hence to legalize abortion. The dissolution of parliament and the 1976 political elections postponed the referendum possibility; the PCI increased its share of seats in Parliament; and in 1978, after several setbacks (including an unexpected rejection by the Senate in June 1977), abortion in Italy became legal under certain limited conditions.

The abortion legislation of 1978 repealed various sections of the fascist penal code, the Codice Rocco, and legalized abortion during the first trimester of pregnancy for reasons of the woman's physical or psychological health; of her economic, social, or family circumstances; of possible malformation of the fetus; or of "the circumstances of conception" (that is, rape or incest). After the first trimester, abortion was legal only in cases of severe threat to the woman's life or of a fetus deformed to the extent of severely impairing the mother's physical or psychological health. These conditions of the new law were a major improvement on the previous law, which declared abortion a "crime against the race"; however, Law 194 did not give the woman full freedom of reproductive choice, requiring her to get approval from a physician and, if she were under 18 years of age, written permission from both parents ("Norme per la tutela sociale della maternità" 1978; Coordinamento femminile del PSI 1982).

Feminists and female activists and deputies within the Left parties objected to the various restrictions which were placed on women's access to abortion: restrictions based on age, time, availability of hospital space, and availability of physicians who did not "conscientiously object" to abortion.[13] It is still unclear, however, *which* organized women were least willing to follow their party's line in making compromises. At least one female activist in the PSI was highly critical of the role of UDI in what she saw as a lack of resistance to restrictions on young women's abortion rights and to the conscientious objector provision.[14] Within the PCI, female activists pressed for the most liberal form of legislation possible but recognized the limitations that opposing political forces imposed upon the possibilities for abortion reform. The PCI strategy in the mid-1970s was to get the best abortion law that could be achieved under the circumstances, and to try to improve the law later.[15] Pro-abortion PCI women faced two problems in pressing the party for liberal abortion reform. The first was the cleavage within the party, based on sex but also partly on generation, that divided young female militants from older male functionaries, party leaders, and conservative members, for whom issues such as divorce and abortion were not easily accommodated by a class analysis. The second difficulty was the lack of visibility of prominent PCI women, such as Nilde Iotti, on the abortion issue.[16] UDI activists in Bologna, for example, blamed women in the PCI parliamentary delegation for not forcing the party to be more resolute in face of the temptation to pander to DC opposition. The suggestion that female PCI deputies helped to prevent the passage of an even less liberal law was completely rejected, and the possibility that PCI *deputate* helped shape more feminist language in the law than the party might otherwise have tolerated was treated very skeptically. UDI activists argued that the prominent women in the PCI were prominent as individuals, that they were not symbolic of and did not generally act for women in the PCI or in Italian life.

Women were also engaged in bringing extraparliamentary pressure to bear upon the parties negotiating abortion reform. The Radical party and the MLD circulated petitions to abrogate the old abortion law by national referendum, which would circumvent parliament completely. UDI, throughout 1975, organized a collection of data and women's personal testimonies on maternity, sexuality, and abortion in Italy, published as *Sesso Amaro* (Bitter Sex); the book was well-received and dramatized the extent of illegal abortions and the need for reform. Throughout the period of the mid-1970s, the MLD organized demonstrations, *autodenuncie,*[17] and a petition (in May 1971) for a popular initiative on abortion (Teodori, Ignazi, and Panebianco 1977, 111–12), as well as abortion counseling clinics in various cities; these provided information about abortion and arranged "abortion flights" to London. The problematic relationship between women's parliamentary and extraparliamentary activism was demonstrated during an all-female, all-party march in Bologna in 1977 (organized by UDI), where women rallied in support of abortion (and in opposition to parties' reluctance to act) at the headquarters of all major parties in the city—including the PCI, which was the final site of the protest. En route, a major argument erupted, and continued later at UDI headquarters, concerning the political (in)correctness of criticizing the PCI. Older UDI members were especially horrified at having the PCI included as a target and at the behavior of some younger members, who had threatened to tear up their PCI membership cards, shouting "Fools, fools!"

The difference in parliamentary responsiveness to issues of divorce and abortion reform was that the latter issue was supported from its inception by organized women, inside and outside parliament as well as inside and outside political parties. While abortion reform initiative was attempted in 1971 by the MLD, abortion legislation was introduced, eventually, by all major parties in parliament; hence the institution became the focus of women's organizing efforts. How effective was parliament in responding to the pressure of organized women? In the case of abortion, we have to consider the following facts.

First, political parties, especially the PCI, had the ability to resist or to modify pressure from their own internal activists and functionaries (including, perhaps, UDI). The PCI leadership, whose following was split on the issue (by sex and by generation), could demonstrate to female activists the *internal* constraints the party faced in moving quickly on abortion; the party also had to grapple with the difficulties of presenting abortion within the framework of a nonfeminist (not necessarily antifeminist) class analysis (J. Hellman 1984).

Second, the PCI was able to point to the *external* constraints faced by the party in promoting abortion: namely, the strong resistance of conservative and confessional parties and the adamant opposition of the Catholic Church to any change in abortion law.[18] The PCI was able to ask its young female militants to moderate their demands in order to get any liberalization at all, with the hope of making additional reforms in the future. (Given that the PCI hoped to repeat its 1976 electoral success in the next elections, this was not a totally unreasonable demand.) Again, the PCI responded to the demands of its young female activists by pushing for abortion reform, but at the price of requiring militants to respond likewise to the demands and requirements of the party's position in parliament and of its internal dynamic.

Third, in the case of the feminist movement (MLD and independent feminists), parliament was less responsive, because these groups were independent of direct party control and discipline and because they demanded more. While women in the PCI, PSI, and UDI were trying, to greater or lesser degrees, to resist age and conscientious objection restrictions on abortion, the MLD and independent feminist groups wanted, in addition, no requirement for prior approval by a physician, access to abortions in clinics as well as hospitals, and no restrictions on length of term; their demand was for the woman's freedom to choose safe, free, accessible abortion (Frabotta 1978). The parties in parliament could not as easily control these demands (and a closer examination of the process would probably reveal that these demands helped female party activists push more successfully for the less liberal reforms); the claims of the autonomous feminists were rejected by parliament early on.

We can conclude, then, that in the case of abortion, political parties were somewhat responsive to the demands of organized women: abortion reform was achieved by the impetus of the feminist movement and the organized pressure of female party activists. The response, however, came at a price: (1) control of the abortion debate by the parties in parliament; (2) the moderation of the demands of women active in the PCI, PSI, and UDI; and (3) the exclusion of direct influence by the independent feminist movement.

Sexual Violence

In 1981, after the successful defense of the reformed abortion law against two referenda designed to annul it, the feminist movement, in coalition with UDI and women in the Left parties, organized a national petition drive[19] for a popular initiative of a model law prohibiting and redefining violence against women.[20] The model law, drafted by feminist lawyers, was initiated with more than 300,000 signatures.

The significance of the initiative must be viewed from the perspective of the feminist movement's experience in the abortion struggle. Organized women did not directly initiate the parliamentary abortion debate; rather, they worked through political parties to which they had preestablished ties and obligations. As a result, women were limited in their ability to bring pressure on the parties to achieve a more liberal abortion law. A major revelation of these limitations came in 1977, when the Senate rejected the abortion bill already passed in the Chamber, despite expectations (based on party strength) that the bill would pass. This promoted a widespread and intense debate among feminists concerning the relationship between the movement and political parties, particularly parties of the Left, a debate that also reverberated inside the PCI, PSI, and UDI (Boccia and Pitch 1980; Bolaffi et al. 1982; Chiaromonte 1982; Ergas and Manieri 1977; Fraire, Gramagli, and Repetto 1977; Trupìa 1982). The debate concerned (and concerns) the extent to which parties act as intermediaries between the movement and parliament, and between the movement and political change on behalf of women. In the context of this debate, the feminist movement sought to introduce a feminist issue directly into parliament: the issue of sexual violence.

At this point in Italian law, there are no provisions for protecting women against sexual violence; rather, the existing law, Title IX of the penal code (written in 1930), prohibits "crimes against public morality and right living" (*buon costume*). The penal code defines these crimes as attacks on society rather than on the physical and psychological person of a woman. "Society" and "morality" are offended when carnal knowledge is had of anyone under the age of 14, of anyone under the age of 16 by someone in a position of authority vis-à-vis the victim, or anyone mentally ill; society is also injured when public officials have carnal knowledge of persons in their official charge or when a man has violent carnal knowledge of a woman to whom he is not married. If, however, the rapist makes restitution to the victim's family and to the victim by marrying her, "all execution [of the law] and its penal effects cease" ("On Crimes against Public Morality" 1930, art. 519–44). The effect of the law, given an increase in reported rapes and in incidents of gang rape, is as follows: (1) the crime goes un-prosecuted if the victim, for whatever reason, chooses not to prosecute; (2) women who are raped must show evidence of violence employed in the crime; (3) gang rape is not mentioned as a separate crime; (4) rape in marriage is not possible; and (5) an act of rape is *not* considered a crime against society if the victim restores the honor of the state by marrying her assailant (*matrimonio riparatore*).

In the late 1970s the issue of violence against women began to be of concern to the Italian feminist movement, which initiated an analysis of sexual violence. The nature of sexual violence was "always less sexual and always more violent" (Bottari 1982), an attack upon women's freedom, self-determination, and sexuality, and a political statement concerning the role of all women in Italy, not just a particular victim. Therefore, the issue of sexual violence in Italy was seen as an attack not *on* society but on women, as individual human beings and as a group, *by* society, through the agency of particular men, who were not unusually "monstrous" or "maniacal" or "fascist" but who were acting out a particularly violent variety of society's general treatment of women: "At base, [sexual violence] constitutes a total lack of respect for the human person, an unequivocal wounding of another's dignity, and hence, a harm to the collective freedom and dignity" (MLD 1981, 1).

This analysis of sexual violence was prompted by a series of events throughout Italy in the late 1970s. In 1976, a "Center against Violence" was founded in Rome, following the verification of 17 rapes in the summer months alone.[21] In 1977 the trial in Rome of the assailant of Claudia Caputi served as a rallying point for mass demonstrations against sexual violence and as a starting point for the feminist movement's legal involvement as an affected party in rape trials. In 1978 the MLD, with the feminist journal *Effe*, organized an International Convention on Violence, which involved 3,000 women in the process of defining and coordinating the feminist movement's plan of work against sexual violence.

The plan was unique in three ways. First, the movement itself was initiating action and was in this case the indisputable source of activism around an issue clearly articulated as feminist—an issue that was not the result of general societal changes such as unemployment, urbanization, or migration but the result of the general patriarchal relationships in Italy between women and men, and between women and the state.[22]

Second, the plan was unusual because the feminist movement proposed legislation directly—without the mediating force of any political party—through a popular legislative initiative and hence presented parliament with a specific task: consideration of a model law on sexual violence, one that was not the result of compromise with such nonfeminist institutions or groups as political parties.

Third, the feminist movement did not rely only on legislative work but organized a second, concomitant effort at modifying the "custom and mentality prevalent in our society," publicizing the issue in the movement's own terms in hopes of mobilizing public opinion in favor of the model law:

> We want . . . to sensitize public opinion . . . and to open a debate on the problem of violence, [to make it clear] that the urgency of the changes we indicate is the urgent necessity of all. It is useless to mislead ourselves [in thinking] that in Parliament they can pass changes that public opinion is unready to accept: also because it is not true that legislators represent the best and most evolved part of the country. Too often, in fact, they have given the country laws which are surely more backward in respect to the general civil consciousness: the abortion law is a clear example. (MLD 1981, 4–6).

Since, therefore, reliance on parliament alone would be fruitless and self-defeating, it was necessary to transform and inform public opinion.

The model law, prohibiting "crimes of sexual and physical violence against the person," would supersede almost all of Title IX of the penal code (conserving only those portions specifying sexual violence against some minors and the mentally ill as crimes), and it redefines sexual violence as a "crime against a person" rather than a crime against public morals. Rape and other violent acts that manifest themselves sexually are defined as a single type of crime (including gang rape, rape within marriage, and rape of prostitutes), and the victim would not be required to prosecute personally; the crime would be automatically prosecuted by the state as soon as it became known. The trial would be public; questions concerning the private life of the victim would be inadmissible in court; and the feminist movement would be a formal, legal party to any and all such trials, on behalf of Italian women. *Matrimonio riparatore* would be abolished.

How did parliament and the parties respond to the feminists' legislative initiative? The PCI almost immediately introduced through its deputy Angela Bottari, its own proposal on sexual violence signed by 35 PCI colleagues, entitled "New Regulations for the Protection of Sexual Freedom." The PCI proposal varied from the feminist initiative in several ways. The most important and general difference was the PCI's removal of sexual violence from the context of violence against women as a logical result of patriarchy, replacing it in a context of general societal violence. The PCI also left the decision to prosecute to the individual and the decision about a public trial to the courts; the formal legal role of the feminist movement in sexual violence cases was rejected.

The PSI likewise reset the debate in terms more general to Italian society (crimes "repugnant to democracy") and less specific to the realities of Italian women. The PSI's "Modifications in the Existing Legislation on Sexual Violence" proposed minor but significant changes: it changed the language to "crimes against sexual freedom"; it advocated the publication of convictions, naming the assailant but not the victim, the abrogation of various sections of the old law (*matrimonio riparatore,* for example). The PSI also proposed a "legal role for women's associations which represent collective interests" (Provincial and Regional Women's Coordination 1979, 30–31) but did not specify *which* associations or that those associations be *feminist.*

In all, seven separate proposals on the issue were introduced in parliament, which had been struggling to compose a single, unified bill for consideration. The task was made more difficult by a series of amendments proposed by the DC, which wanted a unified law covering "crimes against morality" and tried to insert the question of pornography into the debate—which, since the parties are widely split on that issue, would have meant defeat of the entire reform bill (Polara 1983).[23]

There had been no legislative reform on sexual violence by 1983 since the political elections of that year killed the issue. Although new elections were not called in an attempt to avoid resolution of the proposed reforms of the penal code (as had been the case with both divorce and abortion reform), the issue has remained at best inconclusive; a proposal by the PCI and the Sinistra Indipendente was "approved" in the Chamber of Deputies' Justice Committee only because the PSI, DC, and MSI-DN abstained on the vote ("Violenza Sessuale approvato" 1984),[24] and the Chamber passed a modified version of the bill later in 1984. However, an evaluation of the fate of the initiative on sexual violence can be proffered, with the understanding that the call for new elections was not related to an impending success of the initiative.

First, the PCI and the PSI both responded (the PCI immediately) by introducing their own legislation, and both parties had their *deputate* (in the case of the PSI, *deputata*) visible and active. The issue had been difficult for the parties of the Left to control because, technically, the feminist actors were autonomous and offered few points of contact for the parties, which are more structured and formal.[25] Nonetheless, the parties attempted to gain control by redefining the issue on their own terms.

The extent to which the feminist movement can force increased responsiveness to their model law will be determined by the outcome of the movement's second plan: its effort to mobilize support *outside* parliament, in public opinion. This second plan becomes crucial in the postelection period, when parties must reintroduce their proposals on the issue; they are unlikely to do so without the pressure that the feminist movement can bring to bear by mobilizing public opinion and political participation. Given that UDI in particular is less active and coordinated nationally than was the case before its disorganization (Beckwith 1985) and the 1983 elections, the chances for the extensive mobilization necessary for the reintroduction of proposals and their serious reconsideration in parliament are poor. The feminist issue in this case was proposed independently of political parties by a unified feminist movement, concurrent with an attempt to organize and educate public opinion. This unique route to legislative change and the feminist movement's attempt to evade *party* control of the issue have yielded results which, at this particular time, look little different from those obtained through more conventional means.

POLITICAL PARTIES AND RESPONSIVENESS TO
FEMINIST ISSUES

In evaluating the responsiveness of Italian political parties to feminist issues such as divorce, abortion, and sexual violence, we need to consider three questions: First, have political parties done more to promote feminist issues than they have to impede them? Second, have some parties been more responsive than others to the feminist movement? Third, are political parties more likely to respond to feminism if female activists struggle through established party channels, or if they bypass those channels and attempt to legislate directly through the initiative provision in the constitution?

The answer to the first question seems murkily clear. Political parties do promote feminist issues; in some cases, parties promote feminist issues in the absence of an organized feminist movement (as with the PSI and divorce reform), or they propose bills that offend organized women (as with the PSI's proposal in 1980 to draft women). In other cases, where the issue was raised by women, as with abortion and sexual violence, parties reply by introducing their own versions of proposed legislation (in the case of sexual violence, seven parties responded with as many separate proposals). However, these responses were modifications of the original feminist initiative (or evasions or rejections of the original proposal, as in the case of the DC). On the three major feminist issues under study here, parties promoted more than they impeded, but they responded on their own terms, none of which are feminist.

It is certainly the case that some parties have been more responsive than others to demands from the feminist movement. The DC, for example, is clearly an antifeminist party, opposing or attempting to sabotage feminist issues considered in the Chamber. Furthermore, the DC, having lost the battles in parliament, initiated two national referenda to abrogate reform laws on divorce and abortion (and lost again). Nor has the PSI been as responsive to feminist issues as it might appear at first glance. The party has made much of its introduction of divorce and abortion proposals in the Chamber, but its lack of contact and connection with organized women, inside as well as outside the party, makes it unresponsive; it shoots proposals on feminist issues into parliament without having a base among organized women to lend substance and strength to those proposals.[26]

The PCI, it seems to me, is a special case here, because of its ideology and its historical relationship to organized women in both UDI and the party. In addition, it is the strongest Left political party and the only party capable of challenging the legislative power of the DC. These factors have made it attractive to some feminists as well as a major target for criticism. The PCI has, among all the parties considered here, the best record of policy responsiveness to feminist issues, but this responsiveness has been limited by two major factors, neither of which is likely to change in the near future: (1) the PCI's legislative efforts occur in the context of DC opposition, and (2) the PCI is a Eurocommunist party based on the working class, both ideologically and politically. This second factor is particularly important. Given the PCI's ideology, it will always be more responsive to organized feminists than other parties, but it will also always place its response in the context of that ideology—that is, on its own terms—and hence will never be able to respond to feminist issues to the satisfaction of feminists.

In the case of sexual violence legislation, even if the feminist movement is able to succeed in mobilizing public opinion, the PCI's pattern of response on its own (nonfeminist) terms is likely to endure. To respond otherwise, it would have to become a very different kind of party.

The problems for feminists seeking social and political change are immense. If the PCI is the party most responsive to feminist pressure, the future for feminist success appears bleak. With the death of Enrico Berlinguer,[27] the leadership of the party (and perhaps its direction) is uncertain; with the political (but not necessarily electoral) success of the PSI in capturing the prime ministership, the PCI is not likely to come any closer to power than it did under DC prime ministers. What Samuel Barnes said of Italy in the late 1970s is still the case:

> The policy-making game on the national level was largely restricted to players who had been close to the dominant party in the electoral game, augmented by individuals, groups and institutions that carried societal weight and whose interests did not clash with or greatly threaten those of the dominant party. (Barnes 1977, 12)

Since the feminist movement is not among those "players close to the dominant party" but in fact is found repugnant by the DC, the movement alone is not likely to have much success and will be limited in influencing policy through the PCI's mode of responsiveness. Since parties are still the major representatives of political interests and issues, it is impossible for the feminist movement to avoid parties and parliament and still achieve its goals. Unless Italian feminists succeed in organizing a feminist political party (which seems highly improbable, both because of the strong political cleavages that cross-cut sex and because of the movement's explicit rejection of the party way of doing politics), feminists will remain less represented in terms of policy on feminist issues than they wish, regardless of the content of the issue they are pressing and of their method of organizing for its success.

NOTES

Acknowledgments: Gianfranco Pasquino has been reading drafts of my various essays on Italian politics for six years; I am so deeply indebted to him for his guidance and insight that even profuse gratitude seems inadequate. Yet I do thank him profusely, as well as Sidney Tarrow, Judith Adler Hellman, and Stephen Hellman.

1. *Matrimonio riparatore* laws, "enforced" primarily in the south of Italy, are a part of the penal code that invalidates rape as a crime if the victim marries the rapist. Strong social pressures brought upon the victim frequently result in forced marriage to the rapist.

2. For example, the Christian Democratic party has, from time to time, through its Movimento Femminile, argued that women require financial security and stability in order

to raise children. Legislation promoting wages for housework (originally a demand of radical feminists and more recently identified as a conservative, DC-associated issue) or a government stipend of child support to mothers would be examples of concern with issues that open additional opportunities to women, and hence are feminist.

3. Note that this distinction, while useful, is somewhat artificial, since feminists may also serve as parliamentary deputies and as internal party activists; the role of feminist, party activist, and legislator may overlap for some women.

4. The Constituent Assembly wrote and ratified a constitution for Italy that provided for a bicameral parliamentary government, with no major jurisdictional differences between the larger Chamber of Deputies and the Senate; a cabinet government subject to removal by votes of confidence as a custom but not as a requirement; a multimember proportional representation electoral system for the Chamber, with a modified system for the 320-member Senate; the recognition of nonfascist political parties; and a variety of normative policy directives, including free education for all children, health care for all citizens, and equal employment opportunity and pay for women, among others.

5. The Lateran Pacts were the result of negotiations between Mussolini and Pope Pius IX in 1929; the Pacts marked the Catholic Church's tolerance of fascism in exchange for Church control of schools and marriage and family law, and the recognition of Catholicism as the state religion.

6. Two previous proposals had been introduced by Socialist Party members: by Renato Sansone in 1954, and by Sansone and Giuliana Nenni in 1958; see Teodori, Ignazi, and Panebianco 1977, 97 n. 1.

7. Divorce is considered a feminist issue in this essay because the ability to remove oneself from an oppressive or unhappy marriage is part of a woman's ability to control her life options and because the divorce reform legislation made grounds for divorce the same for women as for men.

8. Clark, Hine, and Irving (1974, 338–39) point to the increasing urbanization of Italian society, major changes in the structure of the family, emigration, migration, and the increasing numbers of educated Italian women as factors resulting in the failure of a subsequent referendum to abrogate the Fortuna law. They also cite, for the mid-1950s, 4,000,000 " 'outlaws of marriage,' including the illegitimate children."

9. This changed somewhat with the 1974 divorce referendum, but even then the parties of the Left stressed the antifascist nature of the divorce law and the alliance against the law by the DC and the neofascist Italian Social Movement (MSI); the lay parties, especially the Republicans, stressed the issues of individual choice and separation of church and state.

10. During this period the PSI had, on average, one *deputata* in the Chamber and none in the Senate; despite the PSI's role in promoting and achieving the legislative divorce reform, it can hardly have been the result of pressure from women within the party.

11. Even here, women's role in helping defend the divorce law has been underplayed. The PCI attributed success to a variety of independent, lay, and leftist forces and, according to Stephen Hellman (1977, 169–70), was reluctant to capitalize upon its achievements and to recognize women's contribution. As recently as 1983, Claudia Mancina, writing in the PCI weekly *Rinascita,* celebrated the victory of divorce reform as a "vast, lively, conscious battle of the masses. And, moreover, a *winning* battle"; she spoke of the success of the Left, with no mention of the role of women. One well-known PSI activist claims that the PSI begged its female activists to mobilize in support of a "no" vote in the 1974 referendum (and that the women in the party did all the work on this issue), and that it wasn't

until the PSI realized the strength of women's contribution toward defending the law that they were taken seriously and began to achieve some standing within the party—a standing of limited degree still.

12. The women who made up the committee were from the PCI, the PSI, the Democratic Party of Proletarian Unity (PDUP), the Liberal Party (PLI), the Republican Party (PRI), and the Social Democratic Party (PSDI).

13. It was, in part, the limitation of legal abortion to hospitals that served as the basis for the Radical-sponsored referendum (1981) to abrogate the abortion law.

14. This activist claimed that PSI women and the party itself had attempted to resist these two clauses. A similar criticism of UDI was made by a female PCI functionary in regard to UDI's role (or lack thereof) in the abortion referenda in 1981.

15. When asked about the possibility (in 1982) of additional progressive reform of the abortion law, a female PCI activist stated that any introduction of abortion reform would lead to regressive changes in the law, or to its legislative abrogation.

16. Examples of the conservatism of prominent PCI *deputate* are Adriana Seroni's essays, "Aborto: estremo rimedio" and "Assicurare alla donna una concreta possibilità di scelta," the first of which was published in *Rinascita* in 1975; the second was presented as testimony later the same year before the Chamber's Health and Justice Committees. In "Aborto: estremo rimedio," Seroni (who chaired the national PCI's Women's Commission) argues that the option of abortion is a secondary issue in comparison with the needs for sex education and available contraception, and that abortion is an individualistic choice that would better be placed in the context of the needs of the family and of the state. (These essays are reprinted in Seroni 1977.) For an articulation of the position of the independent feminist movement (a stark contrast to Seroni's position representing the PCI in 1975), see Frabotta 1978, 97–103, where the demand is for "aborto libero, gratuito, sicuro e subito" (the choice of "safe, free abortion, now").

17. *Autodenuncie,* or self-accusations, are a political strategy in which women publicly declare that they have had illegal abortions, a common tool of feminist movements in Italy, France, and the United States, among others.

18. Note that the abortion law was rejected by the Senate on 7 June 1977. The law passed again in the Chamber on 1 April 1978 by 52.8 percent of the 583 votes cast, and was approved by 53.9 percent of the 308 votes cast in the Senate on May 18—a margin of 33 votes in the Chamber and 12 votes in the Senate.

19. In this case, the part of the feminist movement that organized the petition drive included the MLD, UDI, and autonomous feminist groups based in Rome, although women in the PCI and PSI, among others, participated.

20. The Italian constitution provides for the popular initiation of legislation, with a minimum of 50,000 signatures on petitions.

21. Other *Centri contro la violenza* were founded in Milan, Varese, Ancona, Bologna, and Catania; these centers were not "shelters" in the American sense but sources of information, emotional support, and counseling.

22. In later discussions by parliament and the parties, especially the PCI, sexual violence was said to result from an increase in youth unemployment, urbanization, increased personal mobility, juvenile delinquency, and fascism, among other causes (Provincial and Regional Women's Coordination 1979, 19).

23. The amendments were proposed by Carlo Casini, a DC deputy and leader of the anti-abortion Movimento per la Vita.

24. My thanks to Judith Adler Hellman for bringing this article to my attention. Si-

nistra Indipendente is a party group in the Chamber of Deputies composed of non-PCI leftists who ran for election on PCI lists in 1983. MSI-DN (Movimento Sociale Italiano–Destra Nazionale) is an extreme right-wing, neo-fascist party.

25. The MLD, which withdrew from its federated relationship with the Radical party in 1978, is now autonomous and does its political work with other feminist groups, including independent feminist collectives. UDI, formerly associated in a "semiautonomous" way with the PCI, began increasing its independence in the mid-1970s and, in the spring of 1982, "destructured" itself to the extent that its previous relationship with the highly structured PCI is no longer possible.

26. The best example of this was a PSI proposal in 1980 to draft Italian women under the same conditions as Italian men, a proposal that also prohibited women from serving in some technical and military fields (such as combat), which would have violated equal pay provisions of the Economic Parity Act. It was met with a howl of rage from female PSI activists (without whose advice the proposal was made) and independent feminists, and was quickly killed.

27. Enrico Berlinguer, general secretary of the PCI from 1972 to 1984, died of a brain hemorrhage on June 11, 1984. The announcement of his death was met with widespread mourning throughout Italy. His successor is Alessandro Natta.

REFERENCES

Barnes, Samuel. 1977. *Representation in Italy.* Chicago: University of Chicago Press.

Beckwith, Karen. 1979. "Female Communist Deputies to the Italian Parliament: A Thirty-Year Retrospective." Paper presented at the first annual Conference for Europeanists, Washington, D.C.

———. 1981. "Women and Italian Parliamentary Politics, 1946–1979." In Howard R. Penniman, ed., *Italy at the Polls, 1979: A Study of the Parliamentary Elections,* 230–53. Washington, D.C.: American Enterprise Institute.

———. 1985. "Feminism and Leftist Politics in Italy: The Case of UDI-PCI Relations." *West European Politics* 8 (October).

Boccia, Maria Luisa, and Tamar Pitch. 1980. "Movimento femminista, cultura della sinistra, e crisi del sistema politico." *Problemi del Socialismo* 21 (September–December): 113–34.

Bolaffi, Angelo, Luigi Fenizi, Mariella Gramagli, and Margherita Repetto. 1982. "Scacco al re o alla regina?" *Noi Donne,* April, pp. 47–51.

Bottari, Angela. 1982. "Violenza sessuale: Come cambia perchè cambia." *Donne e Politica* 13 (March–April): 26.

Chiaromonte, Franca. 1982. "Nella Constellazione dei 'nuovi movimenti.'" *Rinascita* 39 (no. 47): 16–18.

Clark, Martin, David Hine, and R. E. M. Irving. 1974. "Divorce—Italian Style." *Parliamentary Affairs* 27 (Autumn): 333–55.

Comitato di Difesa della Legge 194. 1982. "Come è nato il Comitato nazionale in difesa della legge." Leaflet, Rome.

Coordinamento femminile del PSI. 1982. *Norme per tutela sociale della maternità e sull'interruzione della gravidanza: Quello che devi sapere se hai bisogna di abortire.* Bologna: Partito Socialista Italiano.

Dogan, Mattei. 1963. "Le donne italiane tra cattolicesimo e marxismo." In Alberto

Spreafico and Joseph LaPalombara, eds., *Elezioni e comportamento politico in Italia*, 475–94. Milan: Edizioni di Comunità.

Ergas, Yasmine, and Maria Rosaria Manierei. 1977. "Movimento e istituzioni." *Nuova donnawomanfemme* 5 (October–December): 118–29.

Fabris, Giampaolo. 1977. *Il comportamento politico degli italiani*. Milan: Franco Angeli.

Frabotta, Biancamaria, ed. 1978. *La politica del femminismo*. Rome: Savelli.

Fraire, M., M. Gramagli, M. Repetto, and G. Tedesco. 1977. "Movimento e istituzioni." *Nuova donnawomanfemme* 5 (July–September): 5–45.

Galli, Giorgio, and Alfonso Prandi. 1970. *Patterns of Political Participation in Italy*. New Haven, Conn.: Yale University Press.

Giele, Janet Zollinger. 1977. "Introduction: The Status of Women in Comparative Perspective." In Janet Zollinger Giele and Audrey Chapman Smock, eds. *Women: Roles and Status in Eight Countries*, 3–31. New York: Wiley.

Giele, Janet Zollinger, and Audrey Chapman Smock, eds. 1977. *Women: Roles and Status in Eight Countries*. New York: Wiley.

Hellman, Judith Adler. 1984. "The Italian Communists, the Women's Question, and the Challenge of Feminism." *Studies in Political Economy* 13 (Winter): 57–82.

Hellman, Stephen. 1977. "The Longest Campaign: Communist Party Strategy and the Elections of 1976." In Howard R. Penniman, ed., *Italy at the Polls: The Parliamentary Elections of 1976*, 155–82. Washington, D.C.: American Enterprise Institute.

Mancina, Claudia. 1983. "Matrimonio per amore, matrimonio per forza, niente matrimonio." *Rinascita* 40 (no. 14).

Marzani, Carl. 1980. *The Promise of Eurocommunism*. Westport, Conn.: Lawrence Hill.

MLD. 1981. "Documento del Movimento della Liberazione della Donna sulla proposta di legge sulla libertà sessuale." Manuscript, Rome.

"Norme per la tutela sociale della maternità e sull'interruzione volontaria della gravidanza. 1978. *Gazzetta Ufficiale della Repubblica Italiana* 119 (no. 140).

"On Crimes against Public Morality and Right Living." 1930. *Penal Code*, Title IX, Articles 519–44.

Pasquino, Gianfranco. 1977. "The Italian Socialist Party: An Irreversible Decline?" In Howard R. Penniman, ed., *Italy at the Polls: The Parliamentary Elections of 1976*. Washington, D.C.: American Enterprise Institute.

Polara, Giorgio Franca. 1983. "Violenza sessuale: La legge in aula, manovre e resistenze nella DC." *L'Unità*, p. 3.

Provincial and Regional Women's Coordination of the Partito Socialista Italiano. 1979. "La proposta di legge del PSI." *Donne e Violenza*. Pamphlet. Bologna: PSI.

Seroni, Adriana. 1977. *La questione femminile in Italia, 1970–1977*. Rome: Riuniti.

Teodori, Massimo, Piero Ignazi, and Angelo Panebianco. 1977. *I nuovi radicali*. Milan: Mondadori.

Trupìa, Lalla. 1982. "La Variabile scomoda per le forze di governo." *Rinascita* 39 (no. 47): 16–18.

"Violenza sessuale approvato il testo in Commissione coi soli voti PCI." 1984. *La Repubblica*.

8 Equality and Autonomy: Feminist Politics in the United States and West Germany

MYRA MARX FERREE

For social movements that are still struggling to establish their legitimacy, there is a temptation to use a comparative perspective to demonstrate the universality and validity of certain concerns. Although similarities are real and important, the emphasis here is on the more often neglected differences between and within two movements. The purpose of this chapter is to sketch certain distinctive contours of debate and consensus within West German and American feminism, while avoiding simplistic assessments of which of the two is "correct."[1] Some of these differences can be traced to historical experiences that have given a particular direction to feminism in each of these two affluent Western countries. Others can be more directly ascribed to the emphases of current political debate and to the dissimilar allies and opponents thus available to feminists in each country. By looking at these differences in tradition and current circumstances, we can see the active feminist movements of both countries in a new light.

After defining some basic concepts and introducing the main organizations in each country, the paper develops its analytical themes in five further sections. The first looks at one central element of American experience, the race analogy, and the political theme of equal treatment that is and has been so closely tied to it. Next, some selected comparisons to the German experience are made to suggest the policy implications of the absence of such a theme in their political discourse. The third section describes a key experience from the historical development of German feminism, the conflict between feminists and socialists; the fourth considers its possible relationship to the political theme of autonomy, central to the self-concept of West German feminists today. The fifth section is again comparative and selects a single policy area, shelters for battered women, where the American emphasis on equality and the West German stress on autonomy seem to have led to quite different outcomes.

VARIETIES OF FEMINISM

To compare the two movements, some common terminology is needed. It is widely agreed that feminism is not so much a single ideology as a perspective that is typically welded together with other assumptions into one of several political orientations (see Jagger and Rothenburg 1984). Within the women's movement in the United States and West Germany there are three major perspectives: radical feminism, socialist feminism, and liberal feminism. Despite common concern with improving the position of women in society, each offers its own distinctive analysis of the nature of women's oppression and the strategies that will lead to effective change.[2]

Radical feminists are those who take the oppression of women to be the root and image of all oppressions. Marriage is typically seen as the paradigm for all claims to own and control the person and labors of another. Patriarchy, a system by which men control women and older men control younger men, is seen as preexisting and pervading all other forms of socioeconomic oppression, socialist and capitalist alike (see, e.g., Millett 1970). Radical feminists emphasize issues involving male violence and see the conflict of interest between women and men as fundamental. Some advocate the construction of organizationally separate power bases for women within male institutions; others find such a strategy a contradiction in terms.

Socialist feminists attempt to combine feminist insights with socialist paradigms, sometimes emphasizing one of these elements more strongly than the other. They are critical of Marxist orthodoxy as exemplified in the program and practice of self-described Communist states, and are also to varying degrees critical of the assumptions and conclusions of Marx and Engels themselves (e.g., Coward 1983). Nonetheless, they accept the necessity for a historical materialist analysis and emphasize that women's freedom cannot be gained without a reordering of capitalst economic relationships, setting their own goals within a context of a socialist agenda. (e.g., Eisenstein 1979; Hooks 1984).

Liberal feminists, finally, are the heirs of the Enlightenment and thus of the American Revolution also. The basic premises of this perspective are self-determination (expressed in personal liberty and representative democracy) and individual rights (Banks 1981). Liberal feminist political analysis centers on the idea of equality under the law: equal rights as citizens (to education and to jobs as well as to the ballot) and equal protection as persons (from the violence and mistreatment to which other individuals might otherwise subject them).

All three of these strands of feminism exist in both the U.S. and West Germany, though their relative importance varies considerably. In the United States, liberal feminists constitute the "mainstream" from which both radical and socialist feminists diverge. The National Organization for Women (NOW), a mass-based liberal feminist group with 220,000 members in 1982, is the largest and arguably the most influential representative of the movement. It is surrounded both by smaller liberal feminist groups with more specialized political goals (such as the National Women's Political Caucus, the Women's Equity Action League, and the Coalition of Labor Union Women) and larger traditional women's organizations that have put liberal feminism high on their agenda (the Young Women's Christian Association, the League of Women Voters, and the National Federation of Business and Professional Women). These organizations, and the sympathetic legislators and other influentials who work with them, form what has been called the women's policy network (Gelb and Palley 1982).

The women's policy network has compiled a mixed record in influencing policy directly. Its most massive effort, on behalf of the Equal Rights Amendment, was defeated, but many significant items of specific legislation have been passed. The women's policy network has also successfully built relationships with the media that allow it to be seen both as the chief exponent of organized feminism and as the representative of women collectively in the political system. Thus, most Americans would take "feminist" to refer to liberal feminists and their organizations.

In West Germany, on the other hand, "feminist" refers primarily to the radical feminist strand. The "autonomous women's movement" is the term used most frequently, and it signifies an informal network of women's centers, publications, bookstores, and, most important, local "projects" created and supported by radical feminists (Altbach 1984; Schenk 1981; Schultz 1984). There is no national membership organization, and the little coordination that exists has been either by word of mouth or through the nationally circulated feminist magazines *emma* and *Courage*. However, *Courage* ceased publication in the spring of 1984 following a financial crisis precipitated in part by its attempt to become a feminist newsweekly, and *emma* usually reports on activities after the fact. While this helps inactive feminists stay in touch with the movement, current activists are usually linked by personal ties to others working in similar projects.

The projects appear in many ways to be the heart of the movement. Projects are collectives: that is, nonhierarchical, value-rational organizations (see Rothschild-Whitt 1979) that work to bring women together to improve their immediate circumstances, to raise their consciousness, and thus to empower them to further change the direction of their lives. Projects are varied, but among the most common are the *Frauenhaeuser* (shelters for battered women) and the women's centers at most major universities.[3] Some projects emphasize work with women in especially oppressed circumstances: support groups for single mothers or lesbians, meeting places for prostitutes, classes for immigrant Turkish women.

In addition, there is an annual "summer university" in West Berlin, a several-day conference attended by up to 3,000 women. Here and in numerous other special-purpose conferences (such as one on reproductive technology in 1985), thematic concerns are taken up that will later be pursued in the magazines, in local discussion groups, and potentially in new projects. Radical feminists organize and dominate these various activities, but some socialist feminists also participate. The continuing debate and discussion between these two groups shapes feminist ideology in West Germany; socialist perspectives continue to inform most radical feminists, even if by opposition and conflict.

Liberal feminists are rarely to be seen at West German feminist gatherings, whether conferences or demonstrations, although recently some deliberate efforts have been made to organize events that are more inclusive. They have an entirely distinct organizational structure most clearly evident in the *Frauenrat*, or Women's Council, an umbrella organization formed from the various traditional women's clubs and associations. Unlike NOW in the United States, the *Frauenrat* seems to have few overlapping memberships or other direct connections to the women in the autonomous women's movement or women in the unions. There is an increasing tendency, however, for cities and states to appoint officials responsible for women's affairs (*Frauenbeauftragten*); they are emerging as a link between the autonomous women's movement and the more traditional women's groups.

While it would certainly be an exaggeration to say that feminism has become socially and politically legitimate in the United States, it appears to be substantially less so in West Germany. Even among feminists, there is considerable consensus on the weakness and "backwardness" of the West German movement relative to the American (e.g., Altbach 1984; Gerhard 1982; Schenk 1981). However, this consensus fails to take into account the very different emphases and organizing principles of the two movements. Radical feminists in West Germany are arguably stronger than their U.S. counterparts; liberal feminists are immeasurably weaker. Consequently, the issues raised and the tactics used differ dramatically between the two countries, and the measures of success are not directly comparable. To understand the strengths and weaknesses of both requires placing each of them in its appropriate historical and political context.

LIBERAL FEMINISM AND THE RACE ANALOGY: THE U.S. MODEL

The dominant American political tradition is classical liberalism. American feminists of the nineteenth century founded their arguments for access to education, political and civil rights, and control of their own property, earnings, and children on the liberal premises embodied in the Declaration of Independence. American socialism does not provide a viable political alternative. Over the course of the past century, working-class radicalism in the United States was both violently repressed and diverted into an often racist populism, leaving the U.S. as the only major Western country without a respected socialist tradition and political party. Thus, almost all feminist appeals to the American public rely on liberal political premises for their justification: for example, stressing a woman's right to control her own body as the basis for legal abortion. Radical and socialist feminists alike find themselves using the terms of liberal discourse (rights, discrimination, and the like) and exploring the potential for fundamental change that such a political framework can, at its best, offer (see, e.g., Eisenstein 1981).

From there it is a small step to working together on concrete political projects such as the defense of abortion rights or the expansion of welfare benefits.

Most central to the development of American feminism, however, is the use of the analogy between sex and race, because it is this analogy that guides the application of liberal principles to specific instances. Historically, the connections were close. Organized American feminism began in the ranks of the abolitionist movement and continued to grow in close proximity to antislavery efforts. When the collectivist strand of feminism reemerged in the 1960s, it did so in part in the ranks of the Black civil rights movement (Evans 1979; Ferree and Hess 1985). The older, more conventional women who founded NOW also explicitly sought to make it an "NAACP for women," which, like the National Association for the Advancement of Colored People, would lobby for nondiscrimination (Friedan 1976, 97). In addition to these organizational "coattails," the women's movement in the United States owes a substantial ideological debt to its Black precursor. Sexism, a word coined in the U.S., intentionally expresses the analogy with racism that white feminists see as central in explaining their oppression in society; it trades on the awareness of discrimination and support for equal rights created by Black activists. The analogy not only helped to bring feminists themselves to an awareness of their own oppression but worked to raise the public's level of gender consciousness.[4]

The disadvantages and struggles of Black people and women of all races are linked not only in American history and popular thought but also in the law and its interpretation. The civil rights struggles of Blacks in the 1950s and the 1960s focused attention on the widespread segregation that received its legal sanction in the doctrine of "separate but equal."[5] A basic tenet of the civil rights movement was that separate facilities were, by design and definition, unequal. Increasingly, the courts and public opinion moved to share that view. Title VII of the Civil Rights Act of 1964, prohibiting discrimination on the basis of race or sex, offered an important new tool for dismantling the existing structure of inequality.

As the U.S. feminist movement developed in the late 1960s and early 1970s, its first action built on this legal foundation (Friedan 1976). The absence of discrimination was defined as equal rights and equal treatment, "equal" being understood to mean that the *same* opportunities, benefits, and facilities would be available to women as to men. Within the context of this interpretation, the Equal Rights Amendment, the first but as yet unratified constitutional acknowledgment of women's equality as citizens, attempts to secure equality by guaranteeing sameness.[6] Because of this, labor unions and those government agencies charged with protecting women workers initially opposed this measure, fearing that essential safeguards and benefits for women would be eliminated (Becker 1983; Sealander 1983). This opposition waned, however, as the lower courts began to strike down protective legislation, such as maximum hours or weight-lifting regulations, as already inconsistent with Title VII (Freeman 1984). Moreover, the image of women workers shifted away from that of reluctant victims to encompass the realities of women's ambition and routine labor force participation (Sealander 1983).

The resultant alliance—however partial, tense, and conflict-prone—between feminists, unions, and the Democratic Party, and other left-center groups seems almost inevitable today. In part, it reflects a commonality of economic interest in social welfare measures by professional women (disproportionately concentrated in the "helping professions") and working-class and poor women (disproportionately in need of help; Erie, Rein, and Wiget 1982). Nonetheless, it seems unlikely that it would have occurred without the entering wedge of the civil rights movement. The race analogy defined women as a minority group whose status could be improved by "sameness" of treatment, created a legal lever for dismantling protective legislation, and raised consciousness about the effects of disparate treatment. In effect, equal rights were no longer deemed irrelevant to the poor, whether Black men and women or white women.

The weaknesses as well as the strengths of the equal rights approach are beginning to be felt in the United States in the present debate over affirmative action. Formally equal treatment in a situation of existing inequality is increasingly viewed by feminists as a means of perpetuating rather than overcoming inequality. This concern arises for women, Blacks, and other "protected groups" in general, but women face an additional problem in the legal treatment of the biological facts of maternity and lactation and the sociological reality that women carry the bulk of the responsibility for child rearing. Comparison with how these issues are handled in West Germany may make the implications of the American model of equal treatment somewhat clearer.

EQUITY AND THE ISSUE OF SEX DIFFERENCES

The Basic Law enacted in 1949 to serve as a constitution for the Federal Republic of Germany contains a section often described as an "equal rights provision" for women, and women had to fight for its inclusion. Yet it has not consistently mandated equal treatment (Schuster 1982). On the contrary, with no separate-but-equal tradition as a pretext for inequality, differences between men and women (real and supposed) were invoked from the start to justify disparate treatment. This includes protective legislation excluding women from entire industries, such as construction and mining, and allowing employers to restrict women to so-called "light"—low-paying—work (see Kurz-Scherf and Stahn-Willig 1981; Lappe 1981). Articles describing the loopholes and weaknesses of protective legislation have only recently appeared (e.g., Demmer, Kuepper and Kutzner 1983; Slupik 1982).

Within the unions and among the public at large, the need for protective legislation is rarely questioned. For example, a woman official of the Deutsche Gewerkschaftsbund, a union leader considered among the most sympathetic to feminism, wrote a critique of some provisions of the laws in the union journal, but even she concluded by supporting "protection" (Dobberthien 1981). There is growing pressure from women in the unions to deal with discriminatory employment practices, but there is also resistance from the union leadership (Kurz-Scherf and Stahn-Willig 1981; Pinl 1977). Additionally, the unions have generally opposed the expansion of part-time work as necessarily exploitive—despite women's interest in such jobs—in lieu of trying to improve the conditions of work for part-timers.[7] This parallels their "protective" strategy but is apparently a point of conflict with feminists, who instead try to show how this policy can work to the disadvantage of women (e.g., Eckart 1982).

In general, protective legislation is accepted, if not always desired, because it contains concrete benefits along with its prohibitions. These benefits are not trivial. For example, pregnant women have the right to transfer to less strenuous jobs with no loss of pay or seniority; a short maternity leave at full pay is guaranteed, and six months' leave at partial pay is available. Though less than many other European countries offer these provisions are generous by American standards (cf. Erler, Jaeckel, and Sass 1982).[8] Indeed, the U.S. has allowed employers to refuse even contractually mandated sick leave and health insurance for childbirth on the grounds that childbirth was not an illness and discrimination against "pregnant people" (not a protected group) was legal. Despite congressional action to override this decision (the Pregnancy Discrimination Act of 1978), maternity benefits remain a contractual matter with individual employers, rather than a state-mandated right. Some American feminists are uncomfortable about pressing for mandatory maternity benefits for fear of providing a further incentive for employers to avoid hiring women.

In the absence of a race analogy, it is difficult to see how feminists and unions in West Germany will resolve the impasse of protectionism. While feminists on principle often support an alliance with labor, they have not persuaded the unions to incorporate women's definition of their own best interests. On the other hand, the existence of the race analogy and the equal treatment theme so closely tied to it in the United States makes it difficult to accommodate the facts of pregnancy and maternity. West German feminists often seem surprised at the failure of the ERA in the United States but may see it in the context of their own fairly innocuous equal rights clause. While they have some doubts about the value of protective legislation and state-mandated maternity benefits, West German feminists would be unlikely to support any measure that would eliminate them.

Additionally, in the absence of the race analogy, no theoretical or practical ties have developed between feminism and the issue of foreign workers (*Gastarbeiter*), in contrast to the American presumption that all "minorities" share certain characteristics: marginal and segregated jobs; use as scapegoats for rising unemployment and other social problems. Although West German feminists do social work with immigrant women, particularly the Turks, there have been few obvious attempts to develop a feminist analysis linking conservatives' efforts to encourage return migration of "guest workers" to their attacks on *Doppel-verdienertum* (married women as "extra" workers) and their anxiety over the low birthrates of ethnic Germans (for partial exceptions, see Beck-Gernsheim 1984; "Lebensborn auf Zeit" 1982) Rather than explicitly linking the concerns of women with those of ethnic minorities, most West German feminists tend to see Turkish or other minority women as backward and helpless victims of the obvious sexism in their native cultures (Hebenstreit 1983).

A further practical consequence of differential treatment of women and men and the estrangement of feminists from the unions in West Germany may have been the greater resonance of the pay-for-housework strategy among feminists. Theoretically, women who worked at home for no pay were actually not helping their families so much as subsidizing employers, who could thus obtain a man's labor more cheaply than if he had to meet his subsistence needs in the market (cf. Bock 1984; Ferree 1983). Thus housewives, along with the peasantry of the Third World, were the truly exploited and revolutionary class (von Werlhof 1982). While unions represented wage laborers, many West German feminists considered themselves the representatives of the interests of housewives and mothers and proposed a wide variety of ways in which the state should recompense women for the unpaid work done at home. In contrast, the pay-for-housework demand was never a serious policy option among American feminists, nor is there any significant constituency for a child care allowance for all women regardless of income or marital status.[9]

The issue of differential treatment by the armed forces is also closely related to the question of what sex differences the government should recognize, if any. For the West German radical feminist mainstream, as for American radical feminists, it is not an ideological problem to assert fundamental differences in the nature of women and men, as long as those differences are seen as positive attributes for women. Most commonly, women are presented as possessing an essential egalitarianism, pacifism, and closeness to nature. In both countries, therefore, radical feminists have strong political commitments in common with the peace and environmental movements. However, in the United States these are two virtually nonoverlapping movements, while in West Germany pacifists and environmentalists work together politically in the Green Party, which also shares the radical feminist commitment to antihierarchical, participatory democracy.[10] The Greens oppose West Germany's military requirement for men, and both the Greens and the autonomous feminists agree that women do not belong in the military under any circumstances.

Piecemeal inclusion of women on a volunteer basis in the West German army, the *Bundeswehr*, has recently been introduced by the conservative government and is actively opposed by virtually all feminists. Feminists argue that the government's motivation for the change reflects the low birthrate and the shortage of male recruits and that women are being exploited as a labor reserve. There appears to be no feminist constituency for the American liberal feminist position that citizens' rights and obligations are linked, nor are the armed forces commonly seen as a potential avenue of economic opportunity, as in the United States. Since in West Germany there is no pressure for consistency in a claim that equal rights demand equal treatment, there is also no pressure to seek equal treatment from the military.[11] With pacifism accepted as a fundamental female attribute, participation in the military is considered inconsistent with feminism.

In sum, liberal feminists, lawmakers, and the general public in the United States have all relied to a great extent on the race analogy in evaluating and changing the status of women. The separate-but-equal idea has little credibility, and thus feminism is understood to mandate the same treatment of men and women. Consequently, women workers in the U.S. find themselves with far fewer restrictions but also fewer benefits than in West Germany. There is also a demand for "equal opportunity" and responsibility in the military by leading American feminist groups, while the radical feminist mainstream in West Germany accepts "protection" from military service as a benefit of being female. The common use of the race analogy in the U.S. facilitated alliances between feminists, unions, and the Democratic Party; in West Germany the belief in women's essential pacifism and closeness to nature encourages feminists to try to work with the environmentalist and pacifist Green Party, while tending to downplay the work, welfare, and immigration issues associated with the Social Democratic party and the unions.

While the relative strength of radical rather than liberal feminism is evident in these policy preferences, such differences arose not simply from the absence of the racial analogy but also from the historical circumstances in which German feminism developed.

THREE FEMINIST TRADITIONS IN GERMANY:
A LEGACY OF CONFLICT

Germany has had an unusually weak liberal tradition, leaving feminists relatively isolated or pushing them into alliances with socialists. Core liberal ideas, long established in the American constitution and its Bill of Rights, were still revolutionary in March 1848, when liberals tried unsuccessfully to form a united democratic state from a multiplicity of German-speaking princedoms. Several notable feminists were active in these liberal struggles, most particularly Luise Aston (1814–71) and Louise Otto-Peters (1819–95). They continued their feminist agitation, after the failure of the 1848 revolution, in the face of active repression. From 1850 to 1865, women's participation in political organizations and women's newspapers were suppressed. While many of their demands (such as the right to an education and to practice a profession) were similar to those raised by American feminists, German feminists were placed in a more actively hostile political environment. Male liberals, themselves outsiders, did not come to the support or defense of the liberal feminists.

In contrast, the socialist tradition in Germany is strong and respected, unlike that in the U.S. The revolutionary year 1848 was marked by the publication of the Communist Manifesto and thus also by the beginning of the division between two competing models of social criticism: socialism as a specific political program based on Marxist analysis, and the liberal political agenda. This division, and the fact that the socialists rather than the liberals achieved political power first, had enormous implications for German feminism.

First, the rapidly expanding Socialist party did not need to build organizational alliances with middle-class sympathizers, especially not feminists, who also labored under political restrictions as women. Even before 1848, the liberal activist Louise Otto-Peters had espoused the cause of women factory workers at least as actively as she had argued for women's rights in higher education and the professions. Afterward, she appealed for solidarity with the newly emerging socialist organizations. Nonetheless, she was more attacked than embraced by the socialists, with the exception of her friend August Bebel and a small circle of his associates. The prevailing socialist position called for either the complete exclusion of women from factory work (rather than the reduction of hours and increase in wages that Otto-Peters demanded) or at least their restriction to certain occupations in which they would not compete with men.[12] In the short run, socialists saw improvement in the situation of working-class women as coming from the improved situation of working-class male wage earners and, in the long run, from the political power of the socialist party.

Socialist women leaders such as Clara Zetkin (1857–1933) mocked the "bourgeois" feminists, regardless of whether they (like Otto-Peters) were sensitive to the needs and concerns of working-class women and willing to work with the socialists or (like Aston and increasing numbers of other feminists) concentrated their efforts solely on education and opportunities in the professions and, later, on sexual emancipation. In the pages of the party newspaper she edited from 1891 to 1916, *Die Gleichheit* (Equality), Zetkin consistently attacked "bourgeois" feminists and demanded that proletarian women put the cause of the party first; their rights as women, she said, would follow. Most apparently agreed; their activities are usually designated the "proletarian women's movement" (Scheu 1983; Thoennessen 1973). Their efforts centered on combatting the virulent strain of anti-woman sentiment within the party while simultaneously denouncing feminists. Thus, one of the world's strongest socialist parties devoted considerable energy to attacking one of the smallest feminist movements in Europe even as it adopted some feminist demands—perhaps most important, women's suffrage.

Feminist writers of the liberal tradition—notably Hedwig Dohm (1833–1919), the first to demand women's suffrage—continued to deal with women's poverty as a crucial social issue, but they did so in ways that were increasingly critical of the socialist strategy. As early as 1869, both Dohm and Otto-Peters protested the socialists' romanticization of man as worker, woman as housewife at the hearth (Thoennessen 1973). In arguing for women's *own* political power, Dohm noted that men's objections to women's employment began only when women earned more than a pittance, a criticism as much of the proletarian anti-feminism of the socialists as of the conservative power structure. Thus socialist and feminist women were actively divided from each other and mutually hostile (Kontos 1979; Scheu 1984).

Among the feminists, the liberals divided into a "radical liberal" wing concerned with sexuality, including men's control of women's childbearing, and a "women's rights" wing with an increasingly narrow agenda. Led by Helene Stoecker (1869–1943), the radical liberals were notable for an unusually extensive analysis of sexual politics (Allen 1985), connecting issues such as abortion rights and support for unwed mothers (two aspects of control over maternity, and thus of the basic conditions of women's existence) and the abolition of prostitution (as a form of sexual slavery like coerced childbearing). The women's rights movement, on the other hand, was more conservative than liberal and thus willing to accept property restrictions on voting as long as men and women were restricted equally. As more conservative feminists were recruited around the single issues of the vote and access to specific professions, the women's rights movement found the prospect of socialists coming to power frightening and supported repressive measures. The movement as a whole became more conservative over time, until its remnants were taken over by the Nazis (Evans 1976).

Since the socialists as a group had actively rejected alliances with all "bourgeois" feminists and thus forced women to choose class or gender politics exclusively, a common ground of mutual support never existed. The acrimonious split between the so-called "proletarian women's movement" within the Socialist party and the so-called "bourgeois women's movement" left scars that are still displayed as contemporary West German feminists argue about who betrayed whom first (e.g., Scheu 1984). Socialist revolution, whether in Weimar or the present German Democratic Republic (East Germany) did not live up to its promises to women; contemporary claims that women should put the party first are met with disdain from feminists. On the other hand, the conservative transformation of the women's rights segment of the movement validated the socialist claim that being "for women" was not necessarily a progressive stance. As a result neither the socialist nor the women's rights model has much historical credibility in the present.

AUTONOMOUS RADICAL FEMINISM: THE WEST GERMAN MODEL

In the United States, feminism reemerged in the 1960s in establishment political circles as the bureaucratic strand, and within the New Left as the collectivist strand (Ferree and Hess 1985; Freeman 1975). West German feminism also has two points of origin, but strikingly, liberal political organizations are not one of them. The nearly total lack of continuity between the West German movement today and that of the 1920s and earlier can be partly attributed to the Nazis. Unlike the U.S., West Germany in the late 1960s and early 1970s did not have a substantial cohort of women who had had experience in progressive politics in the 1930s and 1940s and who were available for mobilization on behalf of women.[13]

On the one hand, West German feminism arose within the New Left, which in West Germany included youth who turned to the tiny DKP (German Communist Party) or to SDS (Socialist Democratic Students), a more structured part of the amorphous APO (Extraparliamentary Opposition). As early as 1968, women within the New Left were beginning to struggle against the pervasive sexism of this supposedly liberating movement (Altbach 1984; Schenk 1981). The sexual exploitation of women within the movement, the indifference of the male leadership to the contributions and needs of mothers, and the increasing definition of "action" for social change as violence all precipitated a women's critique, first of the movement and then of society. As these grievances were similar to some of those facing the collectivist feminists in the U.S., American feminist writings were quickly translated and became widely influential.[14] Feminists coming to the movement via this route were typically well informed about socialist theory and practice, and their own ideas owe much to their continuing struggle within and against the traditional Left.[15]

On the other hand, feminism also grew out of the struggle to abolish the restrictive abortion law known as Paragraph 218, a battle first waged at the turn of the century by the radical liberals and carried on intermittently by the socialists (Kontos 1979). The campaign was revived in 1970–71 by small groups of women in the New Left who also arranged and sometimes performed illegal abortions. In 1971, journalist Alice Schwarzer focused broader public attention on this issue by organizing a special issue of a popular magazine in which women publically admitted that they had had abortions. The abortion question became the touchstone of feminist politics, in part because of the indifference and even hostility of both Left and Right male-controlled political parties to abortion reform. The analysis of heterosexuality as a source of institutionalized oppression that emerged from this struggle (as in Schwarzer's 1977 book, The "Little" Difference and Its Big Consequences) connected the issues of male violence, control of reproduction, and the subordination of women into a radical feminist "body politics." Abortion counseling centers soon became collection points for group trips to neighboring countries where abortions were legal and then were gradually transformed into gathering places for women's consciousness-raising groups.

The result of both the conflict with the New Left and the development of abortion as a theoretical and practical issue was the emergence of what is known as the "autonomous women's movement." This movement has a common core that emphasizes the formation of separate women's institutions, the rejection of both major political parties (the SPD and CDU), and suspicion of the politics of male self-described radicals. Autonomy is the crucial defining characteristic of the movement in its own eyes; it means that the autonomous women's movement is not subordinated to the male-defined needs of 'the whole organization" or, more particularly, to a perceived need for unity in the working class on the part of socialists. In this it is unlike Zetkins proletarian women's movement at the turn of the century or its successor organizations (within the East German regime, the West German unions, and the Social Democratic Party), and also unlike the more conservative denominational and professional women's organizations (typically affiliated with the FDP or CDU). Moreover, organizational autonomy in this sense is typically combined with local autonomy for groups within the movement and a nondirective, nonhierarchical style within the local groups that is seen as supporting individual autonomy as well.

At least until quite recently, the feminists of the autonomous women's movement seem to have at best ignored those women who remained active in mixed-sex organizations. Women within the major parties who expressed sympathy with feminism were goaded to leave the party to show their commitment to women; women in New Left groups were seen as pseudo-feminists trying to take over the movement to advance their own groups. For many, the definition of autonomy seemed to virtually preclude working within institutions to change them while also belonging to separate women's groups. Instead, pressure was to be brought from the outside, where there was no danger of co-optation (Plogstedt 1983). This meant defining as nonfeminist those bureaucratically organized women's groups that established themselves in the mid-1970s under the influence of the rebirth of feminism in West Germany and abroad, such as the *Arbeitsgemeinschaft sozialdemocratischer Frauen* (Association of Social Democratic Women) and the solidly middle-class *Frauenrat* (Women's Council).

Not all radical feminists agreed with this strategy of working from the outside, a strategy common to much of the New Left (and from which the APO, or Extra-parliamentary Opposition, took its name). Some began, essentially as individuals, to make "the long march through the institutions" to positions of potential power and influence. The gradual emergence of these already committed feminists in positions of some authority appears to have been one force reopening debate about how much autonomy is necessary and how it is to be defined. Additionally, as feminists in general have become more integrated into careers, they have also become more concerned with occupational issues and more aware of other women who share their concerns. The election of a frankly conservative (some would say reactionary) national government seems to be another factor directing feminist attention to the need for more responsive policy-makers at the *Land* (state) and local levels, where women officials are more likely to be available as potential allies. A fourth force seems to be the emergence of the Green Party as an institutionalized, while still "countercultural," political force and the desire of many feminists to see their concerns placed higher on this party's agenda.

The past few years have seen several indications that the autonomous women's movement is becoming increasingly willing to work within and through institutions. A group known as the October 6 Initiative was formed in Bonn to weigh political alternatives and to press candidates, especially female candidates, on feminist issues. The strategy of *Quotierung* (giving equally qualified women preference in hiring until proportional representation is achieved) is a major issue, at least in the universities in Hamburg, Berlin, and Frankfort. In some localities, affirmative action plans (*Frauenfoerderplaene*) for government employment have been passed or are now under discussion, and union women are participating actively along with a number of "autonomous" feminists.

Some feminists feel that if they do not find a more institutionalized way of working autonomously yet with other allies, it will be too easy for politically active women to lose touch with feminism and for feminism to lose all touch with practical politics. Sybelle Plogstedt, founder and editor of *Courage*, for example, has expressed concern that autonomous women's projects may have reached the limits of what they can accomplish on their own. She argues for splitting the concepts "feminist," "women's movement," and "autonomous" in order to create more room for cooperation: "To me spiritualists are autonomous but not feminist, many women in the Green Party are feminist but not autonomous . . . many church women neither feminist nor autonomous but in the women's movement" (Plogstedt 1983, 59). She proposed both "theoretical discussion of what the role of feminists is in the now wider women's movement" and consolidation of existing feminist groups into an "Alternative Women's Council." [16]

Still, among West German feminists there appears to be considerable resistance to developing an organizational base as a strategy linked to integrating institutions (see Schultz 1984). It is certainly true that if West German feminists had a national, autonomous, grassroots-based organization—like NOW in the United States—certain of their presumptions and priorities would have to change, but it is not clear that such a move would necessarily tilt the movement in the more liberal direction characteristic of NOW. The predominantly radical feminist movement seems concerned about this possibility and less than enthusiastic about widening the definition of feminism to encompass liberal and socialist groups. On the other hand, there is some evidence that this shift in priorities toward a more integrative strategy has already begun. The continuing concern about the problems of co-optation inherent in an integrative strategy attracts both theoretical and practical attention. This concern can perhaps be best illustrated by comparing the West German and American experience in one particular policy area, that of providing shelters for battered women.

SHELTERS FOR BATTERED WOMEN: RADICAL FEMINISM IN ACTION

One place where the tension between working inside and outside the system has been felt most acutely is in efforts to provide shelter and other forms of support for women leaving men who batter and abuse them. Radical feminists have been at the forefront of these efforts in both the United States and West Germany, and the initial goals of movement intervention were similar in both countries. Their subsequent development has been along two quite divergent lines, however, which highlights the different character of the feminist mainstream in each country.

While the earliest discussions of wife-beating and the development of the shelter strategy in the U.S. took place among radical feminists, liberal feminists were quick to adopt the cause. Both liberals and radicals shared the goal of offering women a transitional environment in which they could safely live, an alternative to continuing to take their husbands' abuse. The radical feminist agenda also regarded shelters as space in which individual women could take charge of their own lives while simultaneously living together with other women, sharing past experiences, and collectively undergoing a consciousness-raising process. From this perspective, it was essential that the shelter be collectively run by its residents, rather than having rules imposed from outside. Thus, not only did residents need autonomy from staff; the staff itself needed autonomy from government or charity organizations and the bureaucratic structures of authority and accountability found there.

The liberal feminists who became involved in the shelters were not particularly committed to these additional goals. The issue for them was government's failure to meet women's needs to the same extent as it met men's needs, even men who were offenders rather than victims. The serious underfunding of programs aimed at women's social welfare, compared to those targeted for male ex-convicts, drug abusers, and juvenile delinquents, was a major sore point. Equity in the amount and nature of government support was the chief liberal feminist issue, and it was this concern, rather than the radical feminist agenda, that shaped the responses of the American feminist mainstream.

As the U.S. media saw in this dramatic "new" problem an ordinary, innocent woman victim whom they thought they could help, they turned their resources upon this issue. In the glare of publicity in the late 1970s, it became relatively easy to obtain funding from the government and private foundations. Since shelter "services" were an expanding (or "hot") topic for funders, nonfeminist groups also hurried to take advantage of the newly supportive climate. Between 1975 and 1978 more than 170 shelters were opened in the United States, but fewer than half of these were explicitly feminist (Tierney 1982). Even the feminist groups found themselves under pressure to establish bureaucratic hierarchies of accountability once they were receiving significant outside funding (Ahrens 1980; Morrison 1982). For liberal feminists this posed less of a problem, since the increase in funding could be understood as a positive move toward equity in providing social services.

Radical U.S. feminists, however, were not primarily interested in equalizing social service delivery and found that increased funding brought increased control by outside agencies. This control was often used to shift the balance of power within the shelters away from residents and radical feminists and toward the more "qualified" and "cooperative" liberal feminists, sometimes to the extent of purging the radicals. Attacks on lesbian activists did not succeed in driving them out of the shelter movement but did force them to adopt a lower profile (Ahrens 1980; Morrison 1982). Increasingly, therefore, as American efforts to deal with wife-beating are being "medicalized," professionalized, decriminalized, and individualized, the radical feminist themes—male violence as a political reality for all women and individual autonomy developed from collective self-help—are muted if not totally lost (Tierney 1982).

The West German approach contrasts with the American in maintaining a strong radical feminist emphasis. At least two-thirds of the shelters are run by autonomous feminist groups (Plogstedt and Douglas 1982); as of 1983 there were approximately 80 feminist shelters as well as perhaps 40 active planning groups for new shelters (Gerhard and Schallhoeffer 1983). In feminist shelters, the issue of control is treated as central, and state funding or other forms of support are accepted only insofar as the autonomy of the organization is not compromised. Shelters that are established and run by other groups are sharply distinguished from those that are feminist, since along with control by outside agencies goes a significant difference in policies and priorities. *Frauenhaeuser* (the feminist shelters—literally, women's houses) seem generally to make a point of accepting all women (even when overcrowding is severe or a woman is drug- or alcohol-dependent), not limiting the length of a stay, sharing work and decision-making collectively, and drawing the fewest possible hierarchical distinctions between residents and volunteers (Hagemann-White 1981). These policies better accord with the radical feminist analysis of male violence, female coping, and collective self-defense than do the policies typical of American shelters, but the price of such autonomy is a considerably lower level of funding, a chronically precarious economic position, and continued reliance on extensive volunteer commitments from the local feminist community merely to keep a shelter open.

Because shelter projects continue to draw heavily on the time and energy of the movement as a whole, the problem of how long a local feminist community can sustain the required level of effort becomes important. Since there is no specific plan for how a transition to government funding or staffing could be accomplished without surrendering feminist control and thus ultimately compromising the operating principles, the commitment to work in the shelters is apparently open-ended.[17] This prospect can be disheartening; it highlights how little real change has occurred while continuing to demand a high level of personal investment. As a result, some West German feminists have started to criticize and withdraw from the shelters, seeing these efforts as futile attempts to provide an adequate level of social services in lieu of demanding that government accept its own responsibility for ensuring the well-being of its citizens (e.g., Bochum Shelter Initiative 1982). Few proposals have yet appeared, however, that clarify how the feminist movement might go about making this demand politically effective.

It would be a distortion to reduce the distinction between the two countries' shelter efforts to a claim that the American movement has been co-opted already while West German feminists have managed to retain their autonomy. This is certainly an element; U.S. funders can and do exert pressure away from the original goals and political vision of the movement. However, many American feminists active in creating shelters for battered women were never committed to the radical feminist agenda in the first place. They were and are liberal feminists who do not see hierarchy and bureaucracy as intrinsically antifeminist. Instead, they consider it as appropriate and desirable to meld their interests as social service professionals with the abused women's interests in obtaining their help and support. Therefore, much of the conflict in the U.S. has taken place within the feminist movement as liberal feminists (typically with professional credentials) struggle with radical feminists (typically without them) for the control of the shelters. Although West German feminists had internal struggles, too, they did not polarize in this way. Because they maintained their commitment to the radical agenda, they have less adequate and secure financial or political support from the government and the public, and thus more of their energies go into sustaining the shelters themselves.

SUMMARY AND CONCLUSIONS

The overall picture of the two movements highlights the differences between them. Rather than quantitative comparison (larger or smaller, stronger or weaker), the issue is one of recognizing the differences in goals, in strategies for achieving these goals, and in the historical and political contexts in which these strategies are situated.

The American movement, like the West German one, has radical, socialist, and liberal strands, but the liberal feminists are dominant both in popular perceptions of what feminism is and in the structure and ideology of the movement itself. The strong liberal tradition continues to create opportunities for feminists to find allies. The ties that exist, however conflict-prone, between U.S. feminist organizations and the Democratic party seem evidence of this. The liberal tradition also makes the movement more open to the outside, perhaps even to the extent that the boundary blurs between feminist and nonfeminist, and co-optation is encouraged. The emphasis on equality of treatment is also inherent in liberal feminism, but it creates certain theoretical and practical problems in moving toward substantive equality that takes account of sexual difference. For example, the reality of women's role as mothers makes the need for a coherent policy of social support and affirmative action increasingly obvious, but American feminists have invested relatively little political effort in fighting for positive governmental interventions to reduce the social costs of motherhood (Joffe 1983; Shanley 1983).

For American women in general, the absence of social support for mothers—

whether in public child care, maternity leave, job protections during pregnancy, or other programs—is a serious lack. But it appears to be difficult to address these issues politically within a liberal framework that defines motherhood as an individual choice. Existing alliances between socialist, radical, and liberal feminists may serve to pull the liberal mainstream into more direct concern with these social welfare issues, even if theory lags behind. Liberal theory and the concern with equity continue to drive the movement forward, most recently into recognition of the "feminization of poverty" (Pearce and McAdoo 1981) and proposals for "comparable worth," a strategy to identify and correct discrimination against jobs held primarily by women rather than just against individual women jobholders (Feldberg 1984).

In contrast, the picture of the West German movement that emerges is one of survival in a much more repressive and hostile climate, with a consequent direction of feminist energies toward affirming the positive value of boundaries and of maintaining autonomy. Radical feminists are the dominant theoretical and organizational strand; their emphasis on boundaries has until recently seemed to place even most socialist and liberal feminists beyond the pale. They have maintained control and self-sufficiency in a way that American feminists have not, but at a tremendous cost in time and energy. Recent observations suggest that they are beginning to feel the limits of strictly autonomous action in producing social change and are reevaluating and revising this strategy (Plogstedt 1983; Schultz 1984). While their self-imposed isolation may be diminishing, it is less clear whether they can expect or achieve a level of support from their putative allies comparable to that available to American feminists.

Feminist concern with boundaries and independence may have left West German women in general almost untouched by the movement. Until now, there has been relatively little emphasis on changing legislation or institutionalizing women's representation in the male-controlled organizations that affect most women's lives. It is not clear whether even those women working for feminist goals in the *Frauenrat,* the unions, or the political parties perceive themselves as part of the same movement as the autonomous feminist groups. Minimal contact and coordination may have hampered some efforts to help women articulate and advance their own interests politically. The issue of part-time work appears to be one case in point. However, growing pressure for affirmative action at the universities (where women still constitute less than 5 percent of the tenured faculty) and elsewhere, and for work in common with the unions to deal with the employment effects of the new technologies, suggests that the definition of autonomy is broadening.

These two feminist movements differently resolve the tension between equality and autonomy. For the most part, feminists in the United States simply assume their autonomy from both party and state. Their struggle focuses on shaping a definition of equality that is consistent with the prevailing liberal conceptualization of equality as identical rights, yet moves beyond that to take account of the responsibility that women carry for the next generation. In contrast, German feminists, for historical and contemporary reasons, dare not take their autonomy for granted. They are struggling to define boundaries between themselves and other political forces that will enable them to maintain their own radical vision while constructing effective alliances with those who share at least some commitment to women's equality. In a tradition in which individual rights have been a lesser concern, German feminists are formulating radical claims to self-determination.

Despite their different situations, strategies, and interpretations, it is clear that both German and American feminists are struggling toward a world in which women's equality and autonomy may both be realized. By comparing the different balances struck between these two concerns in the two movements, we can perhaps begin to clarify the strengths and weaknesses in each approach.

NOTES

Acknowledgments: Particular thanks are extended to Regina Becker-Schmidt, Christel Eckart, Axeli Knapp, Sylvia Kontos, and Wilma Mohr for their careful reading of earlier drafts of this paper. I developed many of the ideas expressed here with their help and was led to correct some of my misconceptions through their kindly and well-informed criticism. Any errors that remain despite their contributions are my responsibility alone.

1. West German henceforward refers to both the Federal Republic of Germany and West Berlin. Unless otherwise noted, all translations are my own. The descriptions of the West German feminist movement not otherwise attributed are based on my observations during two relatively brief periods of residence there (October–December 1982 and May–July 1985).

2. As the rest of the paper will attempt to explain, these terms are inexact and exaggerate some differences while tending to obscure others. Particularly in West Germany, the key distinction is really between the "autonomous women's movement" and all other women's groups. Feminists with both socialist and radical feminist perspectives, as here defined, are found in the autonomous movement, while the term "socialist feminist" is typically reserved for those who have not made a break with the traditional left especially the SPD and unions. I adopt the West German distinction in reference to feminists there.

3. Most universities have a women's group (i.e., *Lesben- und Frauenreferat*) within their student organization (ASTA) and some sort of meeting place exclusively for women (*Frauenraum*). These are not unlike women's centers at American universities. Women's centers distinct from the universities were once common projects in major cities but have now mostly closed.

4. Many movement "classics" use this analogy effectively (cf. Bem and Bem 1970; Hacker 1951; Morgan 1970), but there are serious costs in the overfacile use of this analogy as well: too often this language seems to present all the women as white and all the Blacks as men, making Black women invisible and obscuring important distinctions between the particular forms of oppression that white women, Black women and men, and women and men of other ethnic/racial backgrounds experience (Hooks 1981; Hull, Scott, and Smith 1982; Joseph and Lewis 1981).

5. This "Jim Crow" doctrine was affirmed by the Supreme Court in its infamous

Plessy v. Ferguson decision in 1896 and only began to be dismantled in the wake of the 1954 decision in *Brown v. the Board of Education of Topeka, Kansas*. The important role played by the Supreme Court in both cases highlights the significance of interpretations of the law, rather than niceties of wording, in determining its social impact.

6. While some liberal feminists are unsure that *being* the same as men now are is desirable, it is typically the radical and socialist minority that raises this question. The dominant liberal view seems to be that being *treated* the same as men is essential at present to achieve equality, as witness the priority put on non-gender-based insurance rates and coverage and NOW's *amicus curiae* brief in *Garland v. Bank of California*.

7. Baeker (1981) offers a union perspective on part-time work and its indisputable exploitation of women that recognizes but rejects the feminist critique. He insists that change in the family must occur *before* an expansion of part-time work can be supported, and greater equality in the family depends in turn on fulfillment of the Social Democratic program. This is the classic socialist position.

8. Erler, Jaeckel, and Sass (1982) also found that the level of maternity benefits to which women aspire is strongly affected by the existing level of benefits, which apparently creates a sense of entitlement and raises political expectations. This may help to explain the low level of support found in the U.S.

9. The present conservative West German government (CDU) has actually proposed some child care leave and allowance measures that might be considered feminist in the U.S. Feminists themselves, however, see the restriction of such support to married women and the relatively poor job protection provisions as indications that this support is intended to entice women back into traditional roles rather than facilitate a combination of paid work and child care (see, e.g., Beck-Gernsheim 1984; Schwarzer 1985).

10. The Greens are an attractive political party to most autonomous feminists, but how feminist the Greens really are is a matter of some debate. Feminists have been struggling, with little success, to include among the speakers at peace demonstrations women who will articulate the feminist connections between domestic violence (the *Alltagskrieg,* or everyday war) and international violence (Altbach 1984; Epple 1982; Quistorp 1983). On the other hand, the Greens have taken extraordinary measures to put women into leadership positions, such as dividing the party's electoral lists equally and rotating men out of and women into the official representative slots in the legislature. All four leadership positions were held by women in 1984–85 (the so-called *Feminat*), though naturally not without encountering significant sexism both inside and outside the party (Vollmer 1985).

11. One notable exception is Alice Schwarzer, the editor of *emma* and the single figure most identified with feminism in the popular imagination.

12. For the roots of this proletarian antifeminism in the bourgeois sexual ideology adopted by Marx and his followers, see the informative critique by Benenson (1984).

13. In addition to the relatively trivial takeover by the fascists of once-feminist organizations that had already become remarkably conservative, the Jewish women—once an active and influential part of the movement—were literally destroyed.

14. Although both themes were present in both countries, the problem of sexual exploitation by movement men seems to have engaged more energy and outrage in the U.S. (e.g., Morgan 1970; Piercy 1970), while the absence of social support for mothers and their work animated the earliest West German critics (see Sander 1968; 1978) and encouraged their extensive analysis of housework and child care as socially essential forms of labor for which wages should be paid.

15. Despite their vocal rejection of the "leftist categories of left and right, progressive and reactionary" and pleas for a "radical separation" from the Left (Menshik 1977, 108), radical feminists in West Germany do not show the estrangement from, even unfamiliarity with, socialist terms and methods of analysis that seems evident in American radical feminist circles. However, both countries have an apolitical segment of radical feminism apparently most concerned with individual spirituality and women's culture. The present analysis is focused less on them and more on those radical feminists who do see politics of some sort as their proper sphere of action.

16. In German, "alternative" carries the connotation of countercultural, as in the English phrase "alternative lifestyle." This proposal thus affirms the leftist and noninstitutional bias of the radical feminists even as it proposes creating a formal organization.

17. There are, of course, recurrent demands for no-strings support giving justifications for why this is the right thing, legally and morally, for the government to do (e.g., Gerhard and Schallhoeffer 1984). Many feminist shelters do in fact receive some state and local funding.

REFERENCES

Ahrens, L. 1980. "Battered Women's Refuges: Feminist Co-operatives or Social Service Institutions?" *Radical America* (May–June): 41–47.

Allen, A. T. 1985. "Mothers of the New Generation: Adele Schreiber, Helene Stoecker and the Evolution of a German Idea of Motherhood." *Signs* 10 (no. 3): 418–38.

Altbach, Edith. 1984. "The New German Women's Movement." In E. Altbach, J. Clause, D. Schultz, and N. Stephan, eds., *German Feminism: Readings in Politics and Literature,* 3–26. Albany: State University of New York Press. (Also appears in *Signs* 9 [no. 3]: 454–69.)

Baecker, G. 1981. "Teilzeitarbeit und individuelle Arbeitszeitflexibilisierung: Festschreibung der Benachteiligung von Frauen in Beruf und Familie." *WSI Mitteilungen* 4: 194–203.

Banks, Olive. 1981. *Faces of Feminism.* New York: St. Martin's Press.

Beck-Gernsheim, Elisabeth. 1984. *Vom Geburtenrueckgang zur neuen Muetterlichkeit?* Frankfort: Fischer.

Becker, Susan. 1983. "International Feminism between the Wars: The National Women's Party versus the League of Women Voters." In L. Scharf and J. Jenson, *Decades of Discontent: The Women's Movement, 1920–1940,* 223–42. Westport, Conn.: Greenwood Press.

Bem, Sandra, and Daryl Bem. 1970. "Case Study of a Non-conscious Ideology: Training the Woman to Know Her Place." In D. Bem, ed., *Beliefs, Attitudes and Human Affairs,* 89–99. Belmont, Calif.: Brooks/Cole.

Benenson, Harold. 1984. "Victorian Sexual Ideology and Marx's Theory of the Working Class." *International Labor and Working Class History* 25 (Spring): 1–23.

Bochum Shelter Initiative. 1982. "Down with Social Work: German Feminists Criticize Shelter Politics." *Off Our Backs,* November, p. 19.

Bock, Gisela. 1984. "Wages for Housework as a Perspective of the Women's Movement." In E. Altbach, J. Clause, D. Schultz, and N. Stephan, eds., *German Feminism: Readings in Politics and Literature,* 246–50. Albany: State University of New York Press.

Coward, Rosalind. 1983. *Patriarchal Precedents.* Boston: Routledge & Kegan Paul.

Demmer, H., B. Kuepper, and E. Kutzner. 1983. "Frauenarbeitsschutz: Gesundheits-schutz oder Ideologie?" *Beitraege zur feministische Theorie und Praxis* 9/10: 24–31.

Dobberthien, Marliese. 1981. "Schutz der oder Schutz vor weiblicher Arbeitskraft: Der Frauenarbeitsschutz." *WSI Mitteilungen* 4: 233–42.

Eckart, Christel. 1982. "Teilzeitarbeit: Eine prekaere Strategie gegen Einseitigkeit und Doppelbelastung." *Feministiche Studien* 1 (no. 1).

Eisenstein, Zillah. 1979. *Capitalist Patriarchy and the Case for Socialist Feminism*. New York: Monthly Review Press.

———. 1981. *The Radical Future of Liberal Feminism*. New York: Longman.

Epple, E. 1982. "100 Quadratmeter zuviel des Friedens." *Courage* 7 (July): 6.

Erie, S., M. Rein, and B. Wiget. 1983. "Women and the Reagan Revolution: Thermidor for the Social Welfare Economy." In I. Diamond, ed., *Families, Politics, and Public Policy*, 94–119. New York: Longman.

Erler, G., M. Jaeckel, and J. Sass. 1982. "Ergebnisse der europaeischen Vergleichsstudie zu Mutterschaftsurlaubs- und Elternurlaubsmassnahme." Research report, Deutsches Jugendinstitut, Munich.

Evans, Richard. 1976. *The Feminist Movement in Germany*. Beverly Hills, Calif.: Sage.

Evans, Sara. 1979. *Personal Politics: The Roots of Women's Liberation in the Civil Rights Movement and the New Left*. New York: Vintage.

Feldberg, Roslyn. 1984. "Comparable Worth: Toward Theory and Practice in the United States." *Signs* 10 (no. 2): 311–28.

Ferree, M. M. 1983. "Housework: Rethinking the Costs and Benefits." In I. Diamond, ed., *Families, Politics, and Public Policy*, 149–167. New York: Longman.

Ferree, M. M., and B. Hess. 1985. *Controversy and Coalition: The New Feminist Movement*. Boston: G. K. Hall.

Freeman, Jo. 1975. *The Politics of Women's Liberation*. New York: McKay.

———. 1984. "Public Policy and the Law." In J. Freeman, ed., *Women: A Feminist Perspective*, 3d ed., 381–401. Palo Alto, Calif.: Mayfield.

Friedan, Betty. 1976. *It Changed My Life: Writings on the Women's Movement*. New York: Random House.

Gelb, J., and M. Palley. 1982 (rev. ed. 1986). *Women and Public Policies*. Princeton, N.J.: Princeton University Press.

Gerhard, Ute. 1982. "A Hidden and Complex Heritage: Reflections on the History of Germany's Women's Movements." *Women's Studies International Forum* 5 (no. 6): 561–67.

Gerhard, Ute, and P. Schallhoeffer. 1984. "AUS fuer's Frauenhaus?" *Emma*, January, pp. 30–31.

Hacker, Helen. 1951. "Women as a Minority Group." *Social Forces* 30 (October): 60–69.

Hagemann-White, Carol. 1981. "Confronting Violence against Women in Germany." Paper presented at the First International Interdisciplinary Congress on Women, Haifa, Israel.

Hebenstreit, S. 1983. "Auslaendische Frauen: 'Randgruppe' der Frauenforschung?" *Frauenforschung: Informationsdienst des Forschunginstituts Frau und Gesellschaft* 1 (no. 1): 84–89.

Hooks, Bell. 1981. *Ain't I a Woman: Black Women and Feminism*. Boston: South End Press.

————. 1984. *Feminist Theory: From Margin to Center*. Boston: South End Press.

Hull, G., P. Scott, and B. Smith. 1982. *All the Women are White, All the Blacks are Men, but Some of Us Are Brave: Black Women's Studies*. Old Westbury, N.Y.: Feminist Press.

Jagger, A., and P. Rothenburg. 1984. *Feminist Frameworks*. 2d ed. New York: McGraw-Hill.

Joffe, Carole. 1983. "Why the United States Has No Child-Care Policy." In I. Diamond, *Families, Politics, and Public Policy*, 168–82. New York: Longman.

Joseph, G., and J. Lewis. 1981. *Common Differences: Conflicts in Black and White Feminist Perspectives*. Garden City, N.Y.: Doubleday.

Kontos, Sylvia. 1979. *Die Partei kaempft wie ein Mann.: Frauenpolitik der KPD in der Weimarer Republik*. Basel/Frankfort: Stroemfeld/Roter Stern.

Kurz-Scherf, I., and B. Stahn-Willig. 1981. "Gleiche Arbeit! Gleicher Lohn! und wer macht die Hausarbeit?" *WSI Mitteilungen* 4: 212–22.

Lappe, Lothar. 1981. *Die Arbeitssituation erwerbstaetiger Frauen*. Frankfort: Campus Verlag.

"Lebensborn auf Zeit." 1982. *Emma*, August, p. 15.

Menschik, Jutta. 1977. *Feminismus: Geschichte, Theorie, Praxis*. Cologne: Pahl-Rugenstein Verlag.

Millett, Kate. 1970. *Sexual Politics*. Garden City, N.Y.: Doubleday.

Morgan, Robin. 1970. "Goodbye to All That." *The Women's Rat* (January). Reprinted in *Going Too Far: The Personal Chronicle of a Feminist*, 1977, 121–30. New York: Random House.

Morrison, M. 1982. "Shelters: National Organizing against Domestic Violence." *Off Our Backs*, November, pp. 16–18.

Pearce, D. and H. McAdoo. 1981. *Women and Children: Alone and in Poverty*. Washington, D.C.: National Advisory Committee on Equal Opportunity.

Piercy, Marge. 1970. "The Grand Coolie Damn." In R. Morgan, ed., *Sisterhood is Powerful*, 421–38. New York: Random House.

Pinl, Claudia. 1977. *Das Arbeitnehmerpatriarchat: Die Frauenpolitik der Gewerkschaften*. Cologne: Verlag Kiepenheuer und Witsch.

Plogstedt, Sybelle. 1983. "Wenn Autonomie wird zum Dogma." *Courage* 8 (December): 54–60.

Plogstedt, S., and C. Douglas. 1982. "German Feminism Discussed." *Off Our Backs*, November.

Quistorp, E. 1983. "Von Mackern, Managern und Frauen—gegen Feministinnen—in der Friedensbewegung." *Courage* 8 (November): 6.

Rothschild-Whitt, Joyce. 1979. "The Collectivist Organization: An Alternative to Rational-Bureaucratic Models." *American Sociological Review* 44: 509–27.

Sander, H. 1968. "Rede des Aktionrates zur Befreiung der Frauen." Speech at 23rd Conference of Delegates, SDS (Frankfurt a/M) in *SDS Info*, 26–27, December.

————. 1978. "Muetter sind politische Personen." *Courage* 3 (October): 38–45. (Abridged and translated in E. Altbach et al., eds., *German Feminism* [Albany: State University of New York Press, 1984].)

Schenk, H. 1981. *Die feministiche Herausforderung*. Munich: Verlag C. H. Beck.

Scheu, U. 1983. "Schwestern zerreist eure Ketten." *Emma*, December, pp. 16–25.

————. 1984. "Ohne Macht seid Ihr wehrlos." *Emma*, January, pp. 38–45.

Schultz, D. 1984. "The German Women's Movement in 1982." In E. Altbach, J. Clause, D. Schultz, and N. Stephan, eds., *German Feminism: Readings in Politics and Literature*, 368–77. Albany: State University of New York Press.

Schuster, V. 1982. "Serie Nachkrieg IV: Freiheit, Gleichheit, und unsere verfluchte Lust, gluecklich zu sein." *Courage* 7 (September): 39–47.

Schwarzer, Alice. 1977. *Der "kleine Unterschied" und seine grosse Folgen*. Frankfort: Fischer Taschenbuch Verlag.

———. 1985. "Der zu kleine Unterschied." *Emma*, May, pp. 21–22.

Sealander, J. 1983. *As Minority Becomes Majority: Federal Reactions to Women in the Workforce*. Westport, Conn.: Greenwood Press.

Shanley, M. L. 1983. "Afterword: Feminism and Families in a Liberal Polity." In I. Diamond, *Families, Politics, and Public Policy*, 357–61. New York: Longman.

Slupik, V. 1982. "Gefaehrlicher Schutz." *Emma*, May, pp. 27–30.

Thoennesson, Werner. 1973. *The Emancipation of Women: The Rise and Decline of the Women's Movement in German Social Democracy, 1863–1933*. Translated by Joris de Bres. London: Pluto Press.

Tierney, K. 1982. "The Battered Women's Movement and the Creation of the Wife-Beating Problem." *Social Problems* 29: 207–20.

Vollmer, Anne. 1985. "Mein Jahr Feminat." *Emma*, May, p. 6.

Von Werlhof, Claudia. 1982. "Die Hausfrauisierung der Arbeit." *Courage* 7 (March): 34–43. (Translated and abridged as "The Proletarian Is Dead, Long Live the Housewife" in E. Altbach, J. Clause, D. Schultz, and N. Stephan, eds., *German Feminism* [Albany: State University of New York Press, 1984].)

9 Strategy and Tactics of the Women's Movement in the United States: The Role of Political Parties

ANNE N. COSTAIN

W. DOUGLAS COSTAIN

Since political parties have traditionally been the key institutions in American society that mobilize people to participate in politics, mediate among contending interests, and frame issues to be contested through the electoral process, it is rather surprising that the women's movement directed so little pressure for policy change through the parties prior to the 1980s.[1] The sharp increase in party involvement by some feminist organizations during the 1982 and 1984 election campaigns suggests a reversal of this trend but leaves unanswered the underlying question of why parties played so minor a role in the movement's political strategy during the early years. In this chapter we examine the changing political tactics of the women's movement throughout the period, focusing particularly on the relationship between the movement and political parties.

We have employed two principal sources of evidence in this analysis. The first is the archival material of two feminist organizations: the National Organization for Women (NOW), the first nationally organized group to emerge from the contemporary women's movement; and the Women's Equity Action League (WEAL), a group that formed after a policy split with NOW in 1968.[2] The second is a series of interviews with staff officials of active women's movement groups that have offices in Washington, D.C., spanning the period 1974 to 1984.[3] In addition, we have made use of the major published works detailing the political actions of the women's movement during the 1960s, 1970s and 1980s.[4]

There are several obvious similarities and links between political parties and social movements. Both are important vehicles for organizing people politically. The major function of American political parties is to contest elections, while movements attempt to bring about or halt social or political change. Parties are a type of political institution; movements are semiorganized efforts to challenge institutions and their policies. Movements operate somewhat spontaneously; major parties have a history that shapes their actions, and they answer in future elections for past failures. Clearly, the greater fluidity of social movement organizations and their more limited agenda of political concerns make it easier for them to work through political parties than vice versa. Parties are a part of the institutional apparatus of government that social movements may use to challenge current policy and to apply pressure for political change. Because parties and movements share a number of common characteristics as (1) mobilizers, (2) policy advocates, (3) incubators of new political ideas, and (4) large-scale groups within the body politic, there seems to be a natural fit between social movements seeking political change and parties looking for new issues and new constituencies. The case of the women's movement gives some insight into both the failure of social movements to make more use of political parties in their quest for political influence and the limited receptivity of parties to being used by movements.

POLITICAL TACTICS OF THE WOMEN'S MOVEMENT: AN OVERVIEW

The efforts of the women's movement to reach key political goals encompass a diverse range of tactics. It is not an overstatement to say that one part or another of the women's movement has tried virtually every routine and nonroutine method to attain political influence. However, if one compares its major actions in the 1960s, 1970s and 1980s, one sees a dominant thrust within the movement in each period. Simply, the *formative period* of the women's movement (1966 to 1972) utilized two competitive tactics: protest, and working through political elites. Neither approach emphasized contacts with political parties. The protesters saw parties as integral parts of an oppressive patriarchical political system. The elite women who believed that the system could be changed quickly and quietly through sympathetic public officials thought that a bipartisan approach would be most effective. In the *routinizing period* (1972 to 1977), which overlapped slightly with the formative years, the movement itself had become more cohesive, largely through its failure to achieve its most sought-after goals in the earlier period. There was a fairly broad consensus within the movement that *all* political tactics must now be tried to get a positive response from government. The *institutionalizing phase* (1978 to the present) represents an effort to consolidate the gains won during the preceding stage. Movement groups emphasized legislative lobbying, which had proved successful in the 1970s, and added new initiatives in electoral politics to bring themselves into closer alliance with political parties.

THE FORMATIVE YEARS

The early years of the women's movement were shaped by competiton between two distinct strategies for attaining political influence.[5] One group of activists and organizations emphasized the use of protest tactics developed by the Black civil rights and student radical movements. They believed that if the emerging women's movement used protest tactics and achieved important political change, then the tactics and their advocates would become central to the new movement. A second set of individuals and groups sought to exploit their existing political connections within the policy-making elite to bring about low-key but significant change in national policy; if these "insiders" could demonstrate success in using conventional political avenues for achieving the goals of the movement, then *they* would shape the leadership and strategy of the movement. The formative period was marked by the parallel but separate pursuit of these two divergent strategies.

Those within the movement who favored protest behaved like the political outsiders that they were. They combined confrontational politics with proselytizing through the underground press and informal self-help groups to build a cadre of committed feminists who demanded change in what they saw as an unresponsive and oppressive government. Many of their public actions—such as hexing the New York Stock Exchange, crowning a pig as Miss America, and holding sit-ins at male-only bars and restaurants—caught the eye of journalists and brought the women's movement to the attention of the average American (Hole and Levine 1971, 108–66; Ware 1970).

By contrast, the "older branch" seems quite sedate. Women associated with the State Commissions on the Status of Women organized the National Organization for Women (NOW) in 1966 under Betty Friedan's leadership. Their immediate goals were comparatively modest: "An organization is needed that can supply nation-wide pressure on an immediate basis, an organization that will identify the problems (in the field of equal rights) and relay the information to other interested organizations" (NOW 1966).

In 1968 two other national groups were set up, Federally Employed Women (FEW) and Women's Equity Action League (WEAL) (Fraser 1974; Lawton 1974). The National Women's Political Caucus (NWPC) was formed in 1972. The internal documents and papers of NOW and WEAL show the progressive disillusionment and growing militancy within these groups. While their younger sisters attracted media attention through politics in the streets, these high-powered women with access to top government officials had hoped that, given persuasive evidence illustrating the inequitable treatment of women, government would respond and begin to correct this unfairness.

The executive branch had been their chief target. For example, within hours of NOW's founding,

> telegrams were fired off to the White House demanding the reappointment of staunch feminist Richard Graham to the Equal Employment Opportunity Commission (EEOC); night letters went to the EEOC urging the rescinding of its discriminatory guidelines on "help wanted" advertising; individual communications went to Senators and Congressmen in support of equality for women in jury service. (NOW 1971a)

A report from NOW's president, Betty Friedan (1967) tells the membership of a series of meetings between a NOW delegation and various government officials:

We met for an hour with the Attorney General [Ramsey S. Clark], and for over an hour with [John W.] Macy [Chairman of the Civil Service Commission] and Evelyn Harrison, who has been given the assignment to expedite matters concerning women in federal government generally. We also had a brief session in Washington with Senator Margaret Chase Smith and a strategy talk with Senator [Representative] Martha Griffiths, whom we invited to join us in holding a press conference as a charter member of NOW. As you see by the [press] clippings, she did join us at the press conference and took that opportunity to announce her own new bill to erase inequalities against women in government service. The NOW delegation worked together very professionally indeed in covering the ground agreed upon in our presentations to Clark, Macy and the press, and judging from reports back via the Washington grapevine we may have had some impact.

The government had already taken several actions that seemed responsive to pressures from official groups representing women. As a result of the report of his Presidential Commission on the Status of Women, John F. Kennedy had established the Interdepartmental Committee on the Status of Women and the Citizen's Advisory Council on the Status of Women (East 1983). The most far-reaching action taken by government was the 1967 addition of gender to Executive Order 11246, which is the basis for federal affirmative action.[6]

But despite some scattered shifts in policy, many supporters of the "insider" strategy were clearly dissatisfied that more had not been achieved. It is evident that government officials had little interest in enforcing even the statutes that were on the books. Disquiet was apparent at the second national conference of NOW in November 1967. The conference agenda expanded as members passed a Bill of Rights endorsing reproductive freedom and the Equal Rights Amendment (ERA) to the federal constitution. NOW's acceptance of the ERA for the first time led many labor union women to leave the group (Freeman 1975, 80–81). Organized labor still took the position in 1968 that the ERA needlessly jeopardized hard-won laws protecting women workers. Others left because of NOW's support of legalized abortion.

Elizabeth Boyer was one of this group and went on to establish WEAL as a "conservative" NOW. Boyer (1977) recalled the impetus that led her to found WEAL in 1968: "It soon became apparent to me that I would not be able to convince women such as I knew, in the milieu of the heartland, to adopt the methods and causes which were initially embraced by the first women's organizations (in the East)." The methods objected to were those of protest and demonstration, which had become evident within NOW by 1968, and the issues were abortion and early discussions of sexual orientation.

WEAL took over from NOW as the most moderate voice in the more conservative wing of the movement. As NOW became more willing to join younger women in protest, WEAL tried to keep alive the tradition of conventional pressure for political change. However, the frustration of WEAL's officers is apparent even in the organization's first newsletter in 1970. The newsletter reported on a day of meetings at the Department of Labor where WEAL had been invited to consult on ways to implement the theme of the fiftieth anniversary of the Women's Bureau—"Womanpower: a National Resource."

> WEAL was chiefly concerned with the delay in issuing the Guidelines [on sex discrimination compliance with the 1964 Civil Rights Act], stemming from the meetings in August 1969, and asked if a committee from the group might go to the Secretary's office to request the Guidelines and to obtain, at least, a rough draft of them. WEAL's request was regarded as inappropriate and it was suggested that a note might be left for the Secretary requesting the guidelines. . . . Later, another request that a motion be forwarded asking that the Women's Bureau be elevated to a higher policy-making status was also set aside as being inappropriate to the purposes of the meeting. . . . In general, the meetings did not meet the expectations of WEAL. Perhaps our eager enthusiasm for action on the part of the Bureau was unrealistic . . . or should I say "inappropriate"? (WEAL 1970)

WEAL became involved in litigation in the late 1960s and early 1970s, trying to force government agencies such as those in the Department of Labor and the Department of Health, Education and Welfare to begin monitoring laws prohibiting sex discrimination. The most striking successes were a series of legal challenges to universities' hiring, employment, and firing practices based on the executive order prohibiting sex discrimination by federal contractors.

NOW, by contrast, was sponsoring many protest events. Even in 1967, members throughout the United States had picketed EEOC offices to urge the commission to stop sanctioning sex-segregated want ads.[7] The year 1969 was informally dubbed the "year of protest" for NOW. A Washington march sponsored by NOW in May 1969 was the largest demonstration for women's rights in the United States since the early 1900s. NOW's newsletter reported that women were on the move again:

> A feeling of intense camaraderie was experienced by all. There is nothing more radicalizing than protest the marchers agreed. Marguerite Rawalt, NOW's legal counsel, a woman old enough to be retired, said she had picketed that day for the first time in her life. "I don't know when I've had so much fun," she said (NOW 1969).

Wilma Scott Heide (1972) head of NOW in 1972, described the blend of political activities the organization was engaged in:

> [NOW] has worked within and outside the system to initiate change and implement women's rights and laws and executive orders on public contracts. . . . Our tactics and strategy include polite letters, interruption of conferences and Senate committees, demonstrating and consultations, calling for and coordinating the August 26 Strikes for Equality, rhetoric and positive programs, sisterly and brotherly conscious-raising, experiments with new organizational patterns and leadership styles.

NOW was combining the methods of protest and persuasion in its efforts to change public policy.

Even WEAL, the holdout in adopting disorderly tactics, began to drop its fervent disavowal of "women's liberation" and to accept a more radical political program. In 1970, founder Elizabeth Boyer had told the press: "We do not picket or chain ourselves to the White House gates. . . . And we are not a clutch of people getting together for group therapy" (Salisbury 1970). And its president, Nancy Dowding, asserted: "We don't take positions on issues that polarize people—like The Pill or abortion or husbands washing dishes" (Salisbury 1970). Yet by 1972, WEAL had altered its stand by supporting abortion, and had changed its rhetorical tone as well: "Great concern is justified for both the individual hardships and the mass unjustices and wastefulness which have been allowed to develop [because of sex discrimination]. Rebellion is inevitable, and WEAL stands for responsible rebellion" (WEAL 1972).

These changes reflect an acceptance of a long and far-reaching struggle against sex discrimination. Many activists had started out like Elizabeth Boyer, who thought she was "merely setting up a task force that probably would get its work done in five years" (WEAL 1978). But after five years of intense work the moderates recognized that sex discrimination would not be ended by passing a few statutes, and most radicals realized that no imminent social revolution would eliminate sexism and other social evils.

The radicals saw political parties as a barrier to change rather than a route to power. The parties were also bypassed by the more moderate and politically sophisticated activists who used their access to executive agencies and members of Congress to encourage direct government action on women's issues. Some women within the Republican and Democratic party structures were influenced by the ideas of the movement and pressed their parties to respond to the movement's goals (see Chapter 10). For the most part, though, the role of the parties as electoral mobilizers and symbols of policy direction was deemed irrelevant by individuals and organizations in search of rapid policy change.

Emerging national and local organizations within the women's movement worked together, using protest along with appeals to cabinet secretaries, the EEOC, and the courts, to effect change in policies towards women. The limited success of this strategy and the vanishing barriers between the radical and moderate sectors of the movement set the stage for a period of concerted organizing and of testing the multiple points of access in the political system.

ROUTINIZING POLITICAL PRESSURES

By the early 1970s, women's movement organizations were trying every political avenue to change policy. They approached political parties, Congress, the courts, and the executive branch; they used constitutional amendment, legislative lobbying, and political protest.

Political parties were among the first institutions of government that women's groups approached during this period. The National Women's Political Caucus

(NWPC) was established in 1972 to put pressure on political parties to bring more women into public life and to act more forcefully on questions of concern to women. The 1972 reform of the Republican and Democratic party rules, supported by the NWPC, brought many more women into the parties' presidential selection processes. The caucus also organized women delegates at the 1972 Democratic convention to put pressure on George McGovern to endorse a platform plank supportive of reproductive freedom. The McGovern organization refused and the plank failed, to the intense irritation of the feminists who had worked for the McGovern campaign (Deckard 1979, 364–65). After 1972, most women's groups directed less attention toward the political parties. If a candidate as sympathetic to women's issues as George McGovern would not use the party apparatus to push a key issue like abortion, it seemed unlikely that major policy change would be brought about through the parties.

In any case, Congress was becoming recognized as a much more promising institution for furthering women's issues. Almost 50 years after the Equal Rights Amendment was first introduced, it had finally passed both House and Senate in the spring of 1972. And even though organized women's movement groups had not directed much sustained attention toward the legislative body up to this point, Congress had passed several laws protecting women's rights, often at the urging of women in Congress or other influential women in government (Costain 1982, 29–30; Costain and Costain 1985; East 1983). The ERA itself was a centerpiece of women's historic efforts to improve their second-class citizenship and a rallying point for women's rights supporters.[8] In the early 1970s the ERA and most women's issues had solidly bipartisan support, so lobbying through party channels was largely unnecessary.

Most of the nationally organized women's movement groups began to set up ongoing legislative offices in Washington in 1972 and 1973 (Costain 1980). Despite the lure of lobbying as a way to change policy and get publicity for women's issues, the introduction of lobbying proved as divisive in many organizations as had the start of protest politics a few years before. State and local chapters of NOW and NWPC began dues strikes against the national offices because many members felt that lobbying was another way for the central organization to increase its power at the expense of the chapters, but NOW went ahead with lobbying and experienced a period of turmoil (Costain and Costain 1983). The NWPC downplayed lobbying and reduced internal division more quickly. WEAL moved slowly and cautiously, starting out with a part-time volunteer and waiting until 1976 to hire its first paid but still part-time lobbyist. Not until 1979 did WEAL and NWPC hire full-time paid lobbyists (Bros 1981; Reuss 1981). Women's Lobby, organized by Carol Burris as the lobbying arm for the women's movement, operated throughout the 1970s but disbanded in 1979 when the financial pressures of sustained lobbying without an active membership became too great. Federally Employed Women (FEW), the final Washington-based women's movement group that engaged in lobbying, never had paid lobbyists or lobbied on more than a narrow band of issues. Although these groups were small in number and moved into lobbying very hesitantly, they drew on the experience and guidance of many traditional women's groups, which had long engaged in legislative work. By forming coalitions with the League of Women Voters, the American Association of University Women (AAUW) and the National Federation of Business and Professional Women (BPW)—to name just a few of the more active groups they worked with—women's movement organizations helped trigger a wave of legislative action on women's issues unequaled in U.S. history (Costain and Costain 1985; Freeman 1982).

During the 1970s the courts were also a highly productive arena for change. After the breakthrough case of *Reed v. Reed* in 1971, there followed a steady stream of cases using the equal protection clause of the constitution to knock down sexually discriminatory statutes. A second line of cases, starting with *Roe v. Wade* in 1973, used the constitutional right to privacy to make legal abortions available to women.[9] Women's groups working exclusively on litigation, such as the legal defense funds of NOW and WEAL, shepherded these cases through the courts.[10] One of the rare instances when law-oriented groups worked with lobbying groups involved the passage of an amendment to the 1964 Civil Rights Act. After litigation failed to stop employment discrimination against pregnant workers, legal as well as legislative organizations turned to Congress to plug this loophole. The Pregnancy Disability Act (1978) passed through the efforts of a broad-based coalition supported by labor, civil liberty, anti-abortion, women's, and Black civil rights groups.[11]

The executive branch remained a frequent target of the more organized groups within the women's movement. The two Presidential Commissions on the Status of Women, under John Kennedy and Richard Nixon, issued reports that had far-reaching impact in setting priorities on women's issues. The first (Roosevelt Commission) report, *American Women* (President's Commission 1963) provided strong evidence of legal and economic inequities. Its emphasis on eliminating laws restricting the rights of married women and government support for child care established major objectives of the women's movement for the next decade. The State Commissions on the Status of Women, set up on the recommendation of the Roosevelt Commission report, played a vital role in publicizing women's concerns in many states. The second report, *A Matter of Simple Justice* (President's Task Force 1970), endorsed the Equal Rights Amendment, the removal of gender-based inequity in many federal programs, and federal assistance for child care.

Following President Lyndon Johnson's executive order mandating affirmative action for women, the White House provided very little leadership on major issues of concern to women. Lobbying by organization leaders continued behind the scenes at the executive level but produced few visible results. Without a strongly sympathetic president there was little that could be accomplished through the executive branch.

Political protest was also dying out in the 1970s. There were protests by women's groups, including NOW's annual August 26 strikes; however, most people recognized that with the end of the war in Vietnam, protest politics was fading from the American political landscape.[12]

Women's movement groups were less visible at the 1976 presidential nominating conventions than they had been in 1972. Women delegates themselves did organize into caucuses and negotiate with candidate organizations and other caucuses to promote recognition of women's issues in the party platforms; however, although many of these women were affiliated with movement groups, it seems fair to argue that party endorsement of women's rights was sought for largely symbolic reasons. The political parties were not ignored by the movement, if only because of the media attention lavished on their quadrennial conventions, but few activists in the movement saw them as a vehicle for significant policy change. Other avenues of influence were proving more fruitful.

Women's groups and their allies worked particularly hard during this period to ratify the Equal Rights Amendment and succeeded in activating large numbers of amendment supporters in the states. Their effort also mobilized a backlash against women's rights and divided community opinion on a variety of women's issues (Boles 1979, 61–99). By the end of the 1970s the ERA had become a powerful symbolic issue, both rallying people behind the women's cause and spurring organized opposition to it. But as controversy grew there was little chance that the amendment itself would win the extraordinary majorities necessary to add it to the constitution. Legislative lobbying and litigating had weathered the 1970s as the best hopes for producing policy change. As the Supreme Court became more conservative under Ronald Reagan's administration, Congress began to attract an unprecedented amount of attention from women's groups. This rising interest in legislative politics in turn encouraged many movement organizations to expand their involvement in electoral politics, which had been extremely limited up to this point.

INSTITUTIONALIZING WOMEN'S INTERESTS

Congressional lobbying and electoral politics emerged from the wide range of tactics pursued by the women's movement in the 1970s as the vehicles most likely to advance women's interests in the 1980s. By the late 1970s, representatives of women's groups had established routinized, efficient lobbying coalitions. Catherine East (1984) described her own experience when she assumed the post of legislative director of the National Women's Political Caucus in 1983:

> Pat Reuss [WEAL lobbyist] helped us get plugged in to the different coalitions and information networks from the very beginning. . . . Many of these women's issues at this stage are becoming more and more technical. We have to depend on other organizations to keep us informed on a number of these issues. We depend on a pension rights organization with 501-C-3 tax status to give us information on that

issue. WEAL has a marvelous group on women and the military. There is expertise all over town. For education PEER [Project on Equal Education Rights] helps and Bunny [Bernice] Sandler's group the Project on the Status and Education of Women of the Association of American Colleges.

This specialization of function among women's groups—with some organizations choosing to concentrate on particular areas of policy, some on direct lobbying on the Hill, some on educating their membership, and some on preparing research and pursuing cases through the courts—represents a continuation of the pattern of cooperative lobbying that women's groups have used since the early 1970s (Costain 1980). The chief drawback of such a style is the need for continuous and careful coordination among the separate groups.

By the 1980s, close cooperation had become the norm. The Congressional Caucus on Women's Issues, founded in 1977, did a great deal to help this process along, providing a centralized communication and information center in Congress for the shifting coalitions. By helping separate groups become aware of who was working on what specific issues and then making this known to members of Congress, the Congressional Caucus has speeded up the flow of information and cut down on duplication of effort. On a more general level, the Congressional Caucus creates a climate of concern for women's issues within Congress and beyond. It publishes a newsletter, *Update,* which is circulated on the Hill and to the media, and it distributes a weekly memorandum to its more than 125 congressional members, tracking bills and issues of interest to women as they are introduced and discussed in Congress. The director, Ann Smith (1984) described its links to the press: "By providing information to the press and giving them news releases, we help establish a category in the minds of the presswomen. When members [of Congress] read about women's issues in the press they know that they will be asked about women's issues by their constituents."

A strengthened lobby on women's issues took shape as individual groups within it began to think of their organizations as representing a unique constituency, women. Earlier, these same groups had concentrated on equal rights. They had emphasized that rights possessed by men should be extended to women on the same terms—access to credit, equal pay for equal work, educational opportunity, and equality under the law guaranteed by the constitution through an equal rights amendment. As women began to shift emphasis away from this pure focus on equality and draw attention to a broader range of issues affecting women as constituents, lobbying became even more important. As Ann Smith (1984) explained: "We always call them and think of them as women's issues, not feminist issues. . . . We tell members of Congress how women would be affected by a piece of legislation. We are a constituency just like Blacks and Jews."

Pat Reuss (1984) of WEAL was just as explicit:

We tell members of Congress, you cannot forget women when you are working on social security. You have to think of women when you do a jobs bill. Economic bills must look at their impact on women since so many are now in the work force. . . .

The gender gap is women who are concerned with jobs, fairness, inflation, employment, social security and school lunch programs, not just "women's issues." There
is a real cause and effect which we have to communicate to members of Congress.
We have to teach them that there are women in their districts who care about these
issues—that they can get elected and care about women, that their private parts
won't fall off if they care about women.

The significance of representing women as a separate interest was enhanced
with the appearance of a gender gap that divided the political attitudes and voting
behavior of men and women in the late 1970s. The gender gap added legitimacy
to women's political interests and provided an impetus to extend the efforts of the
women's movement into the electoral arena. Ann Smith (1984) never doubted that
there was a gender gap in the country waiting to be organized:

We knew it had to be. There had to be a gender gap. It is like physicists. They knew
that there had to be subatomic particles because of the way atoms behave. We know
that women have interests. Women, if they have interests, have to vote their interests. . . . Women are still shy about putting their own interests first. They are socialized to deemphasize their own needs."

The political impact of such a gap was obvious immediately to those who
worked with Congress. Catherine East (1984), legislative director of NWPC, observed: "We are likely to get a number of pieces of legislation through Congress.
None is earth shattering. We probably could not have gotten any of them if it
were not for the gender gap." And a lobbyist quoted in the *Congressional Quarterly* explained, "We have gotten a lot of mileage out of this gender gap. We call
it women's vote. Hell, we don't want to close it. . . . We want to widen it" (Cohodas 1983a). WEAL lobbyist Pat Reuss (1984) concluded: "The gender gap and
awareness of women's political sensitivity are now quite prevalent. There is a considered opinion that women are a factor politically. That is the starting point from
which you can approach people on Capitol Hill."

The utility of the gender gap for the lobbying work of organized movement
groups produced an irresistible impetus to broaden the electoral work of these
groups as well. If a 6 or 7 percent spread between women's and men's voting preferences attracted so much attention, a wider gap might attract even more.
Women's groups saw that by influencing the vote, they could make elected officials more receptive to women's special interests. Organizations such as the
Women's Campaign Fund and the National Women's Political Caucus had been
involved in contributing to campaigns and working with candidates for a number
of years, yet their national influence was small, largely because they had so little
money to distribute. But after the 1980 election more women's groups became
involved in electoral politics, and the scale of their involvement grew. A political
action committee established by NOW in 1978 (NOW-PAC) raised and contributed more than a million dollars to national and state campaigns in 1982. The
NWPC's PAC gave out more than a half-million dollars that same year, and the

Women's Campaign Fund collected more than a quarter-million for candidates (Bonafede 1982). In some of the 1982 races a "women's vote" was a decisive factor in the outcome. It helped Democrat Mario Cuomo defeat his gubernatorial opponent, Lewis Lehrman, in New York. It assisted Mark White in winning the governorship of Texas. In other races, although there were sharp differences in the degree of support men and women gave to specific candidates, these differences were not sufficient to produce victories for "female-supported" politicians like Harriet Woods in Missouri and Toby Moffett in Connecticut.

The gender gap, in addition to spurring women's groups to make political endorsements and raise and distribute money to candidates, stirred a new debate over the relationship between political parties and organizations representing women. In the past, most women's groups were scrupulously bipartisan in their political work; since the 1980 election, however, NOW has increasingly allied itself with the Democratic party. In 1982 only 15 percent of the money distributed by NOW-PAC went to Republican candidates (Bonafede 1982). The sharpest break with bipartisanship came with NOW's 1983 endorsement of Walter Mondale for the presidency, prior to the Democratic national convention and earlier than the Republican party's official designation of a presidential candidate. NOW has been a frequent leader in establishing new trends within the women's movement, but this attachment to the Democratic party has caused concern among some other women's groups. The NWPC's Catherine East (1984) noted: "NOW has not been lobbying on a lot of these [women's] issues. They said that they are devoting all their time to the [1984] election and ERA. NOW is so closely linked to the Democratic party that it creates problems in lobbying." And WEAL's Pat Reuss (1984) observed:

> With the endorsement of Walter Mondale they [NOW] jumped right in the middle of politics. It is getting NOW in the center of the electoral contest. They are now restricted in the ways that they can work for their issues—reproductive choice, the ERA, insurance and pension reform. NOW will still "sign on" to issues that we are lobbying for in Washington. You just have to call them and they are quite willing to sign on, but there is not much that they can do on these issues.

NOW's political resources were fully committed to electoral politics with little staff time or money left for lobbying.

Interestingly, the positive impact of the gender gap on legislative lobbying, which led many women's organizations to put more effort into electoral politics, has reached a point where electoral involvement could jeopardize lobbying work. This can be blamed on the lack of "responsible" policy-making parties in America as well as the current weakness of party control in Congress. Interest groups play a crucial role in assembling legislative coalitions and usually need votes from both parties in order to create majorities on specific issues. Thus, women's groups and other lobbying groups benefit from *not* being too closely tied to one political party. Against this, NOW representatives would argue that to receive maximum advantage from involvement in electoral politics, it is necessary to build up credits within a single party. Many women's groups, including NOW, participated in a coalition to register more women to vote in the 1984 election, remaining bipartisan but pursuing a policy that by implication increased the vote for Democratic candidates.

Although the 1984 elections revealed the continuation of an identifiable difference between male and female voting patterns, the "women's vote" was not large enough to influence the presidential election. Despite this limited impact on the outcome of the most visible contest, many media commentators and politicians do credit the gender gap with an important role in deciding several close races (see Mueller 1987). Lobbyists for women's groups are thus able to back up their arguments with a widely held perception of significant electoral clout.

The Republican party, which has been disadvantaged by the growth of a women's voting bloc, has attempted to diffuse the partisan implications of the gender gap by both rhetorical and substantive actions. Prominent women Republicans are used to symbolize the party in public, and a number of Republican politicians have championed particular women's issues in Congress. Democratic party leaders both inside and outside Congress made efforts to add women to the coalition of Democratic support groups. Electorally, the nomination of Geraldine Ferraro as its vice-presidential candidate was intended to symbolize the Democratic party as the women's party. In Congress, Democratic leaders in the House used parliamentary maneuvers in a 1983 vote to revive the Equal Rights Amendment in order to portray the Democrats as the party of equality (Cohodas 1983b). The ability of the organized groups within the women's movement to continue to take advantage of the two parties' competition for the women's vote will depend on their success in harmonizing the often conflicting demands of policy influence via electoral politics and legislative lobbying.

CONCLUSIONS

Despite the importance of political parties in American politics, they have been largely tangential to the successes and failures of the current women's movement. Jo Freeman's analysis (see Chapter 10) helps to explain how feminists attained leverage in the Democratic party. But to understand the past distance between and current entanglement of parties and the movement, we must consider the structure of U.S. parties, their role in the political system in the 1970s and 1980s, and the nature of the women's movement.

Neither the women's movement nor any other social movement in the 1970s achieved significant gains by working through political parties. The American political system frustrates the concerted efforts to change policy that characterize movements. Policy specialization within numerous "subgovernments" rewards those with technical expertise and experience in the labyrinth of decision-making, rather than broadly mobilized interests. Originally an impediment to tyrannical government, the separation of the legislative, executive, and judicial powers has become a complex tangle of largely uncoordinated policy-making arenas, each with its own rules and rituals. The structure encourages and reflects nonprogrammatic, piecemeal decision-making as broad issues are decomposed into problems addressable by specialized policy-making networks. Social movements seeking broad-scale social change, like the women's movement, are forced to adapt their strategy and tactics to fit a decentralized decision-making environment in which no single institution possesses sufficient authority to meet the range of demands posed. Moreover, the existence of multiple, highly autonomous policy-making bodies defies coordination by any political body, including the parties. Political parties may be able to provide access and influence on some issues and for some decision-makers, notably the president, but their role is limited in many other important areas, including the courts and even Congress.

The characteristics of American political parties also make them less than satisfactory partners for social movements seeking political change. The Republican and Democratic parties have evolved into electoral mobilizers, able to present slates of candidates under a party label and to attract votes for these slates. Scholars and commentators have searched in vain for signs that the parties are disciplined, cohesive bodies able to articulate a distinct set of policies for the voters and then to govern the nation in accord with such a program. Despite central control over delegate selection procedures, the parties continue to be highly decentralized organizationally and diverse in policy preferences. Policy is used to attract voters and to symbolize vague unifying emotions, rather than as a principled blueprint for future action.

The observed decline of parties in the 1970s and 1980s has exposed new limitations. Electorally, the parties are losing their traditional ability to guide the choices of voters. The cues to voting provided by party labels mean less as more voters split their tickets and others declare themselves psychologically independent of attachment to either party. Changes in campaign finance laws and the emergence of new campaign technologies also allow more autonomy for candidates. Candidate-centered campaigns organized by the individual rather than the party break down links between candidates running under the same banner. This individualization of campaigning has its parallel inside government in the series of reforms that has decentralized decision-making within Congress, encouraging individual members of Congress to assert their independence. Reforms in the presidential nominating system have also weakened the ties of presidential candidates to their party organizations and loosened some bonds between Congress and the White House. Throughout the 1970s political parties did not seem to be carrying out their basic functions, much less serving as avenues for transforming American society. The women's movement emerged in an era when the parties were not vibrant, powerful, and self-confident political actors. The movement gained symbolic benefits from the parties—rhetorical commitments to women's rights in the party platform and more women delegates at the conventions—but not much more.

The evolution of the strategy and tactics of the women's movement also steered the movement away from close association with the parties. Once it became clear that neither the moralistic exhortations of the 1960s protestors nor the rational approach of the moderates would transform America, the movement achieved, through trial and error, a significant degree of success in changing policy by behaving as a sophisticated interest group. Although there continues to be tension between the special-interest activities of some groups, notably NOW, and their link to the women's movement, the opportunities for access to policy-making that are afforded to America's interest groups allow them a fairly secure niche in Washington. Interest groups maintain legitimacy as the advocates of particular groups as long as they can demonstrate genuine grassroots support for their positions.

In the 1980s the increasing success of the women's movement in mobilizing and arousing mass support for its policy agenda has brought the movement closer to the electoral domain of political parties. The emergence of a gender gap in voting encouraged representatives of women's groups to try to use this highly visible electoral constituency to reinforce its lobbying activities. However, in attempting to perpetuate and widen the gender gap through financial contributions to sympathetic candidates and to use the media to articulate the policy content of the gender gap, women's groups were quickly drawn into the Democratic party's political orbit.

In evaluating the short-term gains of women's groups, especially NOW, within the Democratic party, one must balance the gains represented by having a woman vice-presidential nominee in a losing campaign against postelection changes that threaten the role of organized constituency groups in the party. The new chair of the Democratic National Committee, Paul Kirk, has begun to eliminate the system of formally recognized caucuses within the national organization that had provided a haven for feminist Democrats. Since the Democrats have lost four of the past five presidential contests, they may not be able to deliver enough support for women's movement policies or access to policy-makers to compensate for the loss of political influence caused by the overt partisanship of some women's movement groups.

An enduring "women's vote" can be used to gain a solid place on the national political agenda for women's movement issues. However, if the gender gap endures solely as a component of the Democratic party's constituency, then the ability of women's organizations to call upon Republican support for women's rights policies will be limited. It is an open question whether the benefits from assimilation within a responsive Democratic party are worth endangering a proved record of political gains through a bipartisan interest-group strategy.

NOW is likely to be in the vanguard in making the choice between party politics and interest-group lobbying. The election of Eleanor Smeal to the presidency of NOW and its endorsement of a major legislative effort in 1985–86 to restore strong federal enforcement of antidiscrimination laws may mark a shift away from party politics.[13] Since NOW initiated close ties to the Democratic party, this change in political strategy may reduce tension among women's groups over how partisan the movement should be.

NOTES

1. Although our emphasis differs from that of Jo Freeman, who examines the activity of feminists *within* the political parties, her essay (Chapter 10) and ours should be seen, on the whole, as complementary. We and Freeman find that in the 1980s, party politics is much more central to the strategy and tactics of the women's movement. Freeman's chapter explains how this came about; ours examines why it did not happen earlier.

2. The official archives of NOW and WEAL are housed in the Elizabeth and Arthur Schlesinger Library at Radcliffe College, Cambridge, Massachusetts.

3. Representatives of the following groups were interviewed: Federally Employed Women (FEW), 30 December 1974 and 7 May 1975; National Organization for Women (NOW), 31 October 1974, 5 August 1975, 6 May 1977, and 7 January 1981; National Women's Political Caucus (NWPC), 22 October 1974, 6 January 1981, and 20 January 1984; Women's Equity Action League (WEAL), 25 November 1974, 6 January 1981, and 20 January 1984; Women's Lobby, 3 December 1974 (Women's Lobby disbanded in 1979). Two interviews were also conducted with Ann Smith, director of the Congressional Caucus on Women's Issues (formerly the Congresswomen's Caucus), 7 January 1981 and 20 January 1984; this is a group organized in Congress to keep abreast of women's issues and to perform a liaison role between interested members of Congress and groups representing women.

4. Particularly useful as political histories were Freeman 1975; Gelb and Palley 1982; Chafe 1972; Boles 1979; Boneparth 1982; Conover and Gray 1983; Steiner 1985.

5. See Freeman (1975) for an excellent account of this struggle.

6. On 13 October 1967, President Lyndon Johnson amended his earlier Executive Order 11246 (which required federal contractors and federal assisted construction contracts to take affirmative action to guarantee nondiscriminatory hiring and employment practices) to include sex as a prohibited form of employment discrimination. For a more detailed overview of executive orders and affirmative action, see Kay 1981, 78–86, 987–1010.

7. NOW press releases detail a series of marches, demonstrations, and picketing at regional EEOC offices in New York, Chicago, and San Francisco. Also, throughout 1968, NOW and its chapters staged a variety of protest actions, including a boycott of United Airlines, a week (9–15 February) of protest against male-only public accommodations; a "Fast to Free Women from Poverty Day" on 18 May; and a "national unveiling," burning veils that women wear to church (NOW 1971b).

8. For the meaning of the ERA in its contemporary context, see Conover and Gray (1983, 12–67); Boles (1979). Good historical interpretations may be found in Becker (1981) and Chafe (1972, 112–32).

9. Reed v. Reed, 404 U.S. 71 (1971); Roe v. Wade, 410 U.S. 113 (1973).

10. For a discussion of the relationship between tax status and permissible lobbying activities, see Berry 1977, 45–59.

11. The Pregnancy Disability Act and the background behind its passage are thoroughly discussed in Gelb and Palley 1982, 154–66.

12. Note the sharp dropoff in protest demonstration in the United States beginning in 1973 (from Taylor and Jodice 1983, 22):

Year	1960	1968	1970	1971	1972	1973	1974	1975	1976	1977
No. of demonstrations	105	128	99	152	243	69	60	59	36	51

13. The 1985 national convention of NOW passed the Civil Rights Restoration Act Resolution, laying out a strategy for winning congressional approval for this legislation. If passed, the bill would reverse the Supreme Court decision that restricted the government's ability to curtail funds for non-compliance with anti-discrimination provisions in the law in *Grove City College v. Bell,* 79 LEd 516 (1984). If the bill fails, NOW plans to make the legislation a major issue in the 1986 elections.

REFERENCES

Becker, Susan D. 1981. *The Origins of the Equal Rights Amendment.* Westport, Conn.: Greenwood.

Berry, Jeffrey M. 1977. *Lobbying for the People.* Princeton, N.J.: Princeton University Press.

Boles, Janet. 1979. *The Politics of the Equal Rights Amendment.* New York, Longman.

Bonafede, Dom. 1982. "Women's Movement Broadens the Scope of Its Role in American Politics." *National Journal* 14 (11 December): 2109.

Boneparth, Ellen, ed. 1982. *Women, Power and Policy.* Elmsford, N.Y.: Pergamon Press.

Boyer, Elizabeth. 1977. "In the Beginning . . ." *WEAL National Newsletter* 9, December. In the file "WEAL Newsletters—Master File," Schlesinger Library, Radcliffe College.

Bros, Carol (NWPC). 1981. Interview, Washington, D.C., 6 January.

Chafe, William. 1972. *The American Woman.* New York: Oxford University Press.

Cohodas, Nadine. 1983a. "More Service, Less Construction." *Congressional Quarterly Weekly Report* 41 (19 February): 415–16.

———. 1983b. "New Unity Evident." *Congressional Quarterly Weekly Report* 41 (23 April): 782–83.

Conover, Pamela, and Virginia Gray. 1983. *Feminism and the New Right.* New York: Praeger.

Costain, Anne N. 1980. "The Struggle for a National Women's Lobby." *Western Political Quarterly* 33 (December): 476–91.

———. 1982. "Representing Women: The Transition from Social Movement to Interest Group." In Ellen Boneparth, ed., *Women, Power and Policy,* 19–37. Elmsford, N.Y.: Pergamon Press.

Costain, Anne N., and W. Douglas Costain. 1983. "The Women's Lobby." In Allan J. Cigler and Burdett A. Loomis, eds., *Interest Group Politics,* 191–216. Washington, D.C.: CQ Press.

———. 1985. "Movements and Gatekeepers: Congressional Response to Women's Movement Issues, 1900–1982." *Congress and the Presidency* 12 (Spring): 21–42.

Deckard, Barbara Sinclair. 1983. *The Women's Movement*. 2d ed. New York: Harper & Row.

East, Catherine. 1983. "American Women: 1963, 1983, 2003." Study commissioned by the National Federation of Business and Professional Women's Clubs, Washington, D.C.

———. (NWPC). 1984. Interview, Washington, D.C., 20 January.

Fraser, Arvonne (WEAL). 1974. Interview, Washington, D.C., 25 November.

Freeman, Jo. 1975. *The Politics of Women's Liberation*. New York: McKay.

———. 1982. "Women and Public Policy." In Ellen Boneparth, ed., *Women, Power and Policy*, 47–67. Elmsford, N.Y.: Pergamon Press.

Friedan, Betty. 1967. "Memo to All Board Members," 24 January. In the file "NOW—President's Reports, Letters, etc., 1966–1976," Schlesinger Library, Radcliffe College.

Gelb, Joyce, and Marian Lief Palley. 1982. *Women and Public Policies*. Princeton, N.J.: Princeton University Press.

Heide, Wilma Scott. 1972. "The Feminist Cause *Is* the Common Cause." Speech delivered to the American College Personnel Association, Chicago, 27 March. In Schlesinger Library, Radcliffe College.

Hole, Judith, and Ellen Levine. 1971. *Rebirth of Feminism*. New York: Quadrangle.

Kay, Herma Hill. 1981. *Text, Cases and Materials on Sex-based Discrimination*. 2d ed. St. Paul, Minn.: West Publishing.

Lawton, Esther (FEW). 1974. Interview, Washington, D.C., 30 December.

Mueller, Carol, ed. 1987. *The Politics of the Gender Gap*. Sage Yearbook in Women's Policy Studies, vol. 12. Beverly Hills, Calif.: Sage.

NOW. 1966. "National Organization for Women—June 29, 1966." In the file "National Office and Policy," Schlesinger Library, Radcliffe College.

———. 1969. *Now Acts* 2 (Winter/Spring): 4. In vertical file, Schlesinger Library, Radcliffe College.

———. 1971a. "The First Five Years, 1966–1971." In vertical file, Schlesinger Library, Radcliffe College.

———. 1971b. "NOW Press Releases, 1966–71." File in Schlesinger Library, Radcliffe College.

President's Commission on the Status of Women. 1963. *American Women*. Washington, D.C.: Government Printing Office.

President's Task Force on Women's Rights and Responsibilities. 1970. *A Matter of Simple Justice*. Washington, D.C.: Government Printing Office.

Reuss, Patricia (WEAL). 1981. Interview, Washington, D.C., 6 January.

———. 1984. Interview, Washington, D.C., 20 January.

Salisbury, Wilma. 1970. "Another Lib Voice Heard From." *Cleveland Plain Dealer*, 28 June.

Smith, Ann (Congressional Caucus on Women's Issues). 1984. Interview, Washington, D.C., 20 January.

Steiner, Gilbert Y. 1985. *Constitutional Inequality: The Political Fortunes of the Equal Rights Amendment*. Washington, D.C.: Brookings Institution.

Taylor, Charles, and David Jodice. 1983. *World Handbook of Political and Social Indicators*. 3d ed., vol. 2. New Haven, Conn.: Yale University Press.

Ware, Celestine. 1970. *Woman Power*. New York: Tower.

WEAL. 1970. *WEAL's Word Watcher* 1 (Winter). In the file "WEAL National Newsletter," Schlesinger Library, Radcliffe College.

———. 1972. "WEAL Holds These Truths to Be Self-Evident." In "WEAL—Folder 219," Schlesinger Library, Radcliffe College.

———. 1978. "Tenth Anniversary Conference Draws Largest Attendance Ever." *WEAL National Newsletter* (August). In the file "WEAL National Newsletter," Schlesinger Library, Radcliffe College.

10 Whom You Know versus Whom You Represent: Feminist Influence in the Democratic and Republican Parties

JO FREEMAN

In the last few years feminism has become highly identified with the Democratic party and antifeminism with the Republican party. This development is ironic for two reasons. When the contemporary women's movement emerged in the mid-1960s, its founders had no desire to become closely identified with any political party; many of them viewed both parties as representatives of a status quo that they disdained, and the rest preferred bipartisan activity. The second irony is that the parties with which feminism and antifeminism are currently identified are the opposite of their historical affiliations. In the last ten years not only has feminism become partisan in nature, but the parties have switched sides.

This chapter explores the impact of the women's movement on the major political parties and argues that the polarization has occurred because the political culture of the Democratic party is more receptive to the influence of organized interests than that of the Republican party, and it has been undergoing some significant transformations that have redefined the structure of available opportunities for action. The political culture of the Republican party gives greater weight to personal connections, and the personal connections of Republican feminists have not been to the winners of intraparty political struggles.

"EQUALITY" VERSUS "PROTECTION": THE ORIGINAL FIGHT
The women's suffrage movement was not a united movement. It had two distinct branches with different strategies and different goals that were not abandoned even after suffrage was attained. The moderate branch was by far the largest and is given most of the credit for the Nineteenth Amendment. Its dominant organization was the National American Women's Suffrage Association, which, under the leadership of Carrie Chapman Catt, mobilized the ratification campaign

215

through its state chapters. Even before final ratification, Catt successfully urged her followers to disband the feminist organization and form a nonpartisan, non-sectarian League of Women Voters (LWV) which would encourage women to work within the parties and would support a broad range of social reforms.

The militant feminists, under the banner of the National Woman's Party (NWP), had used civil disobedience, colorful demonstrations, and incessant lob-bying to get the Nineteenth Amendment out of Congress. Once it was ratified, they decided to focus their attention on the eradication of legal discrimination against women through another constitutional amendment (Lemons 1973, 49). Concentrated in Washington and funded more by legacies and wealthy benefac-tors than a large membership, the NWP found this strategy suitable to its particu-lar strengths as well as its feminist ideology. The Equal Rights Amendment, writ-ten by the NWP's guiding light Alice Paul, was strongly opposed by the LWV, the newly created Women's Bureau of the Department of Labor, the National Women's Trade Union League, the National Consumers' Union, and most other women's organizations. Their opposition was based on the one fact about the ERA on which everyone could agree: that it would abolish protective labor legislation for women.[1]

By 1923 both sides had hardened; over the next few decades each devoted itself to undermining the position of the other, with the result that each side's efforts to improve women's lot canceled the other's. For example, in 1932, at the urging of Republican NWP members, President Herbert Hoover issued an execu-tive order denying federal agency heads the right to use sex as a job qualification. In 1934 the Women's Bureau persuaded President Franklin Roosevelt to reverse this decision by arguing that appointments of women to the civil service had de-clined as a result (Lemons 1973, 83).

Over time, the division of opinion on the ERA more and more became one of class or, more specifically, occupation. Women in industry, or associated with women working in industry—particularly unionized industries—opposed the ERA because they supported protective legislation. Business and professional women supported the ERA and opposed protective labor legislation, which they saw as a barrier to effective competition against men in their professions. Indeed, it was the attempt of protectionists to bring women in business establishments (primarily clerical and retail sales workers) under the protective umbrella that pushed business and professional women's clubs from neutrality to support for the ERA. From the businesswomen's perspective, these positions were not indus-trial ones, and their occupants were potential executives and managers who should not be "protected" from promotions and the responsibilities that went with them (Lemons 1973, 199–200).

To a lesser extent the division was also one of party. The social feminists who supported protective legislation were mostly, though not exclusively, Democrats. Although they overlapped only slightly with Democratic party activists and could not keep the ERA out of the Democratic party platform between 1944 and

1960, they and the unions with which they worked closely did exercise some influence within the Democratic party and virtually none in the Republican party.

With some notable exceptions (e.g. Emma Guffey Miller) the NPW members were Republicans. While somewhat disdainful of both parties, Alice Paul and her followers had chosen to follow the British example of blaming the party in power for any legislative failures. Woodrow Wilson was a Democrat, and his repeated failure to support suffrage until circumstances forced him to do so forever tainted the Democratic party in Paul's eyes. The Congress that sent suffrage to the states for ratification was a Republican Congress, and 29 of the first 36 states to ratify it had Republican legislatures. Furthermore, the NWP's ideology of legal equality and independence, and its opposition to government protection, was much more compatible with the Republican philosophy of laissez-faire.

Equally important, the professional and business women who became the ERA's primary supporters were more likely to be Republicans; members of the Senate who voted for the ERA in 1946, 1950, and 1953 were mostly Republicans; and conservative organizations like the National Association of Manufacturers, which opposed any law regulating industry, supported the ERA. In 1928 the NWP even endorsed Hoover for president despite the fact that he had not personally expressed support for the amendment. His running mate, Charles Curtis, had been an ERA sponsor, and his Democratic opponent, Alfred E. Smith, was an ardent supporter of protective labor legislation (Becker 1981, 93–96).

In the late 1930s, Congress looked more favorably on the ERA. In 1938 it passed the Fair Labor Standards Act, which established minimum wages and maximum hours for both sexes. The Supreme Court upheld this act in 1941, reversing its previous position that regulation of the conditions of labor was constitutional only when applied to women. In March of 1938, the Senate Committee on the Judiciary considered the ERA for the first time. It had been reported favorably by the relevant subcommittees in both the House and the Senate in 1936 and 1937, but had not been voted on by a full committee. However, the vote was a tie—9 to 9—with the result that the Senate returned it to committee for further investigation. Although it would be another four years before the full committee again considered the ERA, the momentum behind it increased considerably. There were several reasons for this. The Supreme Court's decision undermined much of the logic behind special legislation for women. The decision in 1937 of the National Federation of Business and Professional Women's Clubs to endorse the ERA brought behind it the weight of one of the largest women's organizations. And the inclusion of support for the ERA in the 1940 Republican platform gave it legitimacy (*Congressional Digest* 1943, 106; Becker 1981, 227).

Even though there were no women on the Republican Resolutions Committee that year, for the first time the platform of a major political party explicitly stated that "[w]e favor submission by Congress to the States of an amendment to the Constitution providing for equal rights for men and women." The Republican party was looking for a way to challenge Roosevelt's campaign for an unprecedented third term, and appealing to women through support of the ERA was one more way to do it. The NWP gave credit for this appeal to two prominent Republicans, Alf Landon of Kansas and Senator Wharton Pepper of Pennsylvania, though it certainly did not hurt for the chair of the Resolutions Committee, Herbert Hyde of Oklahoma, to speak in its favor. This news made the front pages of the *New York Times* (June 27, 1940, 1:6).

Although women's organizations opposed to the ERA did not even personally testify at the Republican convention, they turned out in force at the Democratic one. There Emma Guffy Miller, still Democratic National Committeewoman from Pennsylvania, locked horns with Dorothy McAllister, Director of the DNC Women's Division. McAllister had appointed a women's advisory committee composed of representatives of the national women's organizations opposed to the ERA. It recommended an alternative plank that committed the party to equality "without impairing the social legislation which protects true equality by safeguarding the health, safety and economic welfare of women workers." When Eleanor Roosevelt told the platform committee that the ERA would be "a grave mistake" it accepted the alternative proposal (Harrison 1982, 32–33).

By 1944, the NWP had begun a major campaign to get the ERA passed by Congress, and obtaining endorsements from both parties was considered a crucial step. State chapters lobbied state delegations for both parties and Alice Paul personally interviewed the members of the platform committees. Furthermore, the opposition was in disarray. The DNC Women's Division, under the leadership of Gladys Tillet, stayed out of the fight, and Eleanor Roosevelt, concerned chiefly with the war, failed to speak against the ERA. Since protective laws had been waived in the interest of wartime production their retention was no longer a viable objection, so Emma Guffy Miller was able to argue that support of the ERA would recognize the contribution of women to the war effort. When the Republican party once again endorsed the ERA, Democratic party leaders worried that it would attract women's votes. The final Democratic plank read "[w]e recommend to Congress the submission of a Constitutional Amendment on equal rights for women" (Harrison 1982, 70, 75; *Congressional Digest* 1946, 299, 301).

The conflict between pro- and antifeminist forces was largely external to the political parties even though many of the participants were highly partisan. The main concern of women party activists was the traditional concern of all party activists: winning elections and getting appointments. At the urging of Molly Dewson, director of the DNC Women's Division from 1932 until 1936, women were included on all Democratic convention standing committees. By 1940 women were required to be represented equally on the platform committee, and in 1944 women chaired convention committees and were designated as convention officers. In the Republican party, eight women served on convention committees in 1928. They were represented equally on the platform committee in 1944 and served as officers and chairs in 1948. None of these achievements came easily. They all required intensive lobbying and political maneuvering (Cotter and Bibby 1980).

The lack of power—or interest—of women party activists or appointees in these administrations to effect bills beneficial to women is best seen in the fate of the Equal Pay Act. Equal pay for equal work had been proposed as early as 1868, but it did not become an issue until after World War I and was not taken seriously until after World War II. When the first bill was introduced in 1945, six states already had equal pay laws. The War Labor Board had required that women taking over men's jobs during both World Wars receive the male rate for the job. After the war the Women's Bureau made a federal equal pay law a primary goal, both as an anti-ERA measure and as a desirable goal in itself (Freeman 1975, 174–79). However, each organization in the anti-ERA coalition had its own agenda, and cooperating on an equal pay law was not at the top of their lists. Under neither the Democrats nor the Republicans could they agree on the form and scope of the bill, which was opposed both by the National Association of Manufacturers and the American Federation of Labor (Harrison 1982, chap. 3).

The National Woman's Party, caught between its fear that the effort for equal pay would deflect interest from the ERA and a concern not to be seen as against all bills on women, was publicly neutral and privately opposed—particularly since the proposed bill would be enforced by the party's archenemy, the Women's Bureau. NWP supporters argued that equal pay would undermine women's job opportunities by removing the economic incentive for employers to prefer women to men. Although both parties endorsed the idea of equal pay in their quadrennial platforms, neither made it a priority. Nor did President Dwight Eisenhower, despite his frequent favorable statements. Faced with strong opponents and disunited proponents, the equal pay bill languished in Congress.

The year 1960 was both the nadir of feminism and the beginning of its resurgence. The key person in both these developments was Esther Peterson. As an advisor to presidential candidate John F. Kennedy, she persuaded the Democratic party's Platform Committee to adopt the AFL position and drop its support for the ERA in favor of a vague expression against barriers to employment based on sex and "equality of rights under law, including equal pay." After Kennedy was elected she asked for and received appointment as director of the Women's Bureau and was also made an assistant secretary of labor. Few other women received such important appointments, a lack of action for which Kennedy was roundly criticized by Democratic party women. (Harrison 1982, 258).

Peterson had two major items on her agenda to improve the status of women: passage of the Equal Pay Act and derailment of the ERA. To accomplish the first, she appointed Morag Simchak and with her organized a concerted lobbying campaign that drew upon the expertise and contacts Peterson had developed as a lobbyist for the AFL-CIO. Although the final bill, which passed in 1963 after numerous hearings, was narrower than Peterson and other equal pay advocates had wanted and covered only 61 percent of the female labor force, it did commit the federal government to its first active efforts to improve the economic position of women.

One of Peterson's first recommendations to the new President was the creation of a national commission on women, once proposed by ERA opponents. The 1963 report of the President's Commission on the Status of Women gave Congress an excuse to abstain from further consideration of the ERA; however, it was also a key element in the amendment's resurgence. Its existence prompted governors in all states but one to create their own state commissions on the status of women, which in turn prepared extensive reports documenting discrimination against women in their states. The members of these commissions were invited to annual conferences in Washington by the Women's Bureau, and it was at the third such conference, in June 1966, that the National Organization for Women was formed. Initially, NOW was primarily concerned with changing the guidelines on sex discrimination promulgated by the Equal Employment Opportunities Commission (EEOC), which was created by Title VII of the 1964 Civil Rights Act (Freeman 1975, chaps. 2–3).

The addition of "sex" to the section of the Civil Rights Act prohibiting discrimination in employment on the basis of race, color, creed, and national origin had been more opportunistic than planned. It was not brought up in committee, and no hearings were held. Instead, it was a floor amendment in the House made by a male ERA supporter from Virginia and was subjected to several hours of humorous debate before being passed by a coalition of congresswomen and male opponents of the entire act (Bird 1968, chap. 1).[2]

The EEOC chose to follow what it felt was the true intent of Congress rather than the wording of the law; it ignored the sex provision. Initial guidelines prohibited segregation of newspaper want-ads by race but permitted them by sex. The EEOC also supported state protective labor legislation, forcing opponents to go to court. The courts consistently ruled that these laws were pre-empted by Title VII and therefore invalid. These rulings in turn paved the way for reconsideration of the Equal Rights Amendment (Freeman 1975, 76–79, 186–87).

Since the traditional opponents of the ERA had based their opposition on the need to maintain protective labor legislation, its invalidation neutralized them. Many switched sides. In the meantime, social and legal changes intervened to undermine the basis of the opponents' position. Between 1970 and 1972, opposition was greatly attenuated; what there was was not partisan in nature. With a few notable exceptions, the ERA became a symbolic issue on which everyone could agree. Yet even as this agreement was reached, a new opposition was developing. Ironically, it was from the Right, which had mostly supported the ERA during its lengthy stay in Congress. This opposition grew and eventually consumed more moderate forces, even while the ERA was gaining support from ancient foes to the Left. By 1976, party once again emerged as a major dividing line between opponents and supporters—but they had switched sides. The

Democrats were virtually all in favor of the ERA, and the Republicans were the major source of opposition.[3]

CONTEMPORARY FEMINISM AND THE POLITICAL PROCESS

The new feminist movement that emerged in the 1960s was the spiritual but not the organizational decendant of the post-suffrage feminists. Indeed, the founders of the new organizations were barely aware of the personalities, organizations, and issues—particularly the ERA—that had defined feminism for the previous 40 years. Most of them thought feminism had died with the passage of the Nineteenth Amendment. The contemporary movement had two origins in two different strata of society with different styles of political action. The dividing line between the two was the generation gap, much heralded in the 1960s as separating the political values and styles of those born after World War II from those born before. I call one the older branch and the other the younger branch, both because the former began first and because its primary participants were older.

The founders of the older branch created its first formal organization at the Third National Conference of Commissions on the Status of Women. The National Organization for Women initially conceived of itself as a national lobbying group of politically astute women whose primary focus was to be the Equal Employment Opportunity Commission. After the movement received massive publicity in 1970, it was overwhelmed by women from all walks of life seeking to join and, almost despite itself, developed a mass base. For the next few years NOW operated on two levels that were not well coordinated; at the national level it was a relatively weak and unstable organization trying to cope with the dilemmas of rapid expansion and program development while attempting, with only limited success, to be the major lobbying and litigation organization its founders had envisioned. At the local level NOW chapters were springing up everywhere and vigorously looking for ways to educate their members and focus their energies. After 1975 the national organization began to centralize and strengthen itself, and the chapters began to decline.

The younger branch of the emerging movement began among those younger women who had been involved in the social movements of the early 1960s—student protests, civil rights and antiwar activities. They had become alienated by the male domination of these movements, which espoused the goals of freedom, justice, and equality while expecting women to devote their energies to servicing men. Partially in reaction to their experiences in these movements, the participants of the younger branch rejected the possibility of forming a national organization and were quite hostile to the idea of organization in general. But like the men from whose organizations they came, they had no interest in the major political parties, viewing them as merely handmaidens of an oppressive political system.

The women of the older branch were not alienated from the parties but were suspicious of them, viewing them as bastions of male domination that were closed to women. Since they were well aware that they did not have an organized mass base and that, unlike Blacks, women as a group were not geographically concentrated, they did not see much future in developing an electoral strategy. Nonetheless, some of these women were elected officials, (Bella Abzug and Shirley Chisholm), and others (Gloria Steinem and Betty Friedan) felt that the political parties might present opportunities for action not available through organizations that focused on lobbying. In July 1971 they called together an informal conference of 324 women in Washington. One of the final acts of that conference was to appoint a committee to establish a formal organization. Unlike other organizations, it was to be concerned both with getting more women into public office and with pursuing feminist public policy goals. (Freeman 1975, 161).

The National Women's Political Caucus

Since 1972 was a presidential election year, it is not surprising that after the National Women's Political Caucus (NWPC) was officially constituted in New York the following September, it should emphasize getting women elected as delegates to the national nominating conventions. Although the NWPC wanted very much to be a bipartisan organization, from the beginning it played a greater role in the Democratic than in the Republican party. This happened for two reasons. One is that there were in fact significantly more Democrats than Republicans in the NWPC—to the degree that the Republicans were eventually given "special interest" representation on the national governing committee as a minority group. The second reason is that the Democratic party was more permeable. This permeability was a consequence of both the party's particular political culture and of timing. The Democratic Party was undergoing a major structural transformation; it had an active reform movement that had recently persuaded the party to adopt national rules on delegate selection and representation but did not have any established interpretations of these rules. Change creates opportunities. The NWPC made the most of those that were presented to it.

In an 8 November 1971 letter asking for a meeting with DNC Chairman Larry O'Brien to interpret Guidelines A-1 and A-2, the NWPC's new executive director, Doris Meissner, stated, "Given the fact that women are 52.2% of the total population and are a majority in all but four states, 'reasonable representation' can only mean that women constitute a majority of all but several of the state delegations" (Shafer 1984, 468). This goal was neither expected nor achieved. Nonetheless, at a meeting with O'Brien and other DNC officials, the NWPC did succeed in getting a commitment to interpret a lack of proportional representation of women in state delegations to the 1972 convention as prima facie evidence that the state was not in compliance with the guidelines. The burden would be on any state whose credentials were challenged to show that it had an adequate affirmative action program and that underrepresentation of women was not due to discrimination. Congressman Don Fraser, who became chair of the Party Structure Commission after George McGovern resigned to seek the presidency, obtained the commission's endorsement, which O'Brien sent to state party and elected officials. This put the Democratic party formally in favor of significantly increasing women's participation in the national nominating conventions and, in addition to setting new requirements, opened the door to 82 credentials challenges to more than 40 percent of the delegates from 30 states and one territory at the 1972 convention, as the state parties reluctantly confronted the revolution.[4]

The Republican party is not very hospitable to reform, but it has tinkered with it (Crotty 1983, 206). Its structure and procedures make it very hard to effect the sort of revolution the Democrats engaged in, and its activists have not seen party reform as a route to power, but its concern for appearances often prompt it to simulate its rival. After the GOP's 1968 convention, it too established a Committee on Delegates and Organizations (DO Committee) to review its rules. Unlike its Democratic counterpart, this committee's membership was restricted to members of the Republican National Committee, and its conclusions were purely advisory. However, its chairperson, Rosemary Ginn of Missouri, was an NWPC supporter, and its July 1971 report declared that each state should "endeavor to have equal representation of men and women in its delegation to the Republican National Convention." (RNC 1971). While lacking the force of the Democratic reforms, it did anticipate them by several months.

The 1972 Conventions

Neither party saw equal numbers of women and men in the delegations to its 1972 convention, but both significantly increased women's representation. In the previous two decades the proportion of women delegates had fluctuated between 10 and 17 percent. At the 1972 national nominating conventions, women made up almost 40 percent of the Democratic delegates and 30 percent of the Republican delegates. The presence of so many more women had no profound effect on the overall political orientation of the conventions; male and female delegates' positions on policy issues were quite similar within each party. However, on issues on which a "feminist" position could be identified (abortion, day care, and employment), women were *more* feminist than men. Here too there were party differences, but not enormous ones. Both women and men in both parties favored the feminist position, though more Democrats did so than Republicans, and Democratic men were more likely to be feminists than Republican women. In fact, the only issue on which Republican delegates, women as well as men, were distinctively negative was their general reaction to "women's liberation" (Kirkpatrick 1976, 5).[5]

The NWPC was present at both conventions but represented by different people (except for staff member Doris Meissner). Republican party women lobbied for NWPC goals at the Republican convention, while many nonparty feminists (who were probably registered Democrats) joined with Democratic party women at the Democratic convention. The NWPC had a series of proposals that it wanted to add to both parties' platforms, most of which were accepted. Both platforms included support for the ERA, but neither Platform Committee was willing to include a plank supporting women's right to reproductive freedom. Supporters of reproductive freedom had enough votes on their respective platform committees to file a minority plank and force a floor fight, but the Republican women chose not to do so.

After the platform, the focus of the Republican feminists was on the Rules Committee. The DO Committee had recommended that the party endeavor to represent men and women equally in the state delegations and take *positive action* to achieve the broadest possible participation of everyone in party affairs. Despite some staunch opposition, these recommendations were passed by the Rules Committee and became Rules 32C and 32A. An attempt to add a phrase reassuring the party that no quotas were intended failed.[6]

Democratic feminists had two credential challenges that were of particular concern to them because of their striking lack of women: South Carolina and Chicago. McGovern supported both challenges but finally told his delegates to vote against seating the insurgent South Carolina delegation to avoid a procedural problem. The women were incensed but were powerless to prevent South Carolina's regular delegation from being seated. They also clashed with McGovern's organization over the reproductive freedom plank, which by 1972 had become a highly controversial topic and which was a weight that the Democratic nominee didn't wish to carry into the presidential campaign. After one of the most emotional floor debates of the convention, pro-choice supporters lost the floor vote by three to two. The NWPC had also considered nominating a woman for vice-president, and when they saw that a last-minute campaign organized by three Texas students for Frances "Sissy" Farenthold was attracting interest (she had narrowly lost the Texas gubernatorial primary), they decided to turn their energies in that direction. Farenthold came in second with 13 percent of the vote (Farenthold 1984; Sullivan 1974, 53–54; Tolchin and Tolchin 1974, 40–53; White 1973, 172–74).

Although the Republican feminists achieved more of their tangible goals than did the Democrats, more Democratic delegates (25 percent) than Republicans (10 percent) thought the NWPC had a great deal of influence on the outcome of the convention (Kirkpatrick 1976, 446). This discrepancy occurred partially because the Democrats had already made more extensive changes in the rules than the Republicans were even proposing, but more significantly, it was a consequence of the different styles of the two parties. Republicans favor quiet persuasion; Democrats pursue public confrontation. The Republican feminists were themselves party activists, but they sought women with impeccable party credentials as public spokespersons for their issues, including elected officials and wives of prominent Republican men. While these women led the fights in the committees, the NWPC activists lobbied quietly behind the scene. They eschewed publicity and held only one delegate meeting, on the weekend between the committee meetings and the convention itself, where prominent Republican women reported to the delegates. The Republican feminists planned nothing for the convention itself but did hold a series of box lunches with delegates to discuss how to achieve more influence for women in the Republican Party. Although they had enough support on the platform committee to force a floor fight over abortion, they chose not to. One of the NWPC organizers explained why:

> Because the women delegates were loyal Republican partisans before they were feminists, there was little enthusiasm for introducing an abortion plank on the Convention floor . . . for nominating Ms. Heckler for Vice President, or even for inciting a "spontaneous" demonstration. These Republican women were, on the whole, a group of savvy politicians, who recognized that they were a 30% minority group, and were not about to risk losing any futile battles in a public rout. (Griffith 1972, 14)

The Democratic feminists not only held a meeting of delegates before the convention but virtually every day thereafter. The meetings were not restricted to delegates, and many nondelegates came. There was no real distinction between the actual leaders and the public spokespersons, and the leadership group included public officials, local party activists, and prominent feminists; it did not include wives of prominent party men, nor did it have many women with the extensive party credentials of the Republican spokespersons. The purpose of the meetings was to formulate strategy and organize women delegates into a floor operation. Discussion was often extensive, resulting in acceptance of the leadership's recommendations, but the delegates' other commitments limited their willingness to serve as floor whips. Nonetheless, a primitive floor organization was created sufficient to garner a credible number of votes for Farenthold. While McGovern made it a point to include women in many of his key convention advisory bodies, they were *his* women, not feminist representatives. (Tolchin and Tolchin 1974, 35–37; White 1973, 196). Many of the feminists were also McGovern supporters. Consequently, they were cross-pressured: they found it hard to decide whether their long-range goals would be best served by going along with McGovern or by pursuing immediate feminist concerns. This conflict was also debated in the delegate meetings. On the whole, there was much more awareness both in the press and among those attending the Democratic convention of what feminists were doing than was true at the Republican convention.

The 1976 Conventions
By 1976 the stage had been set for major battles over women's issues by both Republicans and Democrats, but they were very different battles. In the Democratic party, feminists fought for power independently of other struggles going on within the party. In the Republican party, feminists fought for the ERA as part of the contest between Ronald Reagan and Gerald Ford. In the Democratic party,

feminists lost their battle but won the war. In the Republican party, the reverse was true.

Following the 1972 conventions, the NWPC decided to institutionalize its party activities into two task forces, based on the lists of potential supporters its convention efforts had generated. The Democratic Women's Task Force was organized first, largely because the party planned a mini-convention in 1974 to adopt a party charter. The charter was one of the boldest innovations to come out of the furor of 1968. With its adoption, Democratic party affairs would no longer be governed by a hodgepodge of tradition, convention decisions, and DNC rulings. Although many of the provisions in the proposed charter were quite radical, the hottest issue at the 1974 mini-convention was affirmative action.

After 1972, state party leaders had rebelled at what they felt was the rigid imposition of "quotas" for women, minorities, and youth and the assumption that if these were not met, the burden was on state parties to prove that they did not discriminate. Therefore a new reform commission modified the delegate selection rules so that if an approved affirmative action plan had been followed, the results by themselves could not be the basis for a credentials challenge (DNC 1973, rule 18; Crotty 1983, 66–73). This language was incorporated into the proposed party charter, but it was a compromise that the Black and women's caucus leadership at the 1974 conference (including Bella Abzug, Patt Derian of Mississippi, and Barbara Mikulski) felt would preempt most challenges. They threatened a walkout if this section was adopted; the AFL-CIO leadership threatened a walkout if it wasn't. After a great deal of acrimonious debate, national party leaders succeeded in finding further modifications of the wording that were acceptable to all sides. (Sullivan 1976, 33–34, 44, 62–64, 72–73, 78).

The Republican Women's Task Force (RWTF) was organized in 1975 through a letter to Republican women, after the Republican National Committee decided to let each state party interpret the requirement that it achieve equal representation in its own way. Although the task force was nominally composed of several hundred Republican women, throughout most of its subsequent history the work of the RWTF was done and the decisions made by less than a dozen women active in the liberal wing of the party, often independently of the NWPC. Since the NWPC was overwhelmingly Democratic, the RWTF became a cohesive subgroup within it, creating tensions that eventually resulted in its temporary elimination. The Democratic Women's Task Force (DWTF) was less cohesive, had a rotating leadership, and was always subservient to the NWPC leadership.

As it had for Democratic feminists, the political environment changed for Republican feminists between the 1972 and 1976 conventions, but it was a change for the worse. The Equal Rights Amendment, so uncontroversial in 1972, had stimulated an organized opposition by groups that had not participated in the previous 49 years of debate. Phyllis Schlafly, long an active conservative Republican, formed STOP ERA in October 1972, and within a year other right-wing groups—such as the John Birch Society, Pro-America Incorporated, the Christian Crusade, and Young Americans for Freedom—threw their organizational resources into the fight. Organizations of the religious right were also a major source of ERA opponents. The Mormon Church, the Southern Baptists and other fundamentalist Protestant churches, and portions of the Catholic Church actively fought the ERA in state legislatures (Brady and Tedin 1976, 564–75; Freeman 1975, 220–21; McGlen and O'Connor 1983, 373–74;· Marshall 1984, 569; Steiner 1985).

All of the key RWTF members at the 1976 convention were tied to the Ford campaign, personally or professionally. Thus they experienced the same cross-pressures that McGovern feminists had felt in 1972, but they were not troubled by this conflict. Convinced that Ford's reelection was the single most important contribution they could make to the women's movement, they formulated their strategy accordingly. As in 1972, they did not ask women delegates to meet and ratify their decisions but did hold one meeting just before the convention to inform the few people attending of their accomplishments.

There were three issues of potential concern to the RWTF: rules, abortion, and the ERA. The Rules Committee debate on Rule 32 was monitored, but no effort was made to strengthen it or to publicly object to the addition of the anti-quota provision rejected in 1972 (Rule 32d). After the furor that had erupted over the Democrats' alleged use of quotas in 1972, it was too touchy an issue, and as women's representation among delegates had increased by 2 percent, there was no imperative for action. Abortion was a more difficult issue. An RWTF delegate survey had shown that 61 percent supported the Supreme Court abortion decision, compared to only 55 percent who supported the ERA; only one-third of the delegates had bothered to reply, however, and Ford had not taken a pro-choice stance. In order not to "contaminate" the ERA by associating it with abortion, the decision was made to work officially only to keep the ERA in the Republican platform, though unofficially an effort would also be made to keep an antiabortion provision out.

The former effort was successful; the latter was not. The ERA actually lost in the relevant platform subcommittee by one vote; this so shook up the Ford campaign people that they ordered their delegates on the full committee to vote for it. It still won only by 51 to 47. The opponents wanted to take a minority report to the convention floor, but Reagan had decided that he wanted floor fights on only two issues, and the ERA was not one of them. Therefore, it was retained in the 1976 Republican platform.

The same convention saw an antiabortion plank added for the first time; it won overwhelmingly in the subcommittee and was not contested in the full committee. But under the guidance of Congresswoman Millicent Fenwick (N.J.), a petition to remove it garnered enough to bring the issue to the floor. That debate was held after midnight, and a voice vote sustained the antiabortion plank by a substantial margin.

There was no fight over abortion at the 1976 Democratic convention. During the Platform Committee meetings in June a compromise was reached on a single statement that it was inadvisable to amend the constitution in order to overturn the Supreme Court decision. The fight within the Democratic party was over the "50-50 rule" which would have mandated that from 1980 on all delegations would have to be half women. This change was proposed because midway through the 1976 delegate selection process the number of Black, female, Hispanic, and under-30 delegates was running 15 to 35 percent less than in 1972. (In the end, women were 34 percent). Since the new rules made credentials challenges more difficult, the NWPC and the Caucus of Black Democrats went to the June Rules Committee meetings with proposals for improvement and an agreement to support each other's proposals. They both wanted "goals and timetables" for achieving specific results in affirmative action plans. Women also wanted "equal division" of the delegates. After a showdown with Carter aides, Blacks and women won the first point and narrowly lost the second. A minority report was filed so that the issue could be debated on the floor the last day of the convention. The Carter campaign controlled a majority of the votes and did not support the 50-50 rule, but neither did it want a bloody floor fight in a year in which the Democrats sensed victory. After several days of negotiations, Carter compromised by agreeing to *promote* equal division in future conventions, as well as to strengthen the role of women in the Democratic party, his campaign, and his administration.

As at the 1972 Democratic convention there were daily meetings of the women's caucus, to which anyone could come, but delegates and nondelegates voted separately. The latter vote, taken first, was purely advisory; the delegate vote, which was binding, never overturned the recommendations of the leadership. The debate over whether to accept the compromise on the 50-50 rule was largely one between those who were committed to working within the Democratic party and those who were not; those who could benefit directly by more women in the administration and those who could not; those who had been close to the negotiations and those who had not. Ostensibly, it was a debate on how best to promote women's rights. In reality it was a debate over which was a better symbol of power: a convention floor fight that would be lost, or a successful negotiation with the presidential candidate. While spirited, the debate was without acrimony: even though everyone knew that Carter sufficiently controlled the convention to win any vote, his supporters never accused their opponents of trying to divide the party or undermine the campaign, and in turn were not accused of selling out women's interests.[7]

By 1980, "50-50" was no longer controversial. In the winter of 1978 the rules for the December midterm convention had been changed to require equal division, and at a meeting of the Democratic National Committee held just before this convention, the 1980 "call" was amended to require it as well. With feminists in the party continuing to push for equal division, Carter's campaign operatives had decided that the issue was not of sufficient importance to continue fighting over. Furthermore, the death of AFL-CIO President George Meany and the resulting changing of the guard removed the most vociferous opposition to "quotas," and labor's concerns over possible loss of influence in the party were met through other concessions by subsequent reform commissions. By 1980, the party regulars had reconciled themselves to reform. When Carter lost, they did not blame electoral defeat on that year's convention rules as they had in 1972. Indeed, the 1980 election saw a "gender gap" of 8 percent appear between the voting patterns of men and women. Ironically, the very year women achieved the right to half the national convention delegates, they became more than half of the Democratic electorate.

The 1980 Conventions
In 1980 there was a good deal of tension between feminists and both parties. At both conventions feminists had poor relations with the dominant candidate's campaign. This resulted in their virtual exclusion from the Republican convention but at the Democratic convention was merely a stimulus to alternative routes of influence.

Most of the Republican feminists who had been active in the 1972 and 1976 conventions did not go to the 1980 convention. Some had received political appointments from the Carter administration and thus were legally prohibited from participating in politics. Others were discouraged by what they expected to be a hostile atmosphere. As in 1976, the RWTF mailed a questionnaire to convention delegates, 36 percent of whom were women, but the results were so discouraging that it was decided not to release them. A cursory review by RWTF chair Nancy Thompson of the 400 questionnaires that were returned showed a four-to-one opposition to the ERA. Several RWTF members maintained a quiet presence through the hearings of the relevant platform subcommittee, but Phyllis Schlafly's STOP ERA supporters were much more prominent. The RWTF's efforts were hampered by the fact that its members' ties to the Republican party were through the declining liberal wing. Therefore, they recruited former GOP chair Mary Louise Smith, whose Republican credentials were too solid to be dismissed, as their spokesperson.

After discussion with Reagan operatives, the anti-ERA language of the subcommittee was modified to oppose not the ERA itself but "federal interference or pressure . . . against states that have refused to ratify the ERA," while reaffirming "our Party's historic commitment to equal rights and equality for women." Margaret Heckler demanded a meeting with Reagan, which was granted, and afterward she and the RWTF representatives publicly stated that they would support Reagan because they didn't feel that his views and the platform were perfectly congruent.

They kept their word and put together a Women's Policy Advisory Board to help sell Ronald Reagan to American women during the campaign. This incurred the wrath of Phyllis Schlafly, who thought it was a feminist plot. She asked the

Reagan campaign to abolish the board; when that was not done, she pulled her Eagle Forum supporters from their volunteer posts in numerous Reagan campaign offices, leaving some unable to get their phones answered. They were returned after a compromise in which one of her lieutenants, Elaine Donnally, was put on the Women's Board and a separate Board on Family Policy was created for Schlafly supporters. Of those Republican feminists who worked for Reagan's election, only Margaret Heckler received an appointment in his administration, and as a result of right-wing pressure, she was removed from her position as secretary of health and welfare during Reagan's second term.

Within the Democratic party, tension manifested itself in separate meetings for women delegates called by the Women's Caucus of the Democratic National Committee and a feminist Coalition for Women's Rights (comprising NOW, the NWPC, and prominent feminists such as Bella Abzug and Gloria Steinem). NOW had voted the year before not to support Carter because it was unimpressed with his efforts for the ERA. Even before that, there had been an uproar when he fired Abzug from his Women's Advisory Commission. The Carter campaign therefore just assumed that all feminists were Ted Kennedy supporters. This perception was reinforced when Bella Abzug persuaded the coalition to take up as one of its issues a proposal by Kennedy forces to free delegates to vote for the candidate of their choice rather than for the primary winner in their state.

The functioning coalition was primarily a leadership group consisting of the heads of the major feminist organizations, elected officials, funding sources, and media stars, who could be identified by the fact that they had floor passes and met continually during the convention itself. This time feminists had an extensive floor operation, based upon the approximately 20 percent of the delegates who were NWPC or NOW members and staffed by the NWPC. Apart from the leaders, nondelegates had very little to do at this convention.

NOW President Eleanor Smeal and NWPC President Iris Mitgang had decided earlier in the spring to work together at the convention on some feminist issue but didn't choose a particular focus until the platform committee met in July. There a proposal was voted down to add to an already strong ERA plank the promise that "the Democratic party shall offer no financial support and technical campaign assistance to candidates who do not support the ERA." Although the Democratic party has little assistance to give to any candidate, and was not known for enforcing a party line on any issue, as Minority Report No. 10 this proposal became *the* feminist issue of the 1980 convention.

The Carter campaign opposed No. 10, which campaign staff felt was a single-issue "loyalty test" inappropriate for a pluralistic party. The coalition argued that whatever the merits of the actual proposal, it was a "litmus test" on the ERA, and a negative vote would play in the press as a rejection of the ERA. Many Carter delegates, half of whom were women, agreed, and the Carter whips had difficulty keeping their votes in line. The issue was finally settled two hours before the vote when the National Education Association, which had the largest single block of Carter delegates, announced that it would support No. 10. The Carter whips were called off, and convention chair Representative Tip O'Neill phoned Bella Abzug to suggest that both sides agree on a voice vote to save time and the potential embarrassment of a roll call. The subsequent voice vote was really too close to call accurately, but O'Neill did not hesitate in announcing No. 10 passed.

Almost lost in the confusion was the floor vote to add Minority Report No. 11 to the platform. This added party support of government funding for abortions for poor women to the support for the 1973 Supreme Court decision already in the platform. Although the coalition supported No. 11, which had been written by coalition member Gloria Steinem, it didn't lobby on it. That effort was left to the National Abortion Rights Action League (NARAL), which had its own floor operation and similarly stayed away from No. 10. Although Carter personally opposed abortion, this issue was not as polarized as No. 10, partially because it did not commit party resources and partially because it wasn't perceived as a Kennedy proposal.

As in 1976, the fights by feminists at the Democratic convention were struggles over the symbols of power. In 1976, President Carter had acknowledged the importance of women, under feminist leadership, to the Democratic party by personally negotiating with them. This made compromise possible and a floor fight unnecessary. In 1980, feminists felt snubbed. Several participants in the leadership group said they would have compromised had Carter approached them, but when the campaign engaged in tactics they considered heavy-handed, sent negotiators who had no power, and otherwise ignored the women and their issue, they felt a floor fight was necessary if they were to be taken seriously.

In reality, the Carter campaign did not take them seriously. Because of Bella Abzug's prominence and NOW's repudiation of Carter the year before, the coalition was viewed as a Kennedy front. Furthermore, the campaign people believed that Carter and the Democratic party didn't need to prove their support for the ERA and that other issues were simply more important. Sarah Weddington, the person assigned as liaison with the coalition, personally disliked Bella Abzug, was not a key figure in the campaign, and didn't have access to those who were. But the Carter campaign's hold on its delegates, like its hold on the Democratic party, was quite tenuous. In the end the delegates decided that the issues were more important than the candidate and legitimated the right of feminist leaders to define what the party's position on women's issues ought to be. President Carter ratified that decision the following fall when he invited NOW President Eleanor Smeal to the White House to discuss the ERA.[8]

The 1984 Conventions
The 1984 conventions solidified the direction in which both parties had been moving for the previous ten years. The Democrats adopted the feminist perspective on all public issues directly affecting women and made it clear that women, under feminist leadership, were an important part of the Democratic coalition.

The Republican party adopted antifeminist positions on almost every issue. Its public script was written by Phyllis Schlafly. But it did not repudiate women; instead, it has affirmed their importance by showcasing them extensively and devoting more real resources to help women, as individuals, get elected, than the Democratic party has done. Ironically, while feminists both organizationally and individually are now almost totally excluded from the Republican party, their influence is pervasive.

At the convention this influence could be seen not in the content so much as in the quantity of attention paid to women. Although the Republican party has never required that half the delegates be women, 48 percent were female, as were 52 percent of the alternates. Betty Rendel, president of the independent National Federation of Republican Women, disavowed the Democratic quota system as "artificial, discriminatory and . . . a little silly," while describing the way in which Republican women were cajoled into running for delegate spots and men discouraged by top party leaders, including the President. She said party leaders had to exert steady pressure to persuade men originally selected as delegates to step aside for the "envelope stuffers and precinct walkers."

One-third of the major speakers were women, and for the first time the Republican convention had a large booth in the press area solely to provide information on women. The Republican Women Information Services also set up interviews and sponsored or advertised receptions, luncheons, and breakfasts aimed at women. The Women's Division of the Republican Party, since its re-creation in April 1983, has sponsored several projects aimed at women. These include the National Women's Coalition "of professional and activist women drawn from business, the arts, academia, the sports world and politics"; numerous conferences and briefings to form women's networks, develop candidates, and prepare speakers; and the release of reams of material on what the Republican party and Ronald Reagan have done for women. Women and women's issues occupied a larger portion of the platform than at any time since women got the vote; however, the slant was dictated by the Moral Majority and Phyllis Schlafly, whose Eagle Forum supporters were much in evidence.

The Equal Rights Amendment was not mentioned in either the draft or the final version of the platform, but this did not prevent Schlafly from speaking against it before the Human Resources Subcommittee. When one member moved to add a plank endorsing the ERA, it failed for lack of a second. Another attempt before the full committee was defeated 76 to 16. Two other proposals—one to add sex to the equal protection clause of the Fourteenth Amendment, and another merely recognizing that many party members supported the ERA—were also defeated. All motions to soften the hardline pro-life language and the anti–comparable worth plank in the platform met a similar fate. During a meeting of the full committee, comparable worth was denounced by Peggy Miller of West Virginia as "a socialist idea."

Both NOW and the NWPC had decided that it would be futile to attend the convention. Kathy Wilson, president of the NWPC and a liberal Republican, flew in to Dallas to give a press conference and release a 50-page document refuting party claims that women are better off then they were four years ago, but she left before the convention began. The perception by feminists that the Republican party was now so conservative that they could not get a hearing was well founded. Those testifying before the platform subcommittees in opposition to key right-wing planks found themselves barraged with questions about the Democratic ticket rather than the subject on which they were testifying. When former GOP Chair Mary Louise Smith and NWPC representative Mary Stanley, a long-term Reagan supporter from California, testified in favor of the ERA, they were cross-examined on Geraldine Ferraro's finances. Stanley, who had tears in her eyes when she told the subcommittee that *her* Republican Party was the one that supported the ERA and she wanted it back, was later forced to resign from the California Republican State Committee because she made favorable comments about Ferraro. But before she left the convention, Stanley collected the names of 200 pro-ERA Republican women.

In the intervening years the RWTF had for all practical purposes disbanded as a formal group. Because the Reagan administration's attitude toward feminist organizations was that they were arms of the Democratic party, many Republican women who were sympathetic to feminist issues would have nothing to do with the NWPC. In turn, some prominent members of the NWPC were not sympathetic to the difficult situation this presented to Republican feminists who still wanted to remain loyal to their party. As a result, the RWTF transformed itself into something of a loose, informal network of feminist Republicans who felt alienated from both their party and the women's movement.

Feminists' relationship to the Democratic party was quite different. The fact that feminists had displayed so much clout at the 1980 convention gave them an inside spot in the 1984 race, with the consequence that there was very little for them to do at the convention itself. All the candidates trooped to San Antonio, Texas, in July 1983 to seek support from those attending the NWPC convention, and when NOW announced that it would endorse a Democratic party candidate for president, it was courted by all. Six candidates were invited to address NOW's national conference in October 1983 (Reuben Askew was not invited because of his anti-choice stand, and Jesse Jackson had not yet declared his candidacy). Although most observers expected Walter Mondale to get the NOW endorsement, the officers drew up four criteria and met with five of the candidates—Mondale, Alan Cranston, John Glenn, Gary Hart, and Jesse Jackson. Each was also given lists of National Board members and state chairs so that he could lobby NOW. The four criteria involved (1) the candidate's position on and the priority he gave to women's issues, (2) the number of women in key staff positions, (3) his willingness to select a woman vice-president, and (4) his electability. There was some movement within NOW to withdraw the decision to endorse, and some sentiment for Cranston, but the NOW leadership believed strongly that endorsing Mondale was the way to go and persuaded everyone else to go along.

Since the Mondale campaign was prepared to put into the platform whatever planks feminists wanted, the incipient women's caucus decided that its focus should be on persuading Mondale to choose a woman as vice-presidential nominee, though they were uncertain whether to force a floor fight should these efforts fail. Delegate suverys by the NWPC showed that there was considerable support for such a move, and voter polls indicated that a woman would probably help the Democratic ticket more than hurt it. Therefore, public and party officials were lobbied to put pressure on Mondale; helpful information was leaked to the press; and 150 delegates willing to be whips were identified and organized. It was also agreed that this time there would be only one women's caucus at the convention, sponsored by the DNC Women's Division, at which everyone would be organized for the vice-presidential selection. After Mondale announced his choice of Geraldine Ferraro on July 12, the coalition dismantled its whip system.[9]

Because feminists got pretty much everything they wanted prior to the Democratic convention, there wasn't much to do there except celebrate. The organizations that had been ignored as unimportant by McGovern and Carter found themselves treated like members of the family by Mondale and other prominent Democrats. Although the women's caucus met every day as usual, the high point of the convention for feminists was when Mondale and Ferraro addressed them, symbolizing the fact that they were no longer pushy outsiders but part of the party.[10]

The contrasting experiences of Republican and Democratic feminists at the 1984 conventions show how far both had come since 1972, when both had, in different ways, beseeched party leaders to listen to them. At that time the attitude of both parties' leaders had been polite but disdainful; they gave feminists a token by putting the ERA, recently passed by Congress, back in their platforms but otherwise did not take them seriously. By 1984 the parties were listening but responding very differently. On women's issues, the voters were offered a real choice. The Democratic platform adopted the feminist perspective on all public issues directly affecting women, and party leaders took feminist leaders and organizations seriously. Where Democratic feminists shared a sense of euphoria that they had helped make history, Republican feminists experienced rejection and harassment. The 1984 Republican platform took a pointedly antifeminist perspective on all relevant issues; the 1984 Republican convention showcased women but dismissed the women's movement. How this polarization could happen, contrary to the historical tendencies of each party and the preferences of feminist leaders, is the topic to which we now turn.

THE POLITICAL CULTURE OF THE REPUBLICAN AND DEMOCRATIC PARTIES

The impact of the women's movement has been very different on the Republican and Democratic parties. Although both claim to support equal rights for women, they are in fact strongly polarized on this issue. Despite historical traditions to the contrary and a preference by feminists to be bipartisan or nonpartisan, the Democratic party has become strongly identified with feminism and the Republican party with antifeminism.

Although the major political parties have similar aims and similar forms, there are still some profound differences in the mode by which they conduct internal politics. These differences are rooted in two cultural distinctions, one structural and the other attitudinal. First, in the Democratic party power flows upward, and in the Republican party power flows downward. Second, Republicans perceive themselves as insiders even when they are out of power, and Democrats perceive themselves as outsiders even when they are in power.[11]

Structure

Both parties are composed of numerous units, and have a superficial similarity. On the national level each party has three major committees: the National Committee, the Senate and House Campaign Committees. In its efforts to administer internal party activities and provide campaign and organizational services to candidates, the Republican party has by far been the more successful. It raises and spends four times as much money as the Democratic party; it supports a permanent field staff to recruit and train local candidates; and it assists state parties to increase their funding and improve their organizations.

In addition to these formal bodies, the Democratic party, especially on the national level, is composed of constituencies. Each of these constituencies sees itself as having a salient characteristic creating a common agenda that they feel the party must respond to. Virtually all of these groups exist in organized form independent of the party and seek to act on the elected officials of both parties. They are recognized by Democratic party officials as representing the interests of important blocs of voters that the party must respond to as a party. Some groups have been recognized parts of the Democratic coalition since the New Deal (Blacks and labor, for example); others are relatively new (women and gays). Still others (such as ethnics), which participated in state and local Democratic politics when those were the only significant party units, have not been active as organized groups on the national level. With an occasional exception the power of group leaders derives from their ability to accurately reflect the interests of constituency members to the party leaders. Therefore, while leaders are rarely chosen by the participants, they nonetheless feel compelled to have their decisions ratified through debate and votes in the caucuses. The votes usually go the way the leaders direct, but they are symbolically important.

The Republican party has separate units composed of distinct demographic groups—such as the National Black Republican Council and the National Federation of Republican Women—but they are auxiliaries, not constituencies. The purpose of these groups is to elect Republicans, not to communicate group concerns to the party. The Republican party discourages as disloyal and unnecessary any strong identification of its members with any other group. Even in 1976, when Republican feminists were aligned with party leaders, one RWTF organizer commented at the convention that because the GOP is not "an interest group party . . . the RWTF is viewed with skepticism. Party regulars have had a hard time adjusting to the presence of an organized interest" (Pressman 1977–78, 680).

Essentially, the Democratic party is pluralistic, with multiple power centers that compete for membership support in order to make demands on, as well as determine, the leaders. The Republicans have a unitary party in which great deference is paid to the leadership; activists are expected to be "good soldiers," and competing loyalties are frowned upon. This structural difference creates different conceptions of legitimacy. In the Democratic party, legitimacy is determined by whom you represent, and in the Republican party by whom you know and who you are. It is this difference that makes the Democratic party so much more responsive to demands for reform within it, and the Republican party so much more responsive to changes in leadership.

The difference also affects the fate of activists. In the Democratic party the success of individuals whose group identification is highly salient (such as Blacks and women) is tied to that of the group as a whole. They succeed as the group succeeds. When the group obtains more power, individuals within that group get more positions. Thus, social movements that promote members of particular groups can have far more impact on the Democratic party than on the Republican party. The Republican party officially ignores group characteristics, though group members are publicly displayed when the party feels the need to cater to the interest of the voting public in a particular group. Generally, individuals succeed to the degree that the leaders with whom they are connected succeed. Aspirants to leadership seek sponsorship by already acknowledged party leaders and/or make direct appeals to individuals (delegates or voters). The converse is equally true. When a candidate fails or a leader falls from power, those associated with that person lose their claim to consideration. Backing the wrong candidate in the Democratic party is not as disastrous. One does not lose all influence within the party with a change in leaders as long as one can credibly appear to represent a legitimate group.

Attitude

It has been argued that society as a whole has a cultural and structural "center" about which most members of society are more or less "peripheral" (Shils 1970). Republicans see themselves as representing the center, while Democrats view society from the periphery.

Although Republicans do not want to increase state power, they nonetheless feel that what they are and their conception of the American dream is inherently desirable. They are insiders who represent the core of American society and are the carriers of its fundamental values. What they have achieved in life, and wish to achieve, is what every true American wishes to achieve. The traditions they represent are what has worked for America, and the policies they pursue are the ones that ultimately will be best for everyone. They argue that the Republican party and Republican policies represent the national interest, unlike the Democrats, who only serve the "special interests" that are powerful within it. The Republican concept of representation is that of a "trustee," who pursues the long-range best interests of the represented.

The Democrats have a very different world view and a different concept of the meaning of representation. To them, representation means not the articulation of a single coherent program for the betterment of the nation but the inclusion of all relevant groups and viewpoints. Their concept of representation is "delegatory," in which accurate reflection of the parts is necessary to the welfare of the whole. Ironically, this requires a "free market" vision of the political arena as one in which the most collective good comes from maximizing properly represented individual goods. Because there is no common agenda, there is no common conception of a national interest independent of the total interests of the parts. Instead, groups seek to maximize what each gets through bargaining and building coalitions on the assumption that everyone should get something.

Democrats do not have an integrated conception of a national interest in part because they do not view themselves as the center of society. The party's components think of themselves as outsiders pounding on the door, seeking programs that will facilitate entry into the mainstream. They want what's fair, and what's fair is what they want. Thus the party is very responsive to any group, including such social pariahs as gays and lesbians, that claims it is left out. As is typical of outsiders, Democrats are predisposed toward "change" and "experimentation" in the belief that what *is* is not inherently desirable, and something new might lead to something better. At the extreme, this attitude results in the assumption that anything new is inherently better.

Guided by a more unitary conception of representation as the correct articulation of the national interest, Republicans feel that the needs of outsiders can best be met through the promotion of individual success. Insiders generally view their achievements as due to their own merit and efforts rather than to aspects of the social structure or plain luck. Success is its own justification. Thus, what has worked for them, or what they acknowledge as having worked for them, should work for everyone. It is the responsibility of each individual to learn how to succeed and the responsibility of government only to remove the barriers to individual action, not to ensure individual success.

This approach to the world guides not only policy debates but the Republican party's attitude toward those who would exercise influence within it. Since direction comes from the top and group demands are inconsistent with pursuit of the national interest, one affects policy by quietly building a consensus among key individuals and then making a case to the leadership that the proposal furthers the basic values of the party. Maneuvering is acceptable. Challenging is not. This approach acknowledges the leadership's right to make final decisions and reassures them that those preferring different policies do not have competing allegiances. On the other hand, open challenges or admissions of fundamental disagreements indicate that one might be too independent to be a reliable soldier who will always put the interests of the party first.

In the Democratic party, keeping quiet is the cause of atrophy, and speaking out is a means of access. Although the party continues to be one of multiple power centers with multiple access points, both the type and importance of powerful groups within it have changed over time. State and local parties have weakened in the last few decades, and the influence of national constituency groups has grown. The process of change has resulted in a great deal of conflict, as former participants resist declining influence while newer ones jockey for position. Successfully picking fights—symbolic or substantive— is the primary way by which groups acquire clout within the party.

Analysis

Like any other aspirants to power, feminists in the Democratic and Republican parties must operate according to the rules of their respective institutions. The cultural norms determine the structure of available opportunities for action. In 1972 the resources of Republican feminists and their knowledge of how the party operated allowed them to be relatively effective operators within the party. Several had close personal connections to important people and thus could influence the party at least on those things that were not controversial. They chose as public representatives people who had impeccable Republican credentials; they used maneuvering and personal persuasion to attain their immediate goals. They avoided a floor fight on abortion both because they felt that the inevitable loss would not be to their credit and because it would make them appear disloyal.

This strategy would not have worked in the Democratic party, even though many prominent Democrats were feminists and most feminists were also McGovern supporters. (Some supported Shirley Chisholm, which didn't endear them to McGovern but didn't discredit them either.) McGovern's perceived "betrayals" reflected their lack of legitimacy at that time. Feminists within the Democratic party had to build up a power base of women active in the party whom they could legitimately claim to represent before they could have much impact. They began this process with caucus meetings in 1972. But not until, in alliance with the Black caucus, they compelled party leaders to compromise with them at the 1974 mini-convention were they accepted as even junior partners in the Democratic coalition.

In 1976 the personal connections of Republican feminists with the Ford campaign gave them some claim on the campaign's resources to stave off a negative vote on the ERA by the full platform committee, but not in areas that Ford did not support. To maintain their legitimacy as loyal Republicans, they asked NOW— tainted as a leftist "special interest" group—to leave. They also felt it necessary to avoid any connection to the abortion issue because there was no consensus on it among the leaders to whom they had access. Since Congresswoman Millicent Fenwick, a strong pro-choice supporter with excellent Republican credentials, was present and willing to spend her political capital, a separate effort on this issue could be mounted, but her absence from the 1980 convention left pro-choice with no apparent supporters.

Feminists in the Democratic party were looking for an issue in 1976 on which to flex their political muscle. They found it in the 50-50 proposal. It is not necessary to *win* fights to gain clout; their function is to serve as arenas for displaying one's political skills. Therefore, the debate in the women's caucus was over whether a compromise with the presidential nominee or a well-orchestrated but losing floor fight would be the better symbol of power. Even though the outcome was foreordained, the debate and the vote by the caucus were necessary to ratify the compromise itself and legitimate the leaders' right to make it. Republican feminists made no effort to have their "compromise" over which issues to stress ratified because their legitimacy did not derive from whom they represented but from whom they knew.

In 1980 feminists in both parties were looked upon unfavorably by the dominant candidate. In the Republican party it meant their virtual elimination from any consideration. By persuading a prominent Republican woman to intervene with the Reagan campaign, they did achieve some softening of the anti-ERA plank and a symbolic meeting with candidate Reagan, but the circumstances made this appear as a magnanimous gesture by the victor rather than an acknowledgment of their importance. This was confirmed by the subsequent elimination of any access by feminists to the party leadership or administration. Instead, long-time Reagan supporter Phyllis Schlafly became the campaign's and the administration's arbiter (through Reagan adviser Ed Meese) on policy affecting women.

Feminists were similarly cut off from access to the Carter campaign, and did not have any intervenors. But because the Democratic party is pluralistic, there were other routes to power. Upon deciding that Carter had "snubbed" them, feminists sought to reestablish their position by organizing a floor fight. Since they now knew how to put together a floor operation and half the delegates were women, this was a viable option. All they needed was an issue, which they created with a minority report. In the Republican party this strategy would not have worked, because the candidate would have labeled such an issue a loyalty test and would have threatened participants with ostracism. In the Democratic party, where competing loyalties are accepted, individual delegates and delegate blocs (like the NEA) simply ignored Carter's attempts to do this.

By 1984, feminists were so well ensconced in the Democratic Party that they could write the party's platform on women and effectively exclude pro-lifers (of which there were more than a few) from any voice in the party. Although the Democratic party publicly disagrees on more issues than the Republican party does, certain issues and attitudes are "protected." Once a group has been accepted as a legitimate player, it acquires a certain amount of sovereignty over a policy territory and can usually designate those issues and positions within it which are to be part of the "party line." Labor has long had this power, and Blacks have it over most of their issues. In 1984, feminist hegemony over "women's" issues was acknowledged as a result of their successful bids for power in previous conventions. Feminists nonetheless debated whether or not they should instigate another battle and decided to focus on the selection of a woman as the vice-presidential nominee. The coalition that met in the spring had not yet decided whether to wage a convention fight when Mondale preempted them by selecting Geraldine Ferraro.

By 1984, Republican feminists had been read out of effective participation within the party. They were associated with the liberal branch and had backed the wrong candidate. Even those who had not personally been associated with previous feminist activities disassociated themselves from open identification with the feminist movement. A major reason why Republican feminists have had so much more trouble rehabilitating themselves in the Reagan party than others who did not initially support him is that they are assumed to have a major or even primary loyalty to feminism and feminist organizations. Since feminism is not supported by the current leadership, and feminist organizations are viewed as Democratic party front groups, it is virtually impossible to be both an accepted Republican activist and an outspoken supporter of feminist goals. And since the unitary structure of the party makes it impossible to develop an independent power base, feminists can do little until a candidate comes along who is sympathetic to their interests.

Nonetheless, there are many women in the Republican party who are feminists, even if they dare not use the word publicly. Some are seeking to work for women's rights in ways other than supporting the ERA and abortion; indeed, they criticize the Democratic party for what they call a narrow conception of what will benefit women. Others are focusing their efforts on putting women into positions of power. They argue that merely having women in prominent positions will in the long run benefit women more than divisive fights over the ERA and abortion, and they severely criticize feminist organizations such as NOW that have endorsed men in preference to women (including such feminists as Millicent Fenwick and such ERA supporters as Margaret Heckler).

There is some merit to this position, but only some. Sociological studies have shown that women in prominent positions are valuable role models to younger women, but the effects of this are very long range. In the shorter range, the mere presence of women does not by itself achieve specific public policy goals. Between the major women's movements of the twentieth century, women in both parties sought to place their adherents in positions of influence, arguing that women voters would look favorably upon the party that did so. However, the struggles over the ERA, the Equal Pay Act, and the exclusion of married women from the Civil Service during the Depression, indicate that the mere presence of women in governmental positions does not necessarily focus political concern on improving the status of women.

On the other hand, the numerous and rapid public policy successes of the women's movement in the early 1970s were due in part to the presence in government of sympathetic women. Once the women's movement publicly emerged, feminists in the "woodwork" of government provided it with easy access to many key points of decision-making—a major goal of any interest group. But until the movement created a constituency for these women, enabling them to claim a popular demand for new legislation and new approaches, they were unable to persuade the men (who had more votes and power) to pay any attention (Freeman 1975, 234). They might still have been unable to do so had not the new feminist movement emerged at a time when women's issues were of so little concern that there was no organized opposition.

This is no longer the case. As long as there remains "another" women's movement that is antifeminist in nature, like that led by Phyllis Schlafly, it is unlikely that influential Republican women will be able to persuade Republican leaders sympathetic to the other women's movement to support feminist positions. Republican feminists will first have to find or elect Republican leaders who support feminist positions, and they are unlikely to do this until the conservatives suffer a major electoral defeat.

The future of Democratic feminists is rosier but still uncertain. They have won major victories in the Democratic party, but success can be stifling. The Democratic party's traditional approach to insurgent groups is to co-opt them. The price of becoming an insider is that one must abide by the inevitable requirement to curb one's commitment to one's own agenda. The rules of the game require that one not make too many demands, or make demands that are too radical or that seriously conflict with the goals of other coalition groups. The NWPC already knows these rules, which it implicitly followed when it dismantled its whip system at the 1984 convention rather than permit it to be used by the dissident Jackson forces. NOW may also decide to follow them, but the consequence of its doing so will be to remove it from the cutting edge of social change. Because of the demise of the younger branch, NOW is the radical flank of the women's movement. A good radical flank is an essential ingredient in steady social change. Someone (or something) who has nothing to gain by playing the insiders' game must regularly raise new issues and expound new analyses in order to pull the mainstream in a progressive direction. Since an organization cannot be both in the mainstream *and* the radical flank without losing credibility and legitimacy, NOW will have to choose which path to follow.

Another requirement for participating in the mainstream of the party is that one not become an electoral liability. NOW demonstrated its awareness of this rule by endorsing Democratic men running against Republican feminist women, arguing that anyone who supports Reagan's economic program and does not support pro-choice is not really a feminist. Currently, the Republican party is attempting to make feminism an electoral liability by labeling it as just another special interest. Should feminism be discredited in the eyes of the American voter, the feminist organizations' claim to legitimately represent an important bloc of votes and, consequently, their influence in the Democratic party will be undermined. Thus those feminists who do want to remain an important voice in the Democratic party as feminists, not just as women, must continue to take their case to the American public and to organize their supporters to take an active part in local politics.

NOTES

1. Protective labor legislation was a generic label for a host of state laws that restricted the number of hours women could work and the amount of weight they could lift, occasionally required special benefits such as rest periods, and sometimes prohibited their working in certain occupations entirely.

2. For a blow-by-blow account of the floor happenings, see *Congressional Record* (1964). Edith Green (D.-Ore.) was the sole woman to vote against the sex provision. She later became the principal sponsor of another key piece of legislation for women, Title IX of the 1972 Education Amendments Act.

3. Eleanor Smeal (1984, 78), president of NOW and a leader of the ERA ratification struggle during its last five years, claimed that 83 percent of Republican legislators in key unratified states voted against the ERA, while only 45 percent of the Democrats did so.

4. National Party Conventions (1979, 113). See Shafer (1984, chap. 17) for a detailed description of how the burden of proof was shifted through a reinterpretation of the guidelines.

5. Kirkpatrick's conclusions were based on an extensive questionnaire study of delegates to the 1972 conventions. Unfortunately, her study didn't include a question on the ERA, probably because it was not very controversial in 1972.

6. Information on this section is based on interviews with Doris Meissner (1984) and Pat Bailey (1984), and an unpublished paper by Betsy Griffith that was probably written in late 1972. Bailey and Griffith were among those who orchestrated the National Women's Political Caucus efforts.

7. Information in this section is based on my observations and interviews at the 1976 Republican convention in Kansas City and the Democratic convention in New York. Some of this material appeared in *Ms.* magazine, October 1976, pp. 74–76, and November 1976, pp. 19–20.

8. Information in this section is based on interviews and observations I made at the conventions of the Republican party in Detroit and the Democratic party in New York. Much of this material was published in *In These Times*, 30 July–12 August 1980 and 27 August–2 September 1980.

9. This upset the Jackson campaign, as Jackson had hoped it would be used to support his platform minority planks.

10. Information in this section was based on my observations and interviews at the 1984 Republican convention in Dallas and Democratic convention in San Francisco, and on interviews with party and feminist activists in Washington, D.C. during 1984. Some of this material appeared in *off our backs,* February 1985, pp. 11–13, 20.

11. This section is based on an article by the same name published in *Political Science Quarterly* 101, 3 (Summer 1986): 327–56.

REFERENCES

Bailey, Pat. 1984. Interview, 12 December.

Becker, Susan D. 1981. *The Origins of the Equal Rights Amendment: American Feminism between the Wars.* Westport, Conn.: Greenwood.

Bird, Caroline. 1968. *Born Female.* New York: McKay.

Brady, David W., and Kent L. Tedin. 1976. "Ladies in Pink: Religion and Political Ideology in the Anti-ERA Movement." *Social Science Quarterly* 56: 564–75.

Congressional Digest. 1943. Vol. 22, April.

——. 1946. Vol. 25, No. 12.

Congressional Record, 110. 1964. 8 February, 2577–84.

Cotter, Cornelius P., and John F. Bibby. 1980. "Institutional Development of Parties and the Thesis of Party Decline." *Political Science Quarterly* 95: 1–27.

Crotty, William. 1983. *Party Reform.* New York: Longman.

DNC. 1973. Commission on Delegate Selection and Party Structure. *Democrats All.* Washington, D.C.: Democratic National Committee.

Farenthold, Sissy. 1984. Interview, 18 July.

Freeman, Jo. 1975. *The Politics of Women's Liberation.* New York: McKay.

Griffith, Betsy. unpublished paper.

Harrison, Cynthia Ellen. 1982. "Prelude to Feminism: Women's Organizations, the Federal Government, and the Rise of the Women's Movement, 1942–1968." Ph.D. diss., History Department, Columbia University.

Kirkpatrick, Jeane. 1976. *The New Presidential Elite: Men and Women in National Politics.* New York: Russell Sage Foundation and Twentieth Century Fund.

Lemons, J. Stanley. 1973. *The Woman Citizen: Social Feminism in the 1920s.* Urbana: University of Illinois Press.

McGlen, Nancy, E., and Karen O'Connor. 1983. *Women's Rights.* New York: Praeger.

Margolin, Bessie. 1967. Equal Pay and Equal Employment Opportunities for Women. New York University Conference of Labor paper.

Marshall, Susan E. 1984. "Keep Us on the Pedestal: Women against Feminism in Twentieth Century America." In Jo Freeman, ed., *Women: A Feminist Perspective.* 3d ed., 56–81. Palo Alto, Calif.: Mayfield.

Meissner, Doris. 1984. Interview, 7 November.

National Party Conventions, 1831–1976. 1979. Washington, D.C.: Congressional Quarterly, Inc.

Pressman, Jeffrey. 1977–78. "Groups and Group Caucuses." *Political Science Quarterly* 92 (no. 4): 673–82.

RNC. 1971. *The Delegate Selection Procedures for the Republican Party II: Progress Report [of the] DO Committee*. Washington, D.C., Republican National Committee.

Shafer, Byron. 1984. *The Quiet Revolution: Party Reform and the Shaping of Post-Reform Politics*. New York: Basic Books.

Shils, Edward. 1970. *"Center and Periphery": Selected Essays*. Chicago: Center for Social Organization Studies, University of Chicago.

Simchak, Morag MacLeod. 1971. "Equal Pay in the United States." *International Labour Review* 103 (no. 6): 541–47.

Smeal, Eleanor. 1984. *Why and How Women Will Elect the Next President*. New York: Harper & Row.

Steiner, Gilbert Y. 1985. *Constitutional Inequality: The Political Fortunes of the Equal Rights Amendment*. Washington, D.C.: Brookings Institution.

Sullivan, Denis G., et al. 1974. *The Politics of Representation: The Democratic Convention of 1972*. New York: St. Martin's Press.

———. 1976. *Explorations in Convention Decisionmaking: The Democratic Party in the 1970s*. San Francisco: W. H. Freeman.

Tolchin, Susan, and Martin Tolchin. 1974. *Clout: Womanpower and Politics*. New York: Coward, McCann & Geoghegan.

Ware, Susan. 1981. *Beyond Suffrage: Women in the New Deal*. Cambridge, Mass.: Harvard University Press.

White, Theodore J. 1973. *The Making of the President—1972*. New York: Atheneum.

Part Three   # THE STATE AND FEMINIST POLICY OUTCOMES

11 Workers' Movements and Women's Interests: The Impact of Labor-State Relations in Britain and Sweden

MARY RUGGIE

Workers' movements and the development of trade unions are commonly conceptualized by feminists as basically male-dominated concerns, despite their liaison with socialist ideologies. Feminists generally explain trade union disregard of women's interests within the theoretical framework of patriarchy (see Weir and Wilson 1984). This chapter seeks to analyze the involvement of unions with women workers and women's issues within a totally different paradigm, one based on the relations between labor and the state. Stressing an alternative explanation does not necessarily imply an argument against the common feminist approach, but it does suggest an attempt to break out of the confines of conceptualizing patriarchy as the main problem in women's work. When all is said and done, it may well be that what is presented here is itself explainable by the patriarchal roots of the modern state; still, as the following account demonstrates, there are certain detours on route to the final analysis that feminists must come to terms with in order to gain a full understanding of the relationship between labor, the state, and women.

By focusing on the experiences of Britain and Sweden, this chapter traces the development of women's place in the unions and union initiatives on behalf of women workers within the context of organized labor's relations with its representative political party. In both Britain and Sweden, unionism has a long history of developing in concert with supportive socialist-democratic political parties. Both the Labour party in Britain and the Social Democratic party in Sweden have held office for considerable, albeit varying, periods of time because of their labor-based support. In both countries coalitions between the party in power and unions have informed government actions.

Here the similarities diverge. When the Labour party has been in power in Britain, organized labor has always been consulted on certain matters, and a form of tripartitism has been attempted on certain occasions, but labor has never been a consistent and integral partner at the level of the state. The interests of labor have frequently been interpreted (by both organized labor and the Labour

247

party) as particular and outside the realm of the national interest, especially during troublesome economic times. In addition, organized labor itself in Britain has never formed a sufficiently united whole so that it could act at the level of the state as a viable representative of a large portion of the population.

In contrast, labor in Sweden has steadily become a coequal partner in the governing coalition. Its strength and position have been forged, on the one hand, by labor's own unity and centralization, and on the other by the continuity provided by the Social Democrats' long term in power. These two different kinds of labor-state relations—the one tenuous, the other close—have left organized labor in each country with very different sets of opportunities and constraints, with a different agenda and different priorities.

At the same time, the position of women workers in Britain and Sweden and the activism of unions on behalf of women have differed in significant ways. Before the 1950s, women's labor market conditions as well as women's participation in union life was about the same in the two countries—low on both counts. After this time, however, the situation for women workers in Sweden advanced considerably, surpassing by far any comparable changes for women in Britain. In Sweden, economic policies that contained special labor market measures for women, including the development of child care programs, greatly facilitated progress for women workers. But the government did not act alone in developing these policies. At every step along the way, organized labor not only supported but sometimes also fashioned the policy nexus as it concerned labor. In contrast, as the economy changed in Britain in the 1950s and 1960s, labor and the state were preoccupied with concerns that had plagued them for decades. Policy discussion focused on attempts to devise income and price policies to see the nation through economic fluctuations. The special needs of women workers were virtually eclipsed by the constantly more pressing needs of the economy as a whole. The difference in these two nations' interpretations of and approaches to the role of women in the economy can be understood within the context of their different kinds of labor-state relations.

A corollary argument that emerges from this chapter's discussion speaks to the role of women themselves, both within unions and as an organized movement outside unions. It follows from the analysis here that the role of women, and the success or failure of women's organized efforts, must be examined within the broader context of social and political coalitions. The women's movements in Britain and Sweden are very different. In Britain, women within unions remain a separate and unequal partner in forming union positions on women's issues, and the women's movement as a whole is fragmented and segmented (see Chapter 12 in this volume). In Sweden, as women's numerical representation within the unions increased (although not in leadership positions), unions continued an integrationist strategy, adopting policies that benefited women in the same way as they benefited all low-paid workers. The concern that often accompanies such absorption, concern that women's special interests become watered down, is difficult to accept completely, given the results presented below. Outside unions, the women's movement in Sweden is coherent and coordinated, if not exactly centralized. It is interesting to note that both these pictures of organized women reflect the broader contexts of labor-state relations in each country. Where appropriate, I indicate throughout the specific contributions that organized women have made to union and state positions on women's issues.

In the sections below I outline the main features of labor-state relations in Britain and Sweden; then for each country I present the history of women's place in the unions and unions' concerns with women's issues, focusing in particular on equal pay. In the conclusion I turn again to the contention that the analysis presented here offers an alternative understanding of the relations between unions and women workers to that found within the theoretical framework of patriarchy.

LABOR AND THE STATE IN BRITAIN

From its beginnings the relationship between labor and the state in Britain has been punctuated by disunity and misunderstanding. There have been periods of cooperation and accord, to be sure, especially when the Labour party was in power in the 1920s and 1930s. But any historical unity was relative and temporary, and insufficient to prevent the cleavages that developed later. We can trace the ebbs and flows in harmony between labor and the state by focusing on the development of unionism and the Labour party and the relationship between them.

British manufacturing began to industrialize earlier than that of any other country, and while industrialization was slow, it was thorough, affecting even farming. Corresponding to the pace and tone set by industrialism was the development of the working class and its organization into trade unions (Thompson 1963). Two facts about early trade unionism in Britain are important: its organization along craft lines, and the fierce sectionalism and antagonism that resulted. This early divisiveness and its consequence have never been fully overcome. We see it emerging in the "feudal" nature of both British industry and labor relations (Shonfield 1965, 118). The founding of the Trades Union Congress (TUC) in 1868 provided at least a semblance of institutional coordination for organized labor. But the TUC has never been able to effectively centralize labor in Britain: only one-quarter of Britain's approximately 480 unions are affiliated with it. Moreover, unions have remained entrenched in their sectional differences; consequently, the TUC's ability to speak for labor at the level of the state has been constrained. This failure of cohesion has been most obvious and most unfortunate in the various attempts of both Labour and Conservative governments to formulate incomes policies (Martin 1975a). While deals were struck between the TUC and the party in power, agreement was not always forthcoming between the TUC and its affiliates.

In 1899 the TUC founded a Parliamentary Labour party. The early Labour party was a trades union party, not a socialist party; it was devoted to promoting through parliamentary politics the cause of workers for better working conditions (Beer 1965). Later, the party did become socialist, carrying labor with it in its declarations of socialist ideals. But as this unity developed, so too did another discord, this time between the rank and file of the Party and its elected representatives. While the former became more socialist, the latter became only moderately so; while the former wove the interests of labor into an agenda for social change, the latter pitted the particular interests of labor against the "national" interest (Coates 1975). This tension grew and finally culminated in the creation of the Social Democratic party in 1981.

There have been certain key periods in the development of Britain's welfare state when organized labor could have been involved as a central actor in shaping policies concerning production and redistribution. That it was involved only perfunctorily reveals the fundamental cleavage between labor and the state—and further reveals the superficiality of British socialism, a shortcoming that is at the heart of the issue under discussion here. For, as I have argued elsewhere, the development of policies for women has followed the same path and been subject to the same set of constraints as the development of the welfare state (Ruggie 1984).

The area most telling of the strained relationship between labor and the state in Britain is incomes policy and the manner in which it has been consistently imposed without full union backing. Since the issue has relevance to the development of equal pay measures, it requires examination.

By tradition, an earnest attempt is made to keep industrial relations in Britain removed from the political arena. Disputes between employers and employees are settled in collective bargaining without interference from government or politicians. In the early part of this century the principle of abstention of the law in industrial relations prevailed, but the last few decades have brought an increase in legislation both to protect workers and to protect the nation from industrial disputes (as in the Industrial Relations Act of 1969, later repealed). Negotiations are conducted within the framework of these laws. Along with the increased, albeit mild, presence of the state in regulating collective bargaining, the development of a type of tripartite system in Britain has increasingly involved leaders of unions and employers' organizations in concerns at the level of the state, with varying degrees of strength and real participation. Despite these developments, however, the freedom of collective bargaining remains sacrosanct.

Besides modifications in the political context, collective bargaining is also strongly circumscribed by the prevailing economic climate. To put it simply, unions cannot be too aggressive in their demands when economic conditions are poor; their gains have occurred during periods of growth and nearly full employment. This is because wage increases are inflationary; when governments are concerned about inflationary pressures, one measure they try to institute is a wage control policy. Such a policy has its place in the overall array of measures designed to stabilize an economy; to be successful, however, a wage control policy requires the support of labor, and it is more likely to receive such support if a price control policy is included in the measure. In the interests of planned economic growth, a few Labour administrations, most notably those under Harold Wilson in 1964 and James Callaghan in 1974, attempted to capitalize on their relations with union leaders to develop viable policies for wage and price constraint. Although the details of the two attempts differed, the general thrust was similar.[1] In both cases, voluntary efforts to institute wage controls failed. Both failures reflected the fact that "social contracts" existed between government and union leaders, but not between union leaders and their rank and file. Eventually, both governments resorted to imposing an incomes policy and administering it alone. Both times, strikes followed; conciliations were arranged; and the Conservatives regained power with the vow to put the unions back in line.

The main factor behind the failure of incomes policy and the discord it signifies is certainly Britain's poor economic situation. However, Britain's economy is not to be considered an objective determining force on its own. It is the result of policy choices that have shown a remarkable lack of creativity on the part of government leaders of both parties unwilling to take greater control over external factors. What this further means is that the Labour Party has not adopted the sort of socialist program that could keep its relations with workers and organized labor bound by ties of affinity even in times of hardship. When in office the Labour party has provided no better than the Conservative party for policies and programs to support workers and see them through periods of stress and change.

Besides its broken ties with the Labour party and the state, organized labor has suffered from its own disunity and internal discord. Despite the appearance of greater centralization in the 1970s, the TUC never captured the effective voice of or control over the labor movement. The attempts at tripartitism have accordingly been unrepresentative—especially on the part of employers organized in the Confederation of British Industries (CBI)—and unsuccessfully channeled. There have been times, therefore, when workers have felt betrayed not only by their party but also by their top union representatives. Little wonder that the gains British workers have won have been hard fought and jealously guarded— by women no less than men.

WOMEN AND LABOR IN BRITAIN

Where in this picture of mistrust and conflict have women fit in? Nowhere, actually. The workers' movement in Britain has been a predominantly male concern. The political disunity and dissension outlined above has not helped; in fact, it provides an important explanation for the inability of the labor movement to go beyond fragmented interests in order to coalesce a wider united base, necessarily including women. The determination on the part of male workers to maintain the differential between themselves and women workers has smacked of the same motivation as that behind the defense of differentials in general—jealous guarding of turf because of the inability to see, let alone actualize, a common working-class interest in the face of persuasive capitalist co-optation. I outline first the historical relationship between women workers and trade unions before assessing the current situation of grudging, albeit growing, alliance.

From the beginnings of the trade unionism in Britain, women were pitted against men, setting the stage for the diverging development of their interests and movements.[2] As improving technology broke down heavy and complex production into menial tasks, employers preferred to hire women, both because of the lower wages required and also as a tool against men who were forming unions, illegally and contentiously. So in the mills at first and later in the factories, women were functioning as a true industrial reserve army and indeed taking jobs away from men. The result was distrust and resentment on the part of male workers and their unions. Several early unions, most notably the spinners and weavers, excluded women. When the Combination Acts were repealed in 1824, some women workers formed their own organizations. These were largely ineffective—small, financially weak, unable to secure any improvement in working conditions. A few sporadic and, in the end, unsuccessful movements combined the efforts of men and women in organized agitation (an amalgamated Grand National Consolidated Trades Union and Chartism). However, it was not until the latter part of the nineteenth century, when the union movement began to reorganize nationally on craft lines (often throughout an entire industry), that women were included and actively recruited, but only in areas and industries with considerable female representation. Thus, a pattern developed throughout the country: where working-class organization was traditionally strong, as in the textile industries in the north and midlands, women were members of trade unions along with men; elsewhere, they developed separate organizations. After World War I, mergers were more common. However, there are still several unions in Britain with predominantly female membership, representing the persistent occupational segregation of women. There are still several unions with predominantly male membership as well, indicating the continuing effectiveness of apprenticeship and other discriminatory requirements, despite their illegality. To date, about 39 percent of women workers are unionized, compared to about 63 percent of men workers. Working women in Britain continue to be burdened by a dual work load, precluding their ability to be actively involved in unions, which hold most of their meetings in the evenings.

The inclusion of women in previously male trade unions by no means signified adoption of women's interests by these unions. It signifies instead the realization that added numbers of workers could bolster more nonviolent means of industrial agitation. Where women's interests completely coincided with men's, as in the setting of minimum rates in certain industries, the common cause was adopted by the unions concerned. But where interests diverged, as in the issue of equal pay, union support remained token, at best. The development of equal pay for women deserves further elaboration, revealing as it does the force of divisiveness in industrial relations in Britain.

In 1888 the TUC passed a resolution supporting the principle of equal pay for equal work. The principle remained on paper for decades. The first union to accept and successfully press for equal pay was the Civil Service Union, and this not until the 1950s. When increasing numbers of women were joining the labor force and unions in the 1960s, more unions, especially those with increasing female membership, began to support equal pay. But active agitation for equal pay rested on the efforts of women themselves—within the unions, on the streets, and in government. For example, in the 1960s the National Women's Advisory Committee of the TUC became more adamant in pressing for equal pay. Since this committee, founded in 1931, is advisory only, its position—even though accepted by the TUC General Council—would have remained on paper only had not a 1968 strike by women sewing machinists at the Ford Motors plant at Dagenham made action on the paper position imperative. Under normal circumstances the TUC General Council readily supports "industrial action," especially for such principles as equal pay. In this case, however, the TUC was in its all too frequent uneasy position of double agent. It was involved in tripartite discussions on the costs of implementing equal pay and felt it could not support the women strikers' cause without jeopardizing its negotiating position on the same matter vis-à-vis the government and the CBI. The national conference of unionists passed an amendment supporting industrial action for equal pay anyway, and the TUC once again found itself out of step with the rank and file. Officially, the TUC explained its position as favoring traditional and decentralized collective bargaining instead of legislation, saying "representations to Government, advice and guidance to affiliated unions, is as far as the TUC itself can go in the campaign for equal pay. Negotiations with employers are matters for individual unions and only the members of those unions can determine the policy to be followed by their negotiators" (Wootton 1978, 95). One can suggest that the TUC was also suffering from the constraining demands of tripartitism in Britain.

By the time these ambivalences within the trade union movement were emerging, the issue of equal pay had already made its appearance on the government agenda. Among the several reasons precipitating the public interest was the fact that the Labour party, in power throughout the second half of the 1960s, was preparing to join the European Economic Commission (EEC), and Britain would have to be ready to sign the EEC's clause on equal pay when it joined. Hence, the TUC and the CBI arranged bilateral talks to coordinate their positions. To precipitate matters, Secretary of State for Employment and productivity Barbara Castle—the first woman to serve in this post—initiated a series of tripartite discussions to introduce legislation for and begin appropriate implementation of equal pay for women. One important item, the meaning of equal pay, had already been settled in discussions between the TUC and the CBI. The TUC had favored the broad understanding embodied in an International Labour Organization convention, equal pay for work of equal value, but for the sake of expeditiousness it had conceded to the CBI's preference for equal pay for the same work (Wootton 1978).

When reports finally emerged estimating that equal pay would increase wages and salaries by 3.5 percent, the tripartite actors in dismay reconvened for negotiations concerning the timing of implementation. The TUC tried to resurrect discussions of principle (equal pay for equal value) and tried to shorten the number of years it would take to make equal pay operative. It failed on both counts, this time because of the expediency of First Secretary Castle, who had several constituencies to please with an equal pay bill. The bill finally became a law in 1970, just before the Labour government lost office, and was given five years to become fully operational.

As this account indicates, at the upper echelons trade union support for women's interests in Britain has been readily absorbed into and circumvented by the requirements for "cooperation" in tripartite negotiations. At the lower echelons of the labor movement there has also been characteristic foot-dragging, even reactionary measures, on women's issues. The decentralized picture is more mixed, however, reflecting the many differences among unions in Britain. Two main differences have significance for women workers: (1) union control over the regulation of work, especially apprenticeship and training requirements, as well as the closed shop; and (2) wage differentials. Union control over labor requirements has traditionally been used by unionists to protect their members against arbitrary practices by employers. At the same time, of course, the measures served to exclude women from certain jobs and industries. That some unions (most notably printing and engineers) continue these policies to this day reveals as much about disunity in the labor movement as it does about the male domination of unions.[3] The same can be said about the persistent tendency in wage negotiations to maintain differentials between different kinds of workers. This tendency is strongest among unions organizing skilled workers. It is exacerbated by the preference in such unions for separate negotiations with management rather than the establishment of multiunion or joint bodies for bargaining (Daniels 1976). If concerns about the comparability of pay occur between male workers, it is not surprising that they persist where women workers are involved. In 1972 the Office of Manpower Economics conducted a survey at company level of union attitudes toward the equal pay legislation that was slowly being implemented. It found that

> about a quarter of the companies . . . had experienced union pressure for equal pay (and in other cases the question had been raised in the course of general pay negotiations), but in about one in ten it was contended by managements that its introduction had been blocked by the attitudes of male union members. In some cases it was said that the men had resisted pay changes which would have narrowed the differentials between themselves and female employees and had successfully demanded the same percentage increases. (Ellis 1981, 39)

Unions concerned about differentials are more likely to emphasize—for purposes of pay, promotion, and redundancy—those job criteria that place women at a disadvantage: strict interpretations of skill and training requirements, length and continuity of service, mobility requirements, and age bars. Where these criteria are clearly discriminatory, they are now illegal according to the terms of the Sex Discrimination Act. However, when job evaluations have to be conducted to determine pay, the criteria reenter in indirect form.[4] The section of the Sex Discrimination Act dealing with indirect discrimination is as insistent (if not more so) in its presentation of exceptions as in stating the rule.

Were women themselves a stronger force in the labor movement, the status of women's issues might also be higher in the unions. Those unions where female membership is the actual majority, or close to it, are persistent in pressing for greater equality in rights and opportunities for women. Foremost among these are the National Union of Teachers (in which women are 66 percent of the membership) and the National Association of Local Government Officers (50 percent). It is noteworthy that women are most strongly organized in white-collar unions and that these unions are more active in advancing women's concerns than either the TUC or the blue-collar unions it organizes. For example, even though the proportion of women in their membership is about the same (65 percent), the Union of Shop Distributive and Allied Workers has a smaller proportion of women on its executive committee (19 percent) than the National Union of Public Employees (31 percent). Also, while some white-collar unions send delegates to the TUC annual conference, these unions are less integrated under the TUC umbrella than blue-collar unions, enabling the former to become more progressive than the TUC.

In sum, paralleling the tenuous relations between labor and the state in Britain, women within labor have also been secondary, and their interests have been removed from other interests and more pressing concerns. The position of women workers has advanced in Britain, to be sure, and some notable legislative measures have been forthcoming; however, these have tended to follow rather than facilitate and guide the changes in women's employment. Unions, too, have been less than active as vanguards, or even in keeping step with the needs and demands of their female constituency. As we turn now to the case of Sweden, we see a direct reversal of many of the events forming the relationship between labor and the state and women within labor.

LABOR AND THE STATE IN SWEDEN

Labor-state relations in Sweden are noted for their relative stability and consensus, as well as the innovation that results. It should be emphasized that these achievements have come about only after concerted efforts and calculated decisions, and their maintenance requires the same attention. Still, certain structural factors in the historical development of Swedish industrial relations can be identified as enabling the harmonious outcome (Stephens 1979).

Sweden did not begin to industrialize until the latter half of the nineteenth century; once industrialization came, it was swift but concentrated. Labor unions began to form in close concert with the development of industry.[5] The shift was rapid from small craft-based unions to large unions for unskilled workers to coordinated activity among unions in similar occupations to national industry-based unions. By the early part of the twentieth century, consolidated industrial unionism prevailed, paving the way for the development of coordinated industry-wide bargaining.

The first steps toward collective bargaining also occurred early. A central organization for the unions, the *Landsorganisationen* (LO), was formed in 1898. The LO's capacity to function as a central coordinating body was put to the test within a few years. After the first national strike in 1902, apprehensive employers formed their own central organization, the *Svenska Arbetsgivareföreingen* (SAF) to counter the unions. Shortly thereafter, in 1906, the LO and the SAF were engaged in negotiations. The first round of talks concerned the right of organization for workers in a local dispute. And the first of many "compromises" was reached promptly, the SAF recognizing the right to unionization and the LO accepting employers' prerogatives to "hire and fire workers, to manage and distribute the work, and to use workers belonging to any union or to no union" (Jenkins 1968, 135).[6] This is not to suggest that relations between the two organizations were amiable from the start; in fact, there were no further joint efforts until the 1930s. But unlike the situation in Britain, in which employers did not begin to organize until the 1930s, forcing labor to deal with management at the shop floor level, in Sweden the early organization and collaboration provided a good basis for later developments.

After a long period of labor unrest aggravated by economic stagnation, the LO and the SAF returned to the bargaining table in 1936. The immediate instigation behind these talks was the Social Democratic government's warning that legislation would be the only alternative if collective conciliation could not break the tension in industrial relations. The eventual result of the talks was a new spirit of cooperation and the institutionalization of collective bargaining as formulated in the first Basic Agreement, signed in 1938 at Salsjöbaden. Thereafter, centralized negotiations between the LO and the SAF have formed the basic frame within which decentralized bargaining is conducted. Whether adaptations are made at the industrywide or the workplace level, the basic frame is not superseded. Unlike the British situation, systematization of the levels of collective bargaining is facilitated by the fact that agreements are legally binding in Sweden.

After the first Basic Agreement was concluded, the power of the LO steadily increased. The foremost factor behind the LO's position is its special relationship with the Social Democratic Party (SDP). Unionism and socialism took root in Sweden at about the same time. Very soon after trade unions began to form, the Social Democratic party was founded (1889), based largely on union support. In fact, until the LO was formed, the party functioned as a centralizing organization for the unions. From the beginning the LO and the SDP formed a close working relationship, the one actively involved in the efforts of the other to achieve mutually compatible goals. Moreover, from the beginning both organizations and their respective movements decided on goals that were more pragmatic and liberal than radical and revolutionary. Labor's first national strike was over the issue of universal suffrage, which of course was an SDP goal as well. Decades later, cooperative efforts shaped Sweden's innovative economic policies and led to the development of the country's unique welfare state (Tilton 1979).

For a full comparison of the quality of labor-state relations in Britain and Sweden, it is instructive to see how they differed on a similar issue, namely incomes policies. An incomes policy was negotiated and applied in Sweden in the late 1940s in much the same way, for similar reasons, and with similar consequences as in Britain. However, unlike what happened in Britain, the failure of incomes policy in Sweden marked the end of any more such ventures "because the LO refused to consent to any more and no Swedish Social Democratic Government ever tried to impose any form of wage restraint over the LO's objections" (Martin 1975, 40). There have been times when the government has urged wage restraint, but the LO has not always been favorably inclined, as in the unstable period of "wage explosion" provoked by the Korean War. Still, economic factors were taken into account in central bargaining, a practice that became regularized and eventually led to the development of Sweden's alternative to incomes policy: namely, "a structural strategy of economic management" (Martin 1975b, 40).

The whole notion of economic management was one that Sweden had experimented with earlier (under Ernst Wigforss's guidance in the 1930s) and with which key actors were comfortable. So when a new phase of economic management came to be formulated in the 1950s, the ideas were readily accepted and implemented. It is important to note that the new plans originated with two leading LO economists, Gösta Rehn and Rudolf Meidner, presaging the role that labor's interests would have in the economy. While the Rehn-Meidner model proposed a way to reduce both inflation and unemployment simultaneously, it also put the goal of full employment at the forefront should a tradeoff become necessary. The model essentially suggested that labor be moved from industries that are inefficient, have low productivity, and low profits to the more productive and profitable industries. Two kinds of measures were to facilitate this move and direct its purposes. The first came to be known as Sweden's "active labor market policy," a set of government-run programs including career guidance, training, government-monopolized job advertisement and job finding, relief jobs in both the public and private sectors, and adequate financial support during job transition. The second set of measures precipitated the development of the Swedish system of industrial investment. It consists of a Reserve Fund to which companies have allocated some of their profits (in return for a tax advantage) and which the government controls, releasing funds for investment purposes when and where it is appropriate to do so.

To the extent that this model worked, it benefited both labor and business, creating a unique combination of full employment and high economic growth. Moreover, the policy framework functioned as an alternative to incomes policy in at least two ways. First, to prevent high levels of unemployment and growth from generating increased prices or unusual profits, additional measures such as sales and other indirect taxes were used, thus controlling one facet of inflation. Second and most important, in light of these policies, unions willingly accepted some wage restraint, keeping their end of the bargain to contain inflation and contribute to economic growth. The following excerpt from a collaborative research project sponsored by the LO, the TCO (*Tjänstemännens Centralorganisationen*, which organizes salaried employees), and the SAF is remarkable for its tone of unity and the contrast it offers to anything that could emerge from Britain:

> The primary task of the unions is to negotiate as large a share of the production result as possible for their members. But with the strength that these organizations have nowadays in Sweden, they must sense a responsibility for the economy which goes far beyond this primary task. It is true that they have often been accused of demanding too much in wage negotiations and, consequently, of having caused price increases. . . . But in negotiations the unions have been aware of the risk of making such heavy inroads into profitability that the basis for future development in business enterprises deteriorates. The negotiators have long become aware of a point beyond which no claim should be pushed lest it impair the prospects for future wage increases. (Flanagan, Soskice, and Ulman 1983, 303)

Despite these efforts and the mutual understanding involved, Sweden could not remain immune to inflation, nor to increased (though contained) unemployment, nor to consequent tensions in industrial relations. As the economy worsened in the 1970s, so too did the once harmonious compromises of the tripartite actors, resulting in wildcat strikes and a spiral of wage increases and inflation: "By Swedish standards, this must be considered a case of bargaining failure" (Flanagan, Soskice, and Ulman 1983, 327). The deteriorating situation culminated in the defeat of the Social Democrats after 44 years in power, and an even more unstable era of six years under a nonsocialist coalition.

The period of nonsocialist government provided the LO with an opportunity to sort out snags in its relationship with other unions, an effort that eventually served to consolidate the labor movement as a whole. The main issue involved wage and salary equality among different categories of workers (since it pertains to women workers, it is taken up in the next section). This same period also offered the LO and SAF a chance to let the differences between them, which they had kept under control for so long, finally erupt. In 1980, Sweden witnessed a startling general strike as well as an equally startling lockout. The events showed everyone what life was like without effective tripartism, a sobering experience that facilitated the return of the Social Democrats to power in 1982.

The fundamental criterion in consensus-based labor-state-capital relations, such as that discussed above, is the effective integration of labor at the level of the state, a condition that can occur only under a truly committed labor-oriented or socialist government. At present the inclusion of workers' interests within economywide concerns is entering a new phase with the development of wage earners' funds. This is an extension of the concept of industrial democracy into the sphere of collective ownership of industry. Through taxes on payrolls as well as excess profits taxes on companies, funds are to be set up—initially run by trade union representatives—to buy workers' shares in large enterprises. While the future of this scheme is uncertain, its presence on the public agenda reaffirms the place of labor within the governing coalition and the economic development of Sweden.

WOMEN AND LABOR IN SWEDEN

Where, in this picture of concerted efforts on the part of labor, state, and capital in the name of full employment and economic growth, have the special needs of women workers fit in? As a separate category with real and special needs, women workers remained in the background until only very recently. From their beginnings, the LO and the Social Democratic party adopted the position that women's concerns required no special organization outside a class-based labor movement (Streijffert 1974). But this is not to say that the economic position of women workers remained inferior and stagnant. In fact, it improved, but only as a byproduct of the broader concerns of the workers' movement. The main advance has been in the area of equal pay. Before elaborating this issue, I briefly review the background of women's participation in unions in Sweden.

Because unionization in Sweden developed relatively late, at a time when socialism was also in the air, women have never been excluded from Swedish unions, as they have elsewhere. However, women have never formed an effective power base within the workers' movement, neither at the beginning, nor in the later period of union activism. The same kind of male dominance and prejudices against women were to be found in Swedish unionism in the early twentieth century as elsewhere, and the same token statements supporting equal pay were placed on paper to languish for decades. Neither women's membership in unions nor their labor force participation were sufficiently high in the early decades of this century to make them a force to be reckoned with. Moreover, although women organized early in Sweden (the Frederika Bremer Society was founded in 1884, the Women's Association of the Social Democratic Party in 1892), they cannot be said to have formed an effective voice in Swedish society until very recently (in fact, only after the developments discussed below). The story of women workers in Sweden does not become noteworthy until the 1930s and does not take on real significance until the 1960s.

When the Social Democrats first came to power in the 1930s, their main

method of handling economic stagnation was an early form of Keynesian coun-
tercyclical financing, including the adoption of a full employment policy (Tilton
1979). Low-paid women workers in particular were drawn into the labor market
and immediately came under the auspices of the LO; by 1940 women formed
nearly 20 percent of its membership. The LO was involved with the Social
Democrats in developing legislation for basic workers' rights, including some
special protections for women workers (for example, making it unlawful for any
employer to fire a woman who had become engaged, married, or pregnant). But
these early laws were all basic, establishing such principles as equal pension
rights and paid maternity leave.

At the same time that labor laws became established, family policy was also
being formulated. The most important ideas presented by early family commissions were recognition of the need for women workers, both in the national economy and in private households, and recognition of the role of family policy in
facilitating women's work, financially and through day care centers (Liljeström
1978). Again, these policies set more principles than programs, and tended to
encourage a higher birthrate through financial incentives more than they encouraged women to work. But at least the tone was positive (and did not disparage
women's work, as in Britain).

As women's labor force participation gradually increased in the 1940s and
thereafter, the kind of work most women were doing—clerical, professional, and
other white-collar jobs—meant that they were joining unions other than the LO.
Foremost among these were the TCO (*Tjänstemännens Centralorganisation:* the
Central Organization of Salaried Employees) and SACO (*Sveriges Akademikers
Centralorganisation:* Swedish Confederation of Professional Associations).[7]
More women are now organized within these unions than in the LO; in fact,
women are over half of the TCO's membership. But these unions have tended to
lag behind the LO in their concern for women's issues. The reason for this lies
less with any unique characteristics of the white-collar unions than with the special place of the LO in the tripartite system.

By the 1950s, the LO was beginning to conduct talks with the SAF on the
issue of equal pay for women, spurred no doubt by the increased membership of
women in rival unions, as well as by the International Labour Organization's
adoption of a convention on equal pay for women. The talks gradually paved the
way for Sweden to sign the ILO convention in 1960, but it took many years to
eliminate the use of separate pay scales and to establish the principle of "work of
equal value" embodied in the ILO convention. While these efforts of course led
to some improvement in women's pay relative to men's, it is from another area of
the LO's negotiations that women benefited even more. The issue of equal pay for
women, as with other work-related matters in Sweden, was not discussed in a
vacuum distinguished only by its relation to gender. It was contained in the context of developing fair and rational bases for wages and wage differentials, a policy framework that has come to be known as wage solidarity.

Since Sweden had rejected the use of income and price policies to control the economy, another method of holding back spiraling inflation proposed by LO economists in the 1950s was the policy of wage solidarity. It rested on the principle that wage increases and wage differentials had to be based on rational factors consistent across all industries so that wages would not be so out of line with productivity as to create economic strain. The policy rejected the notion that the productivity of any given industry could influence wages in that industry; it argued instead that cohesion among all industries in setting wages would create greater efficiency in the use of labor and improve economic productivity overall. Wage solidarity was not a policy to equalize wages but to systematize them and coordinate them with industrial and labor market policies. Among the criteria for differential wages were the degree of difficulty of the job, vocational training requirements, the danger of accidents, the insecurity of employment, and the nature of the working environment. One major consequence of specifying these factors was to eliminate the (irrational) bases for unequal wages for women and other low-paid workers. Thus, as a result of the gradual institutionalization of the policy of wage solidarity, the wages of all low-paid workers began to rise in relation to higher-paid workers, and women were the major beneficiaries. By 1970, women's pay as a proportion of men's in the industrial sector was 80 percent, and by 1980 it was 90 percent.

Other unions, most significantly the TCO, have supported the policy of wage solidarity—necessarily, for it to be effective. But the TCO's early support was chiefly in principle and for the sake of solidarity. The main difference was the TCO's own emphasis on equal pay for equal work and its efforts to refine job evaluations that justified wage differentiations. Since the TCO conducts its own bargaining sessions with the SAF, different agreements concerning women workers prevailed depending on their affiliated union. Recently, however (and especially because of the equality legislation discussed below), the TCO and the LO have come closer on several issues, including equal pay for work of equal value for women and all low-paid workers. The trend toward even greater centralization among unions is still progressing in Sweden, and it can only further benefit women.

Up to this point, nothing special for women on the part of unions has been discussed because nothing special for women within unions existed before the late 1970s. Special efforts on behalf of women workers are contained in Sweden's very active labor market programs, and unions were involved in developing these programs, since their representatives are members of the National Labor Market Board.[8] By the 1970s, however, the demand for more special measures for women, particularly legislation on equality, increased. One can surmise that women themselves were by then playing a more active role, for organized labor and organized employers have always sought to avoid legislation, on this or any other matter, because they see it as interfering in the collective bargaining procedure. Indeed, by the 1970s the women's movement in Sweden had become more widespread and decidedly more feminist and activist. Moreover, any earlier reservations about legislation among socialists, both women and men, were superseded when a nonsocialist government came into power in 1976. The political benefits to be derived from legislation based on a broad coalition of nonsocialist and socialist women seemed large to the newly elected officials. A law called "Equality between Men and Women at Work" accordingly was passed in December 1980. Interestingly, this law did not supersede but in fact reinforced the mechanism of collective bargaining as the main tool for the achievement of equality. When the equality ombudsperson is called upon to arbitrate a case, she or he must work within the terms of a collective agreement, and if one does not exist that speaks to the point of contention, a new agreement or clause is negotiated. Since 1980 the LO, the TCO, and most other unions have negotiated speical agreements with the SAF pertaining to the situation of women workers. While these agreements are still separate among the unions, there is an increasing effort to standardize their terms. It must be emphasized that these special agreements for women do not stand outside the main collective agreement but are part and parcel of it.

The Swedish method of incorporating the concerns of women workers into the concerns of workers as a whole as interpreted by labor unions has not been without its critics both inside and outside Sweden. The criticism dates back to the beginnings of socialism in Sweden. Unlike its British counterpart, Swedish socialism has consistently emphasized and realized broad coalition building based on common interests. Because of this, women within the labor force have been treated as workers—low-paid and occupationally segregated to be sure, but workers nevertheless. As long as organized labor achieved basic socialist goals, women *workers* benefited, as did all low-paid workers. Hence, some of the concerns that a separate feminist organization would have advocated were fostered by the progress of socialism in Sweden. However, by the 1970s it was becoming clear that progress for *women* within socialism had gone about as far as it could. On the firm foundation of past achievements, women began to press beyond the confines of socialism, and as established members of the labor force, they were heard. Feminist groups supported the development of the equality legislation precisely because they felt that unions had so generalized the concerns of women workers as to ignore the unique problems that women face *as women* rather than as low-paid workers, primarily the problems of sex discrimination and occupational segregation. In addition, as one American commentator has noted, LO's attempts to preempt and contain feminist groups on the labor market, in the unions, and in the workplace can be described as "one-part male apprehension, one-part Swedish concern for union prerogatives, and one-part traditional Social Democratic ideology, which has always subordinated women's rights to class questions" (Scott 1982, 53).

Imperfections and patriarchal ideologies exist in Sweden, to be sure. Nevertheless, the situation of women workers there is so significantly better than the comparative situation in other countries, especially Britain, that attention must be paid to the growth of these achievements. Generalizing the situation of women as workers has been at the root of this growth. The approach has not been unique to the union interpretation, for it is also to be found within Sweden's labor market policies. In many ways, these labor market policies can be analyzed as analogous to the contemporary form of collective agreements. That is, within the general framework of the best use of labor, special measures for women exist. In the field of labor market policies, these special measures include career guidance that encourages women (and men) to train for occupations not traditional for their sex in order to qualify for better job opportunities; hiring quotas and other incentives to employers to hire and train women or men in positions not traditional for their sex; and job creation programs that benefit women workers as much as men. Labor market programs and policies are not an entirely separate sphere of activity from union concerns with wages, job evaluations, and the like. As mentioned above, since union representatives sit on the National Labor Market Board, one can expect some similarity in the approach to women's concerns.

Above all, the basic assumption in all these measures is that women work. The issue of "choice" has been increasingly removed with the gradual recognition that equality between the sexes is based on sex *role* equality. The other side of the coin, greater participation by men in home and family responsibilities, while far from being realized, has been addressed and effected to a greater extent in Sweden than in any other country. In sum, changes in consciousness have had a material and collective base in Sweden, developing in concert with the development of socialism. At the same time, it appears that all of these changes have reached a standoff.

CONCLUSION

If unions are "patriarchal" and, accordingly, treat women's issues perfunctorily, then what accounts for the relative achievements of women workers as a result of union efforts in Sweden? This paper has attempted to demonstrate the inadequacy of patriarchy as a conceptual and theoretical base for understanding the relationship between workers' movements and women's interests. That the concerns of women workers in Britain have fared poorly has been explained here in terms of the broader context of strains and dissensions in labor-state relations. That women's causes have been more successfully promoted in Sweden has been explained here in terms of the broader context of consolidated labor-state efforts to achieve full employment, including women's, together with and for the purposes of economic growth.

This paper has indicated further that the form and fate of women's groups is similarly contained within a broader context of social and political relations. In the case of Britain, feminist activism has not been featured in the development of any of the special measures for women. Even when women have been organized and active in pressing their own concerns, as in the agitation for equal pay in the late 1960s, the efforts were localized and specific to certain companies or groups of workers. In addition, even the most aggressive agitation had little impact on the TUC's position within the tripartite negotiations for equal pay. The final formulation of the Equal Pay Act reflected the tripartite consensus, not the preferred feminist version. This is not to say that British unions have been unresponsive to women workers. Joyce Gelb (see Chapter 12) discusses several areas of union support, such as day care and abortion. None of these areas of support, however, jeopardizes the more important role of the TUC within the tripartite system, a system that is separate from women's issues in both theory and practice. It is perfectly plausible to suggest that had women in Britain been more active and more consistently so, more could have been achieved. But it is less speculative and more to the point to explain why women in Britain have not become a stronger social and political force. Their incapacitation is understandable, given the pattern of fragmented interest structuration prevailing in Britain. Britain is indeed a patriarchal society. But I have suggested that it is the persisting fact of divisiveness, and the persisting onus of self-interest that derives from divisiveness, that explain lack of progress, for women as for all workers—and not the fact of gender alone.

The case of Sweden forms an important contrast—up to a point. Politics in Sweden are based on broad coalitions and a concerted effort to mitigate differences for the sake of rational economic growth. Such progress for women as has occurred in Sweden has advanced within this framework—and Swedish progress has been remarkable compared to that of other countries. But lately the confines of this framework and its limitations on the full achievement of equality for women have become more apparent. In particular, women's occupational segregation in Sweden remains curiously impervious to change. Why? Have we come to the final analysis in which the structure of patriarchy emerges as the root of women's persistent inequality? Perhaps. But it should be kept in mind that Sweden, like most other advanced capitalist societies, has reached an impasse of sorts in the prevailing approaches to achieving social progress. A realignment is underway. We cannot say with any certainty what its future impact will be on the status of women until we can see more clearly the contours of emergent social alliances.

NOTES

1. For detailed discussions of the events outlined here, see Martin (1975a), Coates (1975), and Crouch (1979).

2. The following historical discussion is based largely on Davies (1975).

3. Excluding women's entry to any job is now illegal under the Sex Discrimination Act, both explicitly and implicitly (in that the act recognizes indirect discrimination, which occurs when different training and experience requirements exclude women from certain jobs). However, the enforcement of the act has not been able to control the continued practice of exclusionary requirements.

4. The Equal Opportunities Commission (1981) has been working on ways of eliminating indirectly discriminatory criteria; see the commission's *Job Evaluations Schemes without Bias.*

5. For a full account of the history of unionism in Sweden, see Korpi (1978).

6. The clause remained in effect until 1976.

7. Similar to the LO, these are umbrella organizations for several industry-based unions. See Forsebäck (1980); Heidenheimer (1976); Wheeler (1975).

8. Union representatives were also members of the various commissions that developed day care policy as a special measure for working mothers.

REFERENCES

Beer, Samuel H. 1965. *British Politics in the Collectivist Age.* New York: Knopf.

Coates, David. 1975. *The Labour Party and the Struggle for Socialism.* Cambridge: Cambridge University Press.

Crouch, Colin. 1979. *The Politics of Industrial Relations.* Manchester: Manchester University Press.

Daniels, W. W. 1976. *Wage Determination in Industry.* London: PEP.

Davies, Ross. 1975. *Women and Work.* London: Arrow Books.

Ellis, Valerie. 1981. *The Role of Trade Unions in the Promotion of Equal Pay Opportunities.* Manchester: EOC.

Equal Opportunities Commission. 1981. *Job Evaluation Schemes without Bias.* Manchester: EOC.

Flanagan, Robert J., David W. Soskice, and Lloyd Ulman. 1983. *Unionism, Economic Stabilization, and Incomes Policies: European Experience.* Washington, D.C.: Brookings Institute.

Forsebäck, Lennart. 1980. *Industrial Relations and Employment in Sweden.* Stockholm: Swedish Institute.

Heidenheimer, Arnold J. 1976. "Professional Unions, Public Sector Growth, and the Swedish Equality Policy." *Comparative Politics* 9 (October): 49–73.

Jenkins, David. 1968. *Sweden and the Price of Progress.* New York: Coward-McCann.

Korpi, Walter. 1978. *The Working Class in Welfare Capitalism: Work, Unions, and Politics in Sweden.* London: Routledge & Kegan Paul, 1978.

Liljeström, Rita. 1978. "Sweden." In Sheila B. Kamerman and Alfred J. Kahn, eds., *Family Policy: Government and Families in Fourteen Countries,* 19–48. New York: Columbia University Press.

Martin, Andrew. 1975a. "Labor Movement Parties and Inflation: Contrasting Responses in Britain and Sweden." *Polity* 7: 427–51.

————. 1975b. "Is Democratic Control of Capitalist Economies Possible?" In Leon N. Lindberg, ed., *Stress and Contradiction in Modern Capitalism,* 13–56. Lexington, Mass.: Lexington Books.

Ruggie, Mary. 1984. *The State and Working Women: A Comparative Study of Britain and Sweden.* Princeton, N.J.: Princeton University Press.

Scott, Hilda. 1982. *Sweden's "Right to Be Human": Sex-Role Equality, The Goal and the Reality.* Armonk, N.Y.: M. E. Sharpe.

Shonfield, Andrew. 1965. *Modern Capitalism: The Changing Balance of Public and Private Power.* London: Oxford University Press.

Stephens, John D. 1979. *The Transition from Capitalism to Socialism.* London: Macmillan.

Streijfffert, Helena. 1974. "The Women's Movement—A Theoretical Discussion." *Acta Sociologica* 17: 344–66.

Thompson, E. P. 1963. *The Making of the English Working Class*. London: Penguin Books.

Tilton, Timothy A. 1979. "A Swedish Road to Socialism: Ernst Wigforss and the Ideological Foundations of Swedish Social Democracy." *American Political Science Review* 73 (June): 505–20.

Weir, Angela, and Elizabeth Wilson. 1984. "The British Women's Movement." *New Left Review* 148 (November): 74–103.

Wheeler, Christopher. 1975. *White Collar Power: Changing Patterns of Interest Group Behavior in Sweden*. Urbana: University of Illinois Press.

Wootton, Graham. 1978. *Pressure Politics in Contemporary Britain*. Lexington, Mass.: Heath.

12 Social Movement "Success": A Comparative Analysis of Feminism in the United States and the United Kingdom

JOYCE GELB

    The focus of this chapter is a comparative analysis of the contemporary feminist movements in Britain and the United States. The analysis demonstrates that the "political opportunity structure" (the particular context of institutions, alignments, and ideology) is crucial to an understanding of movement structure, goals, and impact. While the feminist movements in the United States and United Kingdom share many joint objectives, they differ significantly with regard to styles of political activism, leadership orientation, and organizational values (Jenson 1983). These differences interact with contrasting political opportunities to shape the success of feminist claims.

    Based on the comparative research undertaken, the major conclusion of this study is that the structure and values of British politics have served to isolate feminists from the formal political system, from other feminists, and from potential allies.[1] This chapter examines feminist political activism in the U.K. in two contexts. The first is the women's liberation movement—decentralized, localized, and antielitist—sometimes described as anarcho-libertarian (Stacey and Price 1980, 180). Movement groups occasionally come together in national structures such as the National Abortion Campaign (NAC) for abortion rights or the National Women's Aid Federation (NWAF) against domestic violence. In the main, however, they engage local authorities in efforts to obtain funding and other assistance. British feminism is more "nondirected" than its "sister" movement in the United States in its emphasis on personal interaction, expression, and articulation of feminist values and the importance of internal democracy. A second set of feminist groups operates within key political and economic institutions, primarily unions and parties, which play a far more influential political role than their counterparts in the U.S. The chapter suggests the ways in which both aspects of British feminism, the locally and the institutionally based, have affected British politics as well as contrasting the British movement with its American counterpart.

267

THE POLITICAL OPPORTUNITY STRUCTURE

Perhaps the major distinction between the American and British systems as they affect the feminist movement and its impact is the importance in the United Kingdom of centralized government. The relatively centralized process of policy-making in the U.K. emphasizes ministerial responsibility and neutrality, and operates behind closed doors. In the U.S. there is far greater emphasis on public scrutiny and intervention in bureaucratic politics.

A core of politically neutral permanent civil servants and the relatively small size and narrow social background of the political elite present significant barriers to change-oriented policies (Ashford 1981; Sampson 1982). A system of "tripartism"—which includes the government, the Confederation of British Industries (CBI), and unions—excludes other groups from access to policy-making (Beloff and Peele 1980, 28). Unlike appointive offices in the U.S., which are often the result of "clientelism" or pressure group influence, such appointments in the U.K. are limited to "Old Boy" lists of the "Great and the Good." Confidentiality and hierarchy pervade nomination, appointment, and patronage politics. The feedback and friction generated by implementation politics in the United States is almost entirely absent in Britain, given the primacy of appointed, as opposed to elected, officials (Ashford 1981).

Grassroots lobbying, common in the US., has little impact in a system as centralized as that in the U.K. British courts play a far more restricted role than their American counterparts; constitutional review and the use of law to aid social reform movements, especially through class action suits, are virtually unknown. Hence, the policy-making process is organized to make exclusion from access remarkably easy. A consequence of centralization and secrecy is to limit the role of "promotional" or attitude groups seeking change—they tend to be poor in size, finances, and the ability to obtain benefits (Blondel 1974; Christoph 1974, 44).

Although political parties are, by general consensus, declining in importance, they are major agents for the resolution of key political issues (Richardson and Jordan 1979, 12). British parties, more than those in the U.S., tend to be parties of social integration rather than individual representation. Trade unions play a dominant political role, particularly in the Labour party—90 percent of the total Labour party membership and 85 percent of the funds are derived from unions (Punnett 1980, 127). In Britain, 50 percent of workers are unionized, in contrast to fewer than 20 percent in the U.S. The tradition of class-based ideology, socialism, and a strong organized Left involves many British feminists in Labour party and trade movement politics.

The American party system is looser and less dominant in the political system, and the fragmented nature of power lends itself to access to a wider variety of pressure groups. The past decade has seen the further decline of political parties and the rise of single-issue pressure politics. The American political culture stresses incremental, nonradical change as well as compromise.

The scope of government differs as well. In the U.K. the role of national government intervention in the family and social welfare politics has been more firmly institutionalized, providing support for British women in a number of areas that their American counterparts lack. Examples are to be found in the National Health Service, child benefits paid to mothers, (formerly called child tax allowances), maternity grants, and maternity allowances.

Finally, in addition to its structure and institutional framework, emphasis must be placed on Britain as a nation in which only limited value change has taken place (Inglehart 1977, 44).[2] The traditional structure of British society as it affects women's roles includes low educational attainment for women, norms of "good" motherhood and marriage, low wages, and a stratified labor market and class structure. Marriage rates are high and divorce rates low, suggesting the persistence of the traditional family (Hills 1981). A backward, stagnant economy further constrains women's opportunities in a society that continues to be elitist and class based.

The emphasis to be placed here on distinctions related to external factors should not obscure the many similarities between feminism in the two countries. There have been parallel historical developments, including the advent of the suffrage movement, the birth control movement, and the "renaissance" of feminism in the 1960s. In addition, the Seven Demands of the Women's Liberation Movement in the U.K. are generally similar to those advocated by NOW in the U.S.:

1. equal pay;
2. equal education and job opportunities;
3. free contraception and abortion on demand;
4. free 24-hour nurseries, under community control (only the demand for community-controlled nurseries is markedly more radical);
5. legal and financial independence;
6. an end to discrimination against lesbians;
7. freedom from intervention by the threat of violence or sexual coercion, regardless of marital status—an end to the laws, assumptions, and institutions that perpetuate male dominance and men's oppression of women (Feminist Anthology Collective, 1981).

Analysis of public policy on feminist issues reveals similar trends. In the area of equal rights, the U.K. has passed an Equal Pay Act (1970) and a Sex Discrimination Act (1975)—the latter establishing the Equal Opportunities Commission to enforce the new laws. The Employment Protection Act of 1975 gave women a statutory right to paid maternity leave, protection from unfair dismissal during pregnancy, and the right to regain their jobs up to 29 weeks after giving birth.[3] With regard to violence and victimization of women and the right to self-determination, the Domestic Violence Act (1976) strengthened procedures by which women could obtain injunctions to restrain violent husbands, while the Sexual Offenses (amendment) Act provided better safeguards for a rape victim's privacy during trial (Coote and Campbell 1982, 106). The 1967 Abortion Act authorized abortion up to the twenty-eighth week of pregnancy in cases where two doctors agreed that the life of the mother or other children would be at risk or where the baby seemed likely to become handicapped (Randall 1982).

In the U.S., Title VII of the Civil Rights Act of 1964 and the establishment of the Equal Employment Opportunities Commission provided some equal employment protection for women. The Pregnancy Discrimination Act gave pregnant women equal access to insured maternity benefits. Abortion rights were established largely via Supreme Court decisions (in the U.K. they were enacted by legislation) and have been the subject of subsequent (primarily restrictive) congressional action. Domestic violence legislation failed at the federal level, but funding and improved procedures for victims have been the subject of considerable legislative activity at the state level.

Despite the apparently similar nature of public policy related to women, however, it is my contention that the impact of such policy has depended in large measure on systemic factors.

THE EMERGENCE OF WOMEN'S LIBERATION IN BRITAIN
Among the striking distinctions between British and American feminists are the far greater influence in Britain of socialism and Marxism on movement politics and the absence there of a liberal–equal rights organization such as the National Organization for Women (NOW).

The British suffrage movement demonstrated tendencies that are still present in British feminism today. One was an early tie between the Labour party and constitutional feminists (Evans 1977, 126). Another was militancy—perhaps related to the example of Irish nationalism, perhaps born of rage and disappointment when apparently close-at-hand victory failed.

The contemporary British feminist movement received its impetus from radical and New Left politics, especially the Campaign for Nuclear Disarmament (CND) and anti-Vietnam campaigns (Randall 1982, 172; Wilson 1980, 184). Working-class women as well organized in the 1960s: at Hull in 1968 for better conditions for their fishermen husbands, and at Ford's auto machine works in Dagenham, where the demands for equal pay and equal work resulted in the creation of a short-lived Joint Action Committee for Women's Rights (Wandor 1971, 96–97). The revived movement in the U.S. provided the immediate spark for much women's liberation activity in the U.K., which early on developed strength among socialist and university women. A London-based women's liberation workshop coordinated 70-odd local groups and published a journal called *Shrew* (Randall 1982; Wandor 1972). In 1970 the national women's liberation movement held its first national conference at Oxford. The demands that emerged from the conference—24-hour child care, equal pay and education, free contraception and abortion on demand—reflected a practical orientation, new to some movement activists. The British movement developed numerous factions. One chart listed at least 14 different "tendencies" within it (Sebestyen 1979, 16); the resulting conflicts—largely between radical and socialist feminists—have prevented the holding of a national conference since 1978. The conflicts centered largely on whether to scrap the first six of the Women's Liberation demands listed above in favor of concentrating on the seventh, the demand for the cessation of male violence (Randall 1982, 154).

Like the so-called "younger," more radical branch of American women's liberation, the British movement lacked a coordinating structure other than national, regional, or issue-oriented conferences. At the time of this writing, *Spare Rib,* a monthly publication produced by a feminist collective, and the Women's Research and Resource Center (WRRC) in London provide the only organized focus relating to different elements within the movement. (A Woman's Place, also in London, is similarly run by a collective of women and operates a book-shop and reference facility, as well as publishing a weekly newsletter.) The once active WIRES—the Women's Information, Reference and Enquiry Service—has been severely circumscribed.

Despite the absence of a focal point, feminist activities in the U.K. continue energetically. *Spare Rib* and other publications advertise a whole host of feminist activities, and there are numerous groups listed under Women's Liberation in the London and regional phone directories. However, unlike the mass membership–equal rights focus of the visible American movement, the major locus of activity is the small local group, which, eschewing formal rules and leadership, prefers to arrive at decisions by consensus. The movement's character is also defined by the proliferation of small groups, each with a single-issue orientation. It should be noted that even more "traditional" women's groups such as Women in Media and the National Housewives Register (founded in the early 1960s by liberal-minded housewives) operate on the basis of principles of participatory democracy and minimization of hierarchy and rigid structure (Stott 1981).

Feminists have developed legal groups such as Rights of Women (ROW), day nurseries, health and lesbian groups, rape crisis centers, Black and Asian women's organizations, battered women's shelters, and pro-abortion groups. Within specific issue areas such as abortion and domestic violence, national coordinating structures have evolved, but their scope is limited. Women's Aid, established in London in 1972 by Erin Pizzey, was able to attract government and charitable funding. Since breaking with its founder, the Women's Aid movement has proliferated greatly—with 99 groups and 200 refuges in 1980. These organizations operate on feminist principles, with an emphasis on autonomy and self-determination for women (Coote and Campbell 1982, 141, 42).

Local women support the National Woman's Aid Federation (NWAF) through adherence to its aims and attendance at meetings (NWAF 1982). Within the national and half-dozen regional offices, jobs change every two to three years to provide varied experience for all and prevent domination by any one person.

Everyone shares in work, and there is no status distinction among the few staff members. Fund raising is virtually nonexistent because of fear of creating strong central power, although resources from the DHSS (Department of Health and Social Security) help to pay staff salaries.

A second organization that has developed a national structure is the National Abortion Campaign (NAC), launched in the spring of 1975 to defend the 1967 Abortion Act.[4] NAC has a loosely organized mass base and operates from a socialist feminist perspective on principles of participatory democracy (Marsh and Chambers 1981, 1). The nonhierarchical, decentralized structure linking local groups claims a coalition of 400 organizations with membership open to all who support its aims (NAC July 1982). In contrast to the operation of abortion rights groups in the U.S., half of the groups involved in NAC are trade-union related and receive some funding from the unions. Local groups are completely autonomous, deciding their own policy and methods of campaigning. There are no elected officials, no delegated structure. National policy is decided at the annual conference, and meetings are open to all members. An annual general meeting provides a forum for discussion of issues—although there is no mechanism for the resolution of conflicts on issues such as the role of racism and the broadening of the group's agenda to include other types of reproductive freedom. A national office provides backup resources and coordinates, while a steering committee deals with day-to-day work. The staff is limited in policy-making authority, leaving most decisions to annual and regional meetings. Volunteers are heavily relied on, particularly in the absence of financial resources to pay workers.

The contrast with most American pro-abortion groups is marked; the latter (National Abortion Rights Action League [NARAL], Planned Parenthood, and others) tend to be professionalized, hierarchical in structure, and reliant on—although not necessarily directly responsible to—a dues-paying mass-membership constituency. Such groups may fit the model of reliance on a "conscience constituency," which supplies movement resources without material benefit. Effective policy-making is in the hands of the full-time staff, as in the "funded social movement organizations" described by McCarthy and Zald (1973, 22; 1977, 1221–24). Abortion rights groups lobby extensively to prevent progressive weakening of abortion legislation and—again in marked contrast to the British experience, where courts have virtually no role in this policy area—have been active in litigation to preserve and strengthen abortion rights. NAC's strategy is largely extraparliamentary, depending upon proselytizing through demonstrations and picketing (Marsh and Chambers 1981, 48); it has influenced parliament by showing that grassroots support for abortion rights exists, however.

In the U.K., even groups with a national focus are ambivalent about campaigning (lobbying) and the legislative process, although in fact the NWAF and NAC have intervened effectively in the political process. Because NAC's members are (radical) socialist feminists, they have ties to the Labour party and the trade union movement. The potential of this alliance was evident in 1979 when a mass demonstration, with major participation by the Trades Union Congress (TUC) helped to stop a bill that threatened to reduce access to legal abortions.

However, the focus of most British feminist groups is interaction, emphasizing value and lifestyle changes. Consciousness-raising is an important element, and values such as self-confidence, skill attainment, and self-esteem are promoted (Randall 1982, 164). The democratic character of the movement provides flexibility and permits accommodation of all types of grassroots activity, incorporating diverse elements. As Mansbridge (1980, 230–43) has pointed out, small size allows intense interaction, and continued face-to-face contact may prevent elitism. Yet the group *process* may develop as a major focus, as opposed to the attainment of group *ends* (Freeman 1975, 143–46). Conformity to the group may be encouraged. The absence of recordkeeping and repetition of old issues may retard group development (Adlam 1980, 94). An ahistorical perspective may cause repetition of past mistakes. Decision-making may be slowed and the real administrative and political skills of some may be underutilized or ignored (Mansbridge 1980, 247). Individuals may become preoccupied with their own liberation and fail to seek more universal goals related to all women. And local, single-issue-oriented activity may reduce the possibilities for national impact and comprehensive (as opposed to ad hoc) solutions to problems.

Finally, unaccountability to a constituency may create irresponsibility and unrealistic expectations. The inability to agree on goals and to pool resources weakens opportunities for the creation of alliances. If, as suggested here, the "movement" in Britain is a "deliberately dispersed collection of groups, campaigns and political tendencies with no single ideology," the absence of coalitional structures may make it difficult to organize around multiple issues in a continuing fashion (Bouchier 1984, 123, 128–29, 218–23).

In Britain, the politics of personal experience, inward-looking and seeking redemptive lifestyles, has often eclipsed the overtly "political." Women's liberation politics is fragmented, centered on single issues, and without networks in which different views may find expression and audience. The emphasis on personal politics has often, though not always, resulted in reluctance to engage in the politics of the state (Barrett 1980, 228, 245). Although feminist politics may serve as a model for other Left groups in its emphasis on autonomy, flexibility, and democracy, the lack of a coordinating mechanism presents continuing problems (Rowbotham 1979, 90).

COMPARISON WITH AMERICAN WOMEN'S LIBERATION

The structure of grassroots radical feminism in the United States is similar to that in Britain; however, even within radical feminism, recent developments have suggested somewhat different tendencies. Even in battered women's shelters and rape crisis centers that emphasize the feminist ideology discussed above, professionals have combined with feminist influences to provide services and negotiate with bureaucracies, write funding proposals, and develop more enduring organizational structures (Schechter 1982, 38–39). Though conflicts continue over the importance of service, self-determination, and politics, there can be little doubt that such elements as networking, lobbying, and emphasis on legal changes are more evident in the American movement. Activists have mobilized around state legislation and legal change—and have often been less reluctant than their British counterparts to engage with political and bureaucratic forces and to seek legitimacy. Structures have been modified as specialization has created need for more hierarchical organization including staffs and boards. Schechter (1982, 94–95, 100) concludes that government has forced activists to modify practices and formal procedures. In some instances, "modified collectives" have sought a compromise between external imperatives and feminist principles. From local coalitions to statewide and then federal levels, efforts have been generated. There has been willingness to engage political authorities at all levels in order to gain resources and reform legal procedures.

Coalitions, reflecting a variety of influences, include traditional groups such as the YWCA, professional and service providers, radical feminists, and equal rights feminists from groups such as NOW; they emphasize the sharing of resources, access, and skills (Schechter 1982, 113, 148). In the area of aid for battered women, a National Coalition against Domestic Violence (NCADV) lobbied for passage of a Domestic Violence Act (defeated in 1980), built a large network of contacts, sought to build a dues-paying membership base, and wrote proposals to raise money from the federal government and private foundations. The coalition continues to monitor relevant public policy, disseminates information to state and local groups, and seeks to retain a nonhierarchical, multiracial approach (Morrison 1982). Unlike those in Britain, change-oriented American feminists have often been able to rely on government "insiders" to put forward issues and build support within government for movement concerns (Schechter 1982). Hence, issues relating to leadership and structure, engagement with political forces at all levels, and the need for coalition have been treated somewhat differently in the U.S. An area of congruence lies in the fact that in both countries, women's liberation groups have tended to focus on single issues and do not necessarily coalesce with other movement activists in multiple-issue alignments. While a grassroots women's movement still exists in the U.S., it is less visible and to a greater degree has joined forces with the more "middle-class" reformist sector of the original movement. No movement comparable to the latter really exists in the U.K.

Though never dominant, there are groups in the British feminist movement that seek to play a centrist, coordinating role. Among these are the Fawcett Society (with roots in the suffrage movement) and Women in Media. Fawcett remains small, with only about 375 members, its efforts to develop a membership base in northeast England having failed. Women in Media, organized in 1970, has engaged in active campaigning for equal pay and antidiscrimination legislation. Other groups, which do not identify with women's liberation but do support many feminist demands and efforts to achieve them, are current manifestations of more traditional women's activities. Among them are the Women's Institutes (WI) with a membership base of 400,000; the Townswomen's Guilds (TG) with 217,000; the British Federation of University Women with 14,000; and the National Council of Women (NCW) with 5,000 (Stott 1980). While these groups often support women's rights, by and large they eschew relationships with socialist and radical feminists.

Several new developments in the U.K. represent steps toward coalition building among different ideological groups in the women's community. In November 1980 a Women's Action Day was held in London; it involved some 67 organizations from a variety of women's perspectives whose representatives sought to discuss and develop common policies. A "women's agenda" was issued, dealing with issues of equal opportunity in law, education, work, politics, finances, the family, health, and the media. Groups represented included unions, the NAC and ROW, traditional women's groups such as the NCW, and elements of the Liberal and Labour parties. A new political advocacy group—the "300 Group"—has sought to increase the number of women in the House of Commons (now 21 of 635, or about 3 percent). Like its American counterpart, the National Women's Political Caucus (NWPC), it seeks to recruit and train women candidates for political office. The group's membership was estimated at about 3,000 in July 1982; hence, while the group seeks an extensive dues-paying base (dues are £12 per annum), it still lacks a large constituency (Abdela 1982). The "300 Group" has encountered hostility from traditional party groups who resent external intrusion and from feminists who dislike its relatively centralized entrepreneurial style. Nonetheless, it has trained over 1,500 women and helped them to gain interest and confidence in politics. The Equal Opportunities Commission (EOC) and National Council of Civil Liberties (NCCL) also provide opportunities for discussion of specific feminist issues through conferences and forums, and help to link trade unionists with other feminist activists. The Greater London Council (GLC) Women's Committee and other local women's committees (discussed below) have also sought to end centrifugal politics by involving a variety of women's groups as policy participants and recipients. The future of such efforts is unclear.

As suggested above, networking across ideological lines is still rare in the U.K., although it is a concept growing in practical, if not theoretical, adherence. Finally, while traditional women's groups do have a mass constituency base in the U.K. (at least in comparison to other groups), except in a few instances they are reluctant to join forces with those perceived and reinforced by media coverage as lesbian and anti-male. The close relationship that has developed in terms of resource sharing, political access, and even consensus on goals between the so-called traditional women's groups and their feminist allies in the U.S. has as yet no analogue in Britain.

THE ROLE OF WOMEN IN PARTIES AND UNIONS

It is possible to argue that in the British political system, mass membership–equal rights feminism is not necessary or even desirable because women have historically been organized and influential as pressure groups within existing institutions, particularly political parties and trade unions.[5] Despite feminist activism within parties and unions, however, a pattern of isolation from power and "marginalization" continues to mark the position of women, particularly through practices involving statutory seats and women's advisory committees and divisions. Available evidence suggests that while women constitute at least half the membership of the Labour and Conservative parties (Hills 1978), their role within party structures is severely circumscribed. It should be noted that although the Labour party has been close to socialist feminists on some ideological and policy issues, it has no better record on representation and power sharing than the Conservative opposition. Women are poorly represented at the Labour party's annual conferences (11 percent in 1980) and are allotted five of 29 seats on the National Executive Committee (NEC), the party's most powerful policy-making body (Hills 1981, 7). In practice, the "set aside" women's seats are union controlled, and the women selected for these positions are not independent feminists. The constituency-based Women's Section of the Labour party (founded in 1906) holds annual meetings and passes resolutions but has no power to gain acceptance for the policies it endorses.

Because the Labour party is a confederal organization, in recent years women's labor groups have grown and proliferated—from the Women's Action Committee (WAC), associated with the far-left Campaign for Labour Party Democracy (CLPD), to a Women's Rights Study group with Member of Parliament Jo Richardson as chair. A group called Fightback for Women's Rights is active at the party's fringes; it has been especially vigorous in pressing for more channels to the Labour party hierarchy—in the form of five resolutions to be automatically sent to the party's annual conference by the Women's Section—and the election of women members to the National Executive Committee by the Women's Conference. Fightback and WAC also call for an end to all-male parliamentary short lists from which potential and actual party nominees are chosen.[6] The Women's Action Committee of the CLPD has developed a Women's Charter and has been vigorous in promoting its views. A measure of expanded interest in women's activities was evident in the increased number of women's delegates at the annual Women's Conference, from 320 in 1980 to 650 in 1981 (Lever 1982).

The Labour party hierarchy has responded to feminist pressure by appointing a National Women's Officer and more recently designating a Shadow Minister for Women's Affairs. The NEC has appointed a subcommittee on Women's Rights as well. While the extent of feminist participation within the Labour party is impressive and often channels socialist feminist energy into party activities, any victory at the present time (because of the party's disarray) may be a pyrrhic one. In addition, there is some suspicion that groups seeking dominance within the party may be using the women's issues to build their own power base—with little actual regard for feminist concerns.

While women are better represented at the Conservative party's annual conference (38 percent of the delegates were women in 1977–78), this body lacks the policy-making powers of its Labour party counterpart (Hills 1978, 4, 8; Randall 1982, 74). Women constitute about 20 percent of the membership of the Executive Committee of the National Union, which is the highest level in the party hierarchy; its policy-making and administrative powers are limited by the primacy of parliamentary leadership, however.

As in the Labour party, there is a women's national advisory organization with its own annual conference (now called the Conservative Women's National Committee), which often discusses women's issues in the guise of such concerns as education (Hooper 1982). Another group affiliated with the Conservative party, the British section of the European Union of Women, is active on behalf of women's issues as well; it was instrumental in stopping the cuts in Social Security proposed under Margaret Thatcher's government (Rogers 1983, 34) and has pressed for a party rule to include at least one woman candidate on final short lists and for mandated interviews of women by candidate selection committees. In 1982 it also recommended that women's groups within the party undertake candidate education and training for women.

Finally, with regard to women standing for election, women have consistently been underrepresented as candidates in both parties. In the Labour party the union-dominated "A" list nominated only two of 100 women candidates in 1972 and three of 103 in 1977. The constituency-based "B" list contained 9 percent women's names in 1976, and selection for marginal or losing seats is common, as is often the case in the U.S. (Hills 1978). In 1982, Labour with 11 women M.P.s had 25 women on a list of 250 candidates and four new female Labour M.P.s were elected; the Conservative Party, though it attracts more women candidates (largely as a function of class), nominated only 10 percent women, down from 15 percent in 1977 (*Guardian,* 16 April 1982). Only the new Social Democratic party has met women's demands for better representation within the party hierarchy and on party short lists (for nomination). At least two of nine names on every short list are to be women and representational equity for women on the party's National Steering Committee is required (Toynbee 1982).

As most obstacles to women's selection appear to exist at the local level, women activists have sought to mandate positive action with regard to candidate selection. To date, while parties have moved toward expressions of greater concern for nomination of women, in response to pressure, they have not insisted on equality of representation in the final selection process. The success of the "300 Group" in attracting large numbers of women to training sessions for political activism points to the continuing gap between rhetoric and reality in much of British party politics.

COMPARISON WITH WOMEN IN U.S. PARTIES

Political parties are less central to the political process in the U.S. than the U.K., and feminist interest groups such as the National Women's Political Caucus, NOW, and others have played an important role in recruiting women for political office, providing training and some campaign support, and actively campaigning for key political issues such as abortion rights and the ERA. In the U.S., in the main, the tradition of separate women's groups and the principle of numerical reservation of seats for women in party hierarchies have been viewed as anachronistic. However, within the Democratic party, women did move to mandate equal representation of male and female convention delegates in the 1972 McGovern-Fraser guidelines. The 1972 Democratic convention had 40 percent female delegates; the Republican convention in that year had 30 percent (up from 17 percent in 1968). Since then, Republican and Democratic women's task forces have pressed for women's concerns within the parties and provided some funding and training for women candidates (Mandel 1982, 211–13). The Democratic party after 1980 successfully moved to equalize convention representation by men and women and to provide support for such key feminist concerns as the ERA, election of more women to state and local offices, and even abortion rights, as well as nominating the first female vice-presidential candidate, Geraldine Ferraro, in 1984, at least in part due to feminist pressure. At this time, the Reaganite Republican party moved further to the right and away from commitment to feminist concerns.

Despite real gains in representation and support for women's issues (at least in the contemporary Democratic party), the role of convention politics in the American policy-making process is limited and at best marginal. In addition, numerous (if not most) women seeking political office at all levels in the United States have bypassed traditional centers of candidate support and sought other routes to elective offices (Mandel 1982, 49). And for those elected, partisanship is only one influence that defines political behavior in the U.S. Hence, the model of the "300 Group," an all-party organization that trains and recruits women who wish to run for political office, is far closer to the American than to the British pattern.

UNIONS

In the U.S., only about 15 percent of women are unionized; the proportion in the U.K. is 40 percent, with a dramatic increase in the last decade (Hills 1981, 12; Randall 1982, 40). Of 12 million Trades Union Congress (TUC) members in 1980, about 4 million were women (TGWU 1980, 2). From 1961 to 1980 female union membership increased by 110 percent, male membership by only 17.6 percent (Coote and Campbell 1982, 173). Perhaps to a greater degree than in the U.S., the concept of a "family wage" for the breadwinning man has been entrenched and has limited equal job access for women in the labor market (Land 1979).

Socialist feminists have sought to reach women through participation in trade union politics. While a number of unions have a majority of women workers, men remain in control of top positions in individual unions and the TUC. Union women lack representation in key committees, among full-time officers, and at the local shop level as stewards and district committee members. For example, the National Union of Education, with 70 percent female membership, had only four women on its executive committee of 44 in 1980 (Coote and Campbell 1982, 167). The 1981 TUC annual meeting had 116 women among the 1,188 delegates present (TUC 1981–82, 1).

Feminists have sought greater influence in two ways. As in parties, they have advocated "positive action/discrimination," retaining or establishing "set aside" or "statutory" seats on executive committees and seeking other types of special representation through advisory committees, women's conferences, and the like. (In some instances, such efforts do not represent a "new" approach; the TUC Women's Advisory Committee and annual Women's Conference date back to the 1920s and 1930s respectively; Randall 1982, 93). As is true for parties, advisory committees have a solely consultative role and depend on the (often lacking) sympathy of general councils and other policy-making bodies for acceptance. The TUC, with which most British unions are affiliated, responded to a Women's Conference demand by increasing the number of statutory delegate places reserved for women in the TUC Executive Committee from two to five (out of 41) in 1981 (Coote and Campbell 1982, 45–67).

Several major unions—including the two largest, the Transport and General Workers Union (TGWU) and General and Municipal Workers Union (GMWU)—have not a single female executive member among them. However, in white-collar unions whose female membership is growing especially rapidly there have been efforts to create special opportunities for women. These include appointment of a national women's officer (the engineers' union AEUW, or TASS); statutory executive council seats for women (the National Union of Public Employees, or NUPE); establishment of women's advisory committees (GMWU and ASTMS, the technical-managerial union); and creation of equal opportunities or women's rights groups at the district level (NALGO, the local government employees' union). Even consciousness-raising and special training sessions for women have been introduced into several unions—including GMWU and TASS—and the TUC.

The second approach feminists have taken is to seek union support for feminist-related issues. Prompted in part by the 1974 Working Women's Charter—a London-based effort to promote a minimum set of feminist demands in trade unions—the TUC set about revamping its own "Aims for Women at Work." Even before this time it had lobbied for the Equal Pay Act in the 1960s, and the feminist campaign for child care found expression in the TUC's Charter for under Fives (1978), calling for comprehensive and universal child care and flex-time for parents. The TUC has recognized the "outdated" concept of the "family wage" and has called for positive action in employment and education. A TUC ten-point "Charter for Equality" for trade union women (1979) advocated special efforts to include women on decision-making bodies and suggested child care and awareness training programs to aid in increasing women's union participation. In addition, the TUC has held conferences on women's issues, has established guidelines for positive action in employment, and has taken an active role in supporting amendments to the Equal Pay and Sex Discrimination acts.

A dramatic and impressive instance of union support for feminist issues came in a massive demonstration—a joint TUC-feminist march in 1979—to protest the restrictive anti-abortion Corrie Bill then pending in the House of Commons. This marked a unique expression of union support that moved beyond the rhetorical level to practical action.

With regard to key points in the TUC charter—equal job opportunity for women and an end to pay discrimination—only limited progress has been made. As suggested above, male dominance still exists in the unions at all levels, from regional councils to the shop floor and in industrywide negotiating teams. Hence, while support has been forthcoming on some "social issues," impact has been minimal on such economic and industrial matters as pay and maternity leave. Male control limits possibilities for the local- and plant-level implementation of the numerous resolutions passed in union conferences (Turner 1982). It is difficult to escape the conclusion that women's concerns are viewed as secondary to the more significant social and economic issues, with a resulting subordination of feminist demands (Adams and Winston 1979, 141; Scott 1982, 55).

In contrast, in the U.S. the tradition of feminist autonomy from established groups is evident in relationships with the trade union movement as well as parties. Feminists have organized within—but also outside—the labor movement. After facing a set of legal challenges aimed at forcing unions to comply with antidiscrimination measures (particularly the Civil Rights Act of 1964), in 1974 the leading arm of the American labor movement, the AFL-CIO, helped to establish a women's caucus, the Coalition of Labor Union Women (CLUW), within its organization. Like women's groups in British unions, CLUW has pressed for greater sensitivity to women's concerns, increased representation in leadership circles, and an end to job discrimination; it also lobbies for legislation and aids in organizing potential women union members. CLUW has created a women's base and forum for networking within the labor movement, and the result has been more representation of women in union offices and the creation of women's departments and committees within some unions.

In the main, though, CLUW has met with an uneven response, like its British counterparts, and while union support has been engendered for such issues as the ERA and the Pregnancy Discrimination Act and coalitions formed around these issues, there has been limited progress on increased representation of women in leadership ranks and support for such issues as affirmative action. One visible result was the selection of Joyce Miller in 1980 as the first woman on the AFL-CIO's executive council. With regard to issue concerns, the rhetorical level of support in Britain appears greater. Having only 16,000 members, CLUW operates within the constraints of labor union politics and has avoided confrontation with the union hierarchy (Goodin 1983, 146).

In the U.S., a second tradition of labor women has developed, rooted in part in the ambivalence of many professional Americans toward the organized labor movement and perhaps also in the absence of a vigorous socialist (feminist) presence. This tradition involves independent organizations of working women and includes primarily white-collar workers in such groups as Women Office Workers, Nine to Five, and Union WAGE. Unlike unions, which concentrate on collective bargaining, these groups seek to enforce antidiscrimination and affirmative action legislation, demonstrate against employers, and engage in educational efforts relating to safety, organization, and job rights (Gelb and Klein 1983, 34; Seifer and Wertheimer 1979, 168). As unions have perceived the growing strength of autonomous groups of women workers, they have sought to establish links with them, as in the relationship recently forged between Working Women (office workers) and the Service Employees International Union (SEIU) to create a new union, District 925, to organize women. Nonetheless, the independent tradition continues, and together with groups such as Wider Opportunities for Women (WOW) and Catalyst, autonomous groups of working women have been active in finding jobs for women at all levels of the economic ladder, in organizing women, and in fighting job discrimination.

THE IMPACT OF INSTITUTIONAL CONTEXT AND ORGANIZATIONAL DIFFERENCES

The research presented here suggests that the contemporary British and American movements have evolved into different organizational forms. The analysis has emphasized the degree to which external factors—including political institutions, culture, and values—have influenced movement structure and goals.

The most active part of the British feminist movement emphasizes expressiveness, personal transformation, consciousness, and changed belief systems. It eschews formal structure and hierarchy and is centered in small groups that stress life experience and self-help politics. In Gerlach and Hine's (1970, 55) terms, it is segmented—localized, autonomous, and ever-changing—and decentralized. Nonetheless, it lacks the *reticulate* or networking structure that they see as accompanying segmentation and decentralization, largely as a consequence of ideological conflicts and localism. Mediating structures that might resolve conflicts and coordinate action, as well as permit the sharing of resources (particularly at the national level) are absent.

The significance of structural type in affecting organizational effectiveness depends in part on the goals sought. Small structures do maximize personal interaction and community, while larger ones are better able to sustain long-term campaigns at the national level. However, one trend in the U.K. that may effectively interface with existing movement structure is the growing interest of local council governments in aiding feminist efforts. By 1983, women constituted 18.4 percent of local councillors (EOC 1983, 94) and were able to effectively pressure within primarily Labour councils for acceptance of women's concerns. The GLC (Greater London Council), under left/radical Labour domination and significant feminist influence, developed and funded a Women's Committee which in turn funded a variety of women's projects (Interview, Valerie Wise, Chair, GLC Women's Committee, July 1984). In 1984 £8 million was committed to this effort by the GLC. Radical women's projects have been funded, including a women's transportation service and day care for the anti-nuclear women's group at Greenham Common as well as more traditional services. Local London boroughs, including Southwark, Camden, Islington, and Brent, have also established women's committees. Feminists in the U.K. prefer dialogues with local authorities to gain access, funding, and space rather than participation in national elections and representative government. A fear of male hierarchy and co-optation has continued to limit interactions with the political system.

In the U.K., parties and unions occupy a major—if declining—political role, and a tradition of leftist/socialist thought has been strong. While activity in party and trade union politics may be viewed as equivalent to the American liberal–equal rights movement, little evidence for this perspective exists. Rather, it appears that women's participation in these British institutions has been marked by marginalization, with women organized into separate advisory groups and limited to a handful of mandated seats on executive committees. The major union force, the TUC, has endorsed numerous progressive policies on behalf of women, lobbied for them, and even demonstrated on their behalf (in the case of abortion), but has shown greater hesitancy when issues of economic and political power are involved. In addition, tensions exist between socialism and feminism and between the hierarchical unions and parties and feminist ideology. Nonetheless, at their most effective, women's groups within parties may serve as forums through which women's demands and concerns may be highlighted.

In the U.S., a tradition of reform, the absence of a strong socialist Left, and the significance of interest groups in decision-making have combined to produce a different type of movement. Perhaps reflecting the increased weakness of parties and unions politically, feminists have organized as separatist or gender-based groups outside established structures (Adams and Winston 1979, 104). This has given them greater autonomy in terms of strategy, as the mid-1980s trend in the direction of electoral efforts demonstrates. American feminism is characterized by far greater inclusivity of different views than its British counterpart; coalition building and networking are movement watchwords. The American movement has come closer to an accommodation between the more "radical" women's liberation movement and the middle-class reformist one; it has also developed strong ties with such traditional women's groups as the League of Women Voters and the YWCA. The American movement's most visible manifestation is the traditional interest group, organized with hierarchical structure and staff dominance. Organizations such as NOW have moved in the direction of mass membership, while such feminist groups as the Women's Equity Action League, the Center for Women Policy Studies, and the National Women's Political Caucus fit the Zald-McCarthy model of funded social movement organizations that rely on "conscience constituencies" or contributors for resources and on staff for day-to-day decision-making and long-term strategizing (Handler 1978, 8). As the history of the movement against domestic violence demonstrates, even nontraditional groups with grassroots origins are pulled in the direction of political engagement and greater professionalization. American feminists have been eclectic and pragmatic in their use of strategies—from protest to litigation and campaigning.

Definitions of what constitutes social movement "success" may vary. "Success" may refer to legitimization of a group's goals, change in individual or group consciousness, and/or change in public policy outcomes involving redistribution of social goals and changes in power relations (Jenkins 1983, 544). For some, political access for hitherto excluded groups constitutes "success."

Clearly, the British movement has succeeded in creating local activities emphasizing consciousness and lifestyle transformation in numerous (primarily urban) centers throughout the country. The degree of activism and commitment is impressive, even to the casual observer. But also crucial in evaluating mobilization and success in the women's movement is the creation of a "collective consciousness," which incorporates varying degrees of approval for the movement's grievances and goals (Mueller 1983, 4). Such support may involve potential members, allies, and the general public. Measured by this standard, the total membership of British feminist activists has been estimated as one-tenth of one percent (or 20,000) of the female population, indicating a huge distance to go in terms of reaching even a fraction of the women in the U.K. (Bouchier 1984, 178). In contrast, membership in traditional British women's groups is closer to a million. Nonetheless, the mobilization potential of British feminism is evident from the massive pro-abortion demonstration in 1979 and the 1982 antinuclear protest at Greenham Common.

The American movement has grown in size and heterogeneity, particularly in the Reagan era, where apparent disaster has been turned to advantage in terms of group mobilization. NOW's membership, for example, increased from 125,000 (in 1978) to 250,000 over several years. A 1981 poll indicated that 4 percent of women and 2 percent of men contribute to the women's rights movement (about 4.5 million people), and that one of every 300 women is active in some type of feminist activity (Bouchier 1984, 180). Underscoring the acceptance of many

TABLE 12-1
FAVORABLE FEELING TOWARD WOMEN'S MOVEMENT

	Parents	Offspring
U.K.	43%	38.1%
U.S.	45.7%	51.8%

Source: Jennings, Allerbuck, and Rosenmeyer 1979, 497.

feminist views were the results of a *New York Times* poll (19 December 1983): 28 percent of those surveyed indicated that the women's movement had made their own lives better—most often citing improved job opportunities—and these respondents were most likely to be young and educated.

Studies comparing attitudes toward feminism and women's social role in the U.S. and U.K. offer some striking attitudinal differences. One study (see Table 12-1) found British youth much less supportive of women's liberation than their European or American counterparts (less than their parents, as well), suggesting that generational change reflecting positive attitudes towards women's liberation has been far more limited in the U.K.

Another report of European opinion reveals that British women (and men) hold a higher proportion of negative views on feminism than citizens of any other European nation except Italy (Hernes 1982, 520). While strictly comparable data are difficult to obtain, a 1979 poll showed 63 percent of American respondents, compared with 40 percent of the British, agreeing that the part played by women in their nation had changed a lot (International Gallup Poll 1981, 696). Other significant differences emerge when attitudes toward compulsory military service for women are examined—favored in Britain by 35 percent, in the United States by 53 percent (Hastings and Hastings 1982, 262–63)—and the distribution of household responsibilities compared: see Table 12-2. These findings suggest that some of feminism's basic goals, including sex role modification, have met greater resistance in the more traditional U.K. In turn, I have argued, the importance of traditional values has constrained political opportunities for feminists and, together with the rigid nature of the political system, has limited their options. The British movement has a long way to go in gaining the support of women who do not enter into competition with men and thus do not feel unequal, and in convincing the vast majority who are married, have been married, or expect to be married that the feminist movement they perceive as anti-male is relevant to their lives (Hills 1981, 104).

Public policy reflecting feminist concerns has been formulated in both the U.S. and U.K.; hence, in both nations legislative enactments relating to equal pay, sex discrimination, abortion, and domestic violence are in effect. However, the policy process leading to and implementing legislation has been signifantly different in the two nations, thus influencing policy impact. In the U.S., policy

TABLE 12-2
DISTRIBUTION OF HOUSEHOLD RESPONSIBILITIES

	U.K.	U.S.
HOUSEHOLD REPAIRS		
Husband	76%	39%
Shared or equal	11%	47%
CLEANING HOUSE		
Wife	66%	46%
Shared or equal	31%	45%
COOKING		
Wife	73%	58%
Shared or equal	22%	35%

Source: Hastings and Hastings 1980–81, 239; 1981–82, 285.

has largely been the result of lobbying by gender-based groups. As suggested above, policy networks are made possible by the emphasis on coalition formation and the relative openness of the political system to group participation. In both the U.K. and the U.S. it has been more difficult to secure policy implementation than the legislation itself, but in the U.S. the opportunities for intervention in bureaucratic politics are far greater.

In the U.K., because of ideological purism and localized structures, women have not developed comparable political networks. Institutional factors such as the growth of administrative power and executive dominance, and secrecy combined with the strength of parties and parliament, have limited opportunities for direct intervention in policy-making in the U.K. and made monitoring of implementation almost impossible. It is clear that British unions and parties (particularly the Labour party and the TUC) have "literally preempted feminist demands and have put their political clout behind numerous proposals to advance equality between women and men" (Scott 1982, 53). Their efforts were prompted at least in part by European Economic Community (EEC) directives requiring equal pay and job equality. Enactment of public policy has in large measure left the unions and parties free to pursue issues of equality in the workplace and in their own decision-making bodies at their own pace and on their own terms, and issues of power sharing and male dominance have largely been left untouched.

Evidence regarding the disparate rate of change in these areas appears to demonstrate far more impressive economic and professional gains for American women. In Britain, women's hourly earnings in 1983 were 74 percent of men's and gross earnings were 61 percent of men's; comparable figures in the U.S. show hourly earnings at 83 percent, gross earnings at 63 percent (Coote and Campbell 1982, 18; EOC 1983, 89; *New York Times*, 16 January 1984). The female part-time work force in the U.K. was over 40 percent, in contrast to 23 percent in the U.S. In 1975, female managerial and professional employees totaled 13 percent in the U.K. and 20 percent in the U.S. (Ratner 1980, 15). American women have greatly improved their representation in such fields as law—which are particularly compatible with political involvement—with women constituting 14 percent of lawyers and judges; 34 percent of all new law students in 1980–81 were female. In Britain, 7 percent of barristers and only a handful of judges are women (Deckard 1983, 117, 140; Robarts, Coote, and Ball 1981, 10). American women have surpassed men in their representation in college populations and the number of B.A.'s earned; in Britain, women were 40 percent of university students in 1980–81 (Deckard 1983, 117; EOC 1983).[7] While a causal relationship between movement politics, policy enactments, and the growth of a professionally active group of women with economic and political potential is not provable, it may be suggested that the American feminist movement has had a profound impact on changing expectations and possibilities (see *Ms.* Magazine, July 1984).

This essay has sought to demonstrate that external factors—particularly political systems and culture—help both to explain social movement goals and structure and to determine their impact. On the basis of the analysis presented, I conclude that American feminism has been more "successful" than British feminism in gaining public acceptance of many movement goals, reaching larger numbers of supporters and sympathizers, and achieving policy outcomes that may aid in restructuring power relationships.

NOTES

1. The material presented in this essay is the result of ongoing research in the United States and of two visits to the United Kingdom: the first in the spring of 1980, the second in the summer of 1982. Research in Britain was primarily based on interviews with feminist journalists, scholars, and activists as well as women active in political parties, unions and interest groups, elected and appointive politics. The period of analysis covers the 1960s until the end of 1982.

2. Britain has had the smallest amount of generational change of the six European nations surveyed by Inglehart; less than half of Germany's—and, reflecting its more traditional society, the divorce rate (per 1,000 population) was 3.01 in the U.K., as compared with 5.19 in the U.S. in 1980 (U.N. 1982, 303–4).

3. This last provision was made restrictive by the Thatcher government.

4. Most recently, NAC has fought an administrative effort to limit abortion through issuance of restrictive permission forms to be signed by physicians.

5. See Bouchier (1984, 39) for a statement of this view.

6. These proposals were soundly defeated at the 1982 Women's Conference.

7. See also *Digest of Education Statistics 1982* (Washington, D.C.: Govt. Printing Office), Table 3, p. 8. In 1976, 36 percent of British B.A.s were granted to women (Hills 1981, 13).

REFERENCES

Abdela, Lesley ("300" Group). 1982. Interview.

Adams, Carolyn T., and Katherine T. Winston. 1980. *Mothers at Work: Public Politics in the United States, Sweden and China.* New York: Longman.

Adlam, Diana. 1980. "Socialist Feminism and Contemporary Politics." In *Politics & Power #1: New Perspectives on Socialist Politics.* London: Routledge & Kegan Paul.

Ashford, Douglas. 1981. *Policy and Politics in Britain.* Philadelphia: Temple University Press.

Barrett, Michelle. 1980. *Women's Oppression Today.* London: Verso.

Beloff, Max, and Gillian Peele. 1980. *The Government of the United Kingdom.* London: William Field and Nicholson.

Blondel, Jean. 1974. *Voters, Parties and Leaders.* London: Penguin Books.

Bouchier, David. 1984. *The Feminist Challenge: The Movement for Women's Liberation in Britain and the USA.* New York: Schocken Books.

Christoph, James P. 1974. "Capital Punishment and British Politics: The Role of Pressure Groups." In Richard Kember and J. J. Richardson, eds., *Pressure Groups in Britain: A Reader.* London: J. M. Dent.

Coote, Anna, and Beatrix Campbell. 1982. *Sweet Freedom: The Struggle for Women's Liberation.* London: Picador.

Deckard, Barbara S. 1983. *The Women's Movement.* 2d ed. New York: Harper & Row.

EOC. 1981a. Grants for Equality, Manchester.

———. 1981b. *Sixth Annual Report,* Manchester.

———. 1981/1982. *News,* Manchester, Dec.; Jan/Feb.

———. 1983. *Eighth Annual Report,* Manchester.

Evans, Richard. 1977. *The Feminists.* London: Croom, Helm.

Feminist Anthology Collective. 1981. *No Turning Back: Writings From the Women's Liberation Movement 1975–80.* London: Women's Press.

Freeman, Jo. 1975. *The Politics of Women's Liberation.* New York: David McKay Co., Inc.

Gelb, Joyce, and Ethel Klein. 1983. *Women's Movements: Organizing for Change in the 1980's.* Washington, D.C.: American Political Science Association.

Gerlach, Luther, and Virginia Hine. 1970. *People, Power, Change: Movements of Social Transformation.* Indianapolis, Ind.: Bobbs-Merrill.

Goodin, Joan M. 1983. "Working Women: The Pros and Cons of Unions." In Irene Tinker, ed., *Women in Washington,* 140–47. Beverly Hills, Calif.: Sage.

Handler, Joel. 1978. *Social Movements and the Legal System.* New York: Academic Press.

Hastings, Elizabeth H., and Philip K. Hastings. 1982. *Index to International Public Opinion, 1980–81.* Westport, Ct.: Greenwood Press.

———. 1983. *Index to International Public Opinion: 1981–82.* Westport, Ct.: Greenwood Press.

Hernes, Helga Maria. 1982. "The Role of Women in Voluntary Organizations." Preliminary study submitted to the Council of Europe, December (manuscript).

Hills, Jill. 1978. "Women in the Labour and Conservative Parties." Paper prepared for PSA conference.

———. 1981. "Britain." In J. Hills and Joni Lovenduski, *The Politics of the Second Electorate: Women and Public Participation.* London: Routledge & Kegan Paul.

Hooper, Angela (National Women's Officer, Conservative Party). 1982. Interview, July.

Inglehart, Ronald. 1977. *The Silent Revolution.* Princeton, N.J.: Princeton University Press.

International Gallup Poll. 1981. London: George Prior.

Jenkins, Craig. 1983. "Resource Mobilization Theory and the Study of Social Movements." *Annual Review of Sociology* 9: 527–53.

Jennings, M. Kent, Klaus Allerbuck, and Leopold Rosenmeyer. 1979. "Generations and Families." In Samuel Barnes and Max Kaase, eds., *Political Action: Mass Participation in Western Democracies.* Beverly Hills: Sage.

Jenson, Jane. 1983. "Success without Struggle? The Modern Women's Movement in France." Manuscript.

Land, Hilary. 1979. "The Family Wage." *Feminist Review* 6, 55–57.

Lever, Rachel (Fightback). 1982. Interview, July.

McCarthy, J. J., and Meyer Zald. 1973. *The Trend of Social Movements in America: Professionalization and Resource Mobilization.* Morristown, N.J.: General Learning Press.

———. 1977. "Resources Mobilization and Social Movements: A Partial Theory." *American Journal of Sociology* 82: 1212–41.

Mandel, Ruth. 1981. *In the Running: The New Woman Candidate.* New York: Ticknor & Fields.

Mansbridge, Jane. 1980. *Beyond Adversary Democracy.* New York: Basic Books.

Marsh, David, and Joanna Chambers. 1981. *Abortion Politics.* London: Junction Books.

Morrison, Mary (NCADV). 1982. Interview, October.

Mueller, Carol. 1983. "Women's Movement Success and the Success of Social Movement Theory." Working Paper No. 710, Center for Research on Women, Wellesley College.

NAC. 1982. Interview, July.

NWAF. 1982. Interview, July.

Punnett, R. M. 1980. *British Government and Politics.* London: Heineman.

Randall, Vicki. 1982. *Women and Politics.* New York: St. Martin's Press.

Ratner, Ronnie Steinberg, ed. 1980. *Equal Employment Policy for Women.* Philadelphia: Temple University Press.

Richardson, J. T., and A. G. Jordan. 1979. *Governing under Pressure.* London: Martin Robertson.

Robarts, Sadye, Anna Coote, and E. Ball. 1981. *Positive Action for Women.* London: NCCL.

Rogers, Barbara. 1983. *52%—Getting Women's Power into Politics.* London: Women's Press.

Rowbotham, Sheila. 1979. *Beyond the Fragments.* London: Merlin Press.

Sampson, Anthony. 1982. *The Changing Anatomy of Britain.* New York: Random House.

Schechter, Susan. 1982. *Women and Male Violence.* Boston: South End Press.

Scott, Hilda. 1982. *Sweden's "Right to Be Human."* London: Allison & Busby.

Sebestyen, Amanda. 1979. *Notes from the Tenth Year.* London: Theory Press.

Seifer, Nancy, and Barbara Wertheimer. 1979. "New Approaches to Collective Power: Four Working Women's Organizations." In Beatrice Cummings and Victoria S. Schuck, eds., *Women Organizing,* 152–83. Metuchen, N.J.: Scarecrow Press.

Stacey, Margaret, and Marion Price. 1980. *Women, Power and Politics.* London: Tavistock.

Stott, Mary. 1980. *Guardian,* 26 November.

———. *Guardian,* 18 April.

TGWU. 1982. Women's Handbook: Policies and Action for the Transport and General Workers Union 1980. Transport House: Smith Square, London EC 4.

Toynbee, Polly (*Guardian*). 1982. Interview, July.

TUC. 1981–1982. Report for the TUC Women's Advisory Committee, March. Trades Union Congress, Congress House, London WC 1B 3LS.

Turner, Pat (National Women's Officer, GMWU). 1982. Interview, July.

U.N. 1982. *U.N. Demographic Yearbook.* New York: United Nations.

Wandor, Michelle. 1972. *Body Politic.* London: Stage 1.

Wilson, Elizabeth. 1980. *Only Half Way to Paradise.* London: Tavistock.

13 Women Made a Difference: Comparable Worth in San Jose

JANET A. FLAMMANG

One question is frequently asked in the wake of the second wave of feminism in the United States: "What policy difference has women's activism made?" The list of policy accomplishments since the 1960s is impressive, including reforms in areas such as equal pay and credit, employment and educational antidiscrimination measures, affirmative action, abortion, pregnancy disability, pension rights, and child support. However, not all of these achievements for women were brought about by women, or even in the name of women's interest. For example, the 1963 Equal Pay Act was passed under pressure from unions, which wanted to prevent women from undercutting pay for male-dominated jobs. And the word "sex" was added to the 1964 Civil Rights Act, which prohibited discrimination in employment, by a southern congressmember to weaken liberal support for the bill (Freeman 1975).

On the other hand, women can claim credit for successes like Title IX of the Educational Amendments of 1972, the Equal Credit Opportunity Act of 1974, and the Pregnancy Disability Act of 1978 (Gelb and Palley 1982). These legislative victories resulted from women's lobbying and coalition efforts. And women in Congress were credited with the passage of child support and pension reforms in 1984; House Ways and Means Chair Dan Rostenkowski noted that these measures would not have passed "if women in the House and Senate had not kept the pressure up" (Roberts 1984).

Recent policy achievements have underscored the importance of having women in strategic locations, both as activists pressuring political institutions from without, and as officials working from within. The case of "comparable worth" policy in San Jose, California, is no exception to this trend. Women made a difference in this city, home of the nation's first strike for pay equity by city employees, which has been nicknamed the feminist capital of the nation because of its impressive number of female elected officials. This case study will show how the strategic location of women as community activists, elected officials, and union members was indispensable to the strike, settlement, and effective implementation of comparable worth pay adjustments in San Jose. The primary sources for this study are intensive interviews, conducted between 1982 and 1985, with elected officials and union members.[1]

Given the historical significance of the San Jose comparable worth policy, the first part of this chapter discusses the background of the comparable worth issue nationally and in San Jose. The second part examines the strategic location of women in this case—as community activists, as elected officials, and as union members; the third places this case study in a general context of women and local-level policy-making. The conclusion summarizes the factors contributing to the successful outcome of this case study and suggests the lessons it offers for use elsewhere.

COMPARABLE WORTH NATIONALLY AND IN SAN JOSE

Comparable worth, or pay equity, means paying female-dominated jobs the same salary as *comparably valued* male-dominated jobs. It has been called the civil rights issue of the 1980s (Goodman 1984) because it goes beyond the concept of equal pay for *equal* work as specified in the 1963 Equal Pay Act. For the last 30 years, working women have earned only about 60 percent of what their male counterparts have taken home. This gap is attributed in part to the fact that women are concentrated in a narrow range of sex-segregated occupations. Eighty percent of employed women work in female-dominated (greater than 70 percent female) jobs; they are clerical workers, nurses, waitresses, retail salespersons, librarians, teachers, domestics. And these jobs pay less than comparably valued male-dominated jobs (NCPE 1984).

In large firms, the value of a specific job is typically determined through a job evaluation plan. First, points are assigned to a job according to criteria such as knowledge, problem-solving, accountability, and working conditions. Then the points are converted by formula into wage or salary levels. Management consultants are routinely hired by corporations to conduct these job evaluation studies. Only recently have they been hired by state and local governments to evaluate jobs for the purpose of detecting sex discrimination. For example, Hay Associates, the firm hired by the city of San Jose, had previously studied about 7,000 public and private organizations, including IBM and General Electric (Trounstine and Swan 1981). But the San Jose study was the first it conducted to compare job classes by gender.

Every comparable worth job evaluation study to date has found a disparity between comparably valued jobs, with men's earning more than women's. More than 100 pay equity investigations have been undertaken by governments—school districts, counties, municipalities, and states—in at least 30 states (NCPE 1984).

Once a jurisdiction has conducted a pay equity study, the courts have held that jobs should be paid what the study said they were worth. For example, in June

1981 the U.S. Supreme Court ruled in *Gunther v. County of Washington, Oregon* that prison matrons, whose jobs were valued at 95 percent of those of male guards but who were paid only 70 percent of male salaries, were victims of sex discrimination because the county ignored the results of its own study. Furthermore, the court ruled that women had a right to file sex discrimination suits under Title VII of the 1964 Civil Rights Act, which is broader in scope than the 1963 Equal Pay Act because it can be applied to sex-based wage discrimination even when the jobs are not the same (Bunzel 1982; Kahn and Grune 1982). And in 1983, Federal District Judge Jack Tanner found the state of Washington guilty of sex discrimination for failing to implement the findings of its own pay equity study. In 1984 he began to determine how the state should satisfy an estimated $642 million in back pay and $195 million in raises (Pear 1984).

Even before settlements of this magnitude were reached, comparable worth sent shock waves through the business community. In 1978, *Fortune* magazine estimated that "to raise the aggregate pay of the country's 27.3 million full-time working women enough so that the median pay for women would equal that of men would add a staggering $150 billion a year to civilian payrolls" (Smith 1978, 59). Elected officials, too, were fearful of the financial consequences of comparable worth. During the strike in San Jose, Detroit Mayor Coleman Young said of it: "The message is that any time a city gets hung up on an abstract study that makes arbitrary comparisons of jobs but does not take into account the impact on society and its ability to pay, that's dealing in potential anarchy and inviting bankruptcy and the collapse of local government" (Trounstine 1981c). This opposition on the part of business groups and elected officials nationwide was also expressed in San Jose. One council member opposed comparable worth on grounds that it was a burden on taxpayers; that job evaluations were too subjective; that it was inflationary; and that the government's setting of artificial wages was "contrary to our free-enterprise system" (Fletcher 1981). According to union members, San Jose took tremendous heat from the California League of Cities, the National League of Cities, and the Chamber of Commerce over its pathbreaking pay equity decision. And personnel official David Armstrong noted the fear of local firms that comparable worth would drive up salaries of clerical workers in San Jose firms.

In spite of this opposition, comparable worth pay adjustments were successfully bargained for by San Jose city employees in 1981 and implemented over a four-year period. Before we can assess the degree to which women were instrumental in this policy success, a brief look at the political climate of San Jose and the collective bargaining context of this policy decision is in order.[2]

Political Climate of San Jose

The political culture of San Jose has frequently been described as fluid and risk-taking, a reflection of the area's economic activity (Trounstine and Christensen 1982). San Jose's strategic location at the south end of San Francisco Bay enabled it to benefit from two of California's biggest economic booms: the gold rush of the mid–nineteenth century, and the flowering of Silicon Valley's high-tech industries in the post–World War II years. By the 1980s, Santa Clara County, whose major city is San Jose, had one of the highest median incomes in the nation and a well-educated citizenry. Its folk heroes were David Packard and Steve Wozniak—overnight millionaires who turned good ideas into giant electronics industries.

This can-do ethos pervaded politics as well. In the post–World War II years there was no entrenched political machine, and voters were willing to give newcomers a try at running local government. By the mid-1970s, voters were particularly interested in electing candidates who promised to put the brakes on the rapid postwar economic development, which had put a strain on the quality of local services: police, fire, schools, roads, libraries. Many of the candidates who met this description were women, especially homemakers with experience in neighborhood and volunteer groups: they were seen as "clean" and not corrupted by developers. Many of these women decided to run for office in San Jose in 1980, when elections shifted from at-large to district-wide (Flammang 1985). When the new city council was sworn in in January 1981, seven of its eleven members were women. The mayor, Janet Gray Hayes (included in the seven) had been elected in 1974 and in 1978; limited to two terms, she had one year left at her post. She referred to San Jose as "the feminist capital of the nation" because there were female majorities on both the city council and the Santa Clara County board of supervisors (three out of five). She attributed these majorities to the area's entrepreneurship and willingness to give new things a try.

There was another, somewhat paradoxical, side to the area's political culture. In spite of its size of 629,000 in 1980 (the nation's seventeenth largest city), San Jose retained a small-town ethos of trust and good faith: both city and union officials spoke of being hurt, shocked, and betrayed when negotiations degenerated into a strike in July 1981. Several examples illustrate this good faith climate. The committee appointed to assign points to job classes consisted of nine nonmanagement city employees and only one person from management, David Armstrong. Members of the union negotiating teams and Armstrong held each other in mutual esteem. In a formal sense, the city council had stipulated, in agreeing to the job evaluation study by Hay Associates, that it would not be bound to make adjustments when the findings were released, yet the council agreed to the adjustments. Strictly speaking, the union's 1980 contract contained a no-strike clause, yet there was no retribution against the workers who struck the city in 1981 (the city manager threatened to terminate the strikers, but both sides knew the city did not want to carry through on this threat). And while the union talked all along of a strike, even some of its most vocal leaders were truly surprised when it came down to that.

This is not to say that there were not some very tense moments during the negotiations and the strike. The union accused the city of hiring union busters:

there were heated exchanges when union negotiators interrupted a closed city council meeting (Trounstine 1981d); the head negotiators on both sides had to be replaced; and the city finally brought in a Palo Alto attorney who, in the union's view, played serious hardball with an exhausted union negotiating team. But the union's depiction of this attorney indicated that mutuality was the norm and hardball the exception in San Jose.

To summarize the political climate at the time of the city council's comparable worth decision: the area was paradoxically both risk-taking and parochial; basking in its reputation as the feminist capital and cautious with its budget; embarrassed by adverse national publicity and hurt that the fabric of good faith had been torn by a strike.

The Context of Collective Bargaining

According to California law, cities must "meet and confer" with unions to reach salary and benefit agreements. Prior to the early 1970s, what "meet and confer" meant for the city was, in David Armstrong's words, "a father-knows-best kind of thing." City management would determine salaries based on the formula of the mean of the upper two-thirds of public salaries in large jurisdictions in northern California. Then employees would incidentally talk about fringe benefits. The city negotiated with 11 different unions, most of which represented specific crafts or trades: electricians, architects, engineers, police, firefighters. One of these unions was Local 101 of the American Federation of State, County, and Municipal Employees (AFSCME), called the Municipal Employees Federation (MEF). It represented a range of workers: clerk typists, records clerks, telephone operators, accountants, data processors, staff analysts, custodians, aircraft refuelers, water meter readers, engineering technicians, planners, recreation leaders, and librarians.

In the early 1970s, MEF was headed by leaders from blue-collar occupations, such as custodians, construction inspectors, surveyors, and engineering technicians. But beginning about 1977 the unit began to be led by workers from female-dominated white-collar occupations, such as librarians, recreation specialists, and clerical workers. In the spring of 1978, MEF submitted a position paper on pay equity for women as part of its contract proposal. Then–business agent Maxine Jenkins hoped this issue would serve as an organizing tool. But that summer, California voters passed Proposition 13, a property tax reduction initiative, and the city imposed a wage freeze in order to quality for state bailout funds. Pay equity did not make it into the June 1979 contract, but the city signed a side agreement to evaluate MEF-represented job classes, with the provision that no salary adjustments would be made as a result of the study during the term of the contract: that is, through June 1980 (CPER 1981).

In 1979 the city manager, in an effort to curb the exodus of management-level city employees to greener pastures in Silicon Valley's high-tech firms, secured city council approval for a job evaluation study supervised by Hay Associates.

This management study assigned points to the jobs held by 366 managers according to three criteria: knowledge, problem-solving, and accountability. Evaluation was based both on internal equity and market considerations; the study did not compare male- and female-dominated classifications. The report, released in May 1980, recommended adjustments ranging from 9.5 to 30 percent, averaging 14 percent (CPER 1981). The city council immediately voted these adjustments into effect over a one-year period.

When MEF saw the ease with which management raises were approved, they proposed a provision in the 1980–81 contract allowing for the reopening of negotiations once a *non*management study had been completed. City negotiators rejected this proposal, and the union left the bargaining table. At this point, union members directly lobbied city council members, a practice that is technically prohibited during negotiations: the two sides are supposed to communicate indirectly through their respective bargaining agents. Two weeks later, talks resumed, and the union obtained a written agreement that the city would give the union a copy of the Hay report when it was released. At that time, they would bargain over the results, taking into consideration the city's ability to pay and putting the city under no obligations to implement adjustments. In July 1980 a one-year contract was signed granting a 15.5 percent general wage increase and containing a no-strike clause (CPER 1981).

In December 1980 the nonmanagement Hay study was released. Job classes had been assigned points according to four criteria: knowledge, problem-solving, accountability, and working conditions. Results showed that about one-third of the workers fell more than 15 percent either above or below the trend line, which represents the average pay for jobs of equal points. According to the methodology of the Hay study, jobs falling more than 10 percent below trend are paid significantly below their value. Male-dominated classes averaged 8 to 15 percent above and female-dominated classes 2 to 10 percent below, with some as much as 25 to 30 percent below. Mixed male-female jobs clustered near the trend line (Hay Associates 1980).

AFSCME Local 101 represented some 2,000 of the city's 4,000 employees. The study covered all nonmanagement workers at city hall, including 600 not represented by Local 101 (Calvert 1981). About 800 MEF workers stood to benefit from pay equity adjustments (Skipitares 1981). The union was anxious to begin talks with the same council that had authorized the study. Therefore, because on January 1 there would be seven new members on the expanded council (it increased from seven to eleven members with districting), the city reluctantly agreed to reopen negotiations in December.

In January 1981 the talks reached an impasse, and a state mediator was called in. MEF wanted adjustments for 82 classes over four years at a cost of $3.2 million (Trounstine 1981b). Union representatives also said that the trend line should be calculated by using male-dominated classes only, since female-dominated and mixed classes had sex discrimination factored into their salary scales. In their view, only the salaries of men's classes were set by the marketplace, and all wages should be moved up to a trend line based on those jobs. The city counteroffered adjustments for 27 classes over two years at a cost of $750,000. They wanted to raise the lowest classes of female jobs up to 15 percent below trend, with raises ranging from 0.5 percent to 25 percent over two years. About 500 workers would be affected by these adjustments (CPER 1981).

Negotiations continued for six months, with activity stepping up as the July 4 contract expiration date neared. Throughout this period there were rallies and a wildcat strike by librarians, who, along with parks and recreation specialists, had the most to gain from comparable worth adjustments and were in the forefront of activity. In May a strike was averted when the city agreed to negotiate about jobs less than 15 percent below trend (Trounstine 1981a). MEF received a boost from the U.S. Supreme Court's *Gunther* decision on June 8. Taking advantage of this ruling, AFSCME filed a sex discrimination complaint against San Jose with the Equal Employment Opportunity Commission (EEOC), which enforces the 1964 Civil Rights Act. The union offered to withdraw the complaint if negotiations were fruitful (*San Jose Mercury News* 1981). The city interpreted the filing of this complaint as an act of bad faith on the union's part, saying that it would lose $9.3 million in 1981–82 revenue sharing funds if charges were upheld (Trounstine 1981b).

On the eve of the contract expiration date, the two sides were still far apart. The city proposed a 6 percent cost-of-living increase and $1.3 million in comparable worth adjustments over two years. The union proposed a 10 percent cost-of-living increase and $3.2 million in pay equity adjustments over four years (Miller 1981). The city claimed that it was $500,000 in the red *before* wage increases and adjustments; it might have to lay off employees, cut public services, or give smaller raises to those above trend to fund those below (it was never suggested that the wages of those above be *reduced* to fund increases for those below). The union responded that $350,000 had already been set aside from the previous budget for wage adjustments. They noted that the amount requested each year for pay equity adjustments constituted less than 1 percent of the city personnel budget ($95 million in 1981). The union claimed that layoffs would not occur because there was an annual 10 percent vacancy rate in city jobs. Furthermore, a study of city finances by AFSCME national offices showed that the city did have enough funds to cover these adjustments (Tong 1981).

The strike lasted nine days, from 5 to 14 July. Libraries were the most visibly affected; many airline refuelers and clerical workers went out as well. According to the union, 1,700 of AFSCME Local 101's 2,000 workers were on strike on July 7; Mayor Hayes put the number at 1,000 (Carroll 1981). Agreement was finally reached on 14 July. The terms of the settlement were as follows:

1. 7.5 percent cost-of-living increase in 1981–82, 8 percent in 1982–83 (totaling $4 million);

2. $1.45 million compensation for pay equity over two years (effective July 1981 and August 1982);
3. 62 job categories upgraded by adjustments averaging 9.6 percent;
4. 5 percent minimum and 15 percent maximum comparable worth adjustments;
5. adjustments limited to classes at least 10 percent below trend;
6. no adjustments for male-dominated jobs below trend;
7. remaining inequities (i.e., jobs still more than 10 percent below trend) to be discussed in 1983 bargaining sessions.[3]

The city remained open to granting further pay equity adjustments after this 1981 agreement. In 1983 it approved of $116,000; in 1984, $171,000; and in 1985, $341,000 for comparable worth benefits. Together with the 1981 settlement, these adjustments totaled $1,752,000 over five years. The cumulative value of these adjustments (that is, including the costs of higher base salaries to which subsequent comparable worth and cost-of-living increases were added) between 1981 and 1986 was about $6,100,000. Unlike the state of Washington, San Jose followed through with the implementation of its comparable worth policy (Flammang 1986).

Let us now see how women were instrumental to the success of this impressive policy accomplishment: as community activists, as elected officials, and as union members.

STRATEGIC LOCATION OF WOMEN IN THIS CASE STUDY

Much like the Equal Pay Act of 1963, comparable worth in San Jose was primarily a "union issue." AFSCME saw it as a popular way to swell union ranks. According to a former MEF persident, over 500 city workers—men and women—signed up with AFSCME in the course of their three-year struggle to obtain pay equity (Soloway 1981). However, comparable worth was also a "women's movement issue" in three important ways. First, feminist community activists in Santa Clara County had set the agenda for taking women's issues seriously, by providing both moral arguments and political clout. Second, the majority status of female officials on the San Jose city council gave them a greater freedom of action regarding women's issues than is typically the case for token women on governing boards. And third, women in AFSCME, outraged by gender pay inequities, kept up the pressure on the city council throughout the strike, settlement, and implementation stages. In each of these three settings, women sympathetic to women's issues found that by working with similarly situated women—whether in the community, on the council, or in the union—they could marshall the psychological and political support to bolster their efforts for policy changes.

Community Activists Set the Agenda

Women in AFSCME Local 101 told me that organized women's groups played only a very marginal supporting role during the strike period in 1981. Still, though they may not have actively cheered on the strikers at city hall, local women's organizations had an indirect effect on this case by setting the agenda for taking women's issues seriously in Santa Clara County. Their agenda-setting had two components: providing moral arguments, and exercising political clout. That is, activists educated the county about the unfair treatment of women, and they supported candidates sympathetic to women's issues.[4]

One reason why women's groups were powerful in the county was that they filled the void created by the absence of political parties in local politics. At the turn of the century, Progressives had curtailed the influence of party machines in California, through measures such as the direct primary, referendum, initiative, recall, and nonpartisan local elections. While parties were weak in San Jose, their political functions still had to be performed, and women's groups helped by providing the services of ward heelers, forming networks to change policies, educating the public on issues, and recruiting and supporting sympathetic candidates.

The most important agenda-setting women's groups in the country were local chapters of the League of Women Voters (LWV), National Women's Political Caucus (NWPC), National Organization for Women (NOW), and Business and Professional Women (BPW). Also instrumental were the Woman's Alliance (WOMA), a battered women's shelter in San Jose; the Center for Research on Women (CROW) at Stanford University; and the Chicana Coalition, a group of Chicana activists. These organizations provided the moral suasion to keep several important issues in the forefront of people's minds. They organized rallies, testified at council meetings, and held public workshops. They were visible around a variety of issues, including employment discrimination, battered women, affirmative action, bilingual staffs in county hospitals, sexual harassment, pension rights, abortion availability, child care, the Equal Rights Amendment, problems of dual career couples, violence against women, and gay rights. Depending on the issue, citizens were urged to contact their local, state, or federal representatives.

Frequently, women channeled their efforts through the county's Commission on the Status of Women, which was created in 1973 and given indirect subpoena power (through a supervisor). It routinely conducted investigations, held hearings, and organized conferences. Throughout the 1970s the commission mediated an average of 500 sex discrimination complaints a year. Women's groups also found it useful to join ranks with one another. For example, NOW secured LWV and BPW membership lists during its drive to extend the ERA ratification deadline; the Chicana Coalition joined other women's organizations in signing a Mailgram in support of state funds for MediCal abortions; and groups as diverse as the Junior Women's Club, church auxiliaries, NOW, and the Girl Scouts aided WOMA.

The second agenda-setting aspect of local women's groups was exercising political clout. The newsletters of NWPC, NOW, and LWV routinely announced openings for local appointive offices. These organizations provided women with contacts, information about positions, and experience in public speaking. In addition to recruiting women for appointed and elective office, these groups provided endorsements. The NWPC endorsement was sought by both radical and mainstream candidates in the county. Apparently candidates assumed that there was a bloc of women voters in the "feminist capital." Finally, women's organizations donated money to and walked precincts for candidates sympathetic to women's issues. They had a reputation for loyalty and dependability. For example, when a county supervisor faced a 1980 recall attempt because of his support for a county gay rights ordinance, local women's groups rallied to his defense because he was a strong advocate of feminist issues.

In sum, women's groups were salient in local politics. They created a climate where women's issues were taken seriously. Their activities contributed to local officials' open-mindedness when presented with the controversial and then-novel idea of comparable worth. Officials had been sensitized to gender inequalities and felt they could benefit from women's local political clout.

Female Majority on the City Council

There are not many cities with female mayors and council majorities. In 1978 only *six* city councils had female majorities, and only 6 percent of cities had female mayors (Welch and Karnig 1979). Most female officials constitute small minorities on their governing boards. Rosabeth M. Kanter (1977) argues that numerical "tokens" (that is, less than 15 percent) experience more performance pressure, stress, and role entrapment and spend more time resolving problematic interactions than do numerical "dominants" in a group. When women numbered one or two on the San Jose city council and the Santa Clara County board of supervisors, they had to earn the respect of their male colleagues. But once the pioneer women gained this respect and women increased their numbers, they became freer to take distinctive issue positions.[5]

Other studies have found that newly elected women are hesitant to stand out as advocates for women unless they sense support from their constituencies or colleagues (Mezey 1978). With one exception, women elected to the San Jose city council in 1980 were more hesitant in their support for comparable worth than were the holdovers from the council commissioning the Hay study. Veteran members were attuned to the influence of women as a group in local politics, whereas newcomers were concerned to assert that they represented their entire district, not just women. As time wore on, most women on the council became more comfortable with representing women's interests in the "feminist capital" more broadly, and with the idea of comparable worth in particular.

Four council members supported comparable worth from the outset. Three of these were holdovers from the prior council; the fourth was the only self-described feminist among the 1980 cohort joining the council. Three newcomers opposed comparable worth: one man and two women. Two of these opponents were conservative Republicans who believed that pay equity meant harmful government intervention in a free market economy; the third felt that the council should not emphasize women's issues over "people's issues": the economy, housing, unemployment, and education. Finally, four council members were swing votes who eventually voted to fund comparable worth benefits. As it turned out, men on the council actually supported pay equity at least as strongly (three to one) as did their female colleagues (five to two) (Trounstine 1981e).

The breakdown of this final eight-to-three vote raises some interesting possibilities. First, some male officials probably perceived a voting bloc of activist women in San Jose. Two male proponents of pay equity were affiliated with women's organizations. One was on the advisory board of WOMA, and he and the current mayor were NWPC members. Second, a critical mass of three female proponents provided a counterweight to the three staunch opponents, and may have helped to attract the two hesitant women; the initial reservations of one were replaced by a proud support for the concept. And third, San Jose's female majority captured the attention of local and national media, whose queries caused some women to reflect on the role of women in politics *as* women and *as* spokespersons for women's concerns. As the erstwhile hesitant council member said: "I have shifted from seeing the feminist capital as irrelevant to seeing it as a source of pride."

Women on the council at the time of the comparable worth decision ranged from liberal Democrats to conservative Republicans, and from self-described feminists to antifeminists. Much to the consternation of union activists, most of them approached the issue with caution; even Mayor Hayes wanted two years as opposed to four years of benefits on grounds that it was unwise to commit future councils to the policy. Ultimately, however, all but two were supportive. When formal negotiations broke down, it was the female officials who were contacted informally. The union got political mileage from the fact that the nation's first pay equity strike took place in the feminist capital, and this irony was not lost on the women officials, who, along with some of the men, were generally open-minded about women's rights issues. This attitude of openness reflected three factors discussed above: a sensitivity to gender inequities, a fear of alienating female activists and voters, and the experimental, can-do ethos of the area. Thus, women's numbers on the council had a bearing on the outcome of comparable worth in San Jose, both directly (as a critical mass of supporters), and indirectly (as the object of media and union attention).

Union Women Keep Up the Pressure

While community activists created a favorable political climate for comparable worth and female officals influenced the outcome, the group of women most instrumental to this policy success were those of AFSCME Local 101. Union women placed the issue on the city's agenda, participated in the job evaluation process, led the strike, negotiated the settlement, and oversaw the implementation of pay equity adjustments.

The idea of comparable worth for city employees began percolating in San Jose in 1974, when a group called City Women for Advancement (CWA) appeared before the city council, asking why librarians made so much less than engineers (Swan 1981). Women in CWA were high-level clerical workers in city hall who wanted greater pay and prestige. A few were union members. Mayor Hayes remembered their presentation as fair and persuasive, leaving the council with the concrete image of the inequity of paying less to women with master's degrees and Ph.D.'s, and responsibility for supervising many people, than to male park maintenance workers with a grade school education. However, the council did not act on the idea until 1978, when AFSCME brought it to the bargaining table. CWA had difficulty working as a group to pursue the goal of pay equity. Many of its members felt that they could advance at the workplace through their own merit and the good faith of their bosses. Some had a hard time working with something as communal as a union. So they gave up the issue and AFSCME librarians took over, joined shortly thereafter by female parks and recreation specialists.

City librarians had become interested in the issue after attending a convention of the California Library Association in San Francisco in 1977, where San Diego librarians gave a presentation on their lawsuit against the city for pay equity adjustments. The San Jose librarians wondered whether the same injustices applied to them, and they began to gather for informal breakfast meetings. Some 20 to 30 women, originally dubbed "Doughnuts and Dough," later called themselves Concerned Library Activist Workers (CLAW). Most of them were union members who began to take over AFSCME Local 101 as negotiating team members, stewards, and executive board members. The local was receptive to comparable worth. Its president was a librarian, and its business agent saw comparable worth as a way to attract more clerical women to the union.

In April 1979 there was a "sick-out," in which about 80 clerical workers walked off their jobs to protest the city's bad-faith bargaining over pay equity. The issue had been put on the back burner during 1978 negotiations until the fiscal effects of tax-cutting Proposition 13, passed in June 1978, could be determined. The sick-out, triggered by the city council's decision to conduct a management study, pressured the council to study nonmanagement classes as well.

Once a place was secured for comparable worth on the city's agenda, the next step was the job evaluation process. According to David Armstrong, the city never would have conducted the nonmanagement study without union pressure to do so. Furthermore, it was a very revolutionary idea at the time to have a committee of workers rank the jobs. The committee consisted of five men and five women, among whom Armstrong was the only management representative; the nine slots were spread across a variety of jobs such as librarians, parks and recreation officials, legal secretaries, gardeners, and engineers. CLAW and AFSCME held study sessions on how to instruct workers to fill out the evaluations. As it turned out, the departments that completed the evaluations most carefully ultimately got the best pay equity adjustments. Parks and recreation specialists and librarians knew they stood to benefit the most, and their efforts paid off.

Librarians brought expertise to the evaluation process because they had already informally compared their job qualifications to those of higher-paid city workers, and they drew additional data from the national studies of the American Library Association's (ALA) comparable worth project. A 1980 ALA newsletter detailed librarians' pay equity efforts in California, Florida, Maryland, Minnesota, Pennsylvania, Arizona, Washington, and Alberta, Canada (Myers 1980). In 1982 the association made available a pay equity action kit, which included a 142-item annotated bibliography, *Equal Pay for Work of Comparable Worth*, compiled by the Business and Professional Women's Foundation.

The nonmanagement study was still in progress when the management study was released and immediately acted upon by the city council, in May 1980. The council's response fueled AFSCME's hopes for a similarly prompt and favorable response when its study was released the following December, but six months of negotiations eventually deteriorated in the July 1981 strike.

As the strike wore on, the city's low cost-of-living offer united the union members (male and female), who saw the offer as insulting at best and as an attempt at union busting at worst. Women negotiators worried about the female heads of households who took great risks to march in the picket lines; they had gone for a week without a paycheck. Nine days of little sleep and great tension also began to take their toll on the energy of the negotiators themselves, but at no point did male union members pursue female negotiators to accept management's offer. Many of the team's men abstained in votes because they felt this was a women's issue, and women should decide when to stop the strike. The women also had the strong support of the union local's president and of the head city librarian, both men.

The strike settlement raised the prestige of AFSCME in the eyes of the city's other unions, which were competitive and secretive about their contracts with the city. Many of the older trade unions had disparaged AFSCME as inexperienced and a "women's union" (about half of its members were women). An MEF representative who visited some of these unions to drum up their support for comparable worth was met with hostile charges, such as, "Nobody said you have to get pregnant and have children," and "Nobody says you have to work. Why don't you let your husbands take care of you?" Only two city unions—electrical workers and firefighters—supported the comparable worth strike, even though AFSCME had previously honored the other's picket lines. After AFSCME won its $4.5 million settlement, however, other unions took it seriously.

The final stage of the process was overseeing the implementation of the adjustments over two years, and renegotiating the issue in 1983 sessions. MEF women oversaw the successful implementation of pay equity benefits, and they kept the issue alive in the 1983 and 1984 bargaining sessions, bolstered by pressure from rank-and-file women to complete pay equity adjustments. As one negotiator said, "The first year there was this huge outcry among women. It was as if you had been denying them the right to vote when they realized how badly they had been cheated out of 27 percent of their wages for all of their life. The rank and file bring it up every year, 'Finish off the Hay.'" Women in the union were not going to let the issue die until their salaries were at or above the trend line. As of this writing, all female-dominated jobs were within 5 percent of trend. Union leaders have said that adjustments will not be completed until these women's salaries are 10 percent above trend, since the original trend line was depressed by 10 percent because underpaid, female-dominated jobs had been factored into it.

The union and the city agreed that good-faith progress toward the trend line was made in the poststrike period. The union had a good sense of the city's ability to make adjustments (which were less than 1 percent of the total personnel budget and never more than 2.5 percent of the payroll of MEF-represented workers). This spirit of good faith was evidenced by the fact that while neither side knew exactly where everyone was located relative to the trend line, both sides were satisfied in annual negotiations. And the negotiators who kept pay equity alive were women, spurred by their rank and file.

Female negotiators were careful to address the needs of male AFSCME members as well. One male group, the engineering technicians, feared that comparable worth adjustments meant fewer special adjustments or lower cost-of-living increases for them. At the end of the two-year settlement, they left AFSCME and attempted to form their own bargaining unit. But both the city and the union fought to prevent their leaving. The city was already negotiating with 11 unions and did not want to increase that number; the union wanted to avoid a depletion of its ranks. In the 1983 sessions, AFSCME obtained a 3 percent special adjustment for the engineering technicians, who decided to stay in AFSCME after all.

Finally, union women convinced the city that the issue had come to stay, and they applauded the personnel department's efforts to take a national leadership role on comparable worth. They particularly commended the efforts of personnel official David Armstrong, who was trusted by the city council as an expert on the topic. He fielded numerous inquiries from academics, reporters, and officials from other areas. At least 100 times a year he received "phone calls from other cities wondering how to emulate San Jose." Upon his return from a September 1983 comparable worth conference in Oregon, he reported, "We're the target. We've become the experts that people turn to" (Herhold 1983). He coauthored an article assuring public personnel managers that the settlement did not bankrupt San Jose (Farnquist, Armstrong, and Strausbaugh 1983). And when journalists baited him to reveal the feminist plot behind comparable worth in San Jose, he had this response:

I bring in some woman and journalists say, "No, we were looking for the real spokeswoman." I respond, "This *is* the real spokeswoman. She has been here twenty-five years and she has made a difference in this organization. She looks you right in the eye, after never having said anything for twenty-five years, and she is livid. She says, "You'd better square away my pay. We've got this study.'"

Women are extremely angry about this issue. It is a gut-level paycheck issue that all women can unify behind because most women have experienced the clerical ranks, or understand what it is. (Armstrong, 1984)

Union women, both negotiators and rank and file, were responsible for putting San Jose on the map as the first city to strike successfully for comparable worth adjustments. They were aided by the efforts of women on the city council and female activists in the community, who set the stage for taking women's issues seriously.

WOMEN AND LOCAL-LEVEL POLICY-MAKING

This chapter has focused on the question, "What policy difference has women's activism made?" While scholars have frequently raised this query about national policies (see, e.g., Boneparth 1982; Diamond 1983; Gelb and Palley 1982), they have rarely examined the queston in local arenas (e.g., Flammang 1984b; Stewart 1980). This case study suggests three important reasons why more attention ought to be paid to women's efforts at the local level in American politics.

First, this case has shown the importance of having female officials in strategic decision-making positions. Although women still hold fewer than 15 percent of all offices nationwide, since 1970 there has been a dramatic increase in their numbers in local posts. Between 1971 and 1983 the proportion of female mayors grew from 1 percent to 8.67 percent (NWPC 1983); between 1975 and 1980 the proportion of female county officials doubled, from 3 to 6 percent, and that of municipal officials tripled, from 4 to 13 percent (CAWP 1981). By contrast, since 1970 the percentage of women in Congress has hovered at 3 to 4 percent. Given that newly elected women tend to be reluctant to stand out as advocates for women's issues until they sense support form their colleagues (Mezey 1978), and that female officials tend to be more feminist than their male counterparts (CAWP 1983), we can expect to see increasing willingness on the part of local female officials to support women's issues. The fact that the San Jose city council had a female majority drew media attention, which heightened the councilwomen's consciousness as advocates for women. But women do not need majority status to overcome the inhibiting effects of being the "only women" on a governing board. If Kanter's (1977) generalizations about women in corporations can be applied to politics, then 15 percent representation is enough to reduce the inhibitions on "token" women. In sum, scholars should be on the lookout for policy changes resulting from the impressive increase in the numbers of local female officials.

Second, policy changes emerge from the activities of women's groups as well as from the efforts of officials. In the San Jose case, local women activists set the agenda for the council's favorable comparable worth vote. Media and research attention has typically focused on the national influence of groups like NOW and NWPC: Democratic candidates' solicitation of their endorsement in the 1984 presidential race, for example, and their effective lobbying on Capitol Hill. As important as these efforts are, many group achievements are registered at the local level, concerning issues such as reproductive rights, clinic bombings, pay equity, gay rights, health insurance rates, and sexual harassment. Dye (1985) argues that interest group activity may be more influential in community politics than in state or national politics, since the arena is smaller and groups are more obvious. Local-scale activity has the advantage of substitutability: women can substitute their numbers for monetary resources. Most women do not have the disposable income to contribute vast sums to campaigns or causes, but they can show up in impressive numbers at rallies and council sessions. And they have the League of Women Voters' legacy of doing their homework before addressing public audiences, which adds to their credibility. Local interest group activity is particularly strong in American cities with nonpartisan local elections: that is, about 80 percent of cities in all regions except the East, where less than half of city elections are nonpartisan (Dye 1985). Local women's groups help fill the party vacuum by recruiting candidates, educating the public, and pressuring elected officials. Their activities merit more scholarly attention.

Third, certain women's issues have been dealt with more effectively at the local and state levels than at the federal level. This case study has demonstrated that comparable worth was well suited to the local collective bargaining context, and in fact, pay equity achievements have been most notable at the local level, somewhat slower at the state level, and slowest at the federal level. As for "feminization of poverty" issues, Reagan administration cutbacks in federal programs like Medicaid, Aid to Families with Dependent Children (AFDC), and food stamps—the majority of whose recipients are women—have shifted the social services burden to states and localities. These governments have recently become more responsive on many social issues than the federal government, a fact that some analysts have attributed in part to the higher proportion of women and minorities in state legislatures as compared to Congress: the state/congressional ratio for women is 14 percent/4 percent, for Blacks 5 percent/3.6 percent (Pear 1985).

Other women's issues also lend themselves to participation by those familiar with local conditions. Battered women's shelters can take local ethnic, racial, and class differences into account; protection of local family planning clinics can be achieved by escorting clients or securing police investigation of arson; sexual harassment victims can be assisted by providing grievance procedures and legal resources; and pornography can be reduced by passing local ordinances.

This case study has attempted to highlight the importance of the numbers of female officials, the extent of women's group activism, and the kinds of women's policies effectively handled at the local level, all of which have made the local arena of American politics an important focus for policy research. Scholars should not overlook significant local policy accomplishments in their myopic focus on federal policy decisions affecting women.

CONCLUSION

Many factors contributed to the policy success of comparable worth adjustments for San Jose's AFSCME-represented employees. First, San Jose had the fiscal resources to offset the adverse effects of Proposition 13's revenue reductions. City governments in every state except Vermont are required to maintain balanced budgets (Dye 1985). In a study of fiscal stress in 40 major U.S. cities, Stanley (1980) categorized 11 as "declining and vulnerable," 17 as "declining but basically healthy" because of cutbacks, and 12 as "growing." San Jose was in the last category. Cities in the first two groupings can expect more severe fiscal restraints, but a rule of thumb for comparable worth proponents can be derived from the San Jose case: "Implement adjustments incrementally at about 2 percent of the personnel budget annually." This incrementalism would work in nearly all jurisdictions except those in extreme fiscal stress, or in a case like that of Washington state, where ten years of back pay and adjustments would take decades to be implemented at such a slow rate.

Second, San Jose benefited from the novelty of the issue in 1981. Local opponents were caught off guard in a way that could no longer occur once comparable worth had become the subject of national media and political attention. It has been criticized by top Reagan administration officials, such as members of the U.S. Civil Rights Commission (*San Francisco Chronicle* 1985) and Council of Economic Advisors member William Niskanen (Kilborn 1984). According to AFSCME's national office, business opponents have mounted well-organized efforts in several states to extinguish the pay equity prairie fire. However, though other jurisdictions no longer have the advantage of the novelty factor, they have a new advantage: the successful track record in San Jose and other cities, such as Colorado Springs, Colorado, and Long Beach, California (NCPE 1984).

Third, activists in Santa Clara County paved the way for taking women's issues seriously. San Jose is not unique in this regard. There are local chapters of the League of Women Voters, National Women's Political Caucus, National Organization for Women, and Business and Professional Women in hundreds of U.S. localities. Since most American cities use nonpartisan ballots to elect local officials, women's groups can fill the local party vacuum elsewhere as they did in San Jose: by providing the services of ward heelers, establishing networks to change policies, educating the public on women's issues, and recruiting and supporting sympathetic candidates. Women's groups were slow to come around to the support of AFSCME women in the 1981 strike, but they are now mobilized in support of comparable worth, both in San Jose and in most other areas.

Fourth, the majority status of female officials on the San Jose city council gave them greater freedom of action regarding women's issues than is typically the case on governing boards. Such majorities are rare. The token status of most female officials discourages them from taking risks on women's issues. If such women cannot rely on peer support, however, they can look for constituency support, which may be mobilized in areas without the majority status found in the San Jose case.

Finally, women in Local 101 pressured the city throughout the strike, settlement, and implementation stages of the comparable worth policy. AFSCME has continued to press the issue in several other jurisdictions: the states of Washington, Minnesota, New York, Illinois, Connecticut, and Hawaii; and the cities of Los Angeles, Spokane, Portland, Green Bay, New York, and Philadelphia (AFSCME 1984). Invigorated by the San Jose success, AFSCME, along with other unions such as the Service Employees International Union (SEIU), have spearheaded what is now a nationwide movement in more than 100 jurisdictions.

Fiscal constraints and business opposition may cause temporary setbacks, but overall, the prognosis is favorable for women in other localities to make the same impressive policy difference as they did in the San Jose comparable worth case.

NOTES

Acknowledgments: This study was made possible by research grants from the University of Santa Clara and the Sourisseau Academy of San Jose State University.

1. Particularly helpful were city officials David Armstrong, Janet Gray Hayes, Nancy Ianni, Shirley Lewis, Lu Ryden, and Pat Sausedo; and union members Nancy Clifford, Patt Curia, Linda Dydo, Joan Goddard, and Diana Rock.

2. Material in the following two sections is drawn from Flammang 1986.

3. Interview with David Armstrong; Bunzel 1982; Farnquist, Armstrong, and Strausbaugh 1983; Soloway 1981; and Trounstine 1981e.

4. The material in this section is taken from Flammang 1984a.

5. The material in this section is taken from Flammang 1985.

REFERENCES

AFSCME. 1984. *Winning the Fight for Pay Equity.* Washington, D.C.: American Federation of State, County, and Municipal Employees.

Armstrong, David. 1984. Interview with author, 11 July.

Boneparth, Ellen, ed. 1982. *Women, Power and Policy.* Elmsford, N. Y.: Pergamon.

Bunzel, John H. 1982. "To Each According to Her Worth?" *Public Interest* 67 (Spring): 77–93.

Calvert, Cathie. 1981. "Union Blames Pay Disparity on Sex Bias." *San Jose Mercury News,* 5 March.

Carroll, Rick. 1981. "Tough Talk in 'Feminist' San Jose Strike." *San Francisco Chronicle,* 7 July.

CAWP. 1981. "Women in Elective Office 1975–1980." Center for the American Woman and Politics Fact Sheet. New Brunswick, N.J.: Rutgers University.

————. 1983. "Women Make a Difference." Center for the American Woman and Politics Report. New Brunswick, N.J.: Rutgers University.

CPER. 1981. " 'Comparable Worth' Strike Averted in San Jose." *California Public Employees Relations* 49 (June): 16–18.

Diamond, Irene, ed. 1983. *Families, Politics, and Public Policy.* New York: Longman.

Dye, Thomas R. 1985. *Politics in States and Communities.* Englewood Cliffs, N.J.: Prentice-Hall.

Farnquist, Robert L., David R. Armstrong, and Russell P. Strausbaugh. 1983. "Pandora's Worth: The San Jose Experience." *Public Personnel Management Journal* 12 (Winter): 358–68.

Flammang, Janet A. 1984a. "Filling the Party Vacuum: Women at the Grassroots Level in Local Politics." In Janet A. Flammang, ed., *Political Women: Current Roles in State and Local Government,* 87–113. Beverly Hills, Calif.: Sage.

————, ed. 1984b. *Political Women: Current Roles in State and Local Government.* Beverly Hills, Calif.: Sage.

————. 1985. "Female Officials in the Feminist Capital: The Case of Santa Clara County." *Western Political Quarterly* 38 (March): 94–118.

————. 1986. "Effective Implementation: The Case of Comparable Worth in San Jose." *Political Studies Review* 5 (May): 815–37.

Fletcher, Claude. 1981. "Comparable Worth: City Tinkering with the Economy." *San Jose Mercury,* 15 July.

Freeman, Jo. 1975. *The Politics of Women's Liberation.* New York: McKay.

Gelb, Joyce, and Marian Lief Palley. 1982 (rev. ed. 1986). *Women and Public Policies.* Princeton, N.J.: Princeton University Press.

Goodman, Walter. 1984. "Equal Pay for 'Comparable Worth' Growing as a Job Discrimination Issue." *New York Times,* 4 September.

Hay Associates. 1980. "City of San Jose Study of Non-Management Classes." San Francisco.

Herhold, Scott. 1983. "San Jose Sets the Standard in Equal Pay." *San Jose Mercury News,* 11 October.

Kahn, Wendy, and Joy Ann Grune. 1982. "Pay Equity: Beyond Equal Pay for Equal Work." In Ellen Boneparth, ed., *Women, Power and Policy,* 75–89. Elmsford, N.Y.: Pergamon Press.

Kanter, Rosabeth M. 1977. "Some Effects of Proportions on Group Life: Skewed Sex Ratios and Response to Token Women. *Americam Journal of Sociology* 82 (March): 965–90.

Kilborn, Peter E. 1984. "Reagan Aide Assails Equal Pay for Women." *New York Times,* 19 October.

Mezey, Susan Gluck. 1978. "Women and Representation: The Case of Hawaii." *Journal of Politics* 40 (May): 369–85.

Miller, Marjorie. 1981. "City, Union, in Last-Ditch Strike Talks." *San Jose Mercury News,* 5 July.

Myers, Margaret. 1980. Statement of Margaret Myers, Director, Office for Library Personnel Resources, American Library Association, before the Equal Employment Opportunity Commission. 28–29 February, Chicago.

NCPE. 1984. *Who's Working for Working Women?* Washington, D.C.: National Committee on Pay Equity.

NWPC. 1983. *National Directory of Women Elected Officials*. Washington, D.C.: National Women's Political Caucus.

Pear, Robert. 1984. "Administration Plans Challenge for Comparable Pay." *San Jose Mercury News*, 22 January.

――――. 1985. "States Are Found More Responsive on Social Issues." *New York Times*, 19 May.

Roberts, Steven V. 1984. "Women Gain in Power Structure." *New York Times*, 13 August.

"San Jose Workers File Bias Complaint." 1981. *San Jose Mercury News*, 19 June.

"Setback for 'Comparable Worth.'" 1985. *San Francisco Chronicle*, 29 March.

Skipitares, Connie. 1981. "City-Union Talks Near Deadline." *San Jose Mercury News*, 4 July.

Smith, Lee. 1978. "The EEOC's Bold Foray into Job Evaluation." *Fortune*, 11 September, pp. 58–64.

Soloway, Fred. 1981. "They Did It in San Jose." *Public Employee* 1 (August): 4.

Stanley, David T. 1980. "Cities in Trouble." In Charles H. Levine, ed. *Managing Fiscal Stress*. Chatham, N.J.: Chatham.

Stewart, Debra W., ed. 1980. *Women in Local Politics*, Metuchen, N.J.: Scarecrow Press.

Swan, Gary E. 1981. "First to Protest, She's on Sidelines Now." *San Jose Mercury*, 7 July.

Tong, David. 1981. "San Jose May Rewrite Labor History in Salary Dispute." *Oakland Tribune*, 10 May.

Trounstine, Philip J. 1981a. "Strike Averted in San Jose." *San Jose Mercury News*, 6 May.

――――. 1981b. "San Jose Braces for Strike." *San Jose Mercury News*, 3 July.

――――. 1981c. "Union Initiated Job Study That Led to San Jose Strike," *San Jose Mercury*, 12 July.

――――. 1981d. "Council Rejects Offer," *San Jose Mercury News*, 13 July.

――――. 1981e. "City Workers Ratify Contract for $5.4 Million to End Strike." *San Jose Mercury*, 15 July.

Trounstine, Philip J., and Terry Christensen. 1982. *Movers and Shakers: The Study of Community Power*. New York: St. Martin's Press.

Trounstine, Philip J., and Gary E. Swan. 1981. "Job Comparison Study: How It Was Done." *San Jose Mercury News*, 8 July.

Welch, Susan, and Albert K. Karnig. 1979. "Correlates to Female Officeholding in City Politics." *Jourhal of Politics* 41 (May): 478–91.

ABOUT THE CONTRIBUTORS
INDEX

About the Contributors

KAREN BECKWITH is an assistant professor of political science at the College of Wooster. An associate editor of the journal *Women and Politics*, she is the author of *American Women and Political Participation: The Impacts of Work, Generation, and Feminism, American Women in Public Affairs*, and various essays and articles on Italian women and politics.

MARTIEN BRIËT has been affiliated with the Department of Social Psychology at Vrije Universiteit, Amsterdam. With Frederike Kroon and Bert Klandermans she has published on participation in the Dutch women's movement. She is currently affiliated with a bureau for family guidance.

ANNE N. COSTAIN is an associate professor of political science at the University of Colorado in Boulder. Her publications include articles on interest groups, social movements, and gender politics, in the *Western Political Quarterly, American Politics Quarterly*, and *Polity*. She is now working on a book comparing the legislative impact of the women's and environmental movements.

W. DOUGLAS COSTAIN is a lecturer in political science at the University of Colorado, Boulder. He has contributed articles on energy and environmental policy and interest group politics to *Polity, Policy Studies Journal*, and numerous anthologies. His current research is on the environmental movement and the interplay between social movements, parties, and interest groups.

MYRA MARX FERREE is an associate professor of sociology and interim director of women's studies at the University of Connecticut. She was a visiting professor at the University of Frankfurt in 1985, where she temporarily held the first chair in women's studies in the Federal Republic. With Beth Hess, she recently co-authored *Controversy and Coalition: the New Feminist Movement* and co-edited *Analyzing Gender: A Social Science Handbook*. She has also published an article on West German feminist research on women's employment ("Between Two Worlds" in *Signs*, 10, 1985) and numerous articles on her own empirical research on working class women and work in the U.S.

313

JANET A. FLAMMANG is an associate professor of political science at Santa Clara University, where she teaches courses in American politics and women and politics. She edited *Political Women: Current Roles in State and Local Government,* and her articles on feminist theory, female officials, and comparable worth have appeared in *Current Perspectives in Social Theory, Western Political Quarterly,* and *Policy Studies Review.* She is currently writing about comparable worth in California and completing a book on women and politics in Santa Clara County.

JO FREEMAN, a political scientist and lawyer, is the author of *The Politics of Women's Liberation* and editor of *Women: A Feminist Perspective* and *Social Movements of the Sixties and Seventies.*

JOYCE GELB is professor and chair of the Department of Political Science at City College in New York and a member of the graduate faculty of the City University of New York. She has authored books and articles on problems of the powerless, including blacks and women. She is the co-author of *Women and Public Policies* and the author of a forthcoming book on comparative analysis of feminist politics and their impact in the United States, United Kingdom, and Sweden.

JUDITH ADLER HELLMAN is associate professor in the Department of Political Science and the Division of Social Science at York University, Toronto. She is the author of *Mexico in Crisis,* an analysis of the Mexican political system, and is currently completing a book on Italian women's movements, *Journeys Among Women: Feminism in Five Italian Cities.*

STEPHEN HELLMAN is an associate professor of political science and social and political thought at York University. He writes on Italian politics with a particular focus on the Left and Italian communism. Among his recent work is the book *Italian Communism in Transition; the Rise and Fall of the Historic Compromise.*

JANE JENSON is a professor of political science at Carleton University in Canada and research associate at the Center for European Studies at Harvard. She is co-author with George Ross of *The View from Inside: A French Communist Cell in Crisis* and of *Absent Mandate: The Politics of Discontent in Canada* with Harold Clarke, Larry LeDuc, and Jon Pammett. Her recent publications also include "Gender and Reproduction: or, Babies and the State," in *Studies in Political Economy,* Summer, 1986. Her current research concerns the impact of women on the development of the welfare state in Britain, France, and Canada.

MARY FAINSOD KATZENSTEIN is associate professor of government and of women's studies at Cornell University. She is the author and co-author respectively of two books on ethnic politics and preferential policies in India: *Ethnicity and Equality* and, with Myron Weiner, *India's Preferential Policies.* She has written and co-authored various articles on American feminist politics and movement strategy that appear in *Signs* ("The Meaning of Elections for Feminism," Autumn, 1984), in *Moral Theory,* edited by Diana Meyers and Eva Feder Kittay, and in other collections. Her current work explores the role of feminist consciousness as political strategy in different occupational settings.

BERT KLANDERMANS is senior lecturer in the Department of Social Psychology, Vrije Universiteit, Amsterdam. He has published extensively on mobilization and participation in social movements such as those of labor, women, and peace. He is currently engaged in longitudinal research on movement decline. His *Organizing for Change: Social Movement Organizations Across Cultures* will appear in 1987.

ETHEL KLEIN is an associate professor of political science at Columbia University. She is the author of *Gender Politics* and is currently working on a book on what the United States can learn and borrow from European social policy.

FREDERIKE KROON has been affiliated with the Department of Social Psychology Vrije Universiteit, Amsterdam. With Martien Briët and Bert Klandermans, she has published on participation in the Dutch women's movement. She is currently affiliated with a mental health institution.

CAROL McCLURG MUELLER is lecturer in social studies at Harvard University. She has taught at Wellesley, Tufts, and Brandeis. Her published articles and anthology contributions focus on the role of interpretive frames in the creation of political influence and the mobilization of new collective actors in the context of social movements. She recently edited *The Politics of the Gender Gap: The Social Construction of Political Influence*. Her current work explores the interplay between the women's movement and the electoral system with particular emphasis on collective consciousness and political mobilization.

MARY RUGGIE is assistant professor of sociology at Barnard College, Columbia University. She is the author of *The State and Working Women: A Comparative Study of Britain and Sweden*. Her current research, funded by a fellowship from the German Marshall Fund of the United States, is on comparative mental health care systems in advanced industrial societies.

Index

"Hot Autumn," in Italy, importance for women of, 113–14, 127, 138–40, 143

International Conference on Violence, in Italy, 163

Italian Communist party (PCI). *See* Communist party, in Italy

Italian League for Divorce, 157

Italian Republic, and Constituent Assembly, 154–55

Italian Women's Union. *See* Unione Donne Italiane (UDI)

Jenkins, Craig, 92, 93–94, 95
Johnson, Lyndon, 203
Johnson, Marilyn, 101, 106

Kennedy, John F., 199
Klein, Ethel, 42, 43, 94–95

Labor movements, 6–7, 13–15, 43
Labour party, in Britain, 247–51, 276–77
Law of 1920, in France, 75–76, 77, 79, 81, 83, 84
League of Women Voters, 216
Leftist parties, 6, 10–11, 15–16; in France, 10–11, 81–82, 85; in Italy, 111–12, 114, 119, 122, 124, 129, 133, 135, 137, 149, 154, 162; in U.S., 182; in W. Germany, 12, 183, 184
Lipsky, Michael, 17n, 92, 95
Lukes, Steven, 93

McCarthy, John, 93, 95, 103
McGovern, George, 202, 224, 225, 238
Magri, Lucio, 134–35
Manifeste des 343, in France, 83. *See also* Self-accusations
Marshall, T. H., 91
Marx, Gary, 90
Marxism: and antifeminism, 191n12; and orthodoxy/radical feminism, 173; theory of, 93; and view of feminism, 72–73, 128
Matter of Simple Justice, A, 203
Melucci, Alberto, 94
Michel, Andrée, 82
Miller, Joyce, 281
Mondale, Walter, 233, 234, 240
Moore, Barrington, 95
Mouvement pour la libération des femmes (MLF), 65, 86n

Movimento della Liberazione della Donna. *See* Radical party, in Italy

Municipal Employees Federation (MEF), in San Jose, 294–303

National Abortion Campaign, in U.K., 272, 286n
National Abortion Rights Action League (NARAL), 231, 272
National Association for the Advancement of Colored People (NAACP), 176
National Health Service, in U.K., 269
National Organization for Women (NOW), 12, 173–74, 185, 191n, 196, 212n; beginnings of, 96, 198, 220, 221; and Democrats, 207–208, 233, 234; and ERA, 16; growth and change of, 97, 199, 200–201; and NOW-PAC, 206–207; and political parties, 240–41, 278; vs. Republicans, 239
National Woman's party (NWP), 216–19, 230
National Women's Political Caucus (NWPC), 97–98, 104, 201–202, 204, 222–24, 225, 226, 233; recruitment of, of women candidates, 278
Nazis, 182, 183
Noi Donne, 116

Olson, Mancur, 92
"150 Hours" program, in Italy, 127–28
Operaismo. See Workerism
Otto-Peters, Louise, 180–81

Pacifism, as female attribute, 179, 180
Participation motives, 58–61; and collective and selective benefits, 61–62; of women in Netherlands, 56–60
Pasquino, Gianfranco, 167n
Patriarchy, 23, 247, 263
Paul, Alice, 216, 217
Perrow, Charles, 92, 93–94, 95
Peterson, Esther, 219
Piven, Frances Fox, 91–92, 93
Planning Familial, 77–79, 82, 83
Plogstedt, Sybelle, 185
Political institutions, studies of, 4
Political mobilization, 111, 126, 154, 196; attempts, 48–52, 55, 61, 62, 68; and collective identity, 8; at conventions, 218–19, 222, 223–34, 238, 239, 278; and feminist issues, in U.K., 267, 270–75, 277, 280, 282; and "50-50 Proposal," 239; and lobby-